NOTHIN' BUT
BLUE SKIES

NOTHIN' BUT BLUE SKIES

The Heyday, Hard Times, and Hopes of
America's Industrial Heartland

EDWARD McCLELLAND

BLOOMSBURY PRESS

NEW YORK · LONDON · NEW DELHI · SYDNEY

Portions of this book also appeared in *Z*, *Utne*, the *Herald & Review* (Decatur, Illinois), the *Chicago Reader*, *LOST*, *Salon*, and the books *Next: Young American Writers on the New Generation* and *The Third Coast: Sailors, Strippers, Fishermen, Folksingers, Long-Haired Ojibway Painters, and God-Save-the-Queen Monarchists of the Great Lakes*.

Published by Bloomsbury Press, New York

All papers used by Bloomsbury Press are natural, recyclable products made from wood grown in well-managed forests. The manufacturing processes conform to the environmental regulations of the country of origin.

LIBRARY OF CONGRESS CATALOGING-IN-PUBLICATION DATA

McClelland, Ted.
Nothin' but blue skies : the heyday, hard times, and hopes of America's industrial heartland / Edward McClelland. —First U.S. edition.
pages cm
Includes bibliographical references.
ISBN: 978-1-60819-529-9
1. Middle West—Economic conditions.   2. Lake States—Economic conditions.
3. Industries—Middle West.   4. Industries—Lake States. 5. Social change—Middle West.
6. Social change—Lake States.   7. Working class—Middle West.   8. Working class—
Lake States.   9. Middle West—Politics and government.   10. Lake States—Politics
and government.   I. Title.   II. Title: Nothing but blue skies.
HC107.A14M37 2013
330.977—dc23
2012042329

First U.S. edition 2013

1 3 5 7 9 10 8 6 4 2

Typeset by Westchester Book Group
Printed and bound in the U.S.A. by Thomson-Shore, Inc., Dexter, Michigan

To Mr. Matt Mann, J. W. Sexton High School history teacher,
who taught me the story of America

CONTENTS

PROLOGUE

Gus's Bar

For me, the glory days of American industry smelled like paint.

I went to J. W. Sexton High School in Lansing, Michigan, an art deco brick fortress that stood across the street from a Fisher Body auto plant. Fisher Body resembled an enormous backyard shed, clad in a corrugated steel skin whose shade of green was somewhere between the Statue of Liberty and mold. In the summer, Fisher Body's emblem—a landau carriage—bloomed in a floral pattern on the factory's front lawn. In the fall, second-shift workers stood on the balconies to watch the Sexton Big Reds butt heads across the street, in Memorial Stadium. In the spring, I ran laps around the stadium's four-hundred-meter oval, inhaling atomized paint fumes with every gasp—a sweetish metallic tang I still associate with the track team. The industrial atmosphere can't have made me faster. Our band teacher, whose window opened toward the factory, developed a heart condition after years of breathing oxygen scented with Oldsmobile paint jobs.

Facing every gate was a tavern, so Fisher Body's shoprats could speed from punch-out to bar stool in five minutes or less. Gus's advertised "Booze and Burgers." The Shop Stop was renowned for its postshift brawls. The bars were off-limits to students, and so was the Sav-Way, a party store, (the Michigan term for a liquor store), whose coolers were stacked with six-packs.

In Lansing—as in Flint, Detroit, Pontiac, Saginaw, and all the other industrial abrasions on the palm of Lower Michigan—General Motors owned the air, the sky, the land, and the water. The chemically tainted air carried a new-car smell more primal than the showroom aroma. At night, the sky over the twenty-four-hour factories turned pink, an *aurora automobilis* that tattered constellations by outshining all but the lowest-magnitude stars. The biggest building in town was the Oldsmobile Main Plant, which had been the state fairgrounds until General Motors decided to assemble R. E. Olds's buggy alongside the Grand River. When you vaulted over the arched back of the double bridge, built to accommodate shift-change traffic, the Oldsmobile legend shone above the factory in pink neon. And if you looked down, you might see similarly unnatural colors on the water, a rainbow slick I called "Oldsmo-bile." While you were trying to fall asleep, your bedroom filled with the clacket of locomotives carrying Delta 88s along tracks stitched into the coaly riverbank. When you woke up, the drop forge stamped out car parts to a Mordor beat, a half-ton hammer pounding sharply on an anvil, amplified by a copper dawn.

In the 1970s, Oldsmobile was the third-bestselling brand in America, trailing only those titanic rivals Ford and Chevy. Lansing employed twenty-five thousand autoworkers, a constituency so large that candidates for president of the United Auto Workers local bought ads on the radio.

An industrial park is not the most wholesome setting for a secondary education, but in those days, it made perfect sense. Most auto plants are surrounded by suppliers—of tires, radios, door handles, floor mats. Sexton supplied labor. In 1943, when the school was built, General Motors was the largest private employer in the world. For the next thirty-five years, there might as well have been a tunnel from the graduation stage to the assembly line. One week, you had a diploma in your hand. The next, a ratchet. A healthy young man didn't even need to graduate high school to work in the shop.

"I had this student," my history teacher once told me, "a real chucklehead. Just refused to study. Dropped out of school, and a year or so later, he came back to see me. He pointed out the window at a brand-new Camaro and said, 'That's my car.' Meanwhile, I was driving a beat-up station wagon. I think he was an electrician's assistant or something. He handed lightbulbs to an electrician."

That was not the story of my generation. I started high school in 1982, the rock-bottom pits of the Rust Belt era, when Michigan's unemployment rate was 15 percent. Our physics teacher began each semester with this lecture:

"It used to be," he said, "that you could walk out of here, walk across the street, and get a job in that plant. That's not the case anymore. You guys are going to have to study hard and go to college if you want a good job."

Sometimes, as I walked past the plant, I would stare through the high windows, watching an auto frame jerk along in its progress from chassis to Cutlass. That was as close as I ever got. Fisher Body wasn't letting any students inside for field trips or character-building summer jobs. Auto work was not my class's calling. The morning after graduation, there was a line outside the personnel office, but that was just my schoolmates performing their parents' ritual, for a god who no longer listened to prayers for $20-an-hour jobs. "Generous Motors" had dropped that nickname and reverted back to its sterner title: "the General." And the General was not enlisting privates.

The army was, though, so my friend Larry joined up in the winter of our senior year, because he knew his father couldn't get him in at Oldsmobile. When Larry came home, three years later, his old man gave him a hard time about not finding a job right away. Across the generation gap between a baby boomer and a Gen X-er, Larry delivered a speech about how kids his age didn't have it as easy as their fathers.

"I think that you've just lost touch with reality," he told his dad. "I think that you have to know, if everyone had the same opportunity that you did to just walk into a personnel office, fill out a piece of paper, go to work the same day, we'd all be there. Times are different. You didn't have to go to college to earn the life that you have now. You can't just walk into General Motors today."

Still, as long as Fisher Body remained standing, I knew Lansing had not been abandoned, and neither had our ideal of urban life. The twentieth-century auto plant was a great integrator, a great income leveler. Not only did blacks from Tennessee and German Catholics from rural villages build the same cars, they earned the same money as budget analysts at the state capitol—often more, with overtime. Sexton's swath of west Lansing took in the biker neighborhoods by the airport, the ghetto that produced Earvin "Magic" Johnson, the country club, and the governor's mansion. We were a statewide power in basketball and golf. A local joke went, "What's black and white and black and white and black and white? The lunch line at Sexton."

Fisher Body closed in 2005, after General Motors decided it could no longer afford to truck auto shells across town to the assembly plant by the river. GM wanted to put the entire process under one roof. I visited the obsolete factory during its demolition. The green skin remained, but cranes and bulldozers were consuming the innards. Hanging from the weave of a chain-link fence was a sign with this Big Brotherish slogan: "Demolition Means Progress." The warehouse grid of windows was bulleted with broken panes, the glass torn away like paper targets on a shooting range. Peeping through the ragged holes, I saw snarled heaps of metal, the entrails of an assembly line. Down the street, Verlinden School, which had educated the West Side's middle class since the Prohibition twenties, wore a plywood bandage over its first-floor windows. An aluminum bungalow was stickered with a yellow foreclosure notice. Sav-Way, site of so many lunch-break beer runs, subsisted on an inner-city trade of baby food, lottery tickets, canned spaghetti, diapers, and Wild Irish Rose.

Five years later, Fisher Body looked like the Badlands of South Dakota, with Nagasaki in one corner, where the demolition crew had left chunks of concrete riprap and ochre ribbons of steel, twisted at pipe-cleaner angles. Deindustrialization has its own flora, and Fisher Body was now a garden of weeds and wildflowers that grew on the graves of factories: red clover, teasel with its prickly lavender crown, Queen Anne's lace, the most ragged of flowers. It was evening when I walked the fence, so the mellowing dusk glowed through the petals of the black-eyed Susans, illuminating a field of tiny suns.

Across the street from the old south gate, Gus's Bar (Booze and Burgers) was still open, but with a For Sale sign pinned beside the front door. I opened the door, but not even the Mediterranean-white sunshine of a late-spring afternoon could disperse the thirty years of darkness that had accumulated inside Gus's. Three men tending long-necked beer bottles watched a classic car auction on the TV over the bar. The only moving figure in the tenebrous scene was Gus Caliacatsos, a short, bald, bearded Greek who flapped across the perforated kitchen mat in plastic sandals, to check on a hamburger sizzling in grease. On a shelf behind the bar, rock banks were on sale for $25. A sign advertised rooms for rent, $100/wk.

"I was never allowed to come in here when I was in high school," I told Gus.

"I ban the students from Sexton," he said. "One day, they come in, loosen all the saltshakers."

I bought a $2 Budweiser, and Gus sat down with me at the bar. He shuffled through snapshots of his hometown, Preveza, a seaside hamlet of pastel villas, and explained how he had gotten from those bright skies to this dark bar, and why he was trying to go back again.

Gus had arrived in Michigan in 1960, because in 1960, no place on Earth had more to offer an immigrant. After fleeing the Greek Civil War, he worked as a carpenter at the Canadian embassy in Germany. Pleased with a chair he'd built, the ambassador asked Gus, "What can I do for you?"

"I want to go to America," Gus said.

So the ambassador gave Gus a Canadian visa and told him to see the American consul in Montreal.

"Where do you want to go?" the consul asked Gus.

"Where is the most jobs?" Gus asked.

"Detroit, Michigan," the consul told him.

"Is that the capital?"

"Lansing is the capital."

In Greece, Athens was the capital and the leading metropolis. Gus assumed Michigan was the same.

"Then I want to go to Lansing," Gus said.

Gus opened his tavern in 1980, just two years past the all-time high point of GM's employment. It was a shop bar, nothing but. They're working hard in the plant, they deserve a drink, Gus figured. Shoprats raced across the street on their lunch breaks, and sometimes they didn't return to the assembly line. Third shift was known as the party shift, or the bachelor shift, because you got off work early enough to hit the bar and didn't have to be back until late afternoon the next day, long enough to sleep off a hangover. After eleven o'clock, the door never swung back on its hinges, and not even seven barmaids could pour beer as fast as the autoworkers drank it. Who got served first? Whoever shoved his money closest to Gus's face.

When Fisher Body closed, Gus's customers promised to keep drinking in his tavern, but a week later, he had to lay off all fourteen bartenders. After that, it was just Gus and his wife. Then Gus's wife went home to Greece, so it was just Gus, working from seven in the morning until two in the morning, except when he could nap in one of the empty sleeping rooms above the bar. On slow nights, he closed at twelve thirty. Ever since he'd opened the bar, Gus had driven Oldsmobiles, because that's where his money came from. Parked on the sidewalk was a burgundy 1998 Cutlass Ciera. His last, because GM no longer makes Oldsmobiles, and Gus can no longer afford a new car. He was trying to sell the bar, because he hadn't seen his wife in a year.

"The city, they do nothing to save the plant," he complained. "They don't give tax breaks."

"Tax breaks would not have saved that plant!" shouted a man at the bar—Gus's most loyal customer, a retired tool-and-die maker who lived in one of his $100-a-week flops. Bearded, tattooed from bicep to elbow, covering his baldness with a USS *Bennington* cap, he was drinking his GM pension by the pitcher. "That plant was obsolete! It was ancient! I worked there for thirty-five years. They would have had to tear it down and spend a hundred million dollars to build a new one."

"The golden days died." Gus sighed. "Right now, Michigan the most dumb place, because there's no jobs."

In the early 1960s, when the American consul told Gus, "Go to Detroit, young man," Michigan's per capita income was eleventh in the nation. By 2011, when Gus hung the For Sale sign outside his tavern, it was thirty-seventh. The state's poverty rate, once in the bottom five, was in the top twenty. In the parking lot of UAW Local 602, across the street from Gus's, a sign warns "Non-North American Nameplate Vehicles Will Be Towed At Owner's Expense." Fifty years ago, such a sign would have been unnecessary. The only foreign car seen on the streets of Lansing was the Volkswagen Beetle, which was considered an affectation of long-haired piano teachers and graduate students too poor to afford an Oldsmobile with an eight-cylinder Rocket engine. German engineering was at least respected, but "Made in Japan" had the same cachet as "Made in Hong Kong" on the underside of plastic toys. Europe and Asia had destroyed themselves in World War II. The only winner of that conflict, the United States of America, had emerged as the most prosperous society in the history of the world, one that spread its bounty among all classes. No state benefited more than Michigan, because no invention ever accrued more value during its transformation from raw material to finished product than Henry Ford's automobile. That mechanical invention made possible Ford's social invention, the American middle class. From 1960 to 1965, Michigan's per capita income increased 30 percent, more than any industrial state's.

Nikita Khrushchev and Leonid Brezhnev bragged about building a worker's paradise in Soviet Russia, but Michiganders already lived in one: weekly pay stubs the size of Third World annual incomes, two cars in the driveway, a cottage on an inland lake, and each November, a deer-hunting trip to the North Woods, which was stocked like a royal game preserve.

I was born into this world, in the second week of 1967, a year when the nation's unemployment rate was 3.8 percent. I am a coeval of its decline. When I was six months old, Detroit caught fire. When I was six years old, the Arabs stopped sending us oil. When I was fifteen, a presidential candidate declared that my hometown lay at the bottom of "a Rust Bowl." When I was forty-one, General Motors begged the United

States Congress to rescue it from bankruptcy. Although neither I nor anyone in my family ever built cars, as the son of an auto-making town, my life has been shaped by the auto industry's fortunes. Most American lives have. Like red clover and teasel, this book grows from the ruins of Fisher Body, but it's not just about that factory, or about Lansing, or about Michigan. It's about auto plants and auto towns, steel plants and steel towns, even air-conditioner plants and air-conditioner towns, all over America's industrial heartland, that country between the Ohio River and the Great Lakes that once produced so much hardware. It's an attempt to answer, on a historical scale, the question I ask myself whenever I stand on the grounds of Sexton High School and look across Michigan Avenue: What happened to the factory?

1.

The Sit-Down Striker

The Flint Sit-Down Strike, which lasted from December 30, 1936, to February 11, 1937, was to the American labor movement what Lexington and Concord was to the American Revolution. At Lexington, a gang of farmers stood up to the British Empire, the most powerful nation in the world. They lost the battle, but the war they started resulted in the founding of the United States, a new kind of nation, in which no man swore allegiance to a king. In Flint, for the first time, workingmen defeated a major industrial power—in this case, General Motors, the largest corporation in the world. Their victory resulted in the founding of the United Auto Workers and in a new kind of America, one in which every man had a right to the wealth his labor produced.

Whether we still live in that America is one of the subjects of this book, but Everett Ketchum lived in it for most of his career. One of the last surviving Sit-Down Strikers, Everett not only participated in the battle that founded the blue-collar middle class, he enjoyed all the spoils of the peace that followed. As a tool-and-die maker at General Motors, Everett earned $27 an hour in the 1970s: more than any of the necktied budget analysts and wildlife biologists in Lansing's mazes of state government cubicles. After retirement, he was guaranteed free health care for the rest of his life—thirty-eight years so far, only a year less than he worked in the shop.

That's why, into his nineties, Everett was still healthy enough to flirt with waitresses. Everett and I are not related, but in the complicated way that extended families form, he's the grandfather I haven't had since I was a teenager. For years, he and his second wife lived across the street from the woman who became my father's second wife. After Everett was wid-

8

owed, he married my stepmother's mother. Widowed again, he shared our Sunday dinners, our pew at the Presbyterian Church, and our Christmas Eve men's luncheons. Sometimes, his randiness was embarrassing. At one of those luncheons, he used the cream pitcher to tell the waitress an off-color joke about breast milk. And I could never bring a date home without Everett's winking at me and drawling, "Boy, you sure got an eye."

Other times, though, his fondness for waitresses—and the savings from a lifetime of well-paid work—inspired him to benevolence beyond the call of Christianity. A hostess at his favorite pancake house always covered her mouth when she led him to a booth. Everett asked why. Reluctantly, she revealed a mouth with two missing teeth and a cracked incisor. Everett handed her a dentist's card.

"Go there today and make an appointment," he ordered.

Dentures cost $7,000. Everett paid. A busgirl wouldn't smile due to bad hygiene. Everett sent her to a dentist, too. Word got around about the Flap Jack Shack's tooth fairy. The *Lansing State Journal* called. Everett would not allow his name to appear in the newspaper for an act of charity, so the reporter dubbed him "Dental Man."

"I sat there day after day, watching those girls," he told the columnist, "and thought, 'It must be terrible to have to walk around with your hand in front of your mouth.' And these girls were both hard workers. What's money, compared to a chance to help somebody?"

After his legs became so frail he had to trade in his Buick for an aluminum walker, he moved to a retirement home, where actuarial reality made him extremely popular with the widows. One asked to hold his hand during the nightly movie.

"If I hold your hand," he warned her, "I'm going to want to hold something else."

Without the benefits the UAW won from General Motors, Everett would have lived his old age as an unwanted uncle—if he were living his old age at all. He's decided one hundred years will be enough life. After GM went bankrupt in 2008, I told him that his superannuation—both the result and the cause of his consumption of health benefits—was personally responsible for GM's financial crisis. Everett cackled.

"I don't know where I'd be living without it," he said. "I'd be living with one of my nephews or one of my nieces. My two sisters is gone. I really don't know where I'd be if I didn't have what I have. If I had to buy my insurance that I got, I wouldn't be living in this two-thousand-dollar-a-month apartment. But how long are my benefits gonna last, 'cause I'm not working? All the money that I've got is interest money that I saved through the years."

In his own lifetime, which began three months after World War I broke out, Everett went from northern Michigan farm boy to autoworker to prosperous pensioner. America went from agrarian society to foundry of the world to postindustrial nation. And Flint went from a small town where building cars was a cottage industry, to the city with the highest per capita income in the United States, to a depopulated slum with the highest murder rate in the nation. How did all this happen, in the span of one man's years?

EVERETT'S FATHER, Earl Ketchum, wanted to be a farmer, but he couldn't make corn and beans grow in the northern Lower Peninsula's silt. So he worked in the family general store, driving a horse and buggy around the countryside, trading goods for milk, potatoes, and eggs.

When America entered the Great War, it was join the army or work in a factory, so Earl moved his family to Flint, where he built airplane engines at "the Buick," as the locals called the auto manufacturer that would eventually employ two-thirds of the city.

By the early twentieth century, Flint was already on its third great industry, each a descendant of the last. In 1865, a sawmill began operating on the Flint River, slicing the pine woods into lumber. Once the forests were exhausted, Flint used the timber to become the nation's carriage-making capital. When the automobile made carriages obsolete, a Scottish-born tinkerer named David Dunbar Buick added an engine and formed the company that grew into General Motors.

For a factory town, war meant work. In the teens and twenties, Flint's population quadrupled, from 38,500 to 156,600. GM headhunters sought out dirt farmers all over the Middle West and the Mississippi Valley, handing them one-way tickets to Vehicle City, as Flint nicknamed itself. The newcomers slept in shacks, tents, and railroad cars. Earl Ketchum's family rented a tiny house, all he could afford on his factory pay. After the war, Earl tried farming again, failed again, and returned to Flint for good.

Everett grew up a city boy, with no agricultural ambitions. After graduating from high school in 1933, he enlisted in General Motors as an apprentice tool-and-die maker, at fifty cents an hour.

Not only were the wages low, the job could disappear in a day. If a supervisor wanted to hire his brother-in-law, he created an opening by handing a worker a yellow slip, the color of termination. Bachelors were laid off while married men with lower seniority kept their jobs. Wives were laid off because their husbands worked in the plant.

"The supervision, they had no control, either," Everett recalled. "You could come in to work today as a supervisor and have a desk and have a yellow slip on there that said, 'You're all done.'"

Labor's last great campaign to unionize American workers, a 1919 steel strike, had been crushed in the post–World War I Red Scare. But Franklin D. Roosevelt was now president, and his National Industrial Recovery Act gave workers the right to bargain collectively. In 1936, the United Auto Workers sent a missionary to Flint. If the UAW failed to organize Vehicle City, it had no future. General Motors tried to pacify its employees with a pay raise and time-and-a-half for overtime. But it also sacked many of the 150 men who'd been brave enough to join the UAW. What worker would risk his job to join a union too weak to win a contract? GM controlled Flint so thoroughly that the Genesee County Relief Board asked clients whether they belonged to unions or read labor publications. The workers didn't just want more money. They wanted an end to the arbitrary firings. They also wanted an end to assembly line speed-ups. The "speed-up" was profitable for GM—1936 was Chevrolet's first million-selling year—but workers were breaking down under the hectic pace.

"Working conditions [are] so bad a man [can] hardly keep up the pace for nine hours," a Flint autoworker wrote to Secretary of Labor Frances Perkins. "I [haven't] worked an eight hour day for two years. It's not the amount of pay so much. A man hasn't time to get a drink of water and take care of his personal affairs during working hours. At lunch time a man has to shut one of his two machines, take off his apron, and walk a block or two and wash his hands, walk back, find his lunch pail and eat lunch on a piece of sheet metal that has been out in a car/truck for several hours and just unloaded. Abraham Lincoln freed the colored people from slavery and now we are slaves . . . Today in the factories one man does the work of five men."

Only a union could change that.

On November 12, at the Fisher One Plant, three welders conducted a short, pro-union sit-down demonstration. The foreman pulled their time cards from the rack. In protest, an entire department in the plant stopped working. Faced with a shutdown, the plant manager agreed to meet with a UAW representative, who told him production would not resume until the militant welders returned to work. The next day, five hundred autoworkers signed up with the union that had prevented the firings.

The UAW high command had planned the strike for January, when GM's new model-year production would be at its peak, and when Michigan's newly elected New Deal governor, Frank Murphy, would be sworn in. But the week after Christmas, the company forced the union's hand.

On December 30, a rumor circulated through Fisher One that GM was about to ship dies to Grand Rapids and Pontiac so it could stamp out four hundred Buick bodies a day if suddenly radicalized Flint went on strike. The move ended up causing the shutdown it was intended to prevent. At ten P.M. the night shift stopped working and refused to go home. The Sit-Down Strike had begun.

"This strike has been coming for years," autoworker Francis O'Rourke wrote in his diary. "Speed-up system, seniority, overbearing foremen. You can go just so far, you know, even with working men."

Everett was working at the Chevrolet plant known as "Chevy in the Hole," because it was located in a low-lying area beside the Flint River. When the strike spread to Chevy in the Hole, Everett asked his supervisor whether he should keep working or join the union.

"Join it," his foreman told him. "You need it."

For the first week and a half, the strike was peaceful. Inside the plants, the men slept on car seats and filled the long idle days playing pedro and euchre, the Michigan farmers' version of bridge. They watched movies and made up songs mocking GM chairman Alfred P. Sloan and vice president William S. Knudsen. To banjos, mandolins, and guitars, they sang this parody of "Goody Goody," a big hit in 1936:

> We Union men are out to win today, Goody, Goody
> General Motors hasn't even got a chance, Goody, Goody
> Old Sloan is feeling blue
> And so is Knudsen too
> They didn't like the bitter sit-down
> What could they do?

Strike pay was $25 a week, enough for Everett, who still lived with his parents, but not enough for the family men. Grocers and truck farmers sold food to strikers at half price. To oust the strikers, GM sought a court injunction and sent Genesee County sheriff Thomas Walcott after the "trespassers." Fearing the company would use force, the strikers fashioned blackjacks out of hoses, leather, and lead.

On January 11, GM's plant police shut down the furnaces of Fisher Body Two. Winter seeped through the building's brick walls. Wives delivering baskets of food to their striking husbands were turned away by company guards. A thirty-member strikers' police force, wearing armbands to identify themselves as soldiers in a workingman's army, broke open the gate, then barred it with a hose to prevent the cops from following them into the factory. A Flint police captain demanded admission. When the strikers told him to shove off, he fired a gas bomb through a window. Officers gassed 150 pickets on the sidewalk, but as they advanced toward the plant, the strikers inside hurled door hinges, bolts, and milk bottles from an upper window. They hosed down the cops with cold water. Outside, pickets still smarting from the gas attack overturned Sheriff Wolcott's car, while the sheriff was inside.

Outside the plant, UAW organizer Victor Reuther (whose brother, Walter, would later lead the union for twenty-four years) shouted commands from a sound truck. Threatening to destroy the plant if the attack continued, Reuther ordered workers to barricade Chevrolet Avenue with automobiles, so the police couldn't pull their squad cars up to the gates and snipe through the windows.

The police retreated to a bridge spanning the Flint River, north of the plant, but returned an hour later. This time, they launched gas grenades over the gate, covering their attack with pistol fire, to prevent strikers from picking up the projectiles and tossing them back. Several autoworkers standing on the roof were struck by bullets. But even the wind was on the strikers' side. A cold blast from the south blew gas back into the attackers' faces, forcing them to retreat again. Sensing a rout, the pickets chased after the cops, pelting them with snowballs, chunks of concrete, milk bottles, and whatever other garbage they could convert into projectiles. This time, the police turned and fired at their pursuers. Thirteen autoworkers were wounded in what came to be known as the Battle of the Running Bulls.

The day after the skirmish, Governor Murphy dispatched the National Guard to Flint, to prevent more violence between police and strikers. Guardsmen in doughboy uniforms set up machine guns in the streets, but instead of throwing the sit-downers out of the plants, the Guard made sure they stayed inside. This was why the UAW had tried to wait until January. They knew Murphy would take the workingmen's side. (As a consequence of his union sympathies, Murphy was defeated for reelection the next year; President Roosevelt rewarded the beaten liberal by naming him attorney general, then associate justice of the Supreme Court.)

"They came down there and tried to stop it, but they was overwhelmed," Everett would recall seventy-three years after the battle. "Even the city police. We had everybody behind us. If you're in a police car, just move on. I don't care how many police cars you had. Just move on. It was do or die. We had to make it go, to let the union be in control. In a way, it was kind of comical. General Motors, as big as they was, as strong as they was, didn't have a choice. A lot of the guys wanted to go back to work, but the union said no work, no machines. You go to start your machine up, they shut it off and kick your butt out."

A month after the Flint Police and the Genesee County Sheriff's Department lost the Battle of the Running Bulls, General Motors surrendered, too. The company recognized the UAW and raised wages a nickel an hour. It had no choice. From Flint, the center of the GM universe, the strike had spread nationwide. In the first ten days of February, GM produced only 151 automobiles.

"The sit-down strike had idled 136,000 GM workers across the land at a cost in wages of just under $30 million," wrote University of Michigan history professor Sidney Fine in *Sit-Down: The General Motors Strike of 1936–1937*. "GM, as the result of the strike, was estimated to have lost the production of more than 280,000 cars valued at $175 million."

When the armistice was announced, thousands of autoworkers paraded through Flint behind a drummer and a flag bearer. The workers waved the Stars and Stripes and sang "Solidarity Forever."

"It was a whoopee-doo, holler holler, we're all done, we're going back to work starting Monday," Everett said.

Everett Ketchum worked another thirty-nine years in General Motors, but the Sit-Down Strike was the most important event of his career. It made his workingman's fortune possible and was the source of his superannuation. There was never a better time to work for General Motors than the 1940s through the 1970s. There was never a better time to be a laborer, period. After GM recognized the UAW, Everett received a pension plan and health insurance. During World War II, he stayed out of combat by building armored trucks for Chevrolet. Once the war was won, "Flint was booming. They even bused people up from the South, bring 'em up here to work. Everybody was working, everybody had a job, everybody had one or two cars, and you kept getting bigger homes. Oh, boy."

Widowed when his first wife died in an automobile accident, Everett married a woman who ran the 4-H program at Michigan State College and transferred to the Oldsmobile plant in Lansing. As a tool-and-die maker, producing dies that stamped out fenders, he belonged to the shop-rat elite. Skilled tradesman at GM was the best job in town, blue- or white-collar. The tradesmen earned more money than the assembly-line workers, and when GM went bankrupt, in 2008, the retirees held on to their company health insurance, unlike the nonunion salesmen and engineers. With his night-shift bonus—another union perk—Everett bought houses near campus and rented them to MSU students. In the early 1960s, around the time he began wearing the UAW twenty-five-year service ring that still protrudes from his fist like a pewter nut, he joined the company glee club, the Rocketaires, named after the Oldsmobile Rocket engine. Oldsmobile provided the Rocketaires' satin uniforms, gave them time off to rehearse, and paid them to sing at Christmas concerts in the plant's two-thousand-seat auditorium. Every two years, Everett bought a new Oldsmobile in cash, at an employee discount. When he retired in 1976, two years before the American auto industry hit its all-time high of 977,000 workers, the former four-bit apprentice was earning over 50 times his starting wage.

"The whole picture, to me, I was in the right place at the right time," he reflected. "I always had a job right from the time I was a five-year-old kid, I always had a job. My father was a small-town mechanic and he and another fella had a garage and my job was, after school, I come back and cleaned the tools up for the next day. I was twelve, fourteen years old. I got five dollars a day every day that I worked. For me, that was big money. At GM, I come in there at a good time. It was just the right era for a lot of things, and I appreciate that."

America's greatest twentieth-century invention was not the airplane, or the atomic bomb, or the lunar lander. It was the middle class. We won the Cold War not because of our military strength, but because we shared our wealth more broadly than the Communists and, as a result, had more wealth to share. Everett has a Depression boy's gratitude for his good fortune. Born half a century later, I assumed that universal prosperity was the natural condition of American life. Now that another half century has passed, I'm beginning to assume otherwise.

As the unions saw it, the labor movement overthrew an economic order in which the mass of humankind had been born with saddles on their backs, to be ridden by a booted and spurred aristocracy—an order in which the many toiled to provide pleasures for the few. Collective bargaining made obsolete the iron law of wages, which stated that labor could command no more than a subsistence living from capital. It made obsolete the notorious marketplace known as "bidding at the factory gate," in which workers offered their services for ten cents an hour, only to lose the job to a more desperate man who would take nine. If preserving the victory of the Sit-Down Strikers is foolish nostalgia, then perhaps we have to ask whether the golden age of the American worker was a historical aberration, made possible by the fact that we were the only country to emerge from World War II with any industrial capacity. Was that golden age destined to end as soon as the rest of the world rebuilt itself, making blue-collar burghers such as Everett an obsolete class, a relic of the American Century? In this Global Century, will laborers again have to reconcile themselves to their roles as members of an international peasantry, bargaining for work against the exotic Hindoo and the heathen Chinee?

We have to ask, was the American middle class just a moment?

2.

The Arsenal of Democracy

The Oldsmobile Homecoming, which takes place every June in the pond-sized parking lot of a government office building outside Lansing, brings together the dwindling fleet of serviceable, street-legal Toronados, 442s, Cutlass Supremes, Cieras, and Aleros on the American roads. General Motors canceled the Oldsmobile brand in 2004, so the latest of the late-model cars are still being driven by pizza-delivery guys and community-college students with part-time jobs at Best Buy. The Oldsmobiles that attend the reunion are the classics: a 1955 Super 88 convertible, ten feet long at the wheelbase, with womanly curves, a bulbous hood, eye-socket headlamp cylinders, and a chrome belly reflecting a curved blue heaven.

The 1971 Delta 88 was created by a less priapic design team—given the mores of the era, American males no longer had to express their desires in molded steel—but it was the model that carried my infant car seat, so I took several photographs of my father's Oldsmobile. With its snouty hood and crimped tail, the '71 Delta 88 could have been—and probably was—an automotive extra on an early episode of *Hawaii Five-0*. By 1984, Oldsmobile was building 1.2 million cars a year, but those square-edged Cutlasses, indistinguishable from Buicks or Pontiacs, just looked like old cars, abandoned in this parking lot a quarter-century before, long enough for even the intermittent sun of southern Michigan to bake the gloss from their paint jobs.

As a Midwestern cub reporter forced to work weekends, I covered at least a dozen Saturday-afternoon car shows. Eventually, I developed a rule for estimating the nativity of an attendee: subtract fifteen from the model year of his ride. Everyone was posing with the car he wished he could have lost his virginity inside, or the car that, had he owned it in his midteens, would have resulted in the loss of said virginity. Restoring classic autos is the perfect middle-aged hobby, because it directs financial resources toward preserving the virile emblems of youth. (Even if, as is more likely, you actually lost your virginity in your dad's station wagon.) If I'd had the money, I would have shown up in a 1979 Corvette, a car whose lewdly elongated hood resembles the tongue on the Rolling Stones logo, and equipped it with a stereo system powerful enough to blast Montrose's "Rock Candy" loud enough to be heard from one end of a drive-in movie theater to another.

In manufacturing towns, especially automaking towns, and *especially* Lansing, the classic-car rally has a civic purpose that goes beyond the individual statement "This is when I was young, dumb, and full of cum." It's an event that celebrates the peak of the city's virility and fecundity, too. That's why the title "homecoming," which is associated with a return to high school or college, is so appropriate for a gathering of Oldsmobiles. Because Lansing has been stripped of its industrial identity. Now, it's just the state capital.

Classic cars and classic rock—generally of the greasy Eddie Cochran, Gene Vincent, Dion and the Belmonts style—are inseparable elements of baby boomer nostalgia. A loudspeaker played Oldsmobile's greatest hits. Jackie Brenston and Ike Turner's "Rocket 88," which claims to be the first rock and roll song, was inspired by Oldsmobile's greatest innovation, the V-8 "Rocket" engine. (A sign on the side of the plant boasted that Oldsmobile—and Lansing—was "HOME OF THE ROCKET.") "In My Merry Oldsmobile" was the "Little Red Corvette" of the sheet-music era, a celebration of that new pastime—parking—made possible by the hardtopped auto. ("They love to spark in the dark old park / As they go flying along / She says she knows why the motor goes / The 'sparker' is awfully strong.") At a memorabilia table, I found the 1964 LP *Oldsmobile Spotlights the New Stars in Action: Ann-Margret, Anthony Newley, Sergio Franchi, Peter Nero, John Gary, Ketty Lester, Gale Garnett.* If you listened to any of those pop vocalists, you probably drove an Oldsmobile. Oldsmobile may have inspired rock and roll, but unlike the Ford Mustang and the Pontiac GTO, it did not take inspiration in return. In the 1950s—the Rocket-engine era—the Olds was some badass American iron. In its mature years, however, Oldsmobile sat smack in the middle of GM's brand hierarchy, which ran from apprentice electrician to general sales manager: Chevy, Pontiac, Olds, Buick, Cadillac. TV detective Joe Mannix drove an Oldsmobile Toronado. The real-life cops in

Lansing drove Oldsmobiles. The Indy 500 pace car was an Oldsmobile. (The power-ballad band REO Speedwagon did not take its name from an Oldsmobile, but from a truck produced by Ransom E. Olds after he sold out to GM and started a new company, using just his initials. One of the members happened to see the truck's name on a chalkboard in a history of transportation class at the University of Illinois. REO was rightfully worshipped in Lansing, from its bar days to its county-fair dotage. Appropriately, it peaked commercially in the early 1980s, about the same time as the Oldsmobile. At the R. E. Olds Transportation Museum, in Lansing, the docents will point out that the name is properly pronounced "Reo," like the street and the school in Lansing.)

On the windshield of every Oldsmobile at the reunion was the owner's name and hometown. They had driven from Ohio, New York, Georgia, and Florida, and flown from Germany. What else could inspire anyone living south of the forty-second parallel, west of Lake Michigan, or east of Lake Huron to visit Lansing? Not the state capitol, which looks like a snow-globe version of the real thing in D.C. Once the last of these Oldsmobiles rusted away, Lansing would be known as nothing but an answer on a third-grade quiz, along with Jefferson City and Springfield.

A man in a lawn chair explained how to distinguish a 1972 Cutlass sedan from a 1973 Cutlass sedan by studying the taillight design, demonstrating that the difference between gearheads and sci-fi fans is not nerdy obsessiveness but money and practicality. I walked past a 1971 98 hearse. The coffin in the back contained a skeleton wearing a "Go To Hell" cap.

An Oldsmobile historian named Jim Walkinshaw was offering rides in the oldest Oldsmobile in existence: a 1905 curved dash, the open carriage on wheels in which President Theodore Roosevelt rode when he became the first president to visit Lansing (and the last, until Bill Clinton). With a top speed of twenty miles an hour, the curved dash was as sporty as a golf cart.

"Is this thing street legal?" I asked Jim, who was costumed in a motoring cap.

"It's street legal," he told me as we did a gentle doughnut around the parking lot. "Any car is street legal."

The Homecoming's impresario was Don Cooper, a retired autoworker wearing an Oldsmobile sun visor over his winter-white hair. I introduced myself to him in the command tent and insisted he tell me the story of his career at Olds, just because I love listening to baby boom autoworkers talk about how they hired in at the shop. I didn't start my first full-time job until I was twenty-six, and it only paid $12.50 an hour. My last two full-time jobs no longer exist. For a Generation X-er, tales from the 1960s are employment porn.

Cooper started at Oldsmobile on September 13, 1965, less than three months after graduating from high school. According to Oldsmobile Labor Relations, it was the company's largest hiring date since World War II. This was no coincidence. The next afternoon, the business page of *The State Journal*, Lansing's daily newspaper, carried a story headlined "Carmakers Boosting Production."

> U.S. auto production was expected to climb sharply this week with General Motors and American Motors assembly lines humming again.
>
> GM built relatively few Buicks and Chevrolets last week as it picked up the tempo of production following a shutdown for changeover to 1966 models. GM's output last week was only 1,020 cars, but that figure probably will be upped nearly 50 fold this week as all 23 of its assembly plants get back into production.
>
> Ford had two of its assembly plants on overtime operations Saturday as it continued to build up its new car stockpile in advance of public announcement time.

On the front page of the same edition was a story about President Lyndon Johnson pledging unlimited American commitment to prevent the Reds from overrunning South Vietnam and signing a draft-card-burning ban. The war had killed 629 Americans by then.

During the Vietnam War, America could afford guns *and* butter. The late 1960s were the pinnacle of this country's prosperity. What was good for American militarism was good for General Motors. In 1964, GM received $426 million in defense contracts. By 1967, that figure had increased 69 percent, to $776 million. AC Electronics delivered guidance and navigation systems for Apollo capsules. The Allison Division produced turboprop engines for cargo, antisubmarine, and reconnaissance planes. The Hydra-Matic Division received a contract for 469,000 M16A1 rifles, enough to arm every U.S. infantryman in Southeast Asia.

Vietnam was the perfect little war for General Motors. During World War II, the entire auto industry was devoted to building tanks, ships, planes, guns, bombs, and bullets. From 1942 to 1945, Everett Ketchum's Chevrolet plant in Flint built nothing but army trucks. By war's end, he said, "everybody had a four-year-old car and maybe it was a junker to begin with."

Not during Vietnam. Americans *enjoyed* the prosperity that war produced. In 1965, the year LBJ dedicated American troops to combat, GM sold 7,278,000 automobiles, with net sales of $20.7 billion, both company records.

"More GM people earned more money and received more benefits during 1965 than ever before in the history of the Corporation," boasted the next year's annual report. "GM's 1965 worldwide employment averaged 735,000 men and women and payrolls totaled $5,546 million. Its 409,000 hourly workers averaged $3.74—substantially above that reported for all U.S. manufacturing employees by the Bureau of Labor Statistics." (This was when gasoline cost 31 cents a gallon, and a new house averaged $21,500.)

The good times were just beginning. The national unemployment rate did not exceed 4 percent in any of the forty-eight months between 1966 and 1969. If you didn't find a job, a job found you, which was one reason the hippies were so vilified for their refusal to work. In Gary, Indiana, steel mills bought billboard space to beg for workers. (Besides creating jobs, the war made them easy to obtain: the draft targeted young blue-collar males, withdrawing the most able-bodied specimens from the labor pool.)

Don Cooper's job search consisted of cutting class for an afternoon to fill out applications at all four Lansing auto plants: Motor Wheel, Fisher Body, Diamond Reo, and Oldsmobile. Diamond Reo called first, but Cooper's father was the union rep of an Oldsmobile local and wanted his son to work there too, so he told Don to wait. He knew a mass hiring was coming. A week later, Oldsmobile called. After a physical that "amounted to if you could breathe," Cooper was put to work on the frame line. His job consisted of turning the front wheel to the left, lifting the tire rod, pumping oil into the axle, then plugging it so the oil didn't run out. The line moved at ninety-six frames an hour. From six in the morning 'til two in the afternoon, Cooper walked alongside a frame, crouched over, back and forth in a space twenty feet long. To occupy his mind, he sang pop songs, whistled, and swapped trivia questions with the guy squirting axle grease on the other side of the frame. The monotony was worth it. Cooper was earning $5 an hour, plus time-and-a-half for overtime, and double time for Sunday—and he got all the overtime he wanted. In his first model year, Oldsmobile came out with the Toronado, the first car in twenty-nine years to operate with front-wheel drive. In the car culture of the 1960s, when auto engineers were celebrities, this was as significant as the first Technicolor movie or the first moon orbit. The Toronado—a car nicknamed "Mafia," because it was all hood—made the cover of *Time, Newsweek,* and *Look.* It won *Motor Trend*'s Car of the Year, the MVP award for automobiles. As PBA Bowler of the Year, Dick Weber won a Toronado. Miss America visited Lansing to pose with the car. (Professional bowlers and beauty queens were celebrities in the 1960s, too.)

In 1966, Oldsmobile also moved its headquarters from a building that looked like a WPA post office to a midcentury-modern tower with a keypunch room to feed its IBM computers. The general manager's office was adorned with glittering rocket logos in secular stained glass. It was the last year of the mod sixties, an era whose style Olds engineers helped define, and it was the very last year of America's post–World War II optimism, before the Detroit riot, before the Tet Offensive, before the assassination of Martin Luther King Jr.—the last year America believed it could defeat poverty, racism, and Communism, and still send astronauts to the moon in silver-foil suits. My parents moved to Michigan in 1966, when my father followed a college classmate who'd been hired to work as an economist in the state's expanding bureaucracy, overseen by Governor George Romney, the American Motors chairman who had introduced the Nash Rambler, America's original compact car. From auto executive to governor was not a promotion. It was a lateral move. Who was more qualified to run Michigan than one of the businessmen who had built so many factories, designed so many bestselling cars, given lifetime employment to so many men a generation removed from rustic insecurity? The "wave" passage in Hunter S. Thompson's *Fear and Loathing in Las Vegas* was about the San Francisco counterculture, a scene that could not have been more different from a Middle American auto town, but it captured the spirit of the entire nation in the mid-1960s: "There was a fantastic universal sense that whatever we were doing was right, that we were winning . . . We had all the momentum; we were riding the crest of a high and beautiful wave . . ." And then: "With the right kind of eyes, you can almost see the high-water mark—that place where the wave finally broke and rolled back."

In 1967, Don Cooper—safe from the draft thanks to a berth in the Coast Guard Reserve—married his high school girlfriend and bought a house. At the age of twenty, he had settled on a career, a mate, and a home. His life's course was set. He wasn't old enough to drink, but he drank anyway. An autoworker just had to wave his pay over the bar of the Rock Tavern, across the street from the shop. As Gus Caliacatsos would have said, if a man works, he deserves a drink—and at twenty, Cooper was a man.

"A man came into work one day," he said, "and we were talking about the baby boomers. I said, 'I'm a baby boomer.' He said, 'I'm from the X Generation.' He said, 'Your generation will be the last generation that will earn more than the previous generation did. Your generation will probably be the last generation that the majority of them will own their own house. You'll probably never move from your home. My generation will keep moving.'"

(Cooper did move, once. When he was twenty-seven, he built a house on five acres in the country, enough room for his children, and for a pole barn to hold his collection of vintage Oldsmobiles.)

In 1970, Cooper took part in the UAW's last great nationwide strike. It was planned by Walter Reuther, before his death that year in a plane crash, and led by his successor, Leonard Woodcock, who later became ambassador to China. The union wanted a fifty-cent-an-hour raise, annual cost-of-living increases, and the opportunity to retire after thirty years, at age fifty-eight, with full lifetime benefits. (The next contract, negotiated in 1973, allowed workers to retire after thirty years at any age. "Thirty-and-out" would become such a staple of Michigan life that when Johnny Carson retired after thirty years of hosting *The Tonight Show*, that was the headline in the *Detroit Free Press*—as though the King of Late Night were just another stiff who'd put in his time.) At that moment, those requests seemed reasonable. General Motors was the most powerful industrial oligopoly since the days of the Robber Barons. The General built half the cars driven in the United States. Its dominance was so thorough there was talk of the government breaking off each brand into a Chrysler-sized company. A corporation so colossal could not only afford to share its wealth, it could not afford a mass desertion by its workforce.

In September 1970, over four hundred thousand workers—ten times the size of Alexander the Great's army—went on strike and stayed on strike for sixty-seven days, until GM gave them everything they wanted. In those two months, the strike cut the growth in the gross national product from 2.5 percent to 1.4 percent. The auto industry *was* the American economy. As he walked the picket line, Cooper was jeered by passing drivers, but the way he saw it, he was striking for every worker. As GM was the nation's biggest company, the UAW was the nation's biggest union. Its wages and benefits set the standard for all American labor.

"We used to get stoned in the newspapers, every time we'd get something in our contract," he said. "'Well, the autoworkers drove the price up because they got a raise.' But then everybody else would start getting raises, too, after we did."

THE 1970 GM STRIKE took place just as Americans were discovering Japanese cars. Throughout the 1960s, the Volkswagen Beetle was the only foreign car most Americans had ever seen. Volkswagen sold two-thirds of the automobiles imported to the United States, but imports were only 10 percent of the market—a measly fifth of GM's share. The Japanese had tried breaking into the United States with the Toyopet, whose model year and horsepower were identical: fifty-eight. Designed with Iron Curtain flair and engineered for Japan's bombed-out roads, the Toyopet made it to Los Angeles by ship, then stalled on the hills separating the city from the rest of the continent. Americans bought exactly 1,913.

In 1965, Toyota returned to America with the more powerful, more stylish Corona, which sold well among first-time buyers on the Pacific Coast. For precisely that reason, the Big Three didn't take the car seriously. They figured those kids would graduate to a Lincoln or a Cadillac as soon as they could afford it. And California was not Middle America.

"The people who buy Japanese cars probably all live on communes," one Ford executive said, scoffing.

After the little Nash Rambler became the third-bestselling nameplate of 1958, GM responded with the Chevy Corvair, best remembered as a subject of Ralph Nader's *Unsafe at Any Speed*, which revealed that the car's rear-heavy design—the engine was located in the trunk—made it prone to spin out. GM responded by hiring a private eye to dig up dirt on Nader. Chairman James Roche was forced to apologize to the author before a Senate subcommittee. The incident made *Unsafe at Any Speed* a bestseller and put its humorless, ascetic author on the cover of *Time*.

Nader was a contributor to the *New Republic*, so his writing appealed to people who felt cosmopolitan in a cramped foreign car—and would have been embarrassed to buy American for purely patriotic reasons. In 1966, the year GM made Nader a star, those attitudes were already moving from the big cities and the university clubs to mainstream America. Then they hitched a ride in the Corvair.

"It's almost impossible to overstate the magnitude of the Corvair disaster for General Motors, indeed for the entire American auto industry," wrote Paul Ingrassia in *Crash Course: The American Automobile Industry's Road from Glory to Disaster.* "The scandal occurred just as the Vietnam War was fostering a new and profound mistrust of establishment institutions—the government, the military, universities, churches and others. The Corvair added General Motors—and, by extension, all of corporate America—to the list of institutions not to be trusted. In some ways, GM's corporate reputation would never recover."

Culturally and economically, U.S. auto companies were not cut out to build small cars. For the first generation after World War II, American life was defined by one word: "more." An unending expansion of prosperity that not only meant bigger cars and bigger houses, but *two* cars and *two* houses. No one benefited more than the UAW, but every time the automakers granted the union a more generous contract, to prevent a strike that would stop those big cars from rolling off the line, they made it necessary to build even bigger cars, to pay those bigger wages.

The strike hurt the company's competitiveness with Japan in multiple ways. The shutdown cost GM two percentage points of market share, which it never recovered.

The thirty-and-out deal added to GM's pension costs. Because the strike took place in the fall, at the beginning of a model year, it disrupted production of the new Chevy Vega, GM's answer to the Beetle and the Corona.

Keeping the Vega away from customers was not all bad. GM didn't *want* to build a small car, so it built that car shoddily. The Vega was designed with sleeveless piston cylinders, to save weight, but the cylinders lacked a seal that prevented oil leakage, so the car dribbled dark stains onto driveways. Many Vega owners were first-time buyers who became convinced that all GM cars were junk and that, by extension, all American cars must be junk.

THE UNION and the autoworkers negotiated a new contract every three years, which meant the 1970 agreement was the last before the Arab oil embargo, which ended the era of jetliner cars and the monopoly of the American automakers. By then, though, it wasn't just a matter of GM's having nothing more to give, it was a matter of its employees having everything they needed. Since Cooper had hired in right out of high school, he could retire at forty-eight years old, before manual labor wore out his body, and with health care to keep him alive another forty-eight years.

His father's generation—the Sit-Down Strikers—had set the table, so *his* generation could enjoy the feast.

"The union got to a point where we ran out of things to negotiate for," Don said. "What more could we ask for? We had a good wage, we had good health care, we had a good pension. Everything was there. I was there for the best years of Oldsmobile, as far as I'm concerned. I know many people that are production, salaried, engineers that I graduated with, they all say the same thing. We all saw the best Oldsmobile had to offer. I don't think it'll ever come back to what it was."

In the early 1930s, Walter Reuther had campaigned for Norman Thomas, the Socialist presidential candidate, and spent sixteen months in Russia, working as a tool-and-die maker in an auto plant. (Later, as UAW president, he would purge the union of Communists.) Reuther believed in universal health care and affordable housing. It was his genius as a labor leader to fuse capitalism and socialism by agitating for a system in which workers could own big American cars, big American houses, and big American boats while having the security of Soviet medical care, Soviet pensions, and Soviet job guarantees. Genius, of course, only shows itself where there is opportunity, and there was no better place and time to create this way of life than the Great Lakes Region of the United States in the quarter century after World War II.

The Middle West became the industrial heartland of America because, as its name indicates, it was in the middle of things. Most importantly, it was midway between the two essential ingredients of steel—iron ore, mined in northern Minnesota and Upper Michigan, and coal, carved from the mountains of Appalachia. The Middle West also had the element needed to bring those ingredients together: water. After the ore left Duluth on a freighter, where could it go but Chicago, Gary, Detroit, Cleveland, Buffalo, and Ashtabula, the railhead for Pittsburgh?

In 1899, Buffalo attorney John G. Milburn lured the Lackawanna Steel Company from Scranton, Pennsylvania, by promoting his city's location astride the Great Lakes and the Erie Canal. Milburn invited Lackawanna president Walter Scranton to a luncheon in his Delaware Avenue mansion. There, according to Mark Goldman's *City on the Edge* (the only history of twentieth-century Buffalo you will ever need), he assured the industrialist that Buffalo could provide all the essentials for steelmaking, inexpensively and inexhaustibly: iron ore from Minnesota arrived at the docks daily, Niagara Falls generated more power than any other waterfall in North America, and the unlettered immigrants from Poland, Russia, and Austria-Hungary had not yet been infected with the virus of unionism.

The steel company was given 1,300 acres of Lake Erie shoreline and soon after incorporated its own company town—Lackawanna, New York.

Buffalo is the mother of American manufacturing cities. The European immigrants who settled Cleveland, Detroit, Chicago, and smaller urban centers had to pass through Buffalo to get to the mill jobs awaiting farther west, and they copied its layout of ethnic villages and neighborhood taverns. But just as Buffalo was the first city to rise, it was the first to fall. Buffalo pioneered the Rust Belt cycle of decay beginning in the 1950s, at least a decade and a half before everyone else.

As the last stop on the Erie Canal ("all the way from Albany to Buffalo," as the song "Low Bridge" goes), Buffalo was the first freshwater city to achieve national prominence. In the nineteenth century, two Buffalonians—Millard Fillmore and Grover Cleveland—served as president. Their girths are today cast in bronze on the steps of Buffalo's Art Deco city hall. By 1900, Buffalo was the eighth-largest city in the United States. It had the most millionaires per capita. It was the world's busiest grain port. Only Chicago slaughtered more livestock. Every day, dozens of ships unloaded wheat for the bakers and brewers, and steers for the butchers. Competing with Chicago for the title of Greatest Inland City, Buffalo in 1901 threw a World's Fair intended to surpass its rival's 1893 Columbian Exposition. President William McKinley attended the Pan-American Exposition—and was shot by an anarchist as he shook hands in the Temple of Music. Eight days later, the president died of gangrene in a bedroom of Milburn's house. Hours later, and less than a mile away, Theodore Roosevelt was sworn in as his successor.

Buffalonians sometimes blame their city's decline on the Curse of William McKinley, but Buffalo remained an important industrial center for over half a century after it hosted a presidential assassination. Buffalo fermented a good helping of the grain that came through town, in nearly two thousand breweries. Its best-known local beers, Iroquois and Simon Pure, survived until the Budweiser purge of the early 1970s. They were not as long-lived as other hometown swills drunk out of penury or local pride—Iron City in Pittsburgh, Genesee in Rochester, Stroh's in Detroit, Old Style in Chicago—but Buffalo home-brewed first. Buffalo's German brewers invented a fleshy local delicacy to stimulate thirst in their customers: the beef-on-weck sandwich. Tissues of rare roast beef, hot from the oven, packed within a *kummelweck* roll, studded with pretzel salt and caraway seeds. Even the abrasive Midwestern accent—the mother tongue of the Mayors Daley, Jimmy Hoffa, Dennis Kucinich, Iggy Pop, and Jim Belushi—originated in Western New York, as a hard astringent distillation of the nasal Yankee speech brought west from Vermont by the region's pioneers. Today, amateur lexicographers can identify the New York State Thruway exit where waitresses stop serving "soda" and begin serving "pahhp." (Exit 42, Geneva/Lyons, midway between Rochester and Syracuse.) It's the spot where the East ends and the Midwest begins.

During World War II, Buffalo's steel mills made it the ideal city to build the U.S. Army Air Forces, the Royal Air Force, and the Soviet Air Force. At the outset of 1940, Bell Aircraft employed 1,200 workers in its Buffalo factory. By the end of the year, Bell had a new, government-built plant in Niagara Falls, and 31,000 new employees to build the P-39A Airacobra, which would do battle with the Luftwaffe on the Eastern Front. Curtiss-Wright, producer of the P-40 and the Tomahawk, expanded its payroll from 5,300 to 43,000. All three GM plants built airplane engines, and Lackawanna Steel, now owned by Bethlehem, forged the skins of tanks and railroad cars. Buffalo produced 2.5 percent of all American material, making it the fifth city of the war effort.

On December 29, 1940, as the Germans occupied France, bombed Britain, and made plans to attack Russia, President Franklin D. Roosevelt delivered a fireside chat on the topic of America's munitions industry. He used a phrase coined months earlier by his speechwriter playwright Robert E. Sherwood.

"We must be the great arsenal of democracy," Roosevelt said. "For us, this is an emergency as serious as war itself. We must apply ourselves to our task with the same resolution, the same sense of urgency, the same spirit of patriotism and sacrifice as we would show were we at war."

The sobriquet "Arsenal of Democracy" would be claimed by Detroit. Outside that city, along a creek called Willow Run, Henry Ford had built a plant containing the largest room on Earth, to produce the B-24 Liberator bomber. But Roosevelt intended the name equally for the shipyards of Oakland and the steel mills of Buffalo.

Like most Northern industrial cities, Buffalo's population in 1950—580,000—was double its population today. Buffalo's midcentury misfortune was the opening of the Saint Lawrence Seaway in 1959. Its importance as a port was based on its position as the last stop on the Lower Great Lakes. Once the seaway opened, freighters carrying ore and grain bypassed Buffalo's mills and silos, sailing directly to the Atlantic Ocean. The city fathers knew the canal would eliminate the nautical monopoly that had made Buffalo a city in the first place. They'd been trying to stop the seaway since it was first proposed, in the 1920s. In 1953, a desperate Common Council passed a resolution declaring the seaway would be vulnerable to Communist bombs (dropped from planes Buffalo had built for the Soviets a decade before).

"Buffalo's long-dreaded nightmare had finally come to pass," wrote Goldman in *City on the Edge*.

> The city, which for so long had dominated the stream of commerce on the Great Lakes, was now bypassed as a dead-end route. As a result, the entire range of water-fed industries—boat companies, ship chandlers, ship repairers and shipbuilders—suffered the most. In 1962, the American Shipbuilding Company closed, the last vestige of an industry that had been in Buffalo since 1812. Since the middle of the nineteenth century, Buffalo had been the grain storage capital of the world, harboring millions of tons of Midwestern grain in its internationally renowned grain elevators. Now, as increasing amounts of grain were shipped to Montreal via the seaway, Buffalo's significance as a port of storage quickly eroded.

Buffalo fell first. Detroit fell next, and did it with a bang.

3.

The Motor City Is Burning

In January 1966, Detroit's boy mayor, Jerome Cavanagh, was sworn in for a second term. Cavanagh, who at thirty-seven still looked like an Irish seminarian, declared his city was enjoying "the greatest prosperity in Detroit's history." From his office atop Detroit's limestone city hall, Cavanagh could see the riverbank where the French explorer Antoine de la Mothe Cadillac had landed in 1701. If he looked in the other direction, north and west, he could see the fifth-largest city in the United States, spread out for twenty miles along the six-lane Gallic boulevards radiating from the river. "Detroit" was not just the name of a city; it was a met-onym for the automobile industry, builder of the most important con-sumer product ever invented. Cavanagh could see so far not just because Detroit was built on a flat alluvial plain, but because it was in every other way a horizontal city. The tallest skyscraper, the forty-seven-story Penob-scot, had been built the year before the Depression. Since then, Detroit had reached no higher. Detroiters did not move up. They moved out. Detroit had more houses than any American city, and per resident, it had more cars. This was not just a matter of supporting the hometown indus-try. It was a necessity. The derelict Detroit Street Railway system, obso-lete in an atomized city, had retired its last car in 1955. In its place, Detroit built a web of freeways. Once the assembly lines began building cars again after World War II, even a city whose main streets were wide enough for a bus's U-turn needed more room for more automobiles. Many Detroiters migrated to the suburbs along those roads. Detroit had lost 200,000 residents in the 1950s but still had 1.6 million. Along with the people, though, the businesses were leaving, too. In 1954, Hudson's, the downtown department store that was to Detroit what Macy's was to

New York, opened Northland, the nation's first suburban shopping center, just across 8 Mile Road, in Southfield. The auto plants were moving as well. The multistory factories, castles around which industrial peasantry had gathered in wooden bungalows, were out of date, and there was no room in Detroit to build the enormous shop floors that Henry Ford had pioneered at Willow Run. Packard went out of business in the late 1950s, abandoning its four-story plant in northeast Detroit. Around the same time, Chrysler built a plant on farmland in Livonia, west of the city.

By the early 1960s, at the beginning of Cavanagh's first term, Detroit was already one third black. During World War II, when Southerners flocked to Detroit to build tanks and planes, a race riot broke out between blacks who resented their lack of advancement in the factories and whites who resented Northern customs of racial equality, killing thirty-four and injuring hundreds. Afterward, U.S. Attorney General Francis Biddle wrote that "careful consideration [should] be given to limiting and in some cases putting an end to Negro migrations into communities which cannot absorb them, either on account of their physical limitations or cultural background. This needs immediate and careful consideration. When postwar readjustments begin, and jobs are scarcer, the situation will become far more acute . . . It would seem pretty clear that no more blacks should move to Detroit."

But more blacks did, lured by jobs in the liberated auto industry. In the 1950s, Detroit's black population increased from three hundred thousand to five hundred thousand—an increase that did not quite compensate for the white flight it caused. At the same time, Black Bottom, the East Side neighborhood to which African-Americans had been confined since the early twentieth century, was demolished to make way for highways and housing projects. Unwelcome in most parts of Detroit due to restrictive covenants, blacks were packed into new ghettos, even more crowded than Black Bottom, such as Twelfth Street, where the population was twenty thousand per square mile and blacks were charged double the rent vacating whites had paid, because where else did they have to go? After paying the rent man, the newcomers were exploited by liquor store owners, used-furniture dealers, corner grocers, and tavern keepers. Twelfth Street became Detroit's Levee, its red-light district, its Sin Strip, where both blacks and whites sought out marijuana, heroin, numbers runners, and whores—over and underage. The hedonists were followed by the vice squad, who, as one early sixties resident remembered, "rode around . . . busting prostitutes, dope pushers and just plain fucking with people." The police force was 97 percent white. That didn't go unnoticed on Twelfth Street, either.

The black migration to Detroit peaked just as the city's auto employment was declining. Over the course of the 1950s, Chrysler laid off half its forty-six thousand employees in Detroit. Jobs in the new suburban plants were beyond the reach of urban blacks; in the older city plants, the UAW prevented blacks from apprenticing in the skilled trades, which were closed guilds.

There were, however, neighborhoods where blacks and whites lived together in the 1950s and '60s. Northeast Detroit was tributary to Packard, Hudson, the Dodge Main plant in Hamtramck, and three Cadillac plants. Poles began settling there in the late nineteenth century. By the middle of the twentieth, they'd established a Polish Broadway on Chene Street (pronounced "Shane," after the French colonist who farmed there when the soil belonged to Louis XIV). It was one of those self-contained ethnic villages that existed in every Northern city just before and after World War II. The men could walk to work at the factory and the women could do all their shopping in a few blocks of Chene, buying the furniture from Moliszewski, the sausage from Jaworski's Butcher Shop, and dressing the family at Rathenau's. Chene's merchants bragged that their street had more retail businesses per square foot than any American thoroughfare but Fifth Avenue. The children spoke the mother tongue until they went to school, and heard it every Sunday during Mass at St. Stanislaus and St. Hyacinth. The Ivanhoe Café served fish every Friday, and every Saturday, Polish truck farmers and Jewish vegetable peddlers set up stalls at the Chene-Ferry Market.

Then, in the 1950s, the Edsel Ford Freeway—named for Henry's only son—bisected the neighborhood. Packard closed. The Hudson-Nash merger that created American Motors resulted in Hudson's thirty-five thousand jobs moving to the Nash plant in Wisconsin. As the auto plants left, the Black Bottom diaspora began arriving. Janice Harvey, who grew up in one of the neighborhood's first black families, when "everybody was just about at the plant," didn't notice any racial tension as a girl; her grade-school sweetheart was an Italian boy named Angelo. But once she got to Northeastern High School, the black population had reached a tipping point that was causing white parents to move to suburbia.

"When I entered in 1954, and you looked down the hallway, you would see little dark spots," she remembered, "but by the time I ended, in 1958, you would see little white spots."

Marion Krzykowski's family arrived on Chene Street from a displaced person's camp in Germany. His earliest memories were of a mixed neighborhood, where Poles patronized a black dentist and a white kid felt safe pedaling his bike on the colored folks' blocks. Even when blacks bought the houses next door, the Krzykowskis didn't think of moving, because they were still in the center of Polish Detroit.

IN THE HISTORY of the counterculture, the summer of 1967 is remembered as the Summer of Love, after the hippie celebration in San Francisco's Haight-Ashbury neighborhood. That was the title of a section in *Rolling Stone*'s fortieth-anniversary issue, profiling the most fertile music scenes of the magazine's birth year: New York, Los Angeles, London, San Francisco, Memphis, and Detroit.

The Summer of Love may have missed Detroit, but Detroit belonged on that list. From its founding in 1960 to the end of 1966, Motown Records had produced fourteen number one hits, most of them by the Supremes, whose showcase singer, Diana Ross, was a graduate of Cass Technical High School (later the alma mater of the White Stripes' Jack White). Motown's impresario, Berry Gordy Jr., had worked on the line at Ford, and it has been suggested that he transferred the principles of automotive assembly to assembling hit records, employing separate work crews of songwriters (Eddie Holland Jr., Lamont Dozier, and Brian Holland), singers (the Temptations, Smokey Robinson), and backup musicians (the Funk Brothers). Gordy may have organized his business like Henry Ford, but that was not the auto industry's main contribution to Motown's success. Gordy's genius was selling black musicians to white audiences. Detroit's auto plants were a destination for white hillbillies and black sharecroppers, who couldn't help but appreciate each other's music.

Wayne Kramer, the guitarist for Detroit's punk rock progenitors the MC5, learned his instrument from a Southern-born stepfather who serenaded Kramer's mother with Ferlin Husky, Webb Pierce, Eddy Arnold, and the bluegrass standard "Mountain Dew." Then he turned on the radio and listened to John Lee Hooker, Koko Taylor, and Albert Collins.

"The cultural mix as it played out in music in Detroit in the fifties and the sixties and up into maybe halfway through the seventies was unique in the world in its self-referentiality and incestuousness," said Kramer. "If you grew up in Detroit in the fifties and sixties, you listened to the radio. Radio was huge and you had a broad choice. If you wanted to find soul music and real rhythm and blues, you could find it. That's what I would listen to a great deal. There were country stations that were very hard-core country. I was attracted to rhythm and blues. It had a rawness and a passion that you didn't hear in Bobby Vinton. Even the mainstream stations would play a soul record and certainly they played all the Motown hits."

Kramer added another genre to his musical education when he met jazzheads Rob Tyner and John Sinclair. Tyner became the lead singer of the MC5. Sinclair, who had migrated to Detroit from Flint and published the counterculture newspaper *Fifth Estate*, became the band's manager and apparatchik. The MC5 started out playing in parks and at teen clubs, living and rehearsing in a rock and roll collective called the Trans-Love Commune. They developed a sound derived from the industrial cacophony of the city around them: drumbeats at the driving tempo of an assembly line, electric guitars amplified to the volume of 425 cc motorcycle engines. The MC5 became the house band at the Grande Ballroom, Detroit's answer to San Francisco's Fillmore. While Detroit embraced the MC5, the MC5 turned out to be a less successful export than Motown. Their aggressive sound was out of tune with the psychedelic music popular with most hippies. As a result, they bombed outside the industrial Midwest.

"It may have something to do with a kind of anti-intellectualism and anti-elitism," Kramer theorized. "If you just walked up, first impression, you'd say, 'These guys are insane and they're coming on too strong.' It might be off-putting. Europe, we were just too raw for them. They kind of evidenced a more refined sensibility."

Kramer eventually got his due—*Rolling Stone* placed him at number 92 on its "100 Greatest Guitarists of All Time" list, and he's considered a grandfather of punk. But during the Summer of Love, the rest of America was listening to *Sgt. Pepper's Lonely Hearts Club Band* and the Byrds. If the MC5's sound was ahead of its time in its violence, its aggressiveness, and its despair, it could be because Detroit was ahead of its time in those qualities, too.

MAYOR CAVANAGH BELIEVED he was in step with this multiracial Detroit. His upset campaign had been supported by blacks furious about a "crackdown" by Mayor Louis Miriani that resulted in police swarming into their neighborhoods and patting down law-abiding homeowners. The blacks, not yet numerous enough to elect one of their own but numerous enough to defeat a racist mayor, adopted the slogan "Phooey on Louie." The press dubbed the new mayor "Jerry the Giant Killer." Cavanagh named blacks to his cabinet and integrated the police force, whose white officers had staged a ticket-writing strike when forced to share squad cars with black patrolmen. President Johnson showered Detroit with Model Cities grants, hoping to make it the Midwestern front of his War on Poverty. If Cavanagh had been closer to the streets, he might have heard about the "Big Four," a quartet of white cops with a reputation for kicking black ass. If he'd attended one of the monthly meetings held by the East Side's state senator, Coleman Young, he might have heard that Young's constituents thought of the police as "prison guards" whose job was "to keep the damn blacks away from the whites at all costs and what they did to themselves was their problem." But in the summer of 1967, Detroit's establishment believed that no black community in America was less likely to riot.

THE UNITED COMMUNITY LEAGUE for Civic Action had its headquarters in an office above a print shop on Twelfth Street. During election years, the black empowerment organization paid its rent through the largesse of politicians. But 1967 was not an election year, so the group covered its bills by operating a blind pig, throwing weekend parties featuring beer, craps, and dancing. On Saturday night, the twenty-third of July, eighty-five people gathered to celebrate the homecoming of two Vietnam veterans. The police had already raided the club twice. At three forty-five in the morning, they smashed the glass door with a sledgehammer and raced up the stairs. They were surprised by the number of revelers, and by the reaction of the doorman, William Walter Scott III, whose father and uncle operated the establishment.

"The club! Those goddamn peckerwoods are going to raid the club again!" hollered Scott, who would later take credit for inciting the riot in a book titled *Hurt, Baby, Hurt.*

Because of the party's size, the police had to call for three extra squadrols to take everyone to jail. And because the rear door of the club was padlocked and led to a blind alley, they had to lead the arrestees onto Twelfth Street, in full view of wee-hours partiers who saw the police kicking, punching, and clubbing their haul. On one of the hottest nights of the year, the street was already crowded. Once word of a bust spread through the neighborhood, it filled up even more. The crowd taunted the police with racial epithets: "Go home, whitey. Why don't you go fuck with white people?" And, as the cops dragged prisoners into wagons: "They can walk. Let them walk, you white sons of bitches." While the police kept the hostile blacks at bay with nightsticks, Scott jumped onto a car, shouting, "Are we going to let these peckerwood motherfuckers come down here any time they want and mess us around?" Scott then ran into an alley, picked up a bottle, and threw it at a cop. It missed, but Scott had launched the first missile of the Detroit riot. As bottles, bricks, and sticks dented retreating police cars, the mob celebrated its conquest of Twelfth Street by breaking the window of a clothing store and helping itself to brand-new wardrobes.

"For the first time in our lives, we felt free," Scott would write. "It was a free day for everybody to do and be what we wanted, regardless of the world and its laws."

ALMOST ALL THE LOOTERS were black, but to this day, Detroiters insist what happened was not a race riot. It was a class riot, an outburst by people fed up with merchants overcharging them for spoiled meat and lumpy mattresses, fed up with being too poor to buy the clothes and the jewelry they saw advertised on TV—or too poor even to buy a TV. Most of the shops on Twelfth Street were owned by suburban Jews. The rioters cleaned out all their inventory, then set the buildings on fire. The days were black with smoke, the nights red with flames.

The *Detroit Free Press* inventoried the looting: "They took fur stoles and floor maps, diamond rings and dresses, wigs, hamburger, color TV sets; shotguns, cameras, records, cigarettes, soda pop, lamps, toasters, shoes, underwear, guitars, two-pants suits, and $8 scotch and skinless hot dogs."

Skylarking looters partied in the streets with stolen beer, booze, and cigarettes. They were serenaded by musicians playing guitars from music stores stripped of all their instruments and all their jazz records, but none of their classical collections. Unlike in 1943, whites who strayed into the riot zone were mostly ignored. Some even joined the pillage. When the disorder spread east, to Chene Street, mixed mobs of blacks, Poles, and Italians smashed the plate-glass windows and joined forces to carry off couches and twenty-five-inch TVs. Furious shopkeepers recognized old customers enjoying the retail holiday.

The police were too poorly armed to protect firefighters from the rooftop snipers. Armed with newly acquired pawnshop rifles, the snipers took potshots at trucks attempting to douse the fires set that Sunday.

Governor George Romney declared a state of emergency, banned gasoline sales, and called in the National Guard, which arrived in the city with tanks, rifles, and jeeps to relieve police stations under attack by urban guerillas. Auto plants canceled shifts as terrified employees refused to report to work. A nightclub advertised a singing engagement that would begin "after the emergency." Front-porch vigilantes with .22-caliber rifles offered themselves as a security force for the fire department. Black merchants painted "SOUL BROTHER" on their windows, but the temptation of the goods inside was often more powerful than racial solidarity. Detroit Tigers outfielder Willie Horton, who had grown up near Twelfth Street, raced to the neighborhood after Sunday's doubleheader against the Yankees, not even stopping to change out of uniform. The Tigers' home stand against the Orioles was postponed. The teams finally played the third game in Baltimore.

When the farm boys of the National Guard couldn't restore order, Romney reluctantly requested federal assistance. The Republican governor waited until Monday morning to ask the president for help: he was planning to run against Johnson in 1968 and did not want to look like a man who couldn't keep order in his own state. For his part, Johnson was reluctant to send in the army. If he dispatched federal troops to Detroit, wouldn't every governor with a riot on his hands call the White House? Street warfare against American citizens was not the army's purpose. But Johnson was also in a fix: this was the third major riot on his watch, after Watts and Newark, and he had to show white voters he could protect them from black violence.

The president sent 4,700 paratroopers of the Eighty-Second Airborne Division, then scored a political point during a nationally televised speech: "Governor Romney of Michigan and the local officials in Detroit have been unable to bring the situation under control." It was the first time since the 1943 Detroit riot that federal troops had been called out to quell civil disorder. By the time the soldiers arrived on Tuesday, the riot was entering its third day, nearing the end of its life cycle. On Twelfth Street, a Jewish merchant stood in the wreckage of his clothing and variety store, looted of $20,000 in merchandise on a block burned, in the words of a *Free Press* reporter, to "a blackened shell and a vast pit of twisted wreckage, smoldering fires, and foul, stagnant water seeping higher up the basement walls." The shopkeeper's insurance had been canceled because his underwriter considered Detroit a riot risk.

"I'm sixty-three," the man said. "At this age, I lost everything. I don't know what I'm going to do."

On Chene Street, storekeepers reopened just long enough to collect insurance payments, then sold out as quickly as they could, often to Chaldeans—Iraqi Christians—who opened corner groceries and party stores.

"Chene was a stable, mixed neighborhood until the riots," recalled lifelong resident John Givans, who was born in 1961 and spent his earliest years among Slavic neighbors. "We went to West Virginia that summer and when we came back, the National Guard was in Perrien Park. There was a tank on Chene Street."

Forty-three people died in the last week of July, most of them looters shot by police or soldiers. In the infamous Algiers Motel Incident, which became the subject of a book by *Hiroshima* author John Hersey, three black youths were executed by police who mistook them for snipers. Detroit 1967 was America's deadliest civil disturbance until the Los Angeles riot, twenty-five years later.

John Lee Hooker, Detroit's greatest bluesman, memorialized the riot in a mournful song:

> *Ohhh, the Motor City is burning*
> *It ain't a thing in the world that I can do . . .*
> *My hometown is burning down to the ground*
> *Worse than Vietnam*

But the riot itself is less interesting than its aftermath. It was the B.C./A.D. week in Detroit's three-century history. After it was over, Mayor Cavanagh visited Twelfth Street, declaring sorrowfully, "We stand here amid the ashes of our hopes." In the 1960s, black ghettos burned in other big cities—Los Angeles; Chicago; Philadelphia; Washington, D.C.—but none of those riots had the consequences of Detroit's. Beforehand, Detroit had been losing about twenty-thousand white residents to the suburbs each year, a normal rate of defection for a Northern city. The year after the riot, eighty thousand whites left Detroit, for suburbs with well-established policies of keeping out the colored. Dearborn mayor Orville Hubbard stood astride Telegraph Road, his border with Detroit, as obdurately as George Wallace had stood in the doorway of the University of Alabama.

"They can't get in here," Hubbard boasted to an interviewer. "Every time we hear of a Negro moving—for instance, we had one last year—we respond quicker than you do to a fire."

In tony Grosse Pointe, which shares Mack Avenue with Detroit, Realtors had developed a "point system," which took into account religion, ethnicity, skin color, accent, and "Americanization." The system excluded most Poles and Italians, even more Jews, and all blacks.

Not all whites could afford a house in the suburbs, but most could afford a gun. Shotgun sales tripled after the riot. So did membership in the Breakthrough, a paramilitary Caucasian defense league formed to prevent another "Communist-inspired" black riot. Breakthrough's founder, a parks and recreation department employee, wanted "to arm the whites" of Detroit, because if blacks took over, it would mean "guerilla war in the suburbs."

Detroit also had a deeper tradition of black militance than most cities. It was the birthplace of the Nation of Islam, founded by a carpet salesman of unknown racial origin who called himself W. D. Fard. Fard preached that Caucasians had been bred by an evil black scientist named Yacub, as a "race of devils" who would rule the Earth for six thousand years. Fard's Christian analogue was the black separatist preacher Reverend Albert B. Cleage, founder of the Shrine of the Black Madonna. Cleage began denouncing nonviolent, integrationist black leaders as "Uncle Toms" in the early 1960s, even before Stokely Carmichael and H. Rap Brown. After the riot, he advised his followers to stockpile a month's supply of food to prepare for an attack by suburbanites bent on racial revenge.

Before the riot, Cavanagh and Romney had been considered potential presidents. Neither ever won another election. Romney left the governorship in 1969 to become secretary of housing and urban development. He tried to sell President Nixon on integration policies that might prevent more urban riots, but his arguments were thwarted by the white backlash created by his own riot. That same year, a broken Cavanagh announced he would not seek a third term. He died ten years later, aged fifty-one.

Politically, the chief beneficiary of the Detroit riot was Coleman A. Young Jr., the state senator from Black Bottom. Detroit elected one last Caucasian mayor, to succeed Cavanagh, but by 1973, it was a black-majority city. Young won the mayor's race that year and set about ensuring Detroit would remain a black-majority city. The city's first black mayor began his twenty-year rule with an inaugural speech that many whites still quote: "To all dope pushers, to all rip-off artists, to all muggers. It's time to leave Detroit. Hit 8 Mile Road. I don't give a damn if they're black or white, or if they wear Superfly suits or blue uniforms with silver badges. Hit the road."

8 Mile Road is the northern limit of Detroit but also a symbolic border between black and white. Suburbanites would have imported the
Berlin Wall there if they could have, and they heard in Young's speech
an incitement to export criminals into their communities.

Unlike most black leaders of his generation, Coleman Young's politics had not been formed by the civil rights movement. He was a radical
union organizer who had been purged from the Congress of Industrial
Organizations during Walter Reuther's Communist witch hunt in the
late 1940s. Blackballed by the UAW and the Ford personnel department,
Young reemerged as a leader of the National Negro Labor Council.
Called to testify before the House Un-American Activities Committee,
Young won his first citywide street cred when he challenged a Southern
congressman's pronunciation of "Negro" as "niggra." "That word,"
Young said, correcting the segregationist, "is Negro." Young's campaign
issue was police brutality. His opponent was white police chief John
Nichols. The defeat convinced Nichols to follow his constituency to the
suburban Oakland County, where he eventually was elected sheriff.

Black Detroiters refer to the riot as "the rebellion" and to Young's
election as "the liberation," a shattering of white oppression. Young remained in power by perpetuating the racial estrangement that had made
him mayor. He set himself up as Detroit's standard of blackness, label-
ing his political and journalistic opponents racists and Uncle Toms, and
declaring that Detroiters would never disarm as long as whites were
"practicing Ku Klux Klan out in the woods." The mayor knew he had
gained control of the city for the same reason blacks got anything in
America—because the whites had discarded it and moved on—and he
made sure his constituents understood that a vote against Young was a
vote for the suburbanites who had left this mess behind. Young was accused of creating a Midwestern Zaire, a revolutionary autocracy where
the Big Man's photograph stared from the wall of every public building.
After author Ze'ev Chafets visited to research his book *Devil's Night and
Other True Tales of Detroit*, he declared Detroit "America's first Third
World City . . . seething with post-colonial resentments."

"My fortune was a direct result of my city's misfortune—of the same
fear and loathing that had caused all my problems and Detroit's problems in the first place," Young wrote in his autobiography, *Hard Stuff*,
which has to hold the record for use of the word "motherfucker" in a
political memoir. "I was taking over the administration of Detroit because the white people didn't want the damn thing anymore. They were

getting the hell out, more than happy to turn over their troubles to some black sucker like me."

If you want to appreciate how differently Mayor Young was perceived on each side of 8 Mile, mention his name to any metro Detroiter old enough to remember his reign. Whites—who called him "Soulman"—scowl and grumble. Blacks beam. I once talked to a white political consultant who wondered, sighingly, how Detroit's history might have been different if a modest black politician named Richard Austin had not narrowly lost the 1969 mayoral election. When I posed that question to a black college professor, he snorted.

"Richard Austin was a *Negro*. Coleman knew how to talk to the people in the streets."

As the riot created a black nationalist mayor in Detroit, it would create another political creature in suburbia: the Reagan Democrat. In 1971, a federal judge ordered cross-district busing to integrate the Detroit area's schools, meaning white suburban children would be bused into Detroit, and vice versa. Vigilantes, who had fled the city and were determined not to let it follow, broke into a municipal garage, torching several school buses. Five Democratic congressmen from the Detroit suburbs signed a resolution in favor of an antibusing amendment to the U.S. Constitution. George Wallace won the 1972 Michigan presidential primary by campaigning against busing. Wallace did especially well in Macomb County, the white-flight nesting grounds of Detroit's Slavic and Italian autoworkers. In the 1960s, the blue-collar Catholic county was the most Democratic suburb in America, voting avidly for JFK and LBJ. The riot changed that. In the three decades after World War II, Macomb's population increased from one hundred thousand to seven hundred thousand, most of them ex-Detroiters disgusted by how "the blacks" were destroying their native city, and just as disgusted with Democrats who seemed more concerned with giving money to shiftless minorities than helping factory workers losing their jobs to automation and the Japs. Pollster Stanley B. Greenberg discovered the Reagan Democrats in Macomb County, documenting them in the anthropological tone the D.C. intelligentsia often employs when encountering blue-collar voters.

"These white defectors from the Democratic Party expressed profound distaste for black Americans," Greenberg wrote in his book *Middle Class Dreams*. "Blacks constituted the explanation for their vulnerability and for almost everything that had gone wrong in their lives; not being black was what constituted being middle class; not living with blacks was what made a neighborhood a decent place to live . . . For these white suburban residents, the terms *black* and *Detroit* were interchangeable. The city was a place to be avoided—where the kids could not go, where the car got stolen, and where vacant lots and dissolution have replaced their old neighborhoods. The black politicians, like Coleman Young, were doing just fine, they believed, getting rich off special favors, special treatment and special deals. But Detroit was just a big pit into which the state and federal governments poured tax money, never to be heard from again."

Even when the suburbs were offered federal money, they turned it down if the price was welcoming blacks. In 1970, Macomb County's largest city, Warren, had 132 blacks—.07 percent of its population. When Warren applied for a $2.8 million HUD grant, Secretary Romney demanded the city draw up an equal-housing plan. Warren voters responded by passing a referendum banning HUD money. The auto industry isn't the only reason Detroit never built a light rail system: suburbanites didn't want trains carrying blacks across 8 Mile Road.

L. Brooks Patterson, the Oakland County politician who is the negative image of Coleman Young, told Chafets, "In no sense are we dependent on Detroit. They are dependent on us. The truth is, Detroit has had its day. I don't give a damn about Detroit. It has no direct bearing on the quality of my life. If I never crossed 8 Mile again, I wouldn't be bereft of anything."

Patterson, who has served as prosecutor and county executive, is fond of race-baiting initiatives such as trying to revive the death penalty, which Michigan abolished in 1846. It's not hard to imagine Patterson and Young holding secret meetings at a suburban restaurant, such as the Machus Red Fox, where Jimmy Hoffa was last seen alive, and working out this deal over beefsteak and whiskey: "You use me to scare your people, and I'll use you to scare my people."

On the Northeast Side, Chene Street's decline continued with the closing of Dodge Main in the early 1970s. Marion Krzykowski's family moved to the suburbs after his mother was mugged while walking home from the bakery. Krzykowski continued visiting Chene Street to buy Polish magazines at the People's Book Store, which was kept open by an idealistic Socialist and freethinker named John Zukowski. (Despite his beliefs, he sold Mass cards, rosaries, and Marian statues to the parishioners of St. Hyacinth and St. Stanislaus.) Zukowski was shot during a robbery. He never recovered from the wound, and closed his business.

After that, Krzykowski had no reason to visit Chene. Instead, he had reason to stay away.

"After a while, it was just really bad," he said. "It was just really dangerous."

As the Poles moved out, three Catholic schools closed for lack of students. Which caused even more whites to move out, because they wanted to send their children to neighborhood schools—just not integrated ones.

"The white people moved out, and welfare moved in," said John Givans. As a boy, he'd been part of the only black family on his block. Eventually, his was the only family of any color left on the block.

"The welfare people didn't keep up their houses. You don't take care of something you don't own."

Givans was lucky enough to live in a brick house. Most of his neighbors lived in wooden houses. Thrown up by the hundreds of thousands in the industrial boom of the early twentieth century, they rotted in the snowy Northern winters and damp Great Lakes summers. When weather and poverty wore the houses out, the landlords abandoned them to the city's bulldozers, or hired arsonists, who were cheaper than a demolition bill. Arson in Detroit was so common it went from money-saving slum-clearance tactic to unofficial civic festival. Beginning in the early 1970s, the evening before Halloween was known as Devil's Night, when hundreds of houses—most empty, but some occupied—were burned to the ground. The night was so notorious that firebugs dined in the restaurant atop the seventy-three-story Renaissance Center just to see the flat, living map of Detroit embellished with flames. For decades after the riot, the Motor City continued burning.

The Cuyahoga River in Cleveland burned two years after Detroit. Although the fire was extinguished in a few hours, its aftermath also lasted decades.

4.

Burn On, Big River

Most Clevelanders believe the word "Cuyahoga" means "crooked river" in the Mohawk language. Philologically, this is incorrect. To the Mohawks, "Cuyahoga" means "big river," the same title their Huron rivals gave to the Mississippi. (The Mohawks, whose idea of family entertainment was skinning prisoners alive, were neither the poets nor the cartographers the Clevelanders who replaced and romanticized them like to imagine.) Hydrologically, though, "crooked river" is a quite accurate description of the Cuyahoga, so it's a sobriquet that Clevelanders have attached to a brewery (Crooked River Brewing Co.), a novel (*Crooked River Burning*), and the Crooked River Skate Park. The Cuyahoga begins its journey north of its mouth. After tracing a wet, hundred-mile-long V across the Western Reserve, it arrives in Cleveland crumpled into kinks and loops, as though a river with a much truer sense of direction had crashed headlong into Lake Erie. In its dilatory lower reaches, the river scribbles a cursive course through the flats of Cleveland, taking a week to flow through its last five miles.

The Cuyahoga is one of the least-ambitious bodies of water ever to find its way into a Great Lake, but it was in the right place at the right time to become one of the most influential rivers in American history.

In 1844, iron ore was discovered in the Upper Peninsula of Michigan, a promontory of rocks and trees so far removed from the thoroughfares of American commerce that a Virginia congressman called it "beyond the most distant wilderness and remote as the moon." Every attempt to run an iron furnace in the UP failed due to cold weather and lack of coal. Cleveland had access to coal because the Ohio and Erie Canal connected it to Portsmouth, on the Ohio River. Within a decade of the UP iron strike, the Soo Locks opened, allowing ships to pass between Lake Superior and Lake Huron. Boatloads of ore floated down the lakes to the docks of the Cleveland Iron Mining Company. There, coal met ore, and melted it into iron. Once John D. Rockefeller and Andrew Carnegie joined the shipbuilding race, the river was dredged deeper and deeper to accommodate bigger and bigger boats. By the early twentieth century, both banks were occupied by steel mills, preparing the Cuyahoga for the day that would make it world-famous.

To midcentury Clevelanders, the Cuyahoga was not a river. It was not even a body of water. It was, as a staff writer for the *Cleveland Plain Dealer* wrote, "a liquid Mesabi range," shaped like a lower intestine and performing the same function for Republic and for Jones and Laughlin, the two largest steel mills on its banks. Discharge pipes, as misshapen as gargoyle mouths, vomited sulfuric acid into the water. Iron scale and fleece dust tinted the surface a liverish hue that locals described as "terra cotta" or "a maroonish blush." Upstream of the Sherwin-Williams plant, the color depended on which batch of paint had gone bad the night before. Every day, factories polluted the river with 550,000 gallons of wastewater. The pickling acids discharged by the steel mills contained ferrous sulfate, which absorbed so much oxygen that the shoals were open graveyards of fish, bleached of color, gasping to death. Dark oil slicks floated on the water, like whorls of black ink. The calcium sulfate excrescence from Harshaw Chemical topped the river with a cream of white soda. Slaughterhouses pumped blood, animal organs, and offal into the river.

Dredged over twenty feet deep, the Cuyahoga could not work up enough current to flush itself.

The Cuyahoga was not just a sewer. It was a dump, too. Broken pallets and living room chairs were abandoned under bridges. Industrial spools lifted their hips above the surface. The mills cooled themselves with river water, then returned it, steaming, so the Cuyahoga never froze. A city councilman dipped a white sheet into the water and lifted out a rag stained with oil.

If the river looked bad, it smelled even worse.

"It would have had a very distinctive odor," said Wayne Bratton, who captained freighters that tied up in the Cuyahoga. "Back then, it wouldn't have been unusual to have ten to twenty ships in the river. The river bubbled like a cauldron. The river was black, high in petroleum content. Recreational boats did not come in the river, no less canoes. You wouldn't have been able to stand the smell. They used to say if you fell in the river, don't spit it out, because you'll be polluting."

The Cuyahoga first caught fire in 1936. As a welder removed bolts from a freighter's stern, sparks dribbled from his blowtorch, igniting the petroleum cocktail below. The welder tumbled through the smoke, burning his hand and face before crewmen fished him out of the flaming water. The fire fed on the oily wooden piers of an Erie Railroad jackknife bridge but was extinguished by the fire department before it could reach eighty thousand barrels of gasoline stored in riverside tanks. Those stray sparks taught Cleveland a lesson about the Cuyahoga: it needed a fire boat for the next time the river went up in flames.

The next big fire, in 1952, destroyed three tugs and most of a boat-repair yard—a million dollars in damage. Downtown Cleveland looked like Pearl Harbor. An orange tide line of flame spread across the river as the fire expanded, heaping black smoke into the sky. Still without a boat, twenty-two fire companies sprayed water from bridges, beating back the inferno before it could blow up the Standard Oil Co.'s ship fuel tanks. Mayor Thomas A. Burke promised that his administration would clean up the Cuyahoga.

"In the past we have not had the cooperation of industries," Burke said. "Well, we're going to get it in the future."

They didn't. In 1968, Bratton and his maritime industry colleagues were so disgusted by the persistent filth they formed the Oil Study Group, to clean it up themselves. A little vessel known as *Putzfrau*—German for "cleaning woman"—trolled the river, equipped with a two-ton crane and a vacuum tank that allowed it to scoop up one hundred yards of debris and suck up twenty thousand gallons of oil in a single day. The study group experimented with chemicals and absorbent pads to clean up the goop.

A year into the Oil Study Group's existence, the Cuyahoga called attention to itself in a way a gang of conservationists never could have. On June 22, 1969, it caught fire again. A hot rain of sparks fell from a railcar carrying molten steel across a Norfolk and Western bridge, igniting an oil slick. Floating downriver, the burning slick scorched the bridge's pillars and warped its rails. With damage estimated at fifty grand, the fire was no big deal in Cleveland, certainly not as big as the holocaust of '52. And this time, the fire department had a boat to put it out. The *Cleveland Press* ran a photo of the crooked bridge on page 1, with a five-sentence caption. But this so-what-the-river-burned-again fire ignited the American environmental movement and burned a scar onto Cleveland's self-image that has yet to heal.

In response to the antipollution movement begun by Rachel Carson's *Silent Spring*, *Time* magazine had just initiated an "Environment" column. The August 1 column, "America's Sewage System and the Price of Optimism," recounted the fire and described Cleveland's "archaic" sewer system: "Every day for the past month, 25 million gallons of raw sewage have cascaded from a ruptured pipe, spilling a gray-green torrent into the Cuyahoga and thence into Lake Erie."

Clevelanders consider that 1969 column—not the fire itself—the beginning of a decade-long curse on their city. The first stroke of bad luck: the cover of that issue was a photo of Senator Edward Kennedy leaving the funeral of Mary Jo Kopechne, the woman he'd driven off a bridge on Chappaquiddick Island. Had it not been for Chappaquiddick, Clevelanders insist, no one would have read that week's *Time*, thus sparing Cleveland forty years of burning-river jokes.

"The issue of *Time* with Kennedy on the cover, wearing a neck brace, was among the best-selling issues in the formerly Cleveland-based magazine's history," wrote Cleveland novelist Mark Winegardner, both sounding the "Why us?!" cry and lamenting an influential institution's abandonment and betrayal of Cleveland, two civic complexes rooted in the Cuyahoga fire.

The Chappaquiddick excuse, by the way, is nonsense. The issue wasn't one of *Time*'s bestsellers. The unlucky coincidence? The fire occurred as *Time* was responding to its readers' growing ecological consciousness. Cleveland should feel fortunate the column didn't debut the week before, when the moon landing was on the cover. The Cuyahoga, that timely river, burst into flames at just the right moment to become a symbol of the environmental movement. Water turning to fire was the era's most dramatic, otherworldly pollution disaster. Over the next few years, the Cuyahoga inspired Earth Day, the Environmental Protection Agency, and the Clean Water Act of 1972, which contributed half the funds to detoxify the river.

Clevelanders, though, remain fixated on the jokes. After reading *Time*, *Rowan and Martin's Laugh-In* awarded Cleveland its "Fickle Finger of Fate," and sardonic pianist Randy Newman wrote "Burn On" ("The Lord can make you overflow / But the Lord can't make you burn"). The song of course appeared on his most acclaimed album, *Sail Away*. *Sports Illustrated* proposed that Cleveland host the Olympics. The city wouldn't need a torch. It could just light the river.

The Cuyahoga was not the only conflagration that embarrassed Cleveland. Three years later, Mayor Ralph Perk opened the American

Society of Metals convention by cutting a steel cable with a blowtorch. A spark ignited his hair. For a few seconds, until it was beaten to death by the show's embarrassed organizers, a flame danced atop the mayor's head like a sprite. Not only does our river catch fire, Clevelanders moaned, our mayor catches fire, too!

Perk was elected in 1971, succeeding Carl Stokes, the first black mayor of a major American city. An ice peddler who had grown up during Cleveland's robust industrial prime, Perk had the unfortunate task of presiding over its decrepitude. Since the 1950s, Cleveland had lost 20 percent of its people to the suburbs, and an equal proportion of its stores. Cleveland had more acres of officially designated urban blight than any American city. Most of it was on the East Side, where whites accommodated the growing black population not by yielding more territory but by subdividing rental houses into smaller and smaller habitations. As poet Langston Hughes recalled of his Cleveland boyhood, "We always lived during my high school years either in an attic or a basement and paid a lot for such inconvenient quarters."

As in Detroit, businesses were abandoning the East Side's factories. National Screw and Manufacturing moved to a spacious one-story plant in the suburb of Mentor, leaving behind a seven-story target for window breakers and arsonists. Perk spent half a million dollars on demolition, but Clevelanders were abandoning their houses faster than he could tear them down. Cartoonist Harvey Pekar, whose *American Splendor* comic books comprise a graphic novel of life in three-quarter-century Cleveland, absorbed his city's malaise.

"The early and middle seventies—what a lonely, awful time for me!" wrote Pekar, who was between wives during those years. "It seems like it was always snowing and I was always looking out the window by myself."

As businesses let themselves out Cleveland's back door, Perk became so desperate for revenue he sold the city's sewer system and tried to sell its power company, Municipal Light. Peddling public utilities to big business sounded like a campaign issue to Cleveland's young, ambitious, populist clerk of courts. So Dennis Kucinich announced his candidacy for mayor.

Kucinich was only thirty years old, but he was already the most polarizing politician in Cleveland. In newspaper headlines, he was simply "Dennis." Cartoons caricatured the dark forelock that, as the crown of a five-foot-seven-inch, one-hundred-thirty-five-pound body, made Kucinich look like a teenager.

Kucinich had been raised on the West Side, beneath the bell tower of

St. John Cantius, one of the monumental brick churches that define Cleveland's ethnic neighborhoods. He was the oldest of six children in a family so poor they sometimes lived in a car, or were shunted off to an orphanage when their truck driver father couldn't find work. Young Dennis caddied at a country club to pay his way through Catholic school, where he was third-string quarterback on the football team and wrote a John F. Kennedy–inspired essay asserting, "My main ambition is and will be a career in national politics and I am going to aim for the very top."

He decided to start at city hall.

"Dan," he boasted to a boyhood friend, "I am going to be mayor of Cleveland by the time I'm thirty years old!"

When Kucinich filed to run in his first election, a city council race against the Ukrainian machine politician in his ward, he was not even old enough to vote. Roldo Bartimole, a *Wall Street Journal* reporter who'd gotten to know Kucinich when the young man was a copyboy for the paper's Cleveland bureau, went door-to-door with him during that first campaign.

"You know, if I win this, I could go all the way," Kucinich said.

"Dennis, what do you mean by that?" Bartimole asked, although he knew.

"Forget about that," Kucinich said, catching himself.

There were no limits to Kucinich's ambition, only limits to how much he was willing to reveal. Kucinich lost his maiden election, but two years later was elected to Cleveland city council by nineteen votes. At twenty-three, with seven years to make good on his first political goal, he was inside city hall.

After Kucinich went to Congress, and campaigned for president with a promise to establish a Department of Peace, and became a vegan, and told Shirley MacLaine he'd seen a UFO, East Coast journalists were puzzled that a politician who seemed to have purchased his persona from the Whole Earth Catalog was so popular among Cleveland's blue-collar voters.

Dennis Kucinich may have begun his political career in the late 1960s, but he did not learn his politics from the antiwar or the civil rights movements. His idol was Tom L. Johnson, Cleveland's Progressive Era mayor, who built playgrounds in slum neighborhoods, fought the street-car monopoly, and established Muny Light. Kucinich was no liberal. He was an urban populist who exploited the racial fears of his Slavic constituents to win elections. Among its other disreputable functions, the

Cuyahoga was (and still is) a liquid frontier between the East Side's blacks and the West Side's whites. As a city councilman, Kucinich sponsored an antibusing resolution, opposed gun registration, and spoke out against "spreading out public housing into just *any* areas." During a run for Congress, in 1974, he attacked his primary opponent for voting in favor of a Martin Luther King Jr. holiday in Ohio. (Kucinich lost that race.) He tried to defeat a woman running for city council by circulating a photo of George Forbes, the black city council president, staring at her picture. The tag: "What's going on here?" The copy: the woman was a pawn of Forbes and elements of "east of the river." The implication: interracial romance. The result: the woman won. Forbes, who would later become Kucinich's nemesis during his mayoralty, called him "a racist, a man who lacks core passion and a political opportunist who will do anything to further his career."

But Kucinich also saw himself as the champion of lower-class Clevelanders who'd been left behind when their wealthier neighbors and relatives moved to Parma or Shaker Heights. He sponsored a bill for free rapid-transit rides and fought utility rate increases. His campaign literature, with its condemnation of "fat cats" and "bosses," could have been written by a Wobbly pamphleteer.

When Kucinich announced his campaign for mayor (his ninth political race since his twenty-first birthday), he promised to stop the sale of Muny Light; promised to end a tax abatement for National City, Cleveland's largest bank; promised to clean up the river; and promised to stop mobsters from car-bombing each other in pursuit of Cleveland's vacant boss-ship. (The underworld violence was even worse in Youngstown, which was too small to support its own mob but halfway between two cities that could. Warring hoods from Cleveland and Pittsburgh blew each other up with such frequency that a car bombing became known as a "Youngstown Tune-up.")

"It is ominous that the mayor of our city would remain silent while our city becomes a bomb-scarred battleground of the underworld," Kucinich said at his first press conference. "The people desire some action before innocent people are killed by the mob's bombers."

Then, in a phrase no Clevelander can read now without grimacing, Kucinich said, "We cannot allow Cleveland to become a national joke. We cannot wait until the 'for sale' sign is planted in front of city hall. The city is not for sale. The people are not for sale. And they will not be sold out."

The Rust Belt's economic distress is a problem too deep for any mayor or governor to solve, but mayors or governors who can't solve it get fired anyway. Mayor Perk didn't even make the runoff, finishing third in the primary. Kucinich's opponent was another thirty-year-old, state representative Edward Feighan. Kucinich beat up Feighan for supporting National City's tax break, swept West Side ethnics while losing badly among East Side blacks, and became the youngest big-city mayor in America.

Kucinich wasn't just called "the Boy Mayor" because he looked like an urchin from the chorus of *Oliver!* He behaved like an adolescent, too: petulant, impressionable, inflexible, and envious of anyone who received more attention. As his first police chief, Kucinich hired former San Francisco County sheriff Richard Hongisto. Three months later, Kucinich fired Hongisto during a press conference on live TV—while the chief was standing right beside him. Hongisto, Kucinich claimed, had accused his administration of ordering the police to perform "unethical acts," such as cutting off services to a ward represented by one of the mayor's enemies. But the chief had provided no proof. A *Cleveland Press* cartoon illustrated the real reason: Hongisto was popular with the cops and the newspapers, because he personally led late-night manhunts. The drawing depicted a cowboy Kucinich, in a ten-gallon hat marked "D," yanking off Hongisto's star, telling him, "This town isn't big enough for the two of us, chief."

Jim Rokakis, a newly elected twenty-two-year-old councilman from a Polish, Italian, and German ward, was the first member of city council to support Kucinich's recall, a campaign that began immediately after the police chief's firing.

"There were a lot of young people elected to city council that year," Rokakis said. "There was all this anticipation, because Dennis was a real vibrant guy and he was very exciting. The wheel came off almost immediately. Within days. He was combative. He had surrounded himself with people who were like him: they were all difficult. They were angry. It was them versus the world. You had to take sides and if you didn't, you were trampled. There was any number of times I was forced to choose, and I typically was forced into the camp that was anti-Kucinich."

Kucinich's service director was nineteen. His safety director was twenty-three. A week before the recall election, the mayor and his staff stormed out of a city council meeting. Council president George Forbes had cut off the mayor's microphone because the mayor wouldn't stop ranting, "This is a crooked contract!" after the council overrode his veto of a dock lease for Republic Steel.

Kucinich won the recall election by 216 votes, out of 120,000 cast, but by the end of the year, he had the city in another crisis. Cleveland's bankers hated Kucinich's populism. They could not defeat him at the polls, but they did hold $15.5 million in municipal loans. The banks threatened to seize the city's assets unless Kucinich sold Muny Light to the private Cleveland Electric Illuminating Company. Kucinich refused. He'd won the mayor's office by promising *not* to sell city assets—especially the utility. Giving in to the banks would have ruined his image—public and self—as the Tom L. Johnson of the 1970s, the mayor who fought for "the poor and working people" against "the business elite."

"The so-called default was as phony as a three-dollar bill," recalled Roldo Bartimole, who by then was publishing a newsletter on Cleveland politics. "The banks had been rolling that money over every two years, but they didn't do it for Dennis."

If Kucinich didn't sell the utility or cough up the money by midnight on December 15, 1978, Cleveland would become the first American city to default since the Depression. Reporters flew in from all over the country to watch Cleveland go broke. Kucinich, who was learning that celebrity follows confrontation, argued his case on ABC's *Good Morning America*. NBC late-night talk-show host Tom Snyder interviewed Kucinich at Tony's Diner, his favorite West Side restaurant. The police and garbagemen threatened to strike if Kucinich went ahead with layoffs to raise money for the loan payoff. This line appeared in the newspaper: "What's the difference between Cleveland and the *Titanic*? Cleveland has a better orchestra."

Five days after the deadline—after the bankers had presented their notes at the city's treasurer's office and CEI had tagged water trucks for seizure—Kucinich and the council agreed on a compromise that satisfied the banks: a public referendum on selling Muny Light and raising the city's income tax from 1 percent to 1½ percent.

Kucinich won on both issues. Clevelanders voted to hang on to Muny Light and raise their own taxes. But they were also sick of Dennis, whose two years in office would earn him seventh place in a historians' poll of worst mayors in American history. (For an "abrasive, intemperate, and confrontational populist political style, which led to a disorderly and chaotic administration," the citation read.) In November 1979, he was defeated by Republican George Voinovich, a square, polka-loving Serb who would parlay his dull sobriety into three terms as mayor, two terms as governor, and two terms as senator.

"The world settled down," Rokakis said. "The people [Voinovich] brought in were by and large professionals. The city was in default. We went to Columbus and we got a package that got us out of default. I'm not sure Dennis would have done that. He'd taken the 'one against the world' stance. Voinovich was collaborative. He brought people in and over the course of the next eight to ten years, it was a time of peace and harmony."

Kucinich had kept his promise not to sell Muny Light but broken another that Clevelanders held even more deeply: he'd turned the city into a national joke. The Boy Mayor's temperamental brinksmanship was the final embarrassment in a demoralizing decade that began with the Cuyahoga River fire and ended with Cleveland nicknamed "the Mistake by the Lake." The Cleveland *Plain Dealer* tried to lift the city's morale with a bumper sticker slogan: "New York May Be the Big Apple, but Cleveland's a Plum."

Rock musician Michael Stanley tried to lift his city's morale, too. Cleveland's rock and roll history goes back to the early 1950s. Rock was not invented on Lake Erie—that happened in the Mississippi Valley—but WJW disc jockey Alan "Moondog" Freed coined the term "rock'n' roll" to describe the black music he was playing for teenage ethnics. His "Moondog Coronation Ball" at the Cleveland Arena is considered the first rock concert, even though opening act Paul "Hucklebuck" Williams finished only one song before the fire marshal cleared out the brawling, dancing crowd of twenty thousand.

Thirty years later, Cleveland's musical avatar was Stanley, whose trademark vest and permed hair made him look like the prom king who doffed his tuxedo jacket and bow tie so he could get down to rock. The Michael Stanley Band's "He Can't Love You" was the forty-seventh video to air on MTV's first day of programming. ("They didn't have a lot of shit to play," is Stanley's explanation.) Stanley made hit records without moving to New York or L.A. That meant a lot to Cleveland, which had been big-timed by John D. Rockefeller, *Time* magazine, Alan Freed, and even Martin Mull, whose *Fernwood 2 Night*, a satirical TV series about a smarmy local talk-show host, was yet *another* Cleveland joke. Michael Stanley was Cleveland's version of Rust-Belt rockers like Bruce Springsteen (Asbury Park, New Jersey), Bob Seger (Ann Arbor, Michigan), John Cougar Mellencamp (Seymour, Indiana), John Hiatt (Indianapolis, Indiana) and Billy Joel, a Long Island saloon singer sponsored for membership by Allentown, Pennsylvania. Those musicians had grown up listening to two-minute songs about surfing. Without a Pacific Ocean to inspire the next "Fun, Fun, Fun," they composed laments about the Midwest's deepest and most endless characteristic: unemployment. In moaning odes such as "My Hometown," "Makin' Thunderbirds," "Scarecrow," and "Allentown," these heartland rockers—and those wannabes who wished they could have smelled sulfur wafting through the windows of third-period band, from the steel mill they were pounding the piano to stay out of—discovered blue-collar work as a lyrical topic at the exact moment Americans stopped doing it.

When Stanley's band began writing its album *You Can't Fight Fashion*, Ohio's unemployment rate was 14 percent, and the record company insisted on an anthem. So Stanley decided to write a song not just for Cleveland but for Erie, Flint, Gary, Youngstown, and every other town that was losing its auto plant/steel mill/oil refinery and all the drive-ins/bowling alleys/taverns said industrial concern supported.

"The whole Rust Belt situation was bottoming out at that point," Stanley said. "From a civic standpoint, things were pretty lousy. But if something has to be anthemic, it has to cross as many boundaries as possible. It was the whole thing about civic pride, even if there doesn't seem to be anything to be that proud about. Proud of the fact that, if nothing else, you've survived what was going on around you. People always say, 'That's a Cleveland tune.' That says nothing about Cleveland in the song, other than the reference to East Side, West Side, which is how Cleveland's divided up, but I'm sure there's many like that. The whole thing was to keep it as non-Cleveland-centric as possible. It was obvious there were a lot of places going through the same sort of situation we were."

So here's what Stanley sang:

> *This town is my town*
> *She's got her ups and downs*
> *But love it or hate it—it don't matter*
> *This is my town*

The lyrics may not have mentioned Cleveland, but the video was a montage of Clevelandiana. Steaming steel mills. The Russian Orthodox church featured in *The Deer Hunter*. Black lace railroad bridges. A declining orange sun, glowing like a yield signal through smoky clouds as it set beside Terminal Tower, the brick syringe whose needle point is a peak of Cleveland's skyline. Dressed as greasers, the band drove a convertible to the drive-in. (Drive-ins and classic-car shows are to the Midwest what Civil War reenactments are to the South: remembrances of the region's last glorious era.) They walked up to an abandoned factory, where Stanley stuck a "SOLD" sign on the fence and broke the chain with a bolt cutter.

Musically, "My Town" was defined by chugging guitars and brassy, surging saxophones, as much a part of the proto-MTV sound as gelled hair and skinny ties were of its look. Stanley's anthem hit the Top 40 but has not endured as well as Springsteen's wistful "My Hometown," a more evocative industrial-belt anthem released the following year. It's still popular in Cleveland, though, and so is Stanley, who worked as a disc jockey after retiring from rock and roll. A few summers ago, his band headlined Taste of Cleveland. Under a white big top by the river, they played for a thousand or so middle-aged Clevelanders, who sat at picnic tables with Styrofoam plates of pierogi and kolache. Of course, they saved "My Town" for the encore.

"Every once in a while, you try to be a smart-ass and stick it in third. You can see them: 'I don't want it yet. Save that, will ya?'"

A FRIEND FROM CLEVELAND once asked me, "Which city has a better chance of coming back? Cleveland or Buffalo?"

"Well," I responded, "if you put a random group of people in each city, I'd say Cleveland. But since Cleveland is populated by Clevelanders, I'd have to say Buffalo."

This same friend cursed her husband for persuading her to leave New York City for their native Cleveland. In two years back, she had not been able to find a full-time job. Instead, she worked as a bookstore clerk and an archivist for the Rock and Roll Hall of Fame, which Cleveland swiped from runner-up Memphis by stuffing the ballot box in a 1986 *USA Today* vote. Hoping a bomb will fall on her house so she can leave town, she is either a depressed person who happens to live in Cleveland or a person depressed by living in Cleveland. Whichever, she embraces the pessimism that has defined the Cleveland attitude since the 1970s. One of Cleveland's problems is that Cleveland spends far more time worrying what the rest of the nation thinks of Cleveland than the rest of the nation actually spends thinking about Cleveland.

"I think Clevelanders are very sensitive," Michael Stanley says. "They have a very thick thin skin. It goes back to when Kucinich was mayor and the city went into default. That's when it all sort of started."

How defensive are Clevelanders? They make a Cleveland joke before anyone else can make a Cleveland joke—even though no one else was going to make a Cleveland joke. No comic would riff on a topic as stale as the Cuyahoga River fire. But the Great Lakes Brewing Company, located across the street from Cleveland's meaty West Side Market, produces Burning River Pale Ale. Type "Cleveland" into YouTube and the number one result is "Hastily Made Cleveland Tourism Video," with over four million hits. (Forty times as many as "My Town.") Shot by local comedian Mike Polk, it features scenes of people wandering alone downtown in the middle of the day, and these lyrics: "Here's the place where there used to be industry / This train is carrying jobs out of Cleveland / Cleveland leads the nation in drifters." It's not a parody of Cleveland, but a parody of how Clevelanders feel about Cleveland.

"I love this city and pick on it like the little brother I never had," Polk told an interviewer. "But don't mess with my fictitious little brother unless you're also in the family."

Cleveland is even jealous of Detroit, its annual rival for poorest city in America, because Detroit's Roman decay has drawn the cameras of filmmakers and photographers from all over the world. Rotting unnoticed on Lake Erie's other shore, Cleveland is as unromantic as a worn-out strip mall.

When LeBron James appeared on an ESPN special to announce he was leaving the Cleveland Cavaliers for the Miami Heat, TV cameras at taverns all over Cleveland recorded the anguish and deflation of sports fans, who buried their faces in their hands, cried, "I feel like my girlfriend just left me!" then burned the deserter's jersey in parking lot "LeBronfires." All the subsequent parodies—such as Steve Carell discussing his decision to eat at the Outback Steakhouse—made fun of James's self-importance in scheduling an hour-long special around the two-minute sound bite in which he revealed his free-agent signing. James was the joke, but Cleveland's low civic self-esteem made the city feel like the butt. A Cleveland-born sportswriter wrote a book entitled *The Whore of Akron*, which both impugned James's fidelity and reminded readers that he wasn't *really* a Clevelander. Fans in Memphis, Kansas City, or even Milwaukee would not have reacted with such a sense of betrayal. But LeBron had big-timed Cleveland, just like the Browns, who moved to Baltimore, changed their name to the Ravens, and finally won the Super Bowl they'd been unable to attain in their hometown. (The fact that no Cleveland pro sports team has won a championship since 1964 is assumed to be part of the same local curse that caused Ted

Kennedy to drive a young girl off a bridge, thus bringing undeserved attention to the Cuyahoga River.) When the Dallas Mavericks defeated the Heat to win the 2011 NBA championship, bitter Clevelanders dubbed them "the Mavaliers." *If we can't win, let's live vicariously through the losses of our enemies.*

MAYBE CLEVELAND has never gotten over its *decas horribilis*, but the politician and the river that caused it so much humiliation have both been rehabilitated. After losing the mayoralty to Voinovich, Kucinich exiled himself to California, where he lived with actress Shirley MacLaine, who helped him pay the mortgage on the tiny West Side house he'd bought for $23,000. In 1982, the year Kucinich returned to Cleveland, he reported an income of $38. Kucinich was elected to the city council in 1985, but after a failed campaign for governor the next year, he disappeared again, this time to New Mexico, where he spent nearly a decade on "a quest for meaning."

When he finally got back into politics for good, with a run for Ohio state senate, Kucinich ran, defiantly, on his mayoral record. His campaign button was a lightbulb with the slogan "Because He Was Right." It illuminated the fact that holding on to Muny Light had saved Clevelanders millions of dollars in utility fees. The generation-old memory of the little guy who'd stood up to the bankers was cherished by Cleveland's ethnics, who sent Kucinich to Congress in 1996. Never satisfied with the office he occupied, Kucinich then ran for president of the United States, promising a cabinet-level Department of Peace. The first time he did it, in 2004, some Clevelanders were proud of their irrepressible congressman. He had spoken out against the Iraq War when it wasn't politically safe, and if he reveled too much in the spotlight—appearing on a *Dating Game* skit with *Tonight Show* host Jay Leno, for example—well, America was just getting a look at their Dennis, a Cleveland idol. Cleveland being Cleveland, though, others fretted that his quixotic campaign was setting the city up for more embarrassment. (Kucinich didn't win any delegates during that campaign, but he did win a third wife. During a party at Shirley MacLaine's house, he met Elizabeth, red-haired, a head-taller, half-his-age Englishwoman with a tongue stud.)

The second time Kucinich ran for president, in 2008, his hallucination of a St. John Cantius graduate in the White House seemed like an ego trip, especially to Clevelanders who thought they'd heard him promise not to run for president again. Cleveland was leading the nation in foreclosures, they grumbled, while Dennis was eating sushi in Holly-wood with Sean Penn. *Big timing.*

Cleveland forced its UFO-watching congressman to phone home. Kucinich dropped out of the presidential race early that winter to de-fend his congressional seat against four impatient constituents in the Democratic primary. The first week of February, Cleveland State Univer-sity hosted two political debates: a presidential debate in the basketball arena between Barack Obama and Hillary Clinton, which was televised on CNN, and a congressional debate at the music school, between Den-nis Kucinich, a city councilman, a nonprofit executive, a suburban mayor, and a Gold Star mother. It was broadcast on public radio. I was in Cleve-land that week, doing a book signing for *The Third Coast*, a Great Lakes travelogue I'd written, so I attended, as a reporter for *Salon*.

Before I met Dennis, I met his main opponent, City Councilman Joe Cimperman, who had raised enough money to frighten Kucinich into shutting down his presidential campaign. On the night of the Big De-bate between Barack and Hillary, Cimperman sat at the polished slate bar of a nightclub across the street from Cleveland State, hosting an Obama party. In Clark Kent glasses, a sack suit, and a crew cut that needed mow-ing, Cimperman looked like two hundred pounds of Cleveland—the same role Drew Carey played on TV. In fact, he fancied himself a younger, more practical, post–Rust Belt iteration of Kucinich. As a young coun-cilman, Cimperman had idolized Kucinich so much he raised $30,000 for a mayoral portrait. (Kucinich blew off three sittings.) Like his one-time hero, Cimperman came from a working-class, Slavic background—his father was a union machinist, his mother a Slovenian immigrant—and was elected to city council in his twenties. In his pursuit of federal of-fice, Cimperman had also adopted some of Kucinich's abrasive theatri-cal traits. To taunt the incumbent for no longer being down with his hometown, he cut a spoof Western ad titled "The Good, the Bad, the Kucinich," in which he walked into his rival's office with a "Missing Con-gressman" poster. (Kucinich complained about the stunt to the Depart-ment of Homeland Security.) Then he got even more personal, visiting Kucinich's house with a Welcome Wagon basket containing sausage and a map of Ohio.

"For me, the bloom really came off the rose when he announced that he was running for president again, and just the joke he made of this community on Letterman and Leno," Cimperman said. "It was time to come home and he never came home. For an ethnic person, the worst thing you can do is forget where you came from."

Because of its proximity to Obama, the club was filling up with celebrities almost as famous as Kucinich's followers—Timothy Hutton shook everyone's hand, and a Don Cheadle rumor swept the room—but Cimperman had to run to his next event. It took place in a well-restored old house that could have served as the exterior setting for the classic holiday film *A Christmas Story*—which passes for a major tourist attraction in Cleveland. Cimperman, who could make a hockey announcer sound laconic, delivered a speech accompanied by so many finger thrusts and air grabs he looked like his own sign-language interpreter.

"We have an amazing resource in this community," Cimperman said. "We're a place where things are made. While once we were the kings of steel, now we're a growing factor in the medical economy. Through the Cleveland Clinic."

Then came the Q and A . . .

"If you're elected to Congress, will you become yoga partners with Shirley MacLaine?" the host asked.

Another guest seemed anguished about abandoning Kucinich, a politician who had been the strongest voice against a war that she, too, hated.

"In the past, he was a different kind of congressman," the woman said. "This is a very difficult decision for me, because I'm with him one hundred percent on the war. But he hasn't done anything on foreclosures."

The next morning, I drove around the Tenth Congressional District, from St. John Cantius parish to the Madonna-in-a-bathtub suburb of Parma, looking for people who still believed in Dennis. Snowy lawns were brightened by marigold signs shouting "DENNIS!" with a peace symbol dotting the exclamation point. At Kucinich's West Side headquarters, I met Arthur Ebenger, walking out the door with an armful of Dennis!wear—T-shirts, rain slickers—to distribute in the precincts. A retired pipe fitter, Ebenger had grown up playing baseball and basketball with Kucinich—"I went to St. Colman and he went to St. John Cantius"—and remembered him as a feisty, political teenager, fighting to increase access to a neighborhood political center. When Ebenger boxed, Kucinich cheered him on. A die-hard supporter of Kucinich's presidential campaigns—he supported everything Dennis had ever done, including changing his position on abortion from pro-life to pro-choice—Ebenger was convinced his boyhood friend would be the nation's first Slavic president.

"If I live long enough, I'll see him in contention for the presidency,"

Ebenger predicted. "When he believes in something, watch out. Full bore, coming down the track: that's my boy Dennis. This primary's going to be a slaughter. He will beat everybody hands down. Dennis will set the record straight, that he is not what they are trying to make him out to be. He's a full-time Congressman."

A few blocks away was Caffe Roma, the storefront joint where Kucinich often stopped in for spaghetti *aglio e olio*, his favorite vegan Italian meal. (Kucinich's veganism was as much gastrological necessity as New Age affectation: as a young copy editor, he'd had part of his intestine removed after downing ten martinis in thirty minutes to win a newsroom bet.) When one of the cooks had a visa problem, Kucinich straightened it out, owner Joe Coreno told me. Coreno also owned the video store across the street, where Dennis rented his movies.

"He doesn't go to Blockbuster," Coreno said. "That's more than I can say for some people."

"So are you going to vote for him on Tuesday?" I asked.

"I vote for Dennis all the time, no matter what he's running for."

Kucinich's local appeal was the obverse of his national image: he had an emotional bond with older, working-class voters, to whom he embodied the spirit of a city that had survived fire, insolvency, and ridicule; the young professionals, too young to remember the floppy-haired mayor calling the bankers' bluff, disdained him as yet another embarrassment to Cleveland. But even those who accused him of putting idealism before results in Washington admitted that his constituent service was the one effective element of his populism. At home, he was the quintessential Rust Belt politician. When LTV Steel (the product of a merger between Jones and Laughlin and Republic) declared bankruptcy in 2000, Kucinich held hearings until a buyer was found. As a result, 1,500 steelworkers still worked in the plant along the Cuyahoga.

On debate day, snow blew in from Lake Erie, eddying ghostily over the crowned streets. The clouds, the flakes, the salt-crunchy sidewalks, the Eastern European complexions between Browns beanies and acrylic scarves—everything in Cleveland was the same pale hue as a black-and-white documentary about Admiral Byrd's Antarctic expeditions. Kucinich arrived at the music school ten minutes late. He crept down the auditorium steps, smoothing his forelock as the moderator chided, "Not even a congressman can control the weather."

Kucinich's hair was still dark, his suit was baggy, but it was difficult to see the smooth-cheeked Boy Mayor through his gnarled, deep-set sexagenarian features. Whenever he caught sight of his wife Elizabeth sitting in the third row, a blissful glow sparkled across Kucinich's face, as though he'd been dosed with an opiate. When he dropped his eyes, he suddenly looked like a worn Balkan judge, taking notes with a felt-tip pen.

Before Kucinich had a chance to speak, Councilman Cimperman unloaded on him for blowing off his congressional duties to pursue a presidential campaign that barely received the support of 1 percent of the Democratic Party.

"I feel very passionately about the fact that our congressman has been absent," Cimperman said. "We wouldn't have this group up here today if someone hadn't run for president twice, and that person is Mr. Kucinich."

"I led the effort in the United States Congress in challenging this administration's march into this illegal war," Kucinich responded. He spoke loudly and gravely, not like the excitable terrier of local legend, but like the near-elderly pacifist sage he had become. "Is this war not an issue for Cleveland? This war has cost every household already sixteen thousand dollars. We've lost brave young men and women from Cleveland. I made that war an issue in the presidential campaign. Is health care not a Cleveland issue, with one-third of Clevelanders uninsured and underinsured?"

The only time Kucinich raised his voice was when one of his opponents pointed out that he had passed only two pieces of legislation—one allowing a Cleveland museum to show a government film.

"In a Republican Congress!" Kucinich snapped.

After the debate, I waited for Kucinich in front of the proscenium.

"Congressman," I said, introducing myself, "I'm writing an article for Salon.com. Have you heard of our website?"

"Come ahhhn!" he snapped in his well-known Midwestern accent.

"A lot of people in Cleveland have heard of it."

"There are a lot of progressive people here," he said.

Kucinich stepped down from the stage. At five foot seven, he was not as short as he appeared on television, where he was always standing next to aristocratic senators—or his wife. I asked him about his pledge not to run for president a second time.

"I never promised not to run for president," he said. "I said that I had no intention of running and what happened was the Democrats decided they were going to continue to fund the war, and I felt it was important to challenge that. Listen, do you know what this campaign is really all about?"

Kucinich was standing so close I could identify the Teamster pin—his father's union pin—on his suit jacket lapel.

"My opponents are funded by Cleveland developers who've hated me since I was mayor in the 1970s," he said. "These interest groups have a lock on the politics of this city, but they've never had a lock on me. I beat them years ago and they see this as an opportunity to just grab this congressional seat for the purposes of their own moneyed interests."

Even though he had been named one of the ten worst mayors in american history, Dennis Kucinich was a huge success. Not only was he still in politics after forty years, he was one of the most famous politicians in America. How many congressmen have appeared on *The Tonight Show*? After befriending celebrities, he'd married a woman half his age, published an autobiography blurbed by Gore Vidal, and was invited to share his opinions on nationally broadcast talk shows. Yet he still thought of himself as the scrapper taking on the fat cats, to use one of his favorite terms from the seventies. That attitude, that image, had won him a following, made him a first-name-only politician. There was no reason to change now, in late middle age, just as there was no reason to move out of the house he'd lived in for forty years. It was paid for and part of who he was.

Because he had been campaigning for president, Kucinich was badly behind in fund-raising. The celebrity that had made him a target also provided him the wherewithal to fight back. On his campaign site, he posted an appeal for money, claiming he was under attack by corporate interests. The president of the far left knew how to rally his constituents. He quickly collected $700,000, including donations from New Age author Marianne Williamson and singer Bonnie Raitt. Sean Penn flew to Cleveland, joining Kucinich onstage at a heavy metal benefit for a college radio station. As Dennis's friend Arthur Ebenger predicted, the election was a slaughter. Kucinich defeated Cimperman by twenty thousand votes, 50 percent to 35 percent. Another of Ebenger's predictions was wrong, though. Kucinich will never be president, unless the West Side of Cleveland secedes from the union. (Maybe not even then. In 2012, Ohio lost two congressional seats—a decennial Rust Belt tradition. The Republicans in Columbus made sure one of them was Kucinich's. They combined Kucinich's district with the district of a Toledo congresswoman, who defeated him in the primary.)

Despite his international profile, Kucinich is as uniquely Cleveland as Slovenian polka. Cleveland thinks of itself as an underdog among cities, so it likes to vote for underdog politicians. Getting 1 percent in the primaries only endeared Kucinich more to his hometown.

IN THE SPRING of 1971, the second year after the inferno, a reporter and photographer from the *Cleveland Press* canoed the entire Cuyahoga River. It wasn't any cleaner.

"People will dump anything at all into a stream," wrote John Randt. "Among other things that could be identified, we saw bedsteads, white enameled stoves, ice boxes and other appliances.

"We saw paint cans, coffee cans, and all kinds of plastic containers, detergent boxes, and rubber balls. We saw broken wooden boxes, and in one place we saw a discarded old yellow school bus.

"There was still an occasional faint odor of Akron sewage and every rapids foamed up into detergent suds."

Forty years later, I took the same trip—or at least the last leg of it. My guide was a young schoolteacher named Mark Pecot, who runs a kayak adventure service named 41° North, after Cleveland's latitude. We put our boats into the river behind a supper club in the suburb of Valley View, fourteen miles south of Lake Erie as the carp crookedly swims.

That far upstream, the Cuyahoga is a rural waterway. Alone on the river, Mark and I paddled between palisades of forest. Herons skimmed the surface on dragonfly wings. We passed a group of fishermen, standing on the soft bank, keeping one eye on their spidery line and the other on a case of Keystone Ice. Every mile or two, a raised highway transected the river at such an altitude that the cars overhead belonged more to the sky than to our aquatic world. Because the Cuyahoga is so naturally shallow, the bends were clogged with cattails, branches, and tree trunks, lodged against sandbars whose pebbly humps formed midchannel islands. The current eddied around these arboreal sheddings. This was only my second time in a kayak, so I struggled to keep my prow pointed forward in the turgid water.

"Don't fight the current!" Mark shouted as my kayak spun on the water. "Take long, wide strokes to get yourself turned in the right direction!"

Finally, I drove my kayak right into the bank. As Mark tried to free me, I felt water leaking into the cockpit, and then I suddenly tipped over—from upright to sideways, from dry to wet. I lugged the boat to a sandbar and climbed back in. Once, that might have been a medical emergency—"If I fell in that river, I'd go to a doctor," a young man from

Akron told the *Press* in 1971—but now I just had to paddle to the lake in wet jeans.

Six miles from its mouth the Cuyahoga becomes an industrial river. We heard the change before we saw it—a grinding that insinuated itself into our ears and then seemed to be coming from every direction, like an ultra-low-frequency siren. Turning a bend, we saw its source—the ArcelorMittal steel mill. (ArcelorMittal bought the old LTV Cleveland Works in 2005.) To our right, an iron mandible slid along an overhead track, dipped its jaws into a mound of taconite, and carried a mouthful back to the foundry. Now we were paddling beneath railroad bridges as dark as creosote. When Mark spotted a bridge with charred timbers, he floated to a stop and pulled his point-and-shoot camera from a waterproof bag.

"This is it," he said. "This is the bridge where the fire started."

Mark snapped photos and talked about this unremarkable bridge's remarkable afternoon. We were floating at Water Zero of the modern environmental movement. To test the effectiveness of the Clean Water Act, I dipped a finger into the river and stuck it in my mouth. It tasted like well water, clean and minerally.

"It was one of those things that caught the nation's attention," Mark said. "Rachel Carson's book came out. That's why it became a big deal. And it's a good thing that it did. The industries that remain, their practices have changed. For a hundred-plus years, the river was a dumping ground. There's this question of balance. People need to work. You get kind of poignant thinking about Cleveland's place in history. It was the sixth-largest city. It was the playground of the country. That wealth came from the steel that built so many other cities, but it was at the environmental cost of polluting the river. Cleveland was kind of used and cast aside."

It wasn't just the scenery that had changed there on the lowest Cuyahoga. The river had changed, too. Dredged to a depth of twenty-three feet, margined by concrete walls, it was as smooth as an Olympic pool. I was no longer surprised that this river had once been so inorganic that not even flatworms could survive. Now I was impressed that it was the only living thing in downtown Cleveland.

Mark's marine radio alerted him to a freighter. We ducked behind a right angle in the riverbank and watched the seven-hundred-foot-long *Dorothy Ann* fill the channel, fill the sky. Our kayaks bobbed on her echoing wake of wavelets.

"We've been approached about doing a kayak launch, but we've been nervous about novice kayakers dealing with freighters," Mark said.

From then on, we paddled into downtown Cleveland, as though the Cuyahoga were just a street that happened to be colored blue on the map. Our first landmark was the baseball stadium, then the basketball arena, then the Terminal Tower. An old railroad bridge, crosshatched with girders filling panels of sky in a one-sided game of tic-tac-toe. An automobile bridge whose railing resembled the classic façade at Yankee Stadium. A lift bridge, cocked toward the sky like a World War I German howitzer. Greenery clumped on the banks, thick as kudzu. Non-sensical graffiti—"HoBPJ," "OMAR"—in lavenders, reds, and aquas. Grain elevators patched with decals, in drywall patterns.

We passed the *Holiday*, Wayne Bratton's pleasure cruise boat. I called his name and a bald head appeared on deck.

"You're the guy I want to talk to about the river!" I shouted.

"Well, when are we going to do it?" he asked.

"As soon as I finish this kayak trip."

"You've got about two and a half miles to go."

Near the site of Lock 44, where the Ohio and Erie Canal once emptied into the Cuyahoga, warehouses showed their brick backsides to the water. These were the Flats, site of the first great river fire and scene of another catastrophic chapter in Cleveland history. The 1990s were as bounteous to urban America as the seventies had been disastrous. Cleveland opened the I. M. Pei–designed Rock and Roll Hall of Fame, built a baseball stadium that sold out 455 straight games for a team that fell one run short of a World Series title, and transformed its oily, charred, tumbledown riverfront into a nightlife district.

Unfortunately, it took only a dozen years for the Flats to go from hipness to respectability to dereliction. First, underground music venues set up in the old warehouses. They were followed by Joe's Crab Shack and Hooters. Finally, like pimps arriving at a convention, the titty bars moved in. The crowds became rowdier. After three revelers fell in the river and drowned, the city raided the Flats, closing six bars in one night. Now, the derelict Flats were another melancholy Cleveland monument.

"In the nineties, it really seemed like Cleveland was coming back," Mark said. "And then . . ."

I could finish the sentence myself: . . . *it went back to being Cleveland*.

Finally, there was nothing ahead of us but open water and open sky. This was the mouth of the Cuyahoga. Past dunes of gypsum on the right and an abandoned Coast Guard station on the left, we paddled into the choppy lake, turned left, and beached the boats.

I rushed back to the house where I was staying to change out of my wet jeans, then raced back to the riverfront, where I found Wayne Bratton. He was ordering around a two-person crew painting the *Holiday* with the same crusty authority that had once commanded an ore freighter.

"Be careful you don't step where they're painting," he roared at me, at the volume of a man who is both used to command and, at seventy-five, trying to make himself audible above his own hearing loss. He sat down on a padded bench in his galley and explained why I'd been able to kayak a river that was once too rancid even to walk alongside.

Soon after the 1969 fire, the state of Ohio closed a silt distributor and a metal plater who'd been dumping into the river by using a nuisance statute written to shut down whorehouses. Sherwin-Williams was slapped with a $1.5 million lawsuit, to stop it from treating the Cuyahoga as a liquid palette. Republic Steel spent $38 million on a cooling tower and a settling tank that prevented the discharge of scalding water and heavy metals. That summer of the fire, a sewer main broke, spewing twenty-five million gallons of shit every day for months. Cleveland spent billions of dollars on a network of tunnels to hold rainfall that would otherwise have washed through the treatment plants and forced them to release raw sewage. After the fire, Mayor Carl Stokes declared the dirty river as much a threat to his constituents as nuclear war.

"We have the kind of air and water pollution problems in these cities that are every bit as dangerous to the health and safety of our citizens as any ICBM so dramatically poised five thousand miles from our country," said Stokes, who lobbied for federal cleanup money and stronger environmental laws.

Some of those laws were more effective than intended, shutting down factories they'd only meant to regulate. Unable to meet the EPA's air-quality standards, U.S. Steel shipped its mill to China, where polluters can write their names on the sky. Fewer factories on the river meant fewer ships, and fewer ships meant fewer oil terminals: Shell, Mobil, Texaco, Sun, and Gulf all shut down after the steel crisis of the 1980s. The Cuyahoga's revival was tied to Cleveland's economic decline. And of course, with half its peak population, Cleveland is dumping half as much sewage and garbage. Within six years of the fire, the *Putzfrau*'s cleanup mission ended, astonishing its captain.

"The way the river looked in the beginning, I was sure that I would retire and there'd still be plenty of work to do," he told the makers of the documentary *The Return of the Cuyahoga*.

Since the Cuyahoga is a federal navigable waterway, open for ships,

Mark Pecot's "question of balance" had not quite tipped in favor of recreation, but a rowing club has established itself on the Flats, a sign that the lowest Cuyahoga can function as both a shipping channel and a lifestyle amenity. Water is the one advantage every Rust Belt city has over its suburbs and the Sun Belt.

Bratton had seen the Cuyahoga's potential back in 1982, when he bought the *Holiday* and chartered scenic tours of America's unsightliest body of water. Environmental groups traveled to Cleveland from all over the world to see the river that burned. On Saturday nights, Bratton piloted spa cruises.

"I never thought in my life that we'd have these people," Bratton said, lifting his eyes to look at the glittering water. "People swim in the river. Are they goofy? Yeah. They're not well. But they're swimming in the river."

5.

I'm a Flintoid

By winning World War II, the United States also won imperial responsibilities. Among those was the protection of Israel, created by the Allied powers as reparation for Germany's massacre of six million Jews. A Jewish state was resented by the surrounding Muslims, but the Arabs were just emerging from colonialism, so there was nothing they could do about it. From the Crusades to the Allenby Declaration, the Arabs had been kicked around by Westerners for nearly a millennium. But now, the West's economy depended on a resource Allah had placed beneath Arab feet: oil. From 1948 to 1972, sedan-driving Americans tripled their use of oil, from 5.8 million barrels a day to 16.4 million barrels a day. The fuel efficiency of the average American car was 13 miles a gallon. Power plants switched from coal to oil. It was cleaner, and they didn't have to worry about a mine workers' strike. The oil industry had been born in the United States, but by the early 1970s, American cars and TV sets had drunk so much of the country's supply that we were importing six million barrels a day—over a third of our consumption.

In the 1967 Six-Day War, Israel captured the Sinai Peninsula from Egypt. Three years later, Anwar Sadat became Egypt's president and began plotting a revenge war to reclaim his country's lost territory and build his stature as an Arab leader. In early 1973, Sadat asked Saudi Arabia's King Faisal for support. Not only did the king agree to fund a war against Israel, he told the Western press that "America's complete support for Zionism and against the Arabs makes it extremely difficult for us to continue to supply the United States with oil, or even to remain friends with the United States."

Egypt attacked on Yom Kippur, the holiest day on the Hebrew calendar, when Jews rest, reflect, and fast. As Israeli forces retreated, Prime Minister Golda Meir begged President Nixon for help. Reluctantly, Nixon sent ammunition, helping Israel repel the Arab attack. The Saudis retaliated by cutting off oil shipments to the United States. The price of gasoline increased from thirty-six cents to fifty-three cents a gallon—when drivers could get it. Filling stations raised flags—green for "gas available," red for "no gas," yellow for "trucks only." To prevent hours-long lines, stations sold to cars with odd-numbered license plates on Mondays, Wednesdays, and Fridays, even plates on Tuesdays, Thursdays, and Saturdays.

Since World War II, the nation's wealth had increased geometrically, so much of it generated by the auto industry. In 1949, America's automobile fleet stood at 45 million. By 1972, it was 116 million—more cars than we could fill up from our own wells. The alpine graph of the American standard of living had finally reached its plateau.

Nixon, the most farsighted politician of his generation, had predicted this would happen. He had, in fact, decided to spend his second term reconciling his people to the diminishment of the American Dream.

"Nixon had . . . become convinced that one of the reasons he had to serve a full eight years was because he grasped what was true in the intimations of the apocalypticists on the bestseller lists: the imminence of America's decline as the world's number one power," wrote Rick Perlstein in *Nixonland: The Rise of a President and the Fracturing of America*. "He believed Nixon, and only Nixon, in a second term, safely removed from the requirement of ever winning another election, could cushion the blow by teaching Americans to live within limits."

Nixon lowered the speed limit on federal highways to fifty-five miles per hour, extended daylight savings time, and asked Americans to carpool and turn down their thermostats. This was followed by the first Corporate Average Fuel Economy law, which gave automakers until 1985 to double their fleet-wide average to 27.5 miles per gallon.

Our other imperial responsibility was to the nations we defeated: Germany, Italy, and Japan. Failures at world conquest, the Axis countries redirected their national ambitions into industry. Following Winston Churchill's admonition to be "magnanimous in victory," the United States rebuilt their factories and assumed their military duties. During the Cold War, America's best engineers went into aerospace and defense—those fields offered more money, thanks to big government contracts, and offered the patriotic satisfaction of keeping up with the Commies. In Germany, Italy, and Japan, the best engineers designed cars.

And so, when an oil-starved world demanded subcompacts, Germany gave us the Volkswagen Rabbit, Italy gave us the Fiat 131, and Japan gave us the Honda Civic. America gave us the Corvair, the Vega, and the Ford Pinto. The Pinto was the worst car in automotive history. It wasn't just a lemon, like the Edsel, it was a lemon that burned people to death. Ford president Lee Iacocca was so desperate for a small car by the 1970 model year that he accordioned the Pinto's design schedule to twenty-five months, from the usual forty-three. In crash tests, the tube between the gas cap and the tank was torn away in rear-end collisions over thirty miles an hour, spewing gasoline. Ford engineers considered placing the tank above the rear axle, instead of between the axle and the flimsy bumper, or installing a plastic liner in the tanks, but either solution would have added $11 to the production cost. A cost-benefit analysis determined that the Pinto's gas tank would fry 180 passengers, maim another 180, and burn up 2,100 cars. Settling the lawsuits from these infernal accidents would run the company $47.5 million, far less than the $137 million to fix the problem. *Mother Jones*, a muckraking magazine out of San Francisco, published the memo. The next year, a California jury awarded $128 million to a teenager burned over his entire body while riding in a rear-ended Pinto. The only consolation to Henry Ford II was that Pinto replaced his father's name, Edsel, as a synonym for a shoddy car. When Johnny Carson wanted to insult the *National Enquirer* for yellow journalism, he called it "the Pinto of newspapers."

My first car was a Chevy Chevette. Successor to the failed Vega, the Chevette was just as small, and just as flimsy. Its floorboards were so rust-prone my mechanic diagnosed the Fred Flintstone hole as Chevette Floor Cancer. He slid a metal plate under the floor mat, but when I drove through a puddle, dirty water gushed through the unsealed sheet, soaking my trousers. In the summer of 2011, I saw a man trying to crank one final ride out of a primer-gray Chevette on Fort Street in Detroit. I wasn't surprised the car wouldn't run. I was surprised the owner had kept it running for twenty-five years.

The American automakers lost Generation X forever with the crap they put out in the seventies and eighties. I can't convince my import-driving friends and relatives that twenty-first-century American cars are just as good as twenty-first-century Japanese cars, because so many started out in GM beaters. Even my father drove a Toyota, until he got a job with the governor of Michigan, who forced him to trade it for a Ford Escape.

"I don't need to drive foreign cars anymore, anyway," he said. "The American cars are just as good now."

They were just as good thirty years too late.

"The 1970s were the decade that undid Detroit," Paul Ingrassia wrote in *Crash Course*. "During the 1980s and 1990s, the Big Three would mount periodic, and sometimes spectacular comebacks, and undergo especially dramatic crises. But never again would Detroit rule the automobile industry unchallenged and unbowed."

Actually, the 1960s undid Detroit. The city that never recovered from the 1970s was Flint, Michigan.

IN 1980, shortly after the Rolling Stones released their trashy disco vamp "Miss You," a Flint rock and roll station cut a parody—a tribute to the industrial life entitled "I'm a Flintoid."

> *I work Buick all day long*
> *Building car doors makes you strong*
> *I'm a Flintoid.*

To be a Flintoid was to live on the most prosperous planet in the GM universe. In any universe. No city benefited more from the generous contracts negotiated by the UAW. That only seemed fair, because Flintoids had been beaten, gassed, and shot to establish the UAW. Flintoids enjoyed the highest per capita income in the United States. Flint was not the wealthiest city on Earth, but it was the most middle-class. Two out of every three Flintoids drew a paycheck from General Motors or one of its satellites. Eight decades after Billy Durant had the brainstorm of lashing a gasoline-powered engine to a buggy, the Genesee County shoprat population had multiplied to eighty thousand. General Motors owned more real estate in Flint than the Catholic Church owns in Rome. It was running three shifts a day at factories that occupied more ground than every Big Ten gridiron combined. Chevrolet plants were so multifarious that if you built cars in that low-lying area along the Flint River, you worked at Chevy in the Hole (as opposed to Chevrolet Assembly, on the south side). There were multiple Fisher Body plants—Fisher One, site of the Sit-Down Strike, on the East Side, and Fisher Two on the South Side. ACDelco made spark plugs. Truck and Bus installed them in Chevy Blazers. The local identity was spelled out on the black iron arches spanning Saginaw Street, the downtown drag: "VEHICLE CITY."

Fifty miles north of Detroit, and economically independent of the metropolis, the Vehicle City developed a culture distinct from the Motor City's. Even in culinary matters, Flint had its own version of the Coney Island, the hot dog with chili and mustard served in every Michigan diner. Angelo's, the twenty-four-hour hot dog stand, packed its buns with a dry chili that didn't run all over the plates like that mess at Lafayette Coney Island in Detroit. Even the music was different. The Saginaw Valley spawned a thousand garage bands, which made sense in a place where everyone owned two cars. Grand Funk Railroad, which ripped off its name from Michigan's Grand Trunk Railroad, camouflaged its musical sophistication (listen to the singing bass on "We're an American Band") with party-rock lyrics about shagging groupies and trashing hotel rooms. ? and the Mysterians recorded "96 Tears," the definitive two-minute garage rock song, on a front porch in Bay City, with a whistling Vox organ that sounded as though it had been purchased in a pawn shop.

The difference between Flint and Detroit went deeper than hot dogs and rock and roll. As the birthplace of the United Auto Workers, Flint took its unionism seriously. The sons and grandsons of the Sit-Downers believed that their labor had built General Motors and that in return, the company owed them high wages and benefits. Strikes in Flint took nearly twice as long to settle as strikes in other GM towns, but they were so effective that the company's local nickname was "Generous Motors." Unlike their union brothers in Detroit, Flint's UAW members endorsed the civil rights activism of Walter Reuther, one of the organizers of the 1963 March on Washington. Perhaps as a result, Flint never experienced a riot and is to this day equal parts black and white. Flint was segregated—blacks lived north of the river, whites lived south—but in 1966, the Flint City Commission chose an African-American, Floyd McCree, as mayor. McCree threatened to resign after the commission rejected an open-housing ordinance that would have banned racial discrimination in home sales. On February 20, 1968, the ordinance went before the public and passed by forty-three votes, making Flint the first American city to approve open housing in a popular referendum. And there were just as many rednecks, peckerwoods, ridge runners, hillbillies, and crackers working in Flint as there were in Detroit. The difference was that most of Flint's Southern whites were from the Ozark Mountains, which had fewer blacks and less racial conflict than regions

with a history of plantation agriculture. One Flint suburb has a neighborhood nicknamed Little Missouri, because so many residents migrated from the state's boot heel, following the Hillbilly Highway from
rural peasantry to industrial yeomanry. They brought their old-time
religion with them. Baptist and Nazarene churches supplemented the 10
percent tithe with biscuits-and-gravy breakfasts, a meal otherwise unknown north of the Ohio River.

Don Spillman was working in a North Carolina cotton mill in the
mid-1960s—not the same one as Norma Rae, but close enough to sue
her for stealing his life story. He started work when a light flashed on
and stopped when it blinked off. There were no lunch breaks. Spillman
brought his food to the job site and wolfed it when the work slowed
down. If the boss had caught him with a union pamphlet, he could have
been fired. Like Dale Earnhardt and every other young man in his
hometown, Spillman owned a stock racing car, but he couldn't afford
to put gas in it, even though he had a side job driving a bulldozer on a
road crew.

Meanwhile, Spillman's mother had married a guy who'd discovered
this (Cadillac) Eldorado called Flint. Every year, Mom and Stepdad
drove back south in a brand-new GM chariot. After witnessing several
model changes, Spillman finally told them, "Get me one of them jobs
up there."

The jobs were not hard to get.

"They had advertisements in the newspapers," Spillman recalled.
"North Carolina, Arkansas, Tennessee. GM would hire you. It seemed
like most of the people came from Arkansas and Missouri. Back then,
we had people working in two GM plants. They worked one shift in
one, had a lucrative job, then went across town at another one. Oh God,
I'm telling you, you could quit a job one day and get a job across town
in another GM plant. They needed workers. I was a skilled trades job in
the cotton mill, and I tell you, I made good bucks compared to what
you're making down there, but when I came up here, I hired in at $3.90
an hour. I thought I'd died and gone to heaven. And you had protection. You had union protection."

General Motors was such an engine of employment, consuming
labor as gluttonously as steel, rubber, and glass, that it was actually difficult for Flintoids to avoid working in the shop. GM officials trolled the
streets, seeking young men who hadn't volunteered at the personnel
office. Here's a piece of Michigan lore right up there with Marquette
dying in the wilderness or Berry Gordy Jr. impregnating Diana Ross.

The year is 1972. The scene is a filling station on Dort Highway, which is to Flint what the Strip is to Las Vegas: the street that displays the city's soul, a permanent greaser carnival of engine repair shops, biker bars, windowless strip clubs, tattoo parlors, rock and roll nightclubs, Coney Island stands, and oil-change emporiums. A GM executive rolls in for a fill-'er-up and asks the pump jockey, "Why aren't you working in the shop?" The kid shrugs. The driver takes down his number. A week later, GM calls, summoning him for duty. Twenty years later, the kid—by then a father of three—is laid off when his plant closes and his job moves to Texas, but that's a tale for a later chapter.

Likewise, Bernard Egan Hamper III tried to avoid a life in the shop, but deep down, he knew it was as inevitable a result of his lineage as male pattern baldness. Only the names Buick, Chevrolet, and Durant had been associated with General Motors longer than Hamper: his great-grandfather had gone to work there in 1910, followed by both his grandfathers and his father, a work-averse alcoholic who treated GM as an automatic teller machine to hit up between drinking binges. The company was so desperate it put anything that breathed on the line—and didn't care if that breath smelled like Canadian Club or registered a .15 blood alcohol content.

"He would just go from plant to plant," Hamper said. "He would always get a new job. But when I was growing up, my old man, who was a shoprat bum, used to instill in me that 'Look, you don't want to go into that shop. You don't want to get lost in that place. You better study or you'll end up just like everybody else in this town, knockin' screws for the rest of your life.'"

Hamper graduated from high school in 1973. There was no better time to be a young Flintoid. Too young for the draft, but old enough to enjoy the rights your older brothers had won in Vietnam—specifically, the right for eighteen-year-olds to buy beer at one of Flint's many Arab-owned liquor stores. Grand Funk hit number one with "The Loco-Motion." Alice Cooper played at the Whiting Auditorium. Marijuana and cocaine were sold in the auto plants and passed between the vinyl seats of Chevys in high school parking lots. It was a party generation. Not only were two-hour motel rooms, acid caps, and Who tickets available to late adolescents, so were the jobs to pay for them.

Hamper married his pregnant girlfriend right out of high school and spent his late teens and early twenties flailing around financially as a housepainter and a janitor. Finally, in a last-ditch attempt to save his marriage, he gave in and began pursuing his genetic destiny. After wangling an application from an in-law (even then, climbing the family tree was the quickest way into a General Motors plant), he got the Call on a Saturday afternoon, while holding down a bar stool. It was July 9, 1977.

"The state of GM in 1977, it was hot," said David Vizard, a former autoworker who was hired as the *Flint Journal*'s labor reporter that year. "It was rolling. In fact, the biggest problem in the plants was absenteeism. They were working around the clock. They were working these plants overtime. Three shifts. They had relief people on every line, just to cover people who didn't show up. Even if you didn't show up for work, they let it go for a long time. You got warnings, you got screamed at, but they needed people. Especially if you had experience. That robotic exercise of working on the line, it's a very hard thing to maintain for a long period of time."

Hamper was eventually assigned to the rivet line at Truck and Bus. There, he wielded a gun that looked like a giant letter G, shooting eight rivets into eight predrilled holes that connected a Chevy Blazer's cross-member with its side rails. At that stage of automotive parthenogenesis, the truck looked like a metal bed frame. The $8 an hour, plus overtime, didn't bring his wife back, so Hamper worked "the bachelor shift"—four thirty P.M. to one A.M. Also known company-wide as "second shift" or "the party shift," it let the inmates out early enough for last call across the street at Mark's Lounge and allowed them to sleep off the booze until the next afternoon. With no family responsibilities, Hamper spent most of his free time and disposable income on alcohol and punk rock LPs. Plus, he was occasionally able to escape to the bar after four hours of work, because he and a linemate had worked out a scheme they called "doubling up"—doing two jobs at once. GM would have loved to speed up the line, but the union contract specified that workers had to be notified of time studies. Whenever the efficiency expert showed up with his stopwatch, the shoprats began assembling trucks . . . much . . . more . . . carefully.

"It was a great functioning relationship while it lasted," Hamper said. "It was boring, it was stinky, it was shitty, but where in the hell else was I gonna get every Thursday night a check for four hundred dollars? Every time I had a toothache, my foot hurts, doesn't cost me a dime. I said, 'Man, this is a wonderful trade-off.' I think I'm a real product of Flint. You've pretty much got a town that's built on, it's almost inbred that I'm gonna go sacrifice a bunch of monkey motions in order to have my bills paid, and so there's not a lot of need for outside thinking. I think it's just a town of simple folk. I think that's the result of the nature of the beast and the prevalent dormancy attached to factory life. You don't use your brain a lot."

Hamper belonged to GM's last great recruiting class. After the stampede of 1977, the personnel offices of Truck and Bus, Fisher One and Two, Chevy in the Hole, and ACDelco were locked with triple-wrapped chains. Not only was GM refusing to accept aspiring shoprats, it was throwing the existing litter out of the den. No city was hit harder by the recession of the early eighties than Flint. The local unemployment rate reached 25 percent—a "brother, can you spare a dime" level.

Don Spillman's Local 599 had the largest membership in the entire UAW. Its monthly newsletter, the *Headlight*, began a "Hard Times" page, featuring articles entitled "Dealing with Creditors" and "Economic Experts See a Recession Until Spring." On Labor Day 1982, the union set up an "Unemployment City" in Flint Park, where workers spent the night in tents. Evangelist Robert Schuller was lured to Flint from his Crystal Cathedral in California to give a speech titled "How to Cope With Unemployment." His answer: Flint's attitude toward unemployment is "Yes We Can!!" That Christmas, a movie theater threw a party for the children of workers on permanent layoff. A Local 599 meeting on unemployment promised advice on benefits, utility bills, wage garnishment, veterans' rights, as well as "dealing with substance abuse, depression, emotional trauma during unemployment."

The recession struck right after the UAW had negotiated its most generous contract ever. Signed in 1979, it gave workers twenty-six paid personal holidays—a day off every other week—bringing the union closer to its goal of a four-day workweek. Less than three years later, with a third of the UAW's membership on layoff, GM pressured the union into reopening the contract by threatening to close seven plants. The UAW gave up its cost-of-living increase and nearly half its paid holidays, concessions costing each worker $3,800 a year. In exchange, GM spared four plants and agreed to a two-year moratorium on further closings.

"As we are all aware of the economy not getting better, the second shift on Engine Cradle has been laid off," Spillman, by then a shop committeeman, wrote in the January 1982 newsletter. "These members will survive because they are plenty tough . . . we all hope the overinflated salary of GM President Roger Smith is cut more than just a little bit so as to reflect he is as serious about saving the Corporation as well as the UAW is."

Roger Smith was a local villain. So was Ronald Reagan, who had dismissed as not newsworthy "some fellow in South Succotash" losing his job and suggested the unemployed blighter relocate to Texas or California. Although it occurred on his watch, Reagan can't be blamed entirely for the recession of '82, which had its roots in the disruption of the oil supply caused by the Iranian Revolution and the anti-inflationary interest rates set by President Jimmy Carter. Americans could not afford the gas to fill a big car or the loan to buy it. Reagan refused to loosen the money supply until inflation declined. As a result, car sales hit a twenty-year low. In the fall of 1982, the national unemployment rate was 10.8 percent, the highest since the Great Depression. The president urged his gloomy nation to "stay the course," promising that the policies that had extended the recession—reducing taxes and government spending—would eventually end it. Reagan's Cold War shopping spree resulted in $1.3 billion in defense contracts for General Motors—its biggest bonanza since Vietnam. Reagan also forgot about his free-market principles long enough to strong-arm the Japs into limiting auto imports to 1.65 million vehicles a year.

Flint's most belligerent anger was directed toward the Japanese. The same sneaks who'd bombed Pearl Harbor had now blindsided America by building fuel-efficient subcompact cars that did not explode when rear-ended or rust out their floorboards after driving through a puddle.

One of the UAW locals held a fund-raiser, inviting Flintoids to batter a Toyota with a sledgehammer at five dollars a whack. Even the congressman attended. Less publicly, foreign cars were scraped with keys, sabotaged with sugar in the gas tank, and spray-painted with slogans whose racial implications had last been acceptable in polite company during the Second World War. "ASSHOLES BUY JAP CARS" read a graffito on an I-69 overpass between Flint and Lansing. Signs outside UAW halls declared "Non-North American Cars Will be Towed at Owner's Expense." If a schoolteacher or a city employee was seen driving a Nissan or a Honda, the UAW would call his boss to complain. On a popular T-shirt, Uncle Sam hoisted Fat Man and Little Boy, the weapons that had ended World War II, above the legend "Two Bombs Were Not Enough." Having lost the shooting war, the Japanese were now winning a trade war that would eventually make Flint resemble Hiroshima without the radiation.

Only two years into what he'd expected to be a stable, thirty-year relationship with the world's largest industrial concern, Hamper was laid off. In 1981, right after Reagan clamped down the money supply to stop inflation, he was laid off again. He tried to keep busy with a daily and nightly regimen of alcohol, but as the months of unemployment dragged on, even drunkenness got boring. As a short, unathletic high schooler, Hamper's only reprieve from the black-and-white anonymity of the sophomore photo gallery had been winning honorable mention in a *Detroit News* poetry contest. So he borrowed his mother's typewriter to peck away at the monotony. One afternoon, after *Card Sharks* and *Family Feud*, Hamper was so bored he wrote a review of an album by an Illinois rock band called Shoes. As the owner of a large collection of vinyl by the Stooges, the Troggs, and Black Flag, Hamper felt music was the one topic on which he was qualified to rant. So he mailed his screed to the local alternative newspaper, the *Flint Voice*. A few days later, he received a phone call from its editor, Michael Moore. They had never met, but Hamper knew who Moore was. Everyone in Flint knew who Michael Moore was.

Ever since he was a teenager, growing up in the Flint suburb of Davison, Moore had been developing the talent that would one day make him world-famous: getting attention by pissing off the establishment. As a Boys Stater, Moore won an Elks Club essay contest on Abraham Lincoln with a speech on what Lincoln might have thought of the Elks' "Caucasians only" policy. It caused such an uproar that the *CBS Evening News* asked for an interview and Michigan senator Philip Hart invited Moore to testify on a bill to outlaw discrimination by private clubs. Embarrassed by his acne, the sixteen-year-old declined both invitations. Nonetheless, CBS ran a story, and the Elks experienced so much political pressure they began accepting blacks. The pimply young man soon got over his bashfulness. As a high school senior, Moore took advantage of the recently ratified Twenty-Sixth Amendment to run for a seat on the Davison School Board, his candidacy motivated by a paddling from an assistant principal. Moore's victory made him the youngest elected official in the United States. A generation younger than any of his fellow trustees, the long-haired Moore was a volatile element in small-town politics, sitting barefoot on the floor during meetings. He moved to name an elementary school after Martin Luther King Jr. (The motion was not seconded.) He forced the schools to open for extracurricular activities on Wednesdays, against the wishes of Baptists and Methodists, who considered that a church night. (Moore, who had considered becoming a priest, at least had the support of his fellow Catholics.) When the board refused to let Moore tape-record its proceedings, he called the county prosecutor, claiming a violation of the Open Meetings Act. After that, the other board members began holding secret, Moore-less meetings at the president's house. When Moore found out, his fellow members organized a recall election to get rid of him. Moore beat the recall but failed to win a second term. During his four years on the board, though, he did get that assistant principal fired.

The *Flint Voice* grew out of Moore's next project, the Davison Hotline, a crisis center that counseled drug addicts, sheltered runaways, offered birth control advice, and fed the unemployed. Moore decided to promote the hotline with a newspaper called *Free to Be*, named after the seventies women's lib album *Free to Be . . . You and Me*. Doug Cunningham, a college journalist who had met Moore when he walked into the University of Michigan–Flint newspaper office, looking to publicize the hotline, convinced him to turn *Free to Be* into a muckraking alternative newspaper, modeled after the *Seed*, the *Berkeley Barb*, and, of course, its namesake, the *Village Voice*. The first issue of the *Flint Voice* was published on December 10, 1977.

Flint did have an alternative scene that included a free medical clinic, a food co-op, a head shop, and a used paperback store called Middle Earth Books. The Midwest was three to five years behind the East and West Coasts in developing a counterculture, so while the *Voice* was too late to chronicle the sixties, it was right on time for the eighties, a decade that would be far more important in Flint's history.

The *Voice* first made itself obnoxious to city hall with an article exposing the mayor's use of municipal employees in his reelection campaign. The city's ombudsman investigated and leaked a copy of his report to the *Voice*, which published it. Incensed by the leak, and determined to locate the loose valve in his office, the mayor ordered a police raid on the *Voice*'s publisher, seizing the plates from the offending issue. Employing his one true talent—making himself the locus of political outrage—Moore called every reporter he knew. Once again, he was on the *CBS Evening News*, and once again, he declined to testify before Congress, this time for a bill that prohibited police from raiding newspaper offices unless a crime had been committed there. The case was so well publicized that Moore received a phone call from John Lennon, offering to do a benefit concert for the *Voice*, as he'd done nine years before for MC5 manager John Sinclair (coincidentally, another Davison High School graduate). Lennon was murdered before he could make it to Flint, but Moore had already persuaded another world-famous musician to sing for the *Voice*: barging backstage at a Harry Chapin concert, he persuaded the folksinger to perform a dozen benefits. The shows raised half a million dollars, enabling Moore to buy a house for the *Voice* offices.

(Moore had tried to get Michigan's own Bob Seger, but the singer was "taking oxygen" after a concert and thus indisposed to meet with a left-wing newspaper editor.)

After a series of layoffs throughout Reagan's first term, Hamper finally achieved some career stability when Reagan decided his second term would be a great time to order "a shitload of Army trucks" from GM.

"Ronnie needed a new fleet of death wagons," Hamper would write. "It sucked, but so did starving."

With his love of punk rock and his surly attitude toward authority, in particular the authority of GM foremen, Hamper was the missing link between the *Voice*'s hippie pretensions and the blue-collar city in which it circulated. Moore's father had worked at GM and arranged for his son to spend a summer on the assembly line. On his first day of work, young Michael drove up to the factory gate—then turned around and drove away. One of the contradictions in Moore's career was that he wanted to be a voice of the working people . . . but didn't want to work himself. Moore lived a bohemian existence on the $15,000 a year he earned at the *Voice*. Partly because of his niggardly salary, and partly because he fancied himself an internationalist who was above provincial loyalty to GM, Moore drove a Honda Civic. With Hamper as a contributor, Moore could have it both ways. At first, Hamper wrote gonzo articles moaning that local radio played too much AC/DC and "Stairway to Heaven," and reliving a night at the Good Times Lounge, "Flint's Most Dangerous Bar."

"There's been an altercation of some sort just about every night I've been there and if the bouncers aren't working on a commission basis, they oughta be," Hamper wrote about the Good Times. "What this bar lacks in ambience, it makes up for in ambulance. I mean, the tooth fairy would go broke replacing lost teeth with half dollars out in the parking lot."

The article resulted in a libel suit filed by the bar's owner—just the sort of attention Moore loved. Realizing he had discovered a proletarian Céline—the fantasy of every pamphleteer with a Joe Hill poster and a copy of *Eugene V. Debs Speaks*—Moore talked Hamper into writing "Revenge of the Rivethead," a column about life inside GM Truck and Bus. Hamper's writing allowed Moore to live a vicarious shoprat existence, while Moore's editing/hectoring guided Hamper to the subject that would make him the most widely read wage slave of the late eighties and early nineties.

"I could not make sense out of that place without writing," Hamper said of the shop. "I had to do it. I had to get something out of it, because I kept thinking about the look on my dad's face, my grandpa's face, how they went through all those bland years of not having their say or anything, and I said 'I've got to get something out of this besides a paycheck,' and then I stumbled on Moore, and that was the perfect outlet that justified it. Moore wouldn't let me get down or wouldn't let me take any excuses. That's his true gift, and this is what he does with editors or writers or cameramen. He finds people that are talented and he tells them, 'This is what you're gonna do.'"

Moore made Hamper a celebrity years before he made himself famous. In 1983, the *Flint Voice* became the *Michigan Voice*, a statewide paper. I was a junior in high school that year, just getting interested in writing, and I'd pick the paper up at a bookstore in East Lansing, always looking for Hamper's column among the nuclear freeze editorials and Moore's seven-point plan for saving Flint. Newspapers weren't supposed to be fun, but I'd call my friends and read them Hamper's stories about leaving an Ernest Angley revival on a stretcher with a vodka drip, or learning the erotic appeal of Elvis impersonators. ("Tonight," a fan told Hamper, "your wife's gonna treat you like you're Elvis!") Alex Kotlowitz, a former *Voice* reporter who'd moved up to the *Wall Street Journal*, profiled Hamper in a front-page story on blue-collar writers. *Harper's* magazine ran an excerpt from an article on rivet hockey, the factory time-killer of kicking rivets at your linemates' shins. Then, the *Today* show's Betty Rollin profiled Hamper on her "People You Should Know" segment, about members of the heartland herd who displayed talents ordinarily found only in New Yorkers. Hamper was hip to his own novelty, to the fact that editors reacted to a literary shoprat like John Gielgud hearing the Elephant Man recite the Lord's Prayer. *Esquire* or *Penthouse* or *60 Minutes* would call and say, "We were so surprised to see that someone who writes as well as you do . . . ," which Hamper translated as *You know, we always thought you shoprats were such dumb shits and here you are, you have half a brain, and so we'd like to tap it.* An auto factory was a microcosm of society, so Hamper knew he wasn't the only autoworker who could write. Or build ships. Or water-ski.

The Rivethead was sometimes compared to Cleveland's Harvey Pekar as a working stiff–cum–social commentator, but Pekar's eloquence was regarded as less of an evolutionary leap. As a file clerk, he was technically white-collar. Also, Pekar expressed himself in the lowbrow medium of comic books. Since the rivet-guns-to-typewriter shtick was his gravy train to fame, and since NBC News paid for drinks at Mark's

Lounge, Truck and Bus's after-shift tavern, Hamper only half-resented the condescension.

As Hamper's fame as a writer increased, his fortunes as an autoworker became more tenuous. GM was using its failing sales as an excuse to get out of Flint, where the UAW had caused it so many headaches. The fact that Flint was GM's hometown actually worked to its disadvantage. Plants built in the teens and twenties were at the end of their lifespans. Instead of replacing them, GM built new factories elsewhere and gave Flintoids a choice: transfer or layoff. When GM eliminated the pickup-truck line at Truck and Bus, Hamper was told that if he wanted to continue riveting tailgates onto Chevy Blazers, he'd have to do it in Pontiac, forty-two miles to the south.

"I could have stayed put and took my chances here in Flint," he wrote in his column, "but this one unceasing vision kept coming to me, one in which I was cramming sugar paste into the ass-end of a cream stick on the graveyard shift at the doughnut shop while the repo-men were tap dancing down the boulevard with my end-tables and record collection in tow."

(Desperate to replace the auto jobs, Flint built a $13 million Hyatt Hotel and a $82 million amusement park. AutoWorld was a tribute to Flint in its prime, with an antique-car museum and a midway depicting downtown before plywood replaced glass as the most popular filler for window frames along Saginaw Street. Three-mile-an-hour buggies carried visitors through a tunnel where puppets put on a reenactment called "The Humorous History of the Automobile." One trip was enough for most people to realize that AutoWorld combined the charmlessness of the postindustrial Midwest with Disney World's appeal to the first-grade sensibility. The park closed after six months, with attendance less than a third of the expected one million. The Hyatt was passed among several chains before ending its career as a hotel in the 1990s.)

But GM's grandest "fuck you" to Flint was the closing of Fisher One—the plant where the Sit-Down Strike began in 1936. On December 10, 1987, the sixty-four-year-old plant produced its last automobile. The next day, over three thousand shoprats were out of work. More than one remarked on the symbolism of GM's shutting down the birthplace of the UAW. Vizard, the autoworker-turned-labor-reporter, saw it as the endgame of GM's half-century war with the union, which had been fought one strike, one grievance, at a time.

"Why would you want to invest in a place where all they want to do is fight you?" Vizard asks. "There was open sabotage in the plants, even when I worked there. That was your power. If a foreman came along and screwed you over on overtime or a work shift, how do you get him back? You screw up his production schedule. Then it's just a matter of time before you have someone else sitting in his chair. In the military, they called it fragging . . . who didn't go along, who didn't turn his head when the drug locker was open. Flint was so militant. They always referred to [the Sit-Down Strike]. They would always go back to fighting for dignity, for middle-class values, and we've got to keep up the fight. Flint had this entitlement mania, and it was because it was the birthplace of GM, and, essentially, the birthplace of the UAW. They had this sense of 'We've always had GM, we'll always have GM, and they owe us.' It was a plant-wide, screw-you company mentality."

Class conflict was part of GM's culture. The plants were built with separate bathrooms for hourly and salaried employees. Rebellious workers sometimes did worse than get a foreman demoted. There was a supervisor in the Buick Foundry who often made a sweep of the overhead walkways, searching for beds where workers napped. One night, a worker cut a hole in the steel mesh, concealing it with a square of cardboard. The nosy boss fell several stories, injuring himself permanently. After that, management didn't try to stop sleeping on the job.

STANDING IN THE COLD outside Fisher One that day, with a camera crew, was Michael Moore. The year before, Moore had shut down the *Voice* and moved to San Francisco to become editor of *Mother Jones*, one of the investigative magazines he'd been trying to emulate in Flint. It seemed like a perfect fit, since both had made their names as critics of the auto industry. His first issue featured Hamper on the cover. Moore gave the Rivethead a column and sent him to Chicago on a publicity tour. The new gig didn't last long for either Flintoid. After six months, Moore was fired. Part of it was a clash of sensibilities with his sugar-daddy publisher, who was heir to a South African diamond-mining fortune. And part of it was an ego too large to fit into even Michael Moore's roomy blue jeans. The narcissistic journalist had always been motivated by a need to take control of and take credit for every endeavor he was involved in. At the *Voice*, some of the veteran staffers called young volunteers "Moories," because they seemed more devoted to Michael than to the paper. At *Mother Jones*, the staffers saw him as a "one-man show" who blew off editorial meetings and couldn't meet deadlines.

After he was canned by *Mother Jones*, Moore moved back to Flint, depressed and, like so many of his fellow Flintoids, unemployed.

"Jesus Christ," he told Hamper, "I gave up the whole paper and now I got no paper and no job."

"What are you doing now?" Hamper asked.

"I think I'm making this movie," Moore said. "Maybe they'll show it at union halls, like on the wall. I'd like to videotape you for some of this."

"Whatever," said Hamper, who was once again out of work—not because of a layoff, but because he'd freaked out on the assembly line. After nine years in the shop, Hamper suddenly hallucinated that he was trapped in a windowless room full of giant grasshoppers. Diagnosing a panic attack brought on by agoraphobia, a psychiatrist reassigned Hamper from General Motors to the Holly Road Mental Health clinic. Moore filmed his friend at a junior high school basketball court, discussing the crack-up. Moore planned to call the movie *Dance Band on the Titanic* after a line he'd used to end a *Flint Voice* story about AutoWorld. Hamper figured it would just be some Super 8 home movie about GM's assassination of Flint, with Moore as the Abraham Zapruder behind the camera. But Moore was determined not to make a "dying steel town documentary," or even a movie like *Harlan County USA*, which might win an Oscar but would play only at urban art houses hundreds of miles from its subjects' homes.

So how did a movie about an auto company shutting down factories in a city most Americans couldn't find if it were on the front of their hand become the highest-grossing documentary of all time? To answer that question, you have to answer another question: Did Flint become famous because Michael Moore lived there, or did Michael Moore become famous because he lived in Flint?

Moore's self-promoting qualities, which had been on display ever since high school, helped make the movie a hit. Only an overconfident egomaniac would run for the school board at age eighteen. Likewise, only an overconfident egomaniac would become such an important character in his own movie that it wound up being titled *Roger & Me*. Woody Allen is the only other American director whose on-screen persona is so central to his work. At the time, it was unheard of for a documentarian to make himself star, but, as Moore's old coeditor Doug Cunningham observes, "Michael has to be personally front and center of anything he's involved in." For Moore, it wasn't enough to put his name on the movie; he had to put his face on it, too. Moore's gift for social climbing also paid off when he enlisted the help of Kevin Rafferty, director of one of Moore's all-time favorite movies, the early-eighties nuclear-freeze propaganda piece *The Atomic Cafe*. Rafferty was a Harvard graduate and nephew of Vice President George Bush. Moore had introduced Rafferty to a tribe of southern Michigan neo-Nazis for his follow-up feature, *Blood in the Face*, a documentary on white supremacists. In exchange, Rafferty spent a week in Flint showing Moore how to operate a camera and later set him up in a New York editing studio.

If Moore had spent his twenties in Boston instead of Flint, he might have obeyed Rafferty's advice to *not* put himself in the movie. But Flint had been the last city in the United States to get its own PBS station, and Moore had gone broke trying to run an art cinema in the early eighties. (He finally gave up and drove to Ann Arbor to see John Sayles movies.) So he understood that what Flintoids wanted to see was a morally satisfying comedy, with himself as the protagonist and GM chairman Roger Smith as the bad guy. Moore was just as calculating and ruthless an investigative journalist as any of the *60 Minutes* crew, but as a Flintoid, with a nasal, uncosmopolitan accent and a figure developed at Angelo's Coney Island, he could present himself as a clueless but sincere buffoon who thought it was okay to walk into GM headquarters and ask for an interview with the chairman. (To people outside Michigan, at least. *Voice* readers knew that Moore knew better.) Throughout the movie, Moore wore an "I'm Out for Trout" baseball cap borrowed off Hamper's head. Moore borrowed some of his absurd tone from Hamper, too. It was Hamper's idea, first floated in "Revenge of the Rivethead," to invite Roger Smith to Flint for bowling night. Hamper also provided the segue for the movie's blackest humor, describing the moment he turned on the radio during the drive home from his factory crack-up and heard the Beach Boys' "Wouldn't It Be Nice." Moore used the song as a soundtrack to a Parade of Homes tour of Northwest Flint's most distressed residential properties.

Roger & Me is not an honest movie. Its central premise—that Roger Smith refused to grant Michael Moore an interview about the Flint plant closings—is bogus. According to Roger Rapoport's biography *Citizen Moore*, Moore conducted a fifteen-minute interview with Smith at a press luncheon in January 1988, while he was shooting *Roger & Me*, then pressured one of his collaborators to deny the meeting ever happened. Part of the *Flint Voice*'s mission statement went like this: "We believe the commonly accepted notion of objective journalism is bullshit." *Roger & Me* has less in common with the muckraking of Upton Sinclair than it does with the bitter satire of another Midwestern iconoclast, Sinclair Lewis. Substituting Flint's Saginaw Street for Gopher Prairie's Main Street, Moore tried to make fools of the burghers and boosters who had been his enemies when he'd sat on the Davison Board of Education and edited the *Voice*. Moore sneaked his cameras into a country club where unemployed black people were working as living statues for a *Great Gatsby* party. When Flint's smart set dressed as gangsters and paid to spend the night in the new county jail, Moore filmed the event. His interviews with famous folks who dropped in on Flint—Anita Bryant, Pat Boone, Miss America, and native Flintoid Bob Eubanks—were all embarrassing to their subjects, whose square celebrity dated from the days when GM was still a wealthy enough paterfamilias to support Flint in the manner to which it had become accustomed. The movie was framed as single combat between a fat everyman with a microphone and an arrogant CEO—a storytelling device as old as Theseus vs. the Minotaur—but really, it was Michael Moore vs. a small-minded small town, a role he'd been playing for nearly twenty years.

After premiering at the Telluride Film Festival, *Roger & Me* was picked up by Miramax Films for a $1.5 million advance. Now a wealthy man and a celebrity, Moore moved to New York and started developing *TV Nation*, an NBC program that employed the same brand of satirical ambush journalism as *Roger & Me*. The only Flintoid he took with him was Hamper.

Hamper had finally quit GM in 1988, after not even sedatives and forty-ounces could hold back one final monster panic attack at his new job in Pontiac. Retiring to the pool shed behind the house he shared with his new wife—a schoolteacher who'd introduced herself by fan letter—Hamper turned "Revenge of the Rivethead" into a book. *Rivethead* won its author profiles in *People* and the *New York Times*, and a movie option from director Richard Linklater, who thought a shoprat would be a good follow-up to *Slacker*. Linklater even signed Matt Dillon to play Hamper and dragged the star to Flint for a two-day Rivethead tour. Hamper took the film types to Angelo's, where Dillon tried to brush off the "Are you . . ." question by saying, "I get that a lot." Coney dogs sold well among young women that evening. *Rivethead*, however, never became a movie. Like Hunter S. Thompson, to whom he was compared by his publisher, or Charles Bukowski, to whom he was compared by *Businessweek*, Hamper wrote animated prose whose message and energy could not be conveyed onscreen. Truly, he's one of the most colorful stylists ever to plug in a typewriter. The plant manager's State of the Factory address was a "Knute-Rockne-reborn-as-Leo-Buscaglia-on-the-threshold-of-industrial-Guyana rah-rah speech." Flint is a "town that genuflects in front of used car lots and scratches its butt with the jagged peaks of the automotive sales chart." But he had to be a sleight-of-pen magician to distract readers from a subject whose monotony would stump most authors after three hundred words. Only a genius could write an entertaining book about assembly-line labor. But not even a genius can make an entertaining movie about it. Linklater tried two scripts. One ended with an *Officer and a Gentleman*–like romance. The other, which Hamper liked, was heavy on recitations of his garage-rock-inspired prose.

Hamper did get to be a TV star. Moore rented him a New York City apartment and made him a correspondent for *TV Nation*. Once again, Hamper was Moore's house sidekick. In one spot, he visited Manhattan drug stores and sex shops, asking for size S condoms.

"I think Moore just liked having me there because I was from Flint," Hamper said. "He had all those Good Times Charlies and he liked having a good friend around. My relationship with him is two different people. There's Michael Moore and then there's the guy I knew, Mike Moore."

For Moore and Hamper, taking down GM was a ticket out of Flint. Moore, who would get rich as a left-wing auteur, bought a condo on the Upper West Side of Manhattan and a chalet-style cottage on Torch Lake, a northern Michigan resort.

Hamper moved to Leelanau County, another upper Lower Peninsula resort community where his wife had family. He signed a contract for a second book called *America Drinks and Goes Home*, but without his job at the shop, he'd lost his material, and without Moore, he'd lost his literary foreman, demanding quota. A loner and an introvert, Hamper had chosen the rivet gun and typewriter as his tools because shoprats and authors don't have to interact with other humans. Moore founded a film festival in Traverse City, fifteen miles from Hamper's cottage, but Hamper's agoraphobia and fear of crowds prevented him from attending.

A decade and a half after *Roger & Me*, Moore won an Academy Award for *Bowling for Columbine*, his exposé of America's gun culture, and sat next to former president Jimmy Carter at the 2004 Democratic National Convention, as a reward for the anti-Republican agitprop of *Fahrenheit 9/11*. Hamper's only public communication was deejaying a Friday-night soul music show on the local college radio station.

"I think I'm a real product of Flint," Hamper said. "My parents, grandparents, all worked in the shop. I think I was bred to take orders. I think that's why I haven't written another book. No one's telling me what to do. If some guy called me up and said, 'You're gonna write a book and this is what it's about,' I'd probably do it. I'm just used to being told what to do."

NOW THAT THE UAW AND GM MANAGEMENT finally had a common enemy—the Japanese—the union dropped its son-of-a-son-of-a-sit-downer attitude and began cooperating with management. Buick, the most unproductive division in GM, had experienced its last strike in 1974. The next year, GM executives told Local 599 president Al Christner that the company was fed up with high absenteeism, insubordinate employees who slashed foremen's tires, stacks of grievances, and semi-annual strike threats. It was thinking of shutting down Buick Assembly, which had been built in the 1920s. The plant was obsolete, and so was its product, a heavy sedan with a V-8 engine and rear-wheel drive.

That Halloween, Christner held a summit at the Flint Sheraton with Buick's personnel manager. They walked into the meeting wearing devil masks, then whipped them off and shook hands. Once the company and the union stopped demonizing each other, they came up with the Quality of Work Life program, an attempt to end grievances and strikes by giving the guy on the line more say in how the plant was run. Workers could shut down the line, adjust machine settings, reject raw materials—all decisions that had once been reserved for foremen.

"We had union people making schedules up, doing things that salary used to do," Don Spillman said. "We gained a lot of power over what we did here."

Absenteeism, which hurt quality more than any other infraction—even more than drinking on the line—was cut to 2 percent in plants that adopted Quality of Work Life. Grievances—and the time-consuming hearings necessary to settle them—almost disappeared, because "you could settle a lot more issues with the plant manager."

The success of the Quality of Work Life program, plus the desire to emulate Japan's just-in-time manufacturing process, convinced GM to build a new super-plant on the site of Buick Assembly.

Buick City was supposed to be GM's version of a Toyota plant. In the early eighties, the Japanese landed in America, forty years later than originally planned. They were building motorcycles in Ohio, using nonunion shoprats. From top to bottom, from Roger Smith on the fourteenth floor of GM HQ to the guy standing in a trench at the Buick, bolting mufflers to undercarriages, the world's largest corporation had always dismissed the Japanese as copycats, a nation that had not produced an original thought since it got the idea to steal its alphabet from China. Japan did everything America did, at half the size. Now that Americans were cramming themselves into Asian clown cars—you didn't *drive* a Honda Civic, you *wore* it like a square steel suit—GM conceded that the copycat nation was worth copying. As a Local 599 committeeman, Don Spillman was part of the "design team" for Buick City, an eight-factory, 235-acre, $280 million complex on the north side of Flint. GM wanted to break down work classifications by assigning assemblers to six-person teams, in which every member could do every job. The company also wanted "just-in-time" delivery of parts, instead of stockpiling materials in the plant. So Spillman flew across the Pacific Ocean, visiting Honda and Toyota plants to find out why they were winning. The Japanese had assembly lines delivering parts to the assembly line. They had robots welding seams and painting bodies. The workers did calisthenics before each shift. Nobody smiled.

"It used to take us six hours to change a press line," he said. "Set up dies to make a hood, take you six hours. The Japanese were doing it in ten minutes. When they first dropped all this stuff on me, I said, 'That's a cock and bull story.' It took a whole bunch of people working together, the die setters working together, the production men working as a team. We changed a lot of classifications. We didn't combine skilled trades because when you take electrical, machine repair—those are different. But the stock chaser, the buck handler, the assembly line, the paint shop—everybody had to learn all them jobs."

At a Honda motorcycle plant, Spillman was amazed to see parts popping out of the floor, like bowling balls on their return trip up the alley. The workers would snatch the tailpipes or tanks and attach them to the bike.

"We brought back just-in-time inventory," he said. "You don't have a warehouse no more. You got these trucks in here, they're bringing you motors or they're bringing you windshield wiper blades just in time to put 'em on the car. And we brought back technology to change dies in less than thirty minutes."

Buick City resulted in the demise of Fisher One. Instead of building bodies on the East Side of Flint and trucking them to the North Side, which wasted gasoline, manpower, and time, GM would build the entire car in one location.

Buick City opened in September 1985. With twenty-eight thousand workers, drawn from factories all over Flint, the plant was supposed to represent the city's recovery from the recession of Reagan's first term. This hive became the birthing chamber of the LeSabre, a compact, front-wheel-drive sedan at the bottom of the Buick status ladder. Buick City did a great job producing LeSabres. From the time the complex opened, the LeSabre was one of J. D. Power and Associates' highest-ranked automobiles for quality and reliability. There was no problem with Buick City. The problem was with Buick. It was the car your retired high school principal drove to church. Buick's motto should have been "The Last Car You'll Ever Own"—not because of its durability but because the average age of a Buick owner was sixty-seven. David Dunbar Buick, whose fiercely short apparition is reproduced in a bronze statue on a Flint sidewalk, didn't live much longer than that himself. It's an astonishing piece of nostalgia now, but gasoline cost less than a dollar a gallon in the 1990s. Young drivers who had once begun the Buick-to-the-grave cycle in a LeSabre were now buying SUVs. In Buick City's first decade, GM lost another ten points of market share, falling from 40 to 30.7. It also didn't help that Christner had been voted out of Local 599's presidency by workers who were angry about the concessions of the early eighties and thought the Quality of Work Life program "was just another management scheme to eliminate jobs," as one member put it. Christner was eventually succeeded by a Vietnam vet who took the local back to its militant roots, appearing at Flint city council meetings to protest the company's tax abatements. Only a dozen years after it opened, GM decided to shut down Buick City, moving production of the LeSabre to its plants in Hamtramck and Lake Orion, Michigan.

After the word came down from Detroit on November 22, 1997, Flint's UAW region president called it "some Thanksgiving bad news from GM that will cripple our community for decades to come." In an attempt to save the plant, the UAW had taken out ads in the *Wall Street Journal* and *Inventor's Business Daily*, publishing a company memo that ranked Buick City second in quality of GM's nineteen North American plants. It was no use. General Motors had scheduled the Flint autoworker for extinction and was knocking off shoprats as rapidly as western pleasure hunters had exterminated the buffalo. Once Buick City closed, the count would stand at twenty thousand—less than one-quarter of the population just twenty years before. The company's strategy was to disperse Flintoids to plants unafflicted with ancestral memories of the Sit-Down Strike. At Flint Truck and Bus, Hamper had gotten used to reading novels at work thanks to those double-up arrangements with a linemate. Once he was transferred to Pontiac, "the jobs were timed out to make sure the workers wouldn't be allowed a moment's intermission," he wrote. "Anyone caught reading a newspaper or paperback would be penalized. The union was nothing more than a powerless puppet show groveling in the muck."

Flint's bitterness over GM's plan to fire the entire city led to the last great strike against General Motors, not far from where the first had begun. It began at the Flint Metal Fabricating plant, where the company had failed to install $200 million in improvements agreed on in the previous contract. Fearing a strike over its broken promise, GM began removing Chevy Silverado hood dies so it could continue production of the truck elsewhere. Just as in 1936, the very action GM took to avoid the consequences of a strike ended up provoking one.

"We held their feet to the fire about the two hundred million dollars and before Memorial Day, General Motors called some truckers in to take those dies out," said Spillman, who was on the staff of UAW region 1C, which covers south-central Michigan. "I went over, got the shop committee together, and we wouldn't let 'em load the dies onto the truck. We got in front of the trucks and wouldn't let 'em load the dies. So what General Motors did, they waited 'til Memorial Day weekend, brought a scab crew into the plant, and took them dies out like thieves in the night. I told my boss, 'We're going to have to strike that plant if they don't bring 'em back.' Nine thirty on June the fifth, management wanted an extension. I said, 'Only way you'll get an extension, if I can look at that TV set over there and see helicopters airliftin' them damn dies back up here.'"

The strike began half an hour later, as 3,400 workers at Metal Fab walked out. The following week, the walkout spread to Flint East, a parts plant whose employees felt GM's outsourcing of work was just practice for moving all their jobs to Indiana or Tennessee.

"Outsourcing is big," a toolmaker told the *Flint Journal*. "General Motors doesn't seem to even want plants in Flint anymore. Why do you think they've been sending work to other places?"

Unlike Metal Fab, which stamped out hoods and fenders for a limited variety of cars and trucks, Flint East produced speedometers, spark plugs, and filters used in almost every GM vehicle. You cannot sell a car without a speedometer. Because of the just-in-time supply system it had copied from the Japanese, GM had no warehouses full of speedometers. The 5,800 workers at Flint East halted every assembly line in almost every plant in the GM universe.

The strike lasted fifty-four days, the longest since the two-month epic of 1970, and cost GM $2.5 billion. The company returned the dies to Metal Fab, agreed to spend the promised $200 million to improve the plant and to stop outsourcing parts made at Flint East. On the other hand, GM decided to spin off its parts operation into a new company, Delphi, and to build new plants where a small group of workers would assemble parts purchased from outside suppliers. GM engineers were trying to design an autoworker who earned $2 an hour, never got sick, and died on retirement day. Since the Tech Center had not developed even a test model, Human Relations was trying to figure out how to relate to as few humans as possible.

Spillman considered the strike a victory, because Flint Metal Fab and Flint East were still open. But by the second decade of the twenty-first century, there were only six thousand shoprats left in Flint.

"GM pulled out of here 'cause they had done whupped the union," he said. "They thought they had and they wanted to make more money overseas. Flint had a big backing of union people all over, you know, so they needed to break that big bloc of union members up. I'll never understand that, 'cause we worked with management since the early eighties when Quality of Life started, we worked with them to make the company more competitive. We made all the major changes and we still got the shaft."

6.

"A Rust Bowl"

On the East Side of Chicago, life did not run according to the laws that nature imposed on the rest of the world. When night fell on other neighborhoods, those neighborhoods stayed dark until the next morning. On the East Side, the sky burned red when U.S. Steel, Republic Steel, or Wisconsin Steel dumped a load of hot slag, the waste product of steelmaking. The steel mills created their own suns, their own skies, their own weather. In other neighborhoods, housewives hung their washing in the basement when it rained. On the East Side, wives hung it indoors when the wind blew in from the mills, lest their sheets be stained with soot. On bright mornings, the air and the sidewalks glittered with graphite, a metallic mist so thick "you could take a spoon and get a hold of it," recalled an East Sider. Visitors remarked on a musty odor, but to natives, the stench of steelmaking was as natural an atmosphere as oxygen. Men didn't go to work when the sun rose and return home when it set: they pulled the eleven A.M. to seven P.M., the seven-to-three, the three-to-eleven, sometimes a different shift every week, so when you went up on 106th Street at three in the morning all the restaurants were open, and when you knocked on the door of Marino's Tap at the same hour, Marino would sell you a twelve-pack of beer, damn the city's two A.M. license.

The East Side is so named because it lies on the east bank of the Calumet River, a canal-slow body of water that flows into the heel end of Lake Michigan. The ore freighters docked in the Calumet, where they were emptied by Hulett unloaders, huge metal insects feeding from ship holds, rising and dipping like oil derricks. The river ran red from the iron filings dumped by the mills. Concrete banks guided the Calumet along a geometric course, under black lace railroad bridges, past pyramids of rock salt and coal, alongside junkyards piled with compressed cars. The East Side has often considered itself a misunderstood island at the edge of the city, tethered to the rest of Chicago by bridges. This was where the city's dirty work took place. Mayor Richard J. Daley even built an elevated toll bridge over the East Side, so he wouldn't have to drive past the mills en route to his vacation cottage in Michigan. The Skyway walks across the flyover neighborhood on hundred-foot iron legs, so "cars pass like distant jet traffic," the *Chicago Sun-Times* once wrote.

The bridges also kept out the blacks. Even as they were welcomed into the mills, they were not welcomed into the East Side, which remained Polish, Serbian, Croatian, Irish, and Mexican. In 1954, five black families moved into a housing project in Irondale, a sister steel village, and could not be dislodged, even after a week of bombing and rioting. But the blacks never crossed the river.

Since the Calumet River was an international port, the East Side was also a nautical neighborhood, as likely to be visited by sailors from Germany as by anyone from downtown Chicago. Nearby, in South Chicago, were two of the most famous maritime bars on the Great Lakes. Horseface Mary's, named for its proprietor's prognathous homeliness, was across the street from U.S. Steel's main gate. Kate's Tavern, on South Chicago Avenue, was better known as Peckerhead Kate's, after the barmaid's nickname for all her customers. A florid, busty woman, Kate once popped a breast out of her blouse after overhearing sailors speculate on whether she wore falsies. "Here, you goddamned peckerheads," she shouted, grabbing a sailor's hand and clamping it to her teat. "Feel this and see if it's real!" When the Great Lakes were frozen, bachelor sailors wintered over in South Chicago flophouses.

Rob Stanley was born on the East Side in 1947, two years after his father, a U.S. Steel safety man, came home from the war. Of English and Welsh descent, Stanley was an exotic in his ethnic neighborhood. As a student at Chicago Vocational High School, he never thought about going to college, because steelworkers made more money than chemistry teachers. He thought about rumbling with Negro gangs from across the river and playing football in Calumet Park with the local sandlot all-stars, the Bonivirs.

"About five percent of my class went to college," Stanley said. "A lot of the guys on the East Side didn't have plans. What happened is, you were just enjoying life, going out. We had the park, we had all the teams we were on. Our plan was to get a better team, get better ballplayers and work, make enough money to get a car and make it to our games."

When Stanley graduated in January 1965, he had to pay rent or get kicked out of his father's house, so he walked over to Interlake Steel, where he was immediately hired to shovel taconite into the blast furnace on the midnight shift. It was the shittiest job in the mill, but it paid $2.32 an hour—enough for an apartment and a car.

"You'd just go apply," he said. "There was so much work, especially during Vietnam. When I quit Interlake to go over to Republic, they hired fifty guys that day. You'd always see guys with new helmets walking around."

The Vietnam War, which brought so much work to the steel industry, made it easy for Stanley to get hired as a grunt but impossible for him to enroll in a years-long apprenticeship program. The foremen knew his conscription was inevitable. One afternoon in 1967, as Stanley was driving home from work, a friend pulled up alongside his car, waving an envelope.

"I just got drafted," he shouted. "And so did you!"

Sure enough, when Stanley arrived home, the same envelope—the envelope every noncollegiate nineteen-year-old male received that year—was waiting in his mailbox.

Stanley's time "in country" lasted only a year, but the war lasted longer, so there was still plenty of work when he came home to the East Side. For two years, he was part of a construction gang building a blast furnace at U.S. Steel. Seven days a week, Stanley stacked bricks and dug clay out of pits. He figured he had his whole life to work in a steel mill, so he wrote letters to international construction companies, hoping to find a job that would take him back to Hong Kong, where he'd R & R'ed on the way home from the war. After he mailed them out, the Bonivirs' season started, which would keep him on the East Side through the winter. Then he got his girlfriend pregnant, which would keep him on the East Side forever. He had just gotten back from Vietnam and had big plans of traveling the world. He hadn't been planning for fatherhood.

Married now, and with a daughter, Stanley needed something more than a job on a shovel crew. He needed a career, like his father, who'd put in thirty-nine years at U.S. Steel before retiring after open-heart surgery. In 1970, Stanley began a pipe-fitter's apprenticeship at Wisconsin Steel. He didn't know it—nobody knew then—but he could not have hired in at a worse time.

Wisconsin Steel had been purchased by International Harvester in 1902. Fearing price gouging by U.S. Steel, the farm equipment manufacturer wanted a mill to produce plate steel and bar steel for its tractor assembly plants. In the early 1960s, Wisconsin Steel's manager rose to the presidency of International Harvester and spent $30 million to outfit his beloved mill with one of America's first basic oxygen furnaces, which converted iron to steel in under an hour, compared to half a day in an open-hearth furnace. In 1970, Congress passed the Clean Air Act. Chicago's mills so fouled the skies that employees drove old cars to work, because they would be covered in soot, graphite, and iron ore dust by the shift's end. A consultant calculated that pollution controls would cost $150 million. International Harvester decided to sell rather than clean up. While searching for a buyer, the company didn't bother to maintain its white elephant. Several coke ovens exploded, and four men working on a blast furnace died from inhaling toxic gases.

During this time, the local alderman, Edward Vrdolyak, gained control of the Progressive Steelworkers Union, which represented Wisconsin's workers. Even by the degenerate standards of the Chicago city council, Vrdolyak was a shady character. The cunning, ambitious son of a Croatian tavern keeper, he was known around town as "Fast Eddie," for his acquittal on an attempted-murder rap when he was a law student at the University of Chicago and for the mob connections he developed during his rise in politics. Every alderman rewarded his campaign volunteers with jobs, but driving a garbage truck or sweeping floors at city hall didn't pay as well as the mills. So Vrdolyak connived to elect a political ally named Leonard "Tony" Roque as union president. In return, Roque made sure that steelworkers who belonged to Vrdolyak's Tenth Ward organization got the best jobs in the mill. He also hired Vrdolyak's law firm to represent the union.

In 1977, International Harvester finally found a buyer: Envirodyne. The California high-tech company had no experience in steel, but its president, a former Stanford physicist, thought that modern engineering and marketing techniques would turn around the decrepit mill. Panicked that International Harvester was trying to skip out on its pension obligations, Roque negotiated a deal he thought would protect his steelworkers' retirement. But the inexperienced union president didn't understand pension law. Neither did the attorney from the alderman's law firm. They signed away nearly $25 million in benefits, leaving the workers only what the government guaranteed.

Envirodyne secured a $90 million federal loan to build a new blast furnace and water purification system, and install pollution controls that would satisfy the EPA. But due to International Harvester's neglect, the plant was too far gone to save. Blast furnaces broke down over and over again, preventing the mill from filling millions of dollars' worth of orders. As Wisconsin Steel lost money, it cracked down on the union. Rob Stanley and his fellow pipe fitters were asked to work as welders, boilermakers, and riggers for an extra twenty-five cents an hour. Their response: Are you crazy?

A labor dispute finally killed off Wisconsin Steel, but it had nothing to do with steelworkers. On November 1, 1979, workers at International Harvester's tractor plants went on strike after the company demanded they accept compulsory overtime and limits on seniority. International Harvester was still Wisconsin Steel's biggest customer, purchasing 40 percent of the mill's output.

When Stanley showed up for work on March 27, 1980, television news crews were gathered outside the gate.

"Did you hear what happened?" a coworker asked. "It's closed."

Closed? Stanley couldn't believe it. Envirodyne had just spent $90 million on modern equipment. Why would they close the mill? Wisconsin Steel had been in the neighborhood for three generations. How could an institution like that close?

As Stanley left the mill, carrying his bag of clean clothes, a foreman told him, "We'll contact you if something changes."

Nothing ever changed. March 27 was the last day Stanley and his 3,400 co-workers ever spent inside Wisconsin Steel. The mill was bankrupt. Stanley's last two paychecks bounced. He had worked at Wisconsin Steel for nine and a half years—six months short of the ten years that would have qualified him for a pension. The company promised him $4,200 in severance pay. He got a check for $700. And he ended up giving the money to a lawyer when his ex-wife—the woman he'd knocked up after coming home from Vietnam—sued him for back child support. Stanley had been earning $10 an hour in the mill, but once he was laid off, he had to get by on $100 a week in unemployment, plus whatever he could pick up tending bar at the Hot Spot, the tavern underneath his apartment. He even wrote a letter to the Chicago Bears, asking for a tryout, but the team turned him down. His ex-wife had remarried, to an electrician with a house and a boat, so he told her, "I can't pay you what I've been paying you, so I'll just take my daughter and buy her clothes or whatever." But then she divorced a second time, and again sued for child support. Because he hadn't saved his receipts, she won.

Stanley and a few buddies from Wisconsin Steel caught on at a cold-rolling mill in Indiana, but after seven months, he was laid off again. Two layoffs in one year seemed like a message that the steel industry and Chicago had no more use for Rob Stanley. So he moved to Houston, where he found a job hanging Sheetrock. The high gasoline prices destroying the auto and steel industries had rained prosperity on Texas. An out-of-work auto executive drove to Houston every weekend and filled his trunk with Sunday papers. Back in Detroit, he resold the want ads to union men willing to do dangerous jobs for half their old pay. Stanley took $6.50 an hour to stand on a wobbly, fifty-foot-high scaffold with a bunch of illegal aliens. After Houston, he tried California, enrolling in a bartending school that promised him a job once he completed its course. When the classes ended, his instructor told him, "I think you'd be better off looking on your own."

So Rob Stanley, a steelworker who hadn't made steel for over three years, wandered back home to the East Side for no other reason than it was spring and softball season was about to start in Calumet Park. As a thirty-six-year-old bachelor, unemployment didn't bother him that much. Along with three friends, he paid a couple hundred bucks a month to share an apartment near the park. If his car wasn't running, one of his teammates would always drive him to a game.

For the family men, life after the mill was harder. Charles Walley was forty-nine when Wisconsin Steel shut down, a shear man with twenty-two years' seniority, earning $27,000 a year, with overtime, and only a few payments left on his East Side bungalow.

A month after Wisconsin Steel closed, six hundred grumbling steel-workers gathered at St. Kevin's Church to hear Ed Vrdolyak promise to reopen the mill. Still tan from a Florida vacation, Fast Eddie arrived late to the meeting. The steelworkers booed their alderman when he (falsely) explained that he'd just gotten off a plane from Springfield, the state capital, where he'd met with the governor.

"Envirodyne came into the Wisconsin Steel purchase with bullshit and bubblegum—they didn't have a dime," Vrdolyak shouted over the heckling. "I've been talking to everyone, including the president, the mayor, and the governor. I want to get the mill open as soon as possible and get you your back pay because you know that the company wants to keep going. It's too valuable."

When union president Roque finally arrived, he announced plans "to get the mill open within the next three weeks."

Three weeks passed. The mill didn't reopen. Out of work for the first time in his life—even during a four-month United Steel Workers strike, when he'd worked at Republic, Walley had painted houses with an uncle—he began spending despairing days asleep on his couch. Didn't shave, didn't change his clothes, didn't leave the house, afraid of running into neighbors who would ask, "You working?" Instead, he hid in his living room, smoking and watching television until the late-night shows turned to static. International Harvester owed Walley over $16,000 in severance and vacation pay, but the money was tied up in the bankruptcy. Having always counted on a steel mill pension, the Walleys had no savings, no insurance. Chuck's unemployment check was not enough to cover the bills, so his wife, Arlene, sold her high school ring to a "We Buy Gold" shop in Indiana, spending the $35 on groceries. The first Christmas after the mill closed, the Lions Club gave the Walleys a basket full of turkey and canned goods. A sister who waitressed brought leftover chicken. The food pantry at St. Francis provided the filling for grilled cheese sandwiches. Even with loans from family members, the Walleys were forced to pay utility bills with credit cards and take out a second mortgage on their almost-paid-for house.

Having dropped out of high school to pump gas, Walley was unskilled at anything but making steel, so the only jobs he could find were grunt labor, paying half his old wage: toll taker on the Skyway, truck driver, stockroom at a truck factory. He caught on as a janitor in an elementary school, but—his explanation—the poor economy had discouraged couples from having children, so the school closed after three and a half years. (When his teenage daughter, Christine, won a full scholarship to Phillips Exeter Academy, Walley at first forbade her from going, "because when you come back, you'll look down on me for being a janitor!" He relented because a daughter in boarding school was, as she put it, "one less mouth to feed.") Finally, a temp agency hired Walley as a $5-an-hour security guard at a downtown law firm. But he never held a full-time job again. Businesses didn't want to hire ex-steelworkers, especially old ones. When International Harvester finally settled his claim, twelve years after the mill closed, he received $6,800 and a small retirement from the Pension Benefit Guaranty Corporation, a government fund that covered workers who hadn't qualified for a company plan.

"When closing that mill, they took the best years of my life away from me," Walley reflected years later. "My fifties. My fifties should have been the best years of my life. When that mill went down, I didn't owe anybody a nickel. I had three teenage kids. I owed $900 on my house. But by listening to all these politicians and this business about starting the mills back up, hanging around here, instead of selling and getting out of here and start a new life someplace . . . When you put twenty years in a place, you always want to hang in there and think they're gonna go back. It was a mistake most of us made. And when you're out of work and when you're making this $3.50, $5, $4 an hour, you can go in the hole awful fast."

In some ways, even Walley was better off than some of his co-workers. He didn't lose his house, although the roof sprang a leak he couldn't afford to repair. He didn't lose his wife, either. Plenty of Wisconsin Steel families fell apart after the fathers stopped bringing home a factory paycheck. One of Walley's neighbors attempted suicide. The *Daily Calumet*, a neighborhood paper that has gone the way of the steel-town life it chronicled, wrote a ten-years-later story on the men of Wisconsin Steel. Out of 3,400 workers, nearly a quarter died in the decade after the mill closed, most from alcoholism and stress-related illnesses, which went untreated because they no longer had health insurance. Their death certificates could have read "unplanned obsolescence."

Walley's wife stuck with him. Although Arlene had never had to work while he was in the mill, she supported the family as a bookkeeper and a blueprint clerk at an oil refinery.

"He isn't any less of a man in my eyes," Arlene Walley said. "In fact, I think more of him because of what he had to go through."

THE ECONOMIC RECOVERY of the mid-1980s never arrived in South Chicago. A decade before, U.S. Steel South Works, the two-mile-long lakefront plant, had employed ten thousand workers. In 1981, U.S. Steel promised to build a new rail mill at South Works—if the state repealed a rail tax, and if the United Steelworkers took a $1.25-an-hour pay cut. The state and the union agreed, but over the next two years, U.S. Steel lost nearly $1 billion—its worst hosing since the Depression. The company wanted more: a $40 million federal loan, a $33 million state grant to install pollution controls. From the union, it demanded the right to replace craftsmen with contractors and to forgo time-and-a-half for night shifts and weekends, when electricity was cheaper. The union told U.S. Steel to stuff it. Three days after Christmas 1982, U.S. Steel announced it was shutting down South Works. (Steel executives always announced mill closings the week after Christmas, when the holiday moratorium on acting like an SOB was over.) The mill was mostly gone by then, anyway. Most of the workers had been laid off for over a year. Even if

U.S. Steel had built the rail mill, it would have been part of a rump operation, without a blast furnace, basic oxygen furnace, or plate, rod, and bar mill—another reason the union said no. Only the beam mill and an electric furnace remained open, employing eight hundred workers.

Neal Bosanko was a South Chicagoan whose father worked at U.S. Steel before going on sick leave with the throat cancer that killed him. He had grown up in a neighborhood where no one complained about children wheezing with asthma because, as the grown-ups said, "if there's soot on the windows, there's food on the table." Where smoke was as natural to the atmosphere as rain clouds off the lake. Where in the mill-gate taverns, steelworkers downed three shots of whiskey to wash the grit from their throats.

"I thought the world was coming to an end when I saw a blue sky a year after South Works closed," Bosanko said.

Instead of going into the mills like the rest of his family, Bosanko became a VISTA volunteer, organizing food pantries for senior citizens. When Bosanko began his work, in the 1970s, he depended on steelworkers for donations. By the early 1980s, he was feeding steelworkers.

"The bottom dropped out," he remembered. "All of a sudden the steelworker families who used to contribute to the food bank were recipients, because their unemployment had run out, after a few months. We really were a self-sufficient community because we had the mills. But the dynamics of the community changed. I had to challenge the local chamber of commerce to support the food pantries. Before, their attitude had been that they were for leeches, that people using 'em just don't need 'em."

Bosanko was seeing more drinking and drug use. Suddenly impoverished, families pulled their children out of Catholic schools. The white middle class had been leaving for the suburbs since the 1960s. Once the steel crisis struck, those who had stayed either moved out of state or stopped being middle-class. As they went, so went the grocery stores, the restaurants, the department stores—Goldblatt's, Woolworth, Robert Hall. The only reason more steelworkers didn't lose their bungalows was that they'd taken out mortgages with neighborhood banks and credit unions, which held the paper on customers whose hard times were no fault of their own.

In the suburb of Calumet City, two towns south of the East Side, desperate steelworkers turned for help to their priest. Father Leo Mahon was so distressed by his parishioners' plight that he organized the Steel Country parishes into the Calumet Community Religious Conference, which won a $500,000 grant to open a job bank for laid-off steelworkers. In 1985, the conference was looking for a black organizer to serve its inner-city chapter. Unable to find the right candidate locally, the group took out an advertisement in a magazine called *Community Jobs*. The ad was read by a twenty-three-year-old Columbia University graduate at the New York Public Library. Thus, the shutdown of Wisconsin Steel brought Barack Obama to Chicago, where he began his rise to the presidency of the United States. Obama counseled steelworkers still in denial about the disappearance of their industry. Blue-collar aristocrats bejeweled in gold chains and diamond rings, they planned to ride out their layoffs on unemployment and union benefits. In the past, they'd always gone on strike, returned to work, and earned more money than ever. Why would it be different this time? The brightest were retrained as computer programmers. The less fortunate landed near-minimum-wage jobs at the Sherwin-Williams paint factory or Jay's Potato Chips or Brach's Candy. None ever again earned as much money as they'd earned pouring steel.

The East Side's isolation had insulated the rest of Chicago from the soot and stench of the mills. Now the steel industry's disappearance was more remarkable than its presence had ever been. In the early 1980s, Chicagoans assumed their city was headed for the same scrap heap as Detroit, Cleveland, Buffalo, and Gary.

"The city was seen as a vestige of America's industrial past," said Gery Chico, a young lawyer who later became Mayor Richard M. Daley's chief of staff. Between 1967 and 1982, Chicago lost 250,000 jobs and a quarter of its factories. From a population of 3.8 million, Chicago dwindled to less than 3 million, falling behind Los Angeles in population. As Chicago lost industry and railroad traffic, the Loop decayed until its busiest institution was the Pacific Garden Mission, the soup kitchen and homeless shelter where the radio program *Unshackled!* was recorded. The city tried turning State Street into a mall and building condominiums near the mission, but the people who could afford to buy the condos had dismissed urban life as fit only for tramps, drug dealers, welfare mothers, halfway-house mental cases, and immigrants paying their dues in America.

In 1976, after spending sixteen years in London as a foreign correspondent, journalist Richard C. Longworth took a job with the *Chicago Tribune*. The city he had left in 1960 was provincial and coarse—"the Sixties was still the industrial era. It really was the city of Big Shoulders. It was not a cosmopolitan city. A steak and baked potato was as good as it got. It was a polluted city. It was a rough city. Corrupt as hell. The cops were just being reformed. But it was also a middle-class city. There were good salaries. Steady work. It gave a stability to Chicago."

Longworth returned to a Chicago that was still provincial and coarse—except now it was lower-class. As he drove around rediscovering his hometown, he thought, "I've seen worse neighborhoods in Third World cities." After Wisconsin Steel closed, Longworth was so alarmed he wrote a five-part series entitled "Chicago: City on the Brink." Longworth wrote:

> Chicago's basic problem is that it is losing industries, stores and jobs. Because of this, it is losing tax money. Because of this, it won't be able to support itself, to pay for the services of a going city. And because of this, it will lose more industries, stores, jobs and taxes.
>
> Poor schools, political instability, the economic decline of the entire Frost Belt region, the slow decline of Chicago's heavy industry, land shortages, poor city services, and a fixation on the Loop at the expense of the rest of Chicago all contribute to the cycle.
>
> The cycle has been going on for 30 years. There is no reason to think it will reverse when the present recession ends. According to available evidence and many experts, there is no reason to think it will ever turn around.

Chicago was also one of the most racially divided cities in the nation. When blacks arrived from Mississippi and Alabama to build weapons for the World War I doughboys, they were forced to live in a narrow strip of land known as the Black Belt. The ghetto finally burst open in the 1950s and '60s, consuming most of the South and West Sides, despite Mayor Richard J. Daley's efforts to hold back the tide by crowding blacks into housing projects and walling off their neighborhoods with highways. Chicago's greatest monument to segregation was the elevated track that carried the Burlington Northern Railroad through the Southwest Side. It separated Lawndale, a once-Jewish neighborhood that had "turned" in the 1950s, from South Lawndale, whose Polish and Ukrainian residents established the tracks as a racial barrier. After the West Side went up in flames following the assassination of Martin Luther King Jr., South Lawndale began calling itself "Little Village" to dissociate itself from the Negroes on the other side of the tracks.

In 1983, six and a half years after Old Man Daley's death, Chicago elected its first black mayor, Harold Washington. Unlike Coleman Young,

Washington did not represent a Black Power takeover (although plenty of whites saw it that way). He was a fluke winner of the Democratic primary, in which Daley's son, Richard M., and the incumbent mayor, Jane Byrne, had split the white vote.

Taking office during one of the bleakest years of the steel crisis, Washington seemed like more proof that Chicago was finished. A black mayor was like a black neighbor, but on a citywide scale: once he moved in, everything went to shit. Every falling-apart city had one. A white alderman spoke the fears of his constituents when he begged the mayor-elect, "Don't let this city become another Detroit." Washington didn't have a black majority behind him, so he couldn't have behaved like Coleman Young even if he'd wanted. And since Chicago elected its city council ward by ward, rather than citywide, Washington was opposed by a bloc of white aldermen determined to prevent him from diverting the city's dwindling jobs and money from their neighborhoods to the black neighborhoods. Their leader was Fast Eddie Vrdolyak.

A local comedian called the antagonism between the black mayor and the white aldermen "Council Wars," and *Time* magazine nicknamed Chicago "Beirut on the Lake."

"Council Wars really slowed things down for Chicago," Longworth said. "You didn't want to invest in Beirut on the Lake."

RICHARD C. LONGWORTH DUBBED the declining states of the industrial North the "Frost Belt," an antonym to "Sun Belt." Since the Sun Belt was stealing all their jobs, the term seemed to apply not only to desert skies but to President Reagan's "Morning in America," whose sun rose in the South but never reached the Great Lakes. Auto sales were at their lowest since the early 1960s, while housing starts were the worst in fifteen years. If Americans weren't buying cars and houses, auto companies and developers weren't buying steel. High interest rates increased the value of the dollar, which made the American market more attractive to German, Brazilian, and South Korean steelmakers. Beginning in 1979, the U.S. steel market began shrinking, while foreign manufacturers increased their share. By the mid-1980s, America was importing 30 percent of its steel.

Toward the end of his hopeless challenge to Reagan, in 1984, Walter Mondale spoke to three hundred steelworkers outside the LTV mill in Cleveland.

"Mr. Reagan has presided over the virtual dismantling of our industrial base," Mondale said. "He has pursued a policy of official cruelty toward industrial workers. Mr. Reagan's policy toward the industrial belt of America is 'Let it rust.'"

Then, reaching back to a phrase from the 1930s, Mondale accused Reagan of turning the Midwest into "a rust bowl." It was meant to evoke the Depression, still alive in the memories of elderly voters, by echoing "Dust Bowl," the scene of the nation's worst economic suffering during Mondale's boyhood. While Mondale introduced "Rust Bowl" to political discourse, he didn't coin the term. A *Time* magazine article on the early-eighties recession was headlined "Booms, Busts, and Birth of a Rust Bowl."

"As demand for metals lurched lower and layoffs swelled, the once pulsing industrial belt that stretches from Illinois across to western New England took on her grim, ground-down demeanor of a half-century earlier, acquiring the glumly descriptive epithet of Rust Bowl," wrote reporter Christopher Byron, as fond of neologisms as any Timespeaker.

Once Mondale popularized "Rust Bowl," it underwent a journalistic transformation to "Rust Belt," so it conformed to other regional nicknames, such as Bible Belt, Sun Belt, and Frost Belt. In his book *The Nine Nations of North America*, journalist Joel Garreau labeled the continent's industrial quadrant "the Foundry." But as the postindustrial replacement for "the Arsenal of Democracy" and "the Ruhr of America," "Rust Belt" stuck.

ALDERMAN VRDOLYAK'S VOW to reopen Wisconsin Steel had turned out to be empty. He'd failed to save U.S. Steel, as well. The mills had assisted Vrdolyak's political rise. By the time the steel crisis struck his ward, Vrdolyak was not only the most prominent member of the city council, he was chairman of the Cook County Democratic Party's Central Committee: boss of the most powerful political machine in America. No politician in Chicago controlled more patronage, but Vrdolyak demanded a price: votes, from the jobholder and every member of his extended family. The mills had been Vrdolyak's path to power. After the mills closed, Fast Eddie used that power to keep control of his ward by handing out city jobs—which made him even more powerful, because the jobholders didn't report to U.S. Steel, they reported to Eddie.

Latinos were easy—and desirable—recruits. They had a lot of kids, which made the men desperate for work, and they had a lot of aunts, uncles, nieces, nephews, and cousins who could be told, "Vote Vrdolyak." Because of the mills, Latinos had lived in South Chicago longer than in any other part of the city. They had their own church—Our Lady of Guadalupe—and they were tolerated by Stosh and Chester at the ironworkers' tavern, who figured it was them or the colored. Tony Navarro and Al Sanchez both grew up in South Chicago and both worked for the city at Vrdolyak's sufferance. Navarro was a plumber. Sanchez was a community resource specialist in the Department of Human Service, a liaison between city hall and the neighborhood, able to dole out favors. In exchange for Vrdolyak's clout, the young Latinos hustled precincts for the boss.

"When the steel mills were going, nobody needed the politics," Navarro said. "They were making big money in the steel mills. When the mills went down, it was a whole different ball game. People were begging for jobs. I had so many guys I knew in the eighties that lost their families, wives left them because they lost their jobs. They went to drugs, selling drugs. Went to jail."

Selling your family's vote to the Anglo (if you could call a guy named Vrdolyak an Anglo) *jefe* was a minor humiliation compared to destitution, divorce, and the Illinois Department of Corrections. Suddenly popular, Navarro was visited by a frantic steelworker who wanted to know how to get hired by Vrdolyak.

"How big is your family, Danny?" Navarro asked the laid-off dad.

"Thirty, forty," Danny said.

"Write 'em all down, make an appointment to see that motherfucker Al Sanchez," Navarro instructed. "Tell him you'll kiss his ass on State and Madison and everyone in your family will, too. You'll get the job."

Danny did as he was told and was granted a job on a garbage truck.

"Tony," he said the next time he saw Navarro, "I could kiss your ass right now. He's going to give me a job."

Now that Chicago politics had arrived in this most isolated corner of Chicago, Vrdolyak became much more than an emissary to city hall from a distant, misunderstood province. He was the local don. East Siders directed visitors to his keep, which was one of their few remaining tourist attractions. The house was twice as large as the surrounding bungalows. So was the yard: Vrdolyak had taken over an alley to make room for his swimming pool and tennis court. In a blue-collar neighborhood, he was the guy who'd made it big. With his University of Chicago law degree, he built a firm that occupied a block-sized building, with the name "EDWARD R. VRDOLYAK" in two-foot-high letters.

Every election, Vrdolyak had a new plan for Wisconsin Steel.

"I'm going to tell them I'm reopening Wisconsin Steel," he told his precinct captains before appearing at a rally with Mayor Jane Byrne, Harold Washington's predecessor.

"You're a fuckin' liar," one brave captain said to him.

"I don't give a fuck," Vrdolyak said. "I'm going to tell 'em anyway."

Failing to bring back the mills was not Vrdolyak's downfall. Vrdolyak was the face of the white ethnic backlash against Mayor Harold Washington. After the ethnics lost their city council majority to a mongrelized caucus of blacks, Latinos, WASPs, and Jews, Vrdolyak made a decision guaranteed to kill any political career in Chicago: he ran for mayor as a Republican. His Latino precinct captains refused to follow their boss into the party of Ronald Reagan.

"Hey, that's it," Navarro told Vrdolyak. "I cannot knock on a black or a Latino door and tell them, 'We're Republican.' And you just lost your job in a steel mill? I'd get my ass kicked."

Instead, they defected to a bigger boss. After Harold Washington died, Richard M. Daley, son of the Old Man, prepared to run for mayor. Young Daley recognized that Latinos were the swing vote in Chicago. They had joined a black-and-brown coalition to elect Washington, but if Daley could entice them into a white-and-brown coalition, he could take over the city. In the back room of a South Chicago tavern, one of Daley's henchmen made a promise.

"We need you guys," he said. "We're glad you left Vrdolyak. We're going to take you. And we're going to give jobs, jobs, jobs . . . Jobs for you and all the Latinos you can bring with us. We want you guys to be our minority, because we're already sick of that other minority. We don't want that other minority."

"We don't care how you use us," Sanchez told the official. "Our guys are starving. We need the jobs."

That declaration of reality was the birth of the Hispanic Democratic Organization—HDO, for short—the toughest political mob in Chicago. With the mills gone, only the city offered well-paying blue-collar jobs for joes with a high school education—or less. And only Sanchez, who had been promoted to assistant superintendent of streets and sanitation, could distribute those. He reached beyond laid-off steelworkers to members of the Latin Kings, Latin Counts, and Maniac Latin Satan's Disciples—loyal, ruthless gangbangers who would pull any dirty trick in exchange for a spot on a garbage truck.

"That's how Al Sanchez rose to power," Navarro said. "He took every thug that was starving and gave 'em a city job. They'd kill for you. He collected more kickback money, you wouldn't believe. They were so grateful."

The last piece of steel rolled out of South Works in 1992. Within four years, the soil had been scoured of lead, cobalt, and all the other toxins necessary to forge steel. The 573-acre outcropping of slag was now the largest plot of lakefront property in Chicago. The new Mayor Daley wanted to control its development, so his friends, allies, and campaign contributors would get the contracts. In 1999, Daley told the 10th Ward alderman, a sexagenarian time-server, that it was time to retire. Then he ordered Al Sanchez to elect a young man named John Pope, a thirty-year-old city hall aide who had grown up in the neighborhood but never been involved in the community's affairs.

"The mayor had to have a man in place," said Neil Bosanko, who ran for alderman himself that year. "He wanted to make sure whoever was alderman, he had a controlling interest over what happened to South Works. Al Sanchez asked for a meeting with me. Al said, 'The mayor wants John Pope in.'"

Bosanko declined to withdraw from the race. So a lock shop owner who displayed a Bosanko sign was served with a $200 ticket for overflowing garbage—from Al Sanchez's Department of Streets and Sanitation.

That was how Sanchez campaigned. Streets and Sanitation repaired a sidewalk outside a bungalow with four voters living inside. The city's asphalt plant opened early that year so Streets and Sanitation could re-pave Avenue A—even the Indiana side of the street, because Chicagoans drove on that, too. A rival candidate's campaign volunteers defected after Sanchez promised them a city paycheck.

John Pope won the election. ("They bought votes," Neal Bosanko said. "People were afraid. Those HDO people who were gangbangers standing in front of churches. It was intimidating.") As a reward, Al Sanchez was promoted to commissioner of the Department of Streets and Sanitation. Over the next six years, sixty-three HDO members from Sanchez's neighborhood got city jobs.

"Al put every drug dealer, thug, and arsonist from the Tenth Ward to work," Tony Navarro said. "Anybody today that's got a decent job in the Tenth Ward is working for the police department, the fire department, the Chicago Park District, or the county. Anybody outside of that doesn't have a job."

In exchange for their jobs, Sanchez's employees washed his windows and mowed his lawn. This was revealed at Sanchez's federal corruption trial, during which he was also accused of hiring a garbage truck driver whose only previous experience was behind the wheel of a U-Haul. The woman submitted her application in a biker bar that functioned as an

HDO clubhouse. Once on the job, she backed the truck into a co-worker, pinning her against a telephone pole and fracturing her pelvis. Sanchez got two and a half in the federal pen for handing out jobs to political cronies. His mentor, Ed Vrdolyak, also ended up in prison, on a mail fraud charge connected to a real estate kickback scheme. Fast Eddie slowed down in his old age, and the feds caught up with him.

FOUR YEARS AFTER Wisconsin Steel closed, Rob Stanley finally found a new job. He was tending bar at Luke and Nonnie's when a softball teammate walked in and told him the federal government was hiring plumbers. That was close enough to pipe fitting, so Stanley got in with the feds. He married again, to the woman who cut his hair, and bought a craftsman house in the suburbs. In his mid-sixties now, he has no prospects of retiring. Because his pension disappeared along with the steel mill, Stanley had not been able to start saving for retirement until his late thirties.

Even though he'd been working since he was eighteen, "there's no light at the end of the tunnel, so to speak, as far as retiring," he said.

Chuck Walley died in his sixties. His daughter blamed the drinking habit he developed after he was laid off, during the listless days when he lay on the couch and mumbled that he should have been buried along with Wisconsin Steel.

At the foot of the 95th Street Bridge—the lift bridge the Bluesmobile leapt in *The Blues Brothers*—is a red-roofed takeout shack that serves baskets of fried perch and catfish and shrimp and salmon smoked in the curing shed out back. Calumet Fisheries has a perfect vantage for watching the freighters come and go. But the ships no longer float down from Minnesota or Upper Michigan with holds full of taconite to melt into steel. The ships are the *Neve Trader*, a Norwegian vessel with a Latvian crew, delivering girders from Poland, or the *Federal Mackenzie*, from Panama, with shining spools of steel. It's cheaper to import steel than it would have been to modernize the Chicago mills. The sailors wander into Calumet Fisheries looking for beer and cigarettes or cabs and trains that will take them downtown, where they can buy cell phones, MP3 players, and brand-name athletic shoes for their wives and children across the sea. To a merchant sailor, America is a giant shopping mall. The manager gives them the name of the ship terminal and tells them, "Give this to the cab driver when you come back." If she were a stranger in Latvia or Panama, she'd expect the same hospitality.

The old steelworkers come in, too. Not as many as when the mills were running and Calumet Fisheries was open eighteen hours a day. They've died, or retired to Arizona, or moved away to find other work. Since they don't have as much money as they once earned, and since the Great Lakes have been overfished, the shack serves more cheap foreign seafood than it did during the mill days. Lake perch, at nine dollars a pound, is too expensive. Smelt is almost impossible to obtain. The trout comes from Canada. The mill veterans buy it, carry it to the riverbank, and watch the ships bring in the cargo that ended their livelihoods.

"You see older people, they come down to the river, and it's like they're reminiscing," says the manager. "They're watching the ships unload the coils and I want to say, 'A penny for your thoughts.'"

OIL CAN EDDIE LIKED to reminisce, too. Oil Can Eddie was Ed Sadlowski, a steelworker without a mill, a sloganeering, hymn-singing, street-marching, banner-waving, boss-hating labor captain without a union. Had he been born a generation earlier, Eddie would have been a glowering counterpart to George Meany or John L. Lewis, exhorting the picket lines with his bullhorn, cussing out the Yale men across the negotiating table, condescending to bended-knee machine pols who needed his legions on Election Day.

Sadlowski had made a bid for that power. In 1956, after the army was through with him, he followed his father into the mill. They called him "Oil Can Eddie" because, as a machine repairman, he walked around the mill all day dispensing squirts of oil and talking union politics. A big, outspoken neighborhood kid, a beer drinker, a pool shooter, he was the kind of guy who needed a nickname for the loud greetings he heard whenever he walked into a tavern or a union hall. At twenty-five, he was elected president of the ten-thousand-member Steelworkers Local 65. Ten years later, after he beat the union bosses' candidate for district director, the *Washington Post* declared, "A new labor star has been born." Then Sadlowski decided to run for international president of the United Steelworkers, as a reformer. He cut a romantic figure: young, with a dark Bobby Kennedy forelock, a leather jacket, and a mouth that would say "fuck" and "Mozart" in the same sentence. The 1970s were the decade of Archie Bunker, of hard hats pummeling antiwar protesters on Madison Avenue. As the working class rejected liberalism, New York was looking for a genuine proletarian radical. Sadlowski appeared on

60 Minutes. He was interviewed by the *New York Times.* Jane Fonda and John Kenneth Galbraith endorsed his campaign. College-educated Marxists took jobs in the mills, looking to glom onto his blue-collar glamour. He derided the liberals as "colonizers," but he accepted their help.

"Never in my life have I experienced such exhilaration as that campaign," he said years later. "I'd walk in a room, and the adrenaline is going."

Sadlowski's biggest mistake was telling *Penthouse* he didn't mind the steel industry eliminating jobs, as long as it retrained steelworkers for cleaner, more intellectual pursuits.

"Working forty hours a week in a steel mill drains the lifeblood out of a man," he said. "Nothing is to be gotten from that. Society has nothing to show for it but waste."

Instead, he suggested, the labor movement's goal should be liberating workers from hard, sweaty labor, so they could develop their talents as lawyers, doctors, and poets.

"How many Mozarts are working in steel mills?" he had asked another journalist.

Even in 1977, steelworkers were anxious about job loss—their ranks had withered by 20 percent over the previous fifteen years. What kind of airy-fairy talk was this Mozart and poetry stuff, from a guy who palled around with Commies and listened to Pete Seeger albums in his basement? Sadlowski's opponent—the union president's handpicked successor—circulated copies of the interview, implying that Oil Can Eddie *wanted* to eliminate more jobs.

Of course, Sadlowski lost. Young Turks always lose. Old guys don't like to be told it's the new generation's turn. He felt he'd been cheated, but his opponent's biggest margins were in Canada, and there was no way to challenge an election in two countries.

Oil Can Eddie was spending the twenty-first century as a member of the Illinois Labor Relations Board, stuffed into a suit, caged behind a desk. I met him at a Southeast Side history museum, which was open for three hours every Thursday afternoon, in a park field house. He was sitting at the bullshitters' table with a pair of retired steelworkers. White-haired, blunt-featured, he had a heavy granite head that looked as though it had been chipped out of the empty space on Rushmore and grafted to the body of a 250-pound man. The museum director told me that if I talked to anyone on the East Side, it should be Oil Can Eddie. Sadlowski couldn't sit around and drink coffee all afternoon, so he gave me his card and told me to call him. But *soon*. He was going to Florida in a few weeks to spend time with his wife.

When I called, he told me he was going out to Indiana that Saturday, to teach some wet-behind-the-ears ironworkers about their blue-collar heritage. They were gonna go down to the old Republic Steel mill, where the cops killed ten strikers back in '37. Yeah, I could come along, if I gave him a lift.

"But you're gonna have to be there at seven," he said, his voice low and feline, in the way a lion's postprandial purr is feline. "I can't wait around because I have to meet some people. If you fuck up, you fuck up. I'm not trying to be a drill sergeant . . ."

The next time I saw Oil Can Eddie, I was knocking on the door of his bungalow at six forty-five on Saturday morning. I lived thirty miles away, but his lecture had frightened me into punctuality. In Chicago's Bungalow Belt, most houses were built from the same square blueprint, the same sand- or mole-colored brick. I knew I was at Sadlowski's by the placards in the window—"Hate Free Zone" and "Speak Up America: Health Care Is Our Right."

Oil Can Eddie answered the door in his underwear.

"You're here early," he said, leading me through the dining room. The sun had not yet found the south windows, so the house was gray with predawn gloom. The dining table was stacked with union pamphlets and printouts from a left-wing website. It looked like a campaign office.

"Excuse the mess," Sadlowski said as he pulled on a pair of faded jeans with a grass stain on the knee, a windbreaker, and a Cubs cap. "I'm baching it. My wife's in Florida. Do you want some tea?"

"Sure," I said.

He found a clean mug in the cupboard.

"Do you want anything in it?"

"Milk and sugar."

"Ahhh."

His look told me I'd never make a steelworker. It made me self-conscious about the sportcoat and sweater I was wearing.

Sadlowski swallowed a handful of pills with his unsweetened tea, and moaned about the state of his head and his belly.

"Ahh, I'm tired," he said. "I went to a fish fry in Indiana. I was there half the night. That fish is still with me. That's always been a big thing—East Chicago, Northwest Indiana. For one hundred years, the staple was lake perch. Now it's so expensive, I don't know what they use."

In my little red Dodge Neon, we vaulted onto the Skyway to the Indiana Toll Road, above the industrial villages of Whiting, Hammond, East Chicago, and Gary. On the lake side of the highway, steel mills drove spikes into the brightening sky. At U.S. Steel, in Gary, a flame wavered at the tip of a chimney, and battle smoke swept into downtown, obscuring the dome of city hall in a grainy haze. The Calumet Region—"Da Region" in the local urban patois—is linked to Southeast Chicago culturally, historically, and geographically. (It was once described as "a barnacle clinging to the underside of Chicago.") People cross the state line for church services, union meetings, fish fries, and Catholic schools.

"The common bond was the mills," Sadlowski said. "Industry exists in all of us to a degree. We were all fed that bullshit from the cradle. Get ahead by stepping on the other guy. You went to high school, and they would have a recruiter from the mills, have a big assembly. Damn near everybody lived in South Chicago worked in that fuckin'mill. This used to be the biggest steelmaking area in the world. From South Works in Chicago to Burns Harbor, Indiana, there were one hundred thousand steelworkers—now there's maybe twenty thousand. It's horseshit. They took all the money they could out of it and left nothing. That's what all industries do."

A yellow school bus was parked in the lot of the Ironworkers Hall in Hobart. Sadlowski taught labor history to the apprentices, and today he was taking them on a tour of the long-razed plants where their grandfathers and great-grandfathers had worked in peasantry, before the unions. The apprentices were young men with unfinished faces, lanky in blue jeans and work boots, eating bleary breakfasts out of fast-food bags. When Sadlowski boarded the bus, they came to life.

"Wooo, Ed!"—from the back of the bus.

"Don't get smart, now," he growled. "Don't get smart. Anyone owe me a paper? Bring it in Monday. I heard that. It's in the mail. The check's in the mail."

Sadlowski faced down a hefty boy wearing a fluffy beard in progress.

"Hello, Rizzi. Every time I see you, you've got your hand in a McDonald's bag."

"This is the first one!" Rizzi protested. He reached into the sack. "Here, have a burger."

Sadlowski waved him off and addressed the bus.

"Today, we're going to go on a labor heritage tour." He stood in the aisle, and you could hear the union-hall orator who'd drawn in thousands of steelworkers thirty years before. "That's the heritage that belongs to the workingman in this country, and the workingwoman. Someday, some of you might have a kid or two you can take there. That's an important part of your identity."

This was the winter of 2005, a month after George W. Bush was sworn in for his second term and proposed to replace Social Security with private investment accounts. Sadlowski was a staunch New Dealer. The New Deal had made unions possible, promoted the mill worker to the middle class.

"Social Security is the greatest government program in the history of the country," he lectured the young men. "Don't let them bullshit you about personalized accounts. Social Security means just that"—a sweep of his hand encircled the riders—"*social*. Everyone. That's the principle it was established under seventy years ago. You've got to stop thinking about me, me, me. How about us, us, us? I want to go up, you want to go up, let's grab each other and go up together. Who's in Bush's camp? The rich guys. It's not the millwrights or the carpenters."

They had gone up, at least the ones lucky enough to belong to a union. The parking lot was full of pickup trucks—Dodge Rams with swollen hoods and quarter panels, a young man's first purchase with jackpot union wages. At the *Chicago Reader*, the city's alternative weekly, college graduates were earning $9.50 an hour as editorial assistants. None of them seemed interested in forming a union. Neither were my friends who worked in bookstores. On the bus ride back to Chicago, I asked Sadlowski why white-collar workers had never embraced the labor movement.

"The white-collar worker has kind of a Bob Cratchit attitude," he explained. "He feels he's a half step below the boss. The boss says, 'Call me Harry.' He feels he's made it. You go to a shoe store, they got six managers. They call everybody a manager, but they pay 'em all shit."

Steelworkers and ironworkers still thought of themselves as blue-collar underdogs who needed to band together against the plutocrats. That was why these twenty-two-year-olds were driving new trucks, while on the fashionable North Side of Chicago, young graphic designers and computer programmers who fancied themselves "professionals" were riding the L to work. They had status but no money. The ironworkers had money but no status. Take your pick.

The bus pulled into the parking lot of a single-story brick building on Avenue O. It was a day care center, belonging to a local church, but it had once been a union hall, and the new owners still rented a meeting room to the aged remnants of Local 1033. This was a sacred site. Out on the sidewalk, a plaque was bolted to the foot of a flagpole. Sadlowski gathered his students and explained why it was there.

"Back in 1937, on May 26, there was a strike vote at Republic Steel." He gestured across the street. You had to imagine the brick mill, the black sky. The land was back to prairie now, guarded by a snow fence hung with "NO TRESPASSING" warnings. "The company locked the gates. Four hundred workers were locked in, a couple thousand locked out. A rally was called for the thirtieth. Two thousand people converged on Sam's Place. That was the strike headquarters. They marched to the gates, and fifty yards away, the police opened fire. They murdered ten men. The cops were saying a lot of 'em were Communists, because they kept chanting, 'CIO, CIO.'"

The names of the dead were cast on a brass plaque. They were as polyglot as a platoon in a World War II movie: Anderson, Causey, Francisco, Popovich, Handley, Jones, Reed, Tagliori, Tisdale, Rothmund.

Sadlowski led his gaggle inside, to the low-slung auditorium with the flag-flanked stage at the distant end. When he was young, this was where the Christmas parties were held, where the sixteen-inch softball teams returned with their trophies, where tickets were sold for the big once-a-year night at Sox Park. As Sadlowski stood on the tile floor that had been crowded heel-to-toe, ankle-to-ankle, with a thousand steel-shank boots, his eyes focused on something in 1965. The rest of us were too young to see it, so he said, "This was a booming hall when the mills were going. It was really an integral part of the community, more than just a sterile hall. You can raise your voice in a union hall. You can't argue in a bank, you can't argue in a church. Union hall, you have differences of opinion. It's okay. They used to serve great *baccalà* here during the meetings."

"What's *baccalà*?"

Sadlowski glared at the questioner.

"You never ate *baccalà*? Some of youse are Polish and don't even know how to pronounce your name."

There was one black apprentice in the crowd. He recorded Sadlowski's speech on a microcassette.

"That could have been us standing here on a picket," he said when I asked him why he needed a tape. "You gotta get it down, 'cause you might not come here again."

The bus called next at Pullman. Pullman looks nothing like Chicago. A few blocks of row houses whose clay-red bricks burn through faded sheets of whitewash. Pullman offers the illusion that one has taken a wrong turn off 111th Street and is suddenly driving the narrow avenues of working-class Baltimore or Philadelphia. It was never supposed to have been part of Chicago. In the 1880s, when railroad-car manufacturer George Pullman built the houses, the church, and the hotel, it was far south of the city limits, beyond the reach of any authority but his own. Pullman gathered thousands of workers on his manor. They lived in his residences, according to their rank; shopped in his stores; attended plays at his theater; read books from his library; and sent their children to his schools. The workers rebelled. A national railroad strike broke out. President Grover Cleveland sent twelve thousand troops to stamp out the uprising. The workers surrendered, signing pledges never to join a union. Pullman evicted the ringleaders from his village and replaced them with scabs, just as he would have replaced a balky carriage horse with an obedient gelding.

We heard some of this story in the pews of Greenstone United Methodist Church, another monument to George Pullman's impractical vision of the ideal community. It was built of pale jade Pennsylvania serpentine, which has had to be replaced by dyed rock as it disintegrates. Pullman's workers never worshipped here, because the local denominations could not afford to rent a church with a twenty-one-stop organ. The boss was pleased, though, because it completed his village-green diorama.

We heard the rest in the museum of the Pullman State Historic Site, sitting as quietly as grade-schoolers for a twenty-minute movie on the Great Strike.

"This became a worldwide issue of how far you can go with paternalism, by virtue of being an owner," Sadlowski lectured after it was over. "The schools here only went to the eighth grade. If you could read and write and do a little figuring, that was enough to work for Mr. Pullman. There were no high schools and colleges here. That wasn't for us. That was for the elite. Pullman was such a tyrant that he was buried in Graceland Cemetery under rails, encased in concrete, so people wouldn't desecrate his body."

The bus dropped Sadlowski in front of a Polish bakery on 106th Street, a block from his house. But before he stepped off, he had one more message for the ironworkers.

"Get that associate's degree," he told them. "There's a lot better things in life than being a carpenter or a millwright. There's a lot worse things, too. You are the salt of the earth. The smartest people I ever met were guys who ran cranes in the mill."

And then Sadlowski was stamping down the sidewalk, his broad shoulders clenched inside his bulging windbreaker. The morning had been a class in class. Labor unions were a mass movement in the 1940s and 1950s, when a third of American workers carried a card. That was the heyday of the middle class, an interregnum from the dominance of Ivy Leaguers at either end of the twentieth century. Now labor unions are a niche: only 13 percent belong. This is an individualistic era. The communal "we" of Sadlowski's day sounds like socialism to the conservative's ear and serfdom to the liberal's. White South Siders used to define themselves by their loyalty to four institutions: the Catholic Church, the Democratic Party, the Chicago White Sox, and the University of Notre Dame. But people who grew up after World War II are less likely to look for their identities in a church, or a party, or a baseball team, or a college. The white-collar ethic of individual achievement has, generation by generation, replaced the blue-collar ethic of banding together. But the philosophy behind labor unions is timeless: the boss ain't your friend.

7.

Homestead

No place in America has more history per square mile than Homestead, Pennsylvania. That's an easy statement to make, because the entire borough of Homestead, from the S-shaped bank of the Monongahela to the cemetery atop what was once known as Carnegie Hill, is only six-tenths of a mile in area, less than half the size of New York's Central Park. The hill rises three hundred feet in roughly ten times that distance, its incline stair-stepped with row houses and bristling with steeples. Nearly as vertical as Manhattan, Homestead's upwelling makes it twice as large as it appears on a flattened map, which may be why its story is twice as eventful as any other small town's.

The Homestead Works, built on the flats in 1881, was not Andrew Carnegie's first steel mill. That was the Edgar Thomson Works, across the river and upstream in Braddock. But Homestead was Carnegie's largest mill, and since Carnegie was the world's greatest steelmaker, he built it into the world's most productive steel operation. Homestead perfected open-hearth steelmaking, with a Bessemer furnace copied all over the world. The Brooklyn Bridge, the Pacific Fleet, and the Atlas rockets were all built with Homestead steel, the raw material of the American Century.

As Homestead was first in steel, it was also the first scene of the violence that results when a mill owner and his workers disagree on a fair division of the wealth that results from forging the most useful product ever invented. The Homestead Strike of 1892 began with a shootout. After members of the Amalgamated Association stopped working to protest a wage cut, a company of Pinkerton guards attempted to occupy the mill via amphibious landing. The Pinkertons, members of a detective agency founded by Allan Pinkerton, who had made his name by foiling an assassination plot against President-elect Lincoln, were the preferred mercenaries of every nineteenth-century industrialist. Wherever working men rose up to assert their rights—at Homestead, at Pullman in Chicago—Pinkertons were there to beat them down. In the wee hours of July 6, as their barge wallowed across the Monongahela, it was fired on by unionists crouched behind barricades of scrap iron. The Pinkertons fired back, so the workers procured a cannon, filled its muzzle with steel scrap, and bombarded the invading vessel. The barrage killed three Pinkertons. Their bodies were carried back across the river to Pittsburgh. The Pinkertons killed six strikers, who were buried in the cemetery atop the hill.

Carnegie broke the strike by bringing in 1,500 scabs, who entered his mill under the protection of the Pennsylvania militia. By Thanksgiving, the union was licked: the workers Carnegie was willing to rehire slunk back into the mill to continue laboring twelve hours a day, seven days a week, at wages he dictated. The strike was ruinous both to the labor movement and to Carnegie's reputation. While the workers were still picketing, anarchist Alexander Berkman barged into the office of Henry Clay Frick, the business partner who looked after Carnegie's interests while the great man was at his Scottish castle. The anarchist shot Frick twice in the neck, but somehow failed to kill the business magnate. Berkman—the lover of Emma Goldman, his co-conspirator in the shooting—was a freelance assassin who had nothing to do with the Amalgamated Association. Nonetheless, his attempt on Frick's life made the strikers look like allies of treason, mob rule, and bearded immigrants smuggling the virus of socialism into middle America.

On the other side of the pay scale, working-class outrage over the Homestead Strike helped return Democrat Grover Cleveland to the White House that November. Carnegie was reviled as a coward for hiding out in Scotland while Pinkertons gunned down steelworkers in his name. The Homestead Strike, he would write in his autobiography, "wounded me so deeply. No pangs remain of any wound received in my business career save that of Homestead. It was so unnecessary."

Carnegie tried to make amends by building Homestead a magnificent library—one of more than two thousand he built for communities around the world. A slate-roofed manse of autumn-colored brick, atop a terraced hill, the Homestead Library not only had a reading room with a fireplace and leather armchairs, it had a swimming pool, a billiard room, a gymnasium, and a thousand-seat music hall—a dollhouse

Carnegie Hall. The most imposing building in Homestead, it bore Carnegie's name, making it both a peace offering and a reminder to those who would instigate a second Homestead strike that the steel magnate was still laird of the borough.

To prevent further labor trouble, Carnegie imported Poles, Czechs, Slovaks, Ruthenians, and Croatians, reassembling the peasantry of the Austro-Hungarian Empire in his foundry, where they were melted into a panethnic alloy known to the native-born workers as "Hunkies." The Hunkies couldn't read, write, or even speak English, weren't citizens, and thought twenty cents an hour in a Carnegie mill was better than life as a Bohemian farmhand.

The architectural consequence of crowding so many ethnicities into such a small space is that Homestead contains a collection of ecclesiastical buildings that could only be duplicated by a dioramist for the World Congress of Religions. Every nationality arrived toting an Old World creed and, whether Catholic, Orthodox, or Protestant, felt called to prove their faith by building a temple bigger than any of their infidel rivals. No matter how high or low you stand on Homestead's slopes, you'll see a Roman spire, a Presbyterian steeple, or an Oriental dome in the shape of an inverted spinning top, surmounted by a tilted cross, like an antenna for receiving messages from God. The churches are the only structures that rise higher than the shingle roofs or the black cross-hatching of telephone lines. In Homestead, religion and ethnicity were inseparable. At St. Mary Magdalene, whose God's-eye window is set between brick pillars that lack only swirled peaks to be minarets, the Great War Honor Roll is filled with Conroys, Devines, Gallaghers, and Muldowneys. St. John the Baptist Byzantine Catholic Cathedral, its foundation tilted to follow the rising street, was the first church in America built to serve Carpatho-Rusyns, the Austro-Hungarian mountain folk who begat Andy Warhol, the pop artist born across the river in Pittsburgh. The Hungarian Reformed Church's name was chiseled beneath a trapezoidal frieze of gray angels.

"In the days of the mills, they had churches and bars," said Betty Esper, who belonged to St. George's Syrian Orthodox and grew up to become mayor of Homestead. "I don't know if they drank and prayed, or prayed and drank."

After the Homestead Strike was broken, the borough remained free of labor trouble until 1919, when the World War I Armistice allowed workers to demand a share of the 160 percent increase in profits that U.S. Steel had realized from building ships, bombs, and barbed wire to kill Germans. The American Federation of Labor demanded an eight-hour day, a six-day week, and an "American living wage" that included double pay for overtime. U.S. Steel's president, Judge Elbert Gary, refused to meet with the AFL's organizers, even when asked by President Woodrow Wilson. Union sympathizers were fired from the mill. The Homestead burgess prevented the union from renting a hall. When workers met in the street instead, the speakers were arrested and fined. The agitators were condemned as "Hunkies" and Bolsheviks. As if to prove their radicalism, Mary Harris "Mother" Jones, then in the ninth decade of a lifetime dedicated to stirring up labor trouble, appeared in Homestead to support the strike.

Mother Jones was a short, stout former dressmaker who dressed in widow's weeds and may have inspired the name "granny glasses" for her oval spectacles. After losing her family to yellow fever and her home to the Great Chicago Fire, Jones quit domestic life and traveled the country, organizing miners and conducting an anti-child-labor march that led a brigade of mill waifs to President Theodore Roosevelt's Long Island estate. After leading a West Virginia miners' strike, this matron of labor was identified as "the most dangerous woman in America" by the local district attorney. Her motto was "Pray for the dead and fight like hell for the living." When a senator called her the grandmother of agitators, Mother Jones replied that she hoped to live long enough to be their great-grandmother.

In the summer of 1919, Mother Jones spoke to steelworkers throughout the Monongahela Valley but did not find trouble until she arrived in Homestead. Addressing laborers at the corner of Ninth Avenue and Amity Street, near the mill gates, Jones had this to say:

"We are to see whether Pennsylvania belongs to Kaiser Gary or Uncle Sam. Our Kaisers sit up and smoke seventy-five-cent cigars and have lackeys with knee pants bring them champagne while you starve, while you grow old at forty, stoking their furnaces. You pull in your belts while they banquet. They have stomachs two miles long and two miles wide and you fill them . . . If Gary wants to work twelve hours a day, let him go in the blooming mill and work. What we want is a little leisure, time for music, playgrounds, a decent home, books, and the things that make life worthwhile."

For making such socialistic demands, Jones was arrested and jailed in the Homestead borough hall. In court, the judge asked who had granted her a public speaking permit.

"Patrick Henry, Thomas Jefferson, John Adams!" she retorted.

During Mother Jones's trial, workers surrounded the borough hall, demanding her release. The old lady of labor was set free on $15 bond, on the condition that she tell her supporters to go home.

A month and two days later, hundreds of thousands of workers in the Steel Belt, from Lackawanna to Chicago, walked off the job. The nation's steel production was cut in half. In Homestead, the Coal and Iron Police—a strikebreaking militia that replaced the Pinkertons after the violence of 1892—dragged strikers from their homes, beat them up, and threw them in jail. The borough banned outdoor gatherings and prohibited foreign languages at indoor meetings. After the Russian Revolution and Germany's defeat in World War I, a wave of nativism had swept the country. The Great Steel Strike of 1919 coincided with the passage of the Eighteenth Amendment, which banned the Irishman's whiskey, the Italian's wine, and the German's beer. It also coincided with the Palmer Raids, in which the Justice Department arrested Russian immigrants suspected of plotting an American soviet. (The raids snared Goldman and Berkman, Frick's would-be assassins. After serving fourteen years in prison for the shooting, Berkman had resumed his radical activities, founding the No Conscription League to oppose the World War I draft. During the steel strike, the anarchists were deported to Russia and Frick finally died—"deported by God," as Berkman put it—thus settling old scores from 1892.) In Seattle, shipyard workers called a general strike that shut down the city. In Boston, a police strike was suppressed by Governor Calvin Coolidge. It was a radical spring and summer. With unions and aliens held in such suspicion, it was easy for the steel companies to turn Protestant America against strikers who spoke babel languages and worshipped in exotic, Oriental temples. American workmen should take no part in a "Hunkie strike," the newspapers lectured. On a flier distributed by the steel companies, Uncle Sam told workers, "Go back to work," in Polish, Croatian, Italian, Lithuanian, and Hungarian.

"The end of the steel strike is in sight," it read. "Failure was written across it before it was a day old. American workers who understood the radical element that is seeking to operate under the cloak of organized labor are now back. Few of them even left their work—only a few foreign-born—mostly aliens—who allowed themselves to be swayed by the un-American teachings of radical strike agitators."

The propaganda worked. The coal miners and the railroad workers refused to support the strike. After seeing blacks and Mexicans take their old jobs, thousands of steelworkers returned to the mills. By Christmas, the strikers had dwindled to a third of their original strength. In January, the Amalgamated Association called off the strike. Defeated for the second time in two generations, it was never again a force in American labor.

AFTER THE 1892 STRIKE, Carnegie had begun hiring blacks at the Homestead Works, not because he was enlightened on the race question, but because illiterate blacks, like illiterate Hunkies, were grateful enough not to join unions. The blacks were put to work shoveling coal into furnaces—the hottest, dirtiest job in the mill, labor even more exhausting than the sharecropping they'd left behind in the South. In his search for ethnicities to exploit, Carnegie brought to Homestead the roster for the town's second-most-famous export: a baseball team. At the turn of the twentieth century, the sandlot leagues were just as segregated as the major leagues, so black steelworkers organized their own club. For the first ten years, they called it the Blue Ribbons. Then it was the Murdock Grays. Finally, the team was taken over by Cumberland "Cum" Posey, scion of the richest black family in Homestead. Most blacks lived in the Ward, the riverfront flats that would be razed to expand the works during World War II. The Poseys, who owned a coal company, lived atop the hill, on 11th Avenue, almost as high as the numbers ran in Homestead. Posey would become manager of the Homestead Grays, the Yankees of the Negro Leagues. The team's most renowned player was Josh Gibson, a steelworker's son from Pittsburgh's Hill District, who was said to have hit eighty-four home runs in one season. But the Grays also fielded Hall of Famers Judy Johnson, Oscar Charleston, Martin Dihigo, Rube Foster, and James "Cool Papa" Bell. Because of their aggressive barnstorming, the Grays were the winningest team in the Negro National League for nine straight seasons, from 1937 to 1945. They averaged eight games a week, once enduring a fourteen-hour round-trip bus ride for a single-night contest in Buffalo. Homestead was too small to hold the team: they started out playing home games at Edgar Thomson Field, in Braddock, then used Forbes Field, when the Pirates weren't busy with it, and finally moved to Washington, D.C., which had a bigger black population than Pittsburgh. Even in their new home, they were the Washington Homestead Grays, never forgetting their steeltown origins.

TWICE DEFEATED in their efforts to unionize, Homestead's steelworkers didn't try again until the 1930s, when they had a prolabor president to protect them. With 1892 and 1919 still in living memory, steelworkers had learned "not to join unions rashly, as that meant strikes, and hardships, and losing out in the mill," according to a labor study. The Flint Sit-Down Strike, a victory by the more assertive autoworkers, convinced U.S. Steel to recognize the Steel Workers Organizing Committee, progenitor of the United Steelworkers of America.

On Labor Day 1941, the workers celebrated their victory by erecting a granite cenotaph to the martyrs of the Homestead Strike. They placed it at the foot of the High Level Bridge, which crosses the Mon into Pittsburgh, so everyone going in and out of Homestead could read about the skirmish that Carnegie and company had wished to forget.

ERECTED BY THE MEMBERS OF THE STEEL WORKERS ORGANIZING COMMITTEE LOCAL UNIONS IN MEMORY OF THE IRON AND STEEL WORKERS WHO WERE KILLED IN HOMESTEAD, PA, ON JULY 6, 1892, WHILE STRIKING AGAINST THE CARNEGIE STEEL COMPANY IN DEFENSE OF THEIR AMERICAN RIGHTS.

So reads the inscription, beneath an etching of a burly puddler stirring molten iron with a long rake.

Once they won the right to strike, the steelworkers used it—over and over again. In the decade and a half after World War II, they struck five times—in 1946, 1949, 1952, 1956, and 1959. The last was the most expensive strike in American history and has been blamed for destroying the domestic steel industry two decades later. The issue was, to use a technical term, featherbedding. In exchange for a big raise, the steel companies asked the union for the right to reduce the number of workers assigned to a task ("featherbedding" refers to the practice of making life for workers easier by hiring more hands than strictly necessary for the workload, thus allowing everyone to work at a more humane pace) and to install machinery that might cost a worker his job. No sale, said the union's president, suave, pipe-smoking David McDonald, and its general counsel, future Supreme Court justice Arthur Goldberg. Half a million workers walked out. They stayed out for four months, until President Dwight D. Eisenhower invoked the Taft-Hartley Act. Starved of steel, General Motors laid off 40 percent of its autoworkers, causing a recession in Detroit. The air force slowed down construction of a missile base in Colorado. With no steel shipments, the railroads lost half a billion dollars and cut employment to its lowest level since 1900. Once the furnaces went cold, customers began buying steel from foreign manufacturers. It was, they discovered, as good as American steel, and cheaper.

"Imports more than doubled over the previous year, to 4.4 million tons, making the United States a net importer of steel for the first time since the 1800s," wrote John P. Hoerr in *And the Wolf Finally Came: The Decline of the American Steel Industry*.

Technically, the union won the strike, preserving the work rules and gaining an automatic cost-of-living adjustment. But foreign steel had found a market in the United States. From then on, whenever the union talked strike, customers would stock up on steel, creating more demand than American companies could supply.

"Steel users increasingly turned to foreign steelmakers, who frequently demanded long-term supply contracts," Hoerr wrote. "Imports surged to 10.4 million tons in 1965, to 18 million tons in 1968, and to 18.3 million tons in 1971. The 1971 imports constituted 18 percent of the domestic market, an intolerable intrusion in the view of both steel companies and the USW."

UNLIKE THEIR COUNTERPARTS at Wisconsin Steel, who showed up at work one day to find a padlocked gate, the workers in Homestead knew their mill was going down. To stop it from closing, they used every protest tactic short of violence.

Mike Stout found his way to Homestead in 1977, looking for a secure job after spending eight years trying to make it as a folksinger in New York City. He was hired as a crane operator in the one-hundred-inch plate mill. In the late 1970s, the steel industry was going through its last employment boom. Unlike previous waves, this one brought in blacks, women, and members of the counterculture—including college-educated "colonizers" who took steel jobs to spread socialism in the mills. The new workers arrived just before the industry's collapse. Homestead's steelworkers combined the militance of the antiwar movement with a working-class resentment that had been simmering since 1892, to turn their local into "the hardest of the hard core," as a Mon Valley historian would put it.

"Not only was the rank-and-file upsurge at Homestead embedded in the workplace itself, it seemed to be the continuity of the spirit that evolved out of the workplace, over years and decades of work and struggle at Homestead, dating back through the consent decree battler, the CIO drive, and the strike of 1892," Stout would later say. "It was something I felt the minute I walked into the mill and started working there, it was something in the air."

In the bitter 1977 election for the presidency of the United Steelworkers, Homestead voted for Ed Sadlowski by a margin of two to one. After Oil Can Eddie's defeat, workers inspired by his "throw out the old hacks" campaign began plotting to take over their own local, 1397. They began by publishing an underground newspaper, *Rank and File*, which won a following when it editorialized against U.S. Steel's plan to recover $385,000 in overpayments from Homestead employees—anywhere from $40 to $800 a worker. The paper also published cartoons lampooning unpopular foremen, ran articles with headlines such as "LOCAL PRESIDENT BETRAYS MEMBERSHIP," and used as a logo the Homestead Strike memorial, thus connecting its cause to the borough's martyrs.

The Young Turks' candidate for president was a welder named Ronnie Weisen. Weisen was a pugnacious street tough, a pompadoured greaser who had boxed Golden Gloves in his youth. After his boxing career ended, he continued to pursue his interest in brawling by picking fights in Homestead bars. At union meetings, Weisen railed against the leadership as "a bunch of sellouts"; he was so disruptive that the local president finally asked the police to attend, to prevent fistfights from breaking out.

Weisen and his Rank and File Caucus took over the local in 1979, winning big. On election night, Stout performed his campaign song "We Are the 1397 Rank and File" for two hundred steelworkers crammed into the campaign headquarters on Amity Street, not far from where Mother Jones had been arrested. He would remember it as one of the highlights of his music career.

For his loyalty to the Rank and File Caucus, Stout was appointed assistant grievance man in his department, making him an ombudsman between the workers and their foremen. Six months later, U.S. Steel announced it was shutting down thirteen mills, including all of its operations in Youngstown, Ohio, and the forty-eight-inch mill in Homestead. With little seniority, Stout was laid off for over a year. It was the beginning of a slow-motion economic bloodletting.

When Stout returned to the mill, he found himself fighting nickel-and-dime firings intended to cut down the work force. He managed to save the job of an epileptic who was let go after suffering a seizure at work. But when U.S. Steel laid off 1,800 workers, there was nothing Stout could do to save them.

By late 1982, it was clear to Stout that U.S. Steel was intent on shutting down not only entire departments but entire mills. Braddock's Edgar Thomson Works seemed doomed. The executives in Pittsburgh were telling plant managers, "Get your man-hours down or shut down." *Fortune* magazine illustrated a story about the company with the U.S. Steel logo cracked in half. "There are no more sacred cows," board chairman David Roderick was quoted as saying. "If you aren't down to 4.5 man hours per ton of steel produced, you're finished." Crews were cut from twelve to two or three people. Entire shifts were eliminated, forcing those still employed to work overtime.

Most of those laid off from the Homestead Works never stepped foot inside a mill again. Stout was now grievance man for the entire Slab and Plate Zone, so his job was protected. To help those who were not so lucky, he started a food bank with money from a benefit concert. Not only did the concert raise $12,000, it was covered by the *CBS Evening News* and the *Today* show. In the spring of 1982, the unemployed were hotter than they'd been since the Depression. Bruce Springsteen chipped in $10,000 of the gate from a Pittsburgh show and allowed the union to collect money outside the concert hall.

As in South Chicago, the Mon Valley steel crisis inspired local pastors to found an organization that used Saul Alinsky's *Rules for Radicals* as a guidebook for fighting mill closings. Chicago is a Catholic town, so its movement was run by the Catholic Church. Homestead, city of competing faiths, produced the Denominational Ministry Strategy, led by Protestant ministers, with no archbishop to moderate their militance. The pastors' first action was against Mellon Bank, which had foreclosed on Homestead's Mesta Machine Company for failure to make payments on a $20 million mortgage. Mesta, an eighty-five-year-old company that employed thousands of Homesteaders, went bankrupt and closed. At first, the pastors organized a demonstration outside the bank's Homestead branch. Unionists withdrew over $100,000 in savings and held a press conference accusing Mellon of bankrupting Mesta and denying its laid-off workers their severance pay and pension benefits. The withdrawals spread, costing Mellon millions in deposits. The bank agreed to a settlement with Mesta's workers.

The Denominational Ministry Strategy's organizer, a hard-ass named Chuck Honeywell, was pleased with the victory but thought the union needed to stage more theatrical protests. Laid-off steelworkers changed five-dollar bills for rolls of pennies at Mellon branches, then counted the coins at the teller's window, while customers in line seethed. The workers rented safe-deposit boxes, in which they locked mackerel and trout.

"Smelliest fish we could find," Stout explained. Deer hunters who used skunk oil to camouflage their scent began pouring the odoriferous concoction on the bank's carpets, a trick that became known as "Smellin' Mellon." Pranking Mellon Bank was fun, but Honeywell's next step was too much for even a labor militant like Stout.

"It's not enough to attack the banks," Honeywell told Stout. "We've got to start going inside the churches and attacking the leaders right inside their churches and places of worship."

"You lose me here," Stout responded. "You're crazy."

But Honeywell hadn't lost the combative, confrontational Weisen or several other hard-line local leaders. On Easter Sunday 1984, they infiltrated Shadyside Presbyterian Church. Located in one of Pittsburgh's wealthiest neighborhoods, Shadyside was attended by executives of U.S. Steel and Mellon Bank. During the service, the president of USWA Local 2227 strode to the nave and began reciting a sermon about confronting evil. The husky unionist quoted German theologian Dietrich Bonhoeffer's conclusion that assassinating Hitler was a Christian response to Nazism.

"Heresy!" parishioners cried, until the union leader told them he was reading a sermon written by their previous pastor. During other services, workers laid cast-off steel on the altar while carrying a sign that read "All We Have Left. Scraps of the Mills."

The militants were getting plenty of publicity—the *New York Times* and *60 Minutes* documented Homestead's proletarian uprising, while presidential candidates Gary Hart and Jesse Jackson came to town to be photographed showing solidarity—but the attack they sprang that holiday season wiped out most of the sympathy they'd won in the community: three men in gas masks invaded a Christmas pageant at Shadyside Presbyterian. They tossed water balloons laced with skunk oil, splattering and terrifying children at the party. Weisen was unapologetic.

"What about our women and children?" he asked. "They don't get any banquets at Christmas."

Just two months later, Weisen was reelected as president of Local 1397. Stout won a term as chairman of the Grievance Committee. That was the last straw for U.S. Steel. The company had been planning to close the Edgar Thomson Works in Braddock. Instead, it closed Homestead. The reason, a company official told Stout: your confrontational union.

"Because of Ronnie Weisen, the militancy of our local, they decided to shut down Homestead," Stout said. "I wouldn't say the militancy went too far. I would say the idiocy went too far, with attacking kids at Christmas parties and stuff like that and attacking people inside churches. Any time you attack innocent people, I think it's ridiculous. I actually don't think we were militant enough. They were going to shut us down anyway. We lost nine out of ten workers. We lost ninety percent of the steel industry."

As grievance chairman, Stout's job was protected by the union contract, so he was among the last group of workers to leave the Homestead Works on the day it closed in 1986. Most of his union brothers and sisters left the Mon Valley, but Stout, who had bounced from Kentucky to New York to Homestead, decided to stick around and keep fighting for steelworkers. A year after the mill closed, his unemployment ran out, leaving him "destitute" and dependent on friends. Even though he was totally broke, Stout decided to run for the state legislature in Harrisburg. He lost the Democratic primary by thirty-nine votes. Stout also tried to find a buyer to reopen the mill. He formed an organization called the Steel Valley Authority to bring back the region's manufacturing base but failed at that, too, due to U.S. Steel's determination that the Homestead Works never make steel again. When it was finally torn down in the mid-1990s—with ex-steelworkers working on the demolition crew—the cranes that Stout had operated were shipped to Poland.

"The whole shift in the ruling class at that time was to begin exporting jobs and going global and basically shut down our manufacturing base, and they deregulated everything from the trucking industry to the banks," Stout said. "That paved the way for the burgeoning of this whole slave-wage labor, Third World, put the jobs over there because we've got people who'll work for twenty cents an hour. I'd say the policies of the Reagan administration at that time pretty much paved the way and greased the skids. They eliminated every law, they allowed banks and S & Ls to ship overseas. They busted the air-traffic controllers' union. They couldn't bust our union, so they pulled the floor out from under us."

Stout eventually opened a print shop on Eighth Avenue, Homestead's main drag. Rent was cheap, because the department stores and the theaters and the restaurants had closed and boarded up their windows. He got his equipment from the Catholic archdiocese and the United Steelworkers International in Pittsburgh, which were both shutting down their in-house printing, and went into business with a couple other ex–mill workers. Stout also resumed his music career, writing prolabor anthems, which he performed as the World's Grievance Man. He toured Germany four times and released nine CDs, including *Soldiers of Solidarity* and *American Dreams: Keeping the Promise*. But he's never earned as much money as he did at U.S. Steel.

IT'S HARD not to meet Mayor Betty. As mayor of Homestead Borough, her only responsibilities are breaking tie votes during council meetings and overseeing the police force. You can get her home phone number from the Rivers of Steel National Heritage Area Museum on Eighth Avenue (a steel museum is the surest sign that steel is dead in Homestead). When you call, she'll invite you to the house on Eleventh Avenue, halfway up the hill. Mayor Betty Esper has lived alone in the upstairs unit since her mother died. A slender woman, with a raptor's profile and flossy white hair that covers her head like a shower cap, Mayor Betty never had a family of her own. Homestead is her family. She doesn't have long-distance phone service or the Internet, because nothing outside her borough interests her, except the Syrian Orthodox church in Pittsburgh, which she began attending after Homestead could no longer support a congregation. Mayor Betty sits on her second-floor balcony and keeps an eye on the neighborhood children. You can tell someone important— or at least someone colorful—lives up there, because overhanging the railing are a seamstress's dummy wearing a rubber Einstein mask, a stuffed Kermit the Frog holding a ladybug flag, and a faux-leather helmet in the yellow and black colors of the Pittsburgh Steelers. (Everyone in the Mon Valley owns at least one article of Steelers apparel or memorabilia. Not only are the Steelers the most successful NFL franchise, with six Super Bowl victories, their name and history flatter the industrial heritage of a region that doesn't have much industry left.)

"I got the dummy from the dump and set it up for Halloween," Mayor Betty explained. "And it became a thing with me."

Mayor Betty spent over thirty years as a clerk of the Homestead Works, working finally for the men in charge of shutting down the mill. ("The only person there was me and [my boss] and five or six laborers that threw stuff in Dumpsters.") In 1990, she became "the first lady mayor in the Steel Valley"—a woman finally got the job because it was worthless by then. The "Welcome to Homestead" signs identified the borough as the "Steel Center of the World." But without the steel mill that had made it famous, Homestead was broke. The borough had no money, and neither did anyone who lived there.

"The steelworkers, they lost their houses," Mayor Betty remembered. "A lot of my friends, they were young, they had to be retrained. They got security jobs. Didn't pay pfft. Some got divorces, some became alcoholics, some committed suicide. Many of them divorces."

Two years into Mayor Betty's first term, Homestead went bankrupt. The state of Pennsylvania took over its finances. The borough laid off half the street department and had to rely on a government grant just to keep its ten police officers on the job.

Once the skies over Homestead turned blue again, the folks across the river and up the hill—architects, city planners, historians, economists, anthropologists, sociologists, and philanthropists who would never have visited a filthy steel town—adopted the little borough as a reclamation project. There were study groups and committees, historical exhibits, film proposals, lectures, brown-bag lunches, dinners, economic analyses, historical surveys, and histories. The Harvard Business School published a case study of disinvestment and redevelopment plans in the Monongahela Valley.

One of the slumming architects was a Carnegie Mellon University professor named David Lewis. Lewis had grown up in England, where he graduated from Leeds University, in the steelmaking Midlands. The future of industrial cities, he believed, was the most important urban planning issue of the late twentieth century.

In his desire to find new purposes for abandoned steel towns, Lewis had an ally from his native country. In the early 1980s, the Prince of Wales had been asked to substitute for his flu-ridden father at the Royal Institute of British Architects' annual dinner. At the time, Sheffield and Birmingham, the cities where steel was invented, were in the same slough as Cleveland, South Chicago, and Homestead. Instead of offering the architects stodgy royal praise, as the Duke of Edinburgh might have, the modern prince challenged them: how many of you, he asked, have offices in the North of England, "where the real problems lie?"

When Lewis read about the speech, he was thrilled. Was not the Mon Valley America's North of England? The Royal Institute of British Architects and the American Institute of Architects were planning the Remaking Cities Conference in Pittsburgh. Lewis invited Prince Charles. The prince not only agreed to attend, but once he was there, he agreed to visit Homestead. Riding in the royal Jaguar as it crossed the High Level Bridge, on its way to a handshaking visit with students at Steel Valley High School, Lewis told the prince about the Mon Valley's similarities to Sheffield and Glasgow. The prince was very disturbed, Lewis recalled. He suggested founding two organizations to wipe away postindustrial blight. Britain's would be called the Prince of Wales Foundation.

"You chaps make yours the Remaking Cities Institute," Prince Charles suggested.

Lewis was so convinced of Homestead's potential for revival that the next year, he bought an old rooming house for $40,000, converted it to a single-family home, and moved in.

"My colleagues all thought I was bloody well crazy," he said. "I wasn't crazy at all. I was doing what I wanted to do. The life had gone out of Homestead. Shops closed, boarded up. I thought all the world's attention would leave the Mon Valley."

The save-Homestead movement had generated some airheaded proposals. Even the *Pittsburgh Post-Gazette* lampooned the idea of using the empty mills as pavilions for a flower show to commemorate the one hundredth anniversary of the Homestead strike. But when Lewis examined a map of the Mon Valley, he noticed that Homestead possessed two geographical benisons: the borough had once been peripheral to Pittsburgh, but now that suburbia had spread south and east of the Three Rivers, it was at the center of the metropolitan area. And with the mill closed, Homestead had the longest stretch of unused riverfront on the Monongahela. Through a member of the West Homestead Borough Council, Lewis got to know Ray Park, president of the company that had bought the Homestead Works and was tearing it apart for scrap. (The Homestead Works actually crossed the borders of three boroughs— Homestead was bracketed by West Homestead and Munhall, which contained the Carnegie Library and the managers' brick homes. U.S. Steel had created multiple municipalities in the valley, to prevent any one from telling it how to run the mill.)

"I don't know what I'm going to do with three hundred empty acres," Park said.

"Put a compass on Homestead, swing it ten miles, and you'll have a million people," Lewis informed him. "It's twelve minutes from downtown Pittsburgh and eight minutes from Carnegie Mellon."

Lewis drew up a plan for a shopping center inside one of the old mill buildings. That turned out to be impractical, because the building could not be air-conditioned, but the idea of a shopping center remained. It took another step when West Homestead convinced Allegheny County and the state of Pennsylvania to scour the old mill site of its toxins. The Homestead Works was the first brownfield in Pennsylvania to be completely remediated. Lewis suggested Park film a flight over his empty, unpolluted three hundred acres of riverfront and take it to a meeting of a national conference of convention center businesses. Developers loved it. In 1999, only thirteen years after the works closed, greater Pittsburgh's largest outdoor mall opened in Homestead. The Waterfront, as it was called, had a Bed, Bath & Beyond, a Men's Wearhouse, a Macy's, a Dave & Buster's, a Mitchell's Fish Market, and an AMC Loews Theater. It had a Chick-fil-A, a Barnes & Noble, and a Courtyard by Marriott Hotel starting at $169 a night. To remind shoppers that they were buying four-hundred-thread-count sheets on the site of a steel mill, and to remind sub-minimum-wage baristas that they'd taken the place of union crane operators, Lewis persuaded the mall's developer to leave standing a dozen blast-furnace smokestacks. The flat-topped obelisks stand in a file along the access road, looking like abstract sculptures of branchless, crownless trees. The only other structures left over from the Homestead Works are a gantry overhanging the river, and the Pump House. The red brick station where the Pinkertons made their landing in 1892 is now rented out for private parties. In a grand irony of labor history, the International Workers of the World celebrated its centennial there, in 2005.

The first successful repurposing of a steel mill, the Waterfront drew 1.5 million visitors a year to a town everyone had avoided in its industrial heyday. To Pittsburghers over thirty, Homestead meant steel. To children and teenagers, Homestead meant shopping. The mall's sales tax receipts rescued the borough from insolvency but did little to change everyday life in Homestead, which had become poorer, blacker, and more run-down since the Works closed. The Waterfront's attraction ended at the waterfront. Few shoppers crossed the railroad tracks and drove up onto Eighth Avenue. The Avenue, as Homesteaders call Eighth, had nothing to offer but a diner, a candy store, a lingerie shop, and a dark, surly bar where the drinkers stared at every newcomer, even when Penn State football games were on the TV. Chiodo's, the after-work tavern by the mill gate, closed down, unable to stay alive even on the patronage of day-tripping Rust Belt romantics seeking an authentic proletarian drinking experience.

"There's two trains of thought on the mall in Homestead," Mayor Betty said. "I love the Waterfront. Personally, everyone in Homestead is so glad they've got the Waterfront. At the same time, people drive through the town and there are empty houses and it's unkempt."

To Stout, the mall didn't change Homestead one bit. "Homestead's one way on this side of the tracks and another way on the other side of the tracks. One's still an impoverished, run-down steel-mill town and the other side is a glitter mall."

Realizing his work had not ended with the mall, Lewis began buying historic storefronts on Eighth Avenue. For $1, plus back taxes, he purchased a burned-out building, refurbished it, and rented it to a hairdresser and a T-shirt shop. Then he bought the building across the street. One side became a gourmet kitchen boutique, owned by his wife. The other became the Tin Front Café, a vegan restaurant where Lewis's stepson was the chef. Homestead began attracting hipster shops that could no longer afford Lawrenceville, the hip neighborhood across the river and up the heights in Pittsburgh. A thrift store specializing in retro fashions opened on Eighth Avenue. A mod furniture emporium followed next door. Homestead—the Homestead above the railroad tracks, not the Homestead of the shopping mall—was written up in a Pittsburgh lifestyle magazine.

There were other benefactors with roots in Homestead. Charlie Batch, the star quarterback from Steel Valley High, went on to play second string for the Steelers. Batch spent his NFL money to transform an old bakery into $1,500-a-month riverfront apartments, with a basement gym. William V. Campbell had left Homestead for California, where he became chairman of Intuit, the tax and business software company. Campbell sent his Silicon Valley money back to the Mon Valley, building a football field for the high school and a gym for the middle school.

"Billy always said when he made money, he'd come back, and boy did he come back," Mayor Betty said.

Stout had once dismissed the Save Homesteaders as "carpetbaggers." He considered the Waterfront "the kiss of death" for bringing industry back to Homestead. But even he was impressed with Lewis's work.

"I think it's real good," Stout said. "I think he's probably the lone person in the area that's trying to revitalize the Avenue. He's got all my respect. He put his money where his mouth is."

A quarter century after the mill went down, Stout is one of the only links between Homestead's steelmaking past and its boutique present. Ronnie Weisen, the union president, moved on with his life, finding a job as a jackhammer operator with the city of Pittsburgh, but he died of cancer in 2000. Mayor Betty—the other link—ate lunch with U.S. Steel pensioners at the Elks Club on the second Thursday of every month, until the Elks closed. A few Christmases ago, they held their last meeting. Her generation of Homesteaders still thinks of their town as the Steel Center of the World. But Mayor Betty also renamed the High Level Bridge after the Homestead Grays, who have a larger place in posterity than the strike or the works. (You can still buy a Grays jersey. You can't buy a bar of steel made in Homestead.) To Stout, who still wasn't living as well as when the works had sprinkled a black snow across Pittsburgh, Homestead was a microcosm of what America had become: a nation of shopkeepers who sold each other things, instead of making things.

"Young people who were born after the manufacturing base was destroyed, I don't think they have a clue about what this place was like," he said. "All they know is there's no jobs out there. They don't know why. I mean, you have to have a college degree to get a job at McDonald's today. You can't grow an economy, grow a middle class, without making things, producing stuff. It's just impossible. I haven't seen it anywhere."

There's an old adage that says, "We can't all take in each other's laundry." It's been proven in Homestead.

8.

New Jack Cities

Before the Vietnam War began, Detroit's single-year record for murders stood at 158, set in 1929, during Prohibition, when the Jewish-dominated Purple Gang was smuggling booze across the river from Canada. Detroit's OGs, the Purple Gang murdered its way into control of the city's underworld by massacring three rival bootleggers. The hired hit man later took part in Chicago's St. Valentine's Day Massacre. Lords of gambling, prostitution, narcotics, and even the wire service that transmitted horse racing results, the Purple Gangsters were so fearsome that Al Capone bought Canadian whiskey from them, rather than trying to muscle in on their smuggling operation. The end of Prohibition was the end of the Purple Gang. It was also the end of gang warfare in Detroit—until heroin started coming home with the soldiers.

During Vietnam, GIs returned with an addiction to the Asian poppy and infected the streets with their craving. Greg Erving turned seventeen that year, and like most of the young men who weren't sent to 'Nam, he went to work in the shop. His job at Chrysler didn't last long. Erving disappeared to Toronto to play drums in a jazz band and get away from a woman who was nagging him for child support. When he returned, three months later, Chrysler informed Erving he'd been fired for going AWOL. In need of a new trade, he became a drug dealer. Music and narcotics went together, so he knew some guys who could hook him up. At first, he just sold marijuana. After his brother was arrested for dealing heroin, Erving took over that operation. He was a successful dope dealer—all the money he needed, all the pussy he wanted—until he met a woman who asked, "Why don't you try balling when you're high?" He tried it. He liked it. After that, he was nothing but a junkie and drunk.

"The riot didn't destroy Detroit," Erving says. "That's bullshit. There was a riot in 1943. It didn't do anything. The riot was the riot. *Drugs* destroyed Detroit. The auto plants left, and people needed to make a living, so they started to hustle. You had white people coming in from the suburbs to buy heroin. By 1974, it was off the chain."

With its bounty of military contracts, the Vietnam War had at first looked so promising for Detroit. But beginning in the mid-1960s, as heroin was introduced to the city, and more and more multistory factories went dark, Detroit's murder score increased geometrically. In 1966, it inched ahead of the record body count from the days of Prohibition, with 175 killings. The next year—the year of the riot—it was 220. The year after that—when heroin began to take hold—303. By 1974, the year Erving described as "off the chain," 714 people were murdered in Detroit. Motown was so terrifying that even Motown left town—Berry Gordy Jr. moved his record label to Los Angeles, leaving only that monument to civic obsolescence, a museum. The Motor City picked up a new, unwanted nickname: Murder City.

Heroin's answer to the Purple Gang was Young Boys Inc., or YBI, a crew founded by street thug Milton "Butch" Jones after he returned to Detroit from serving a four-year sentence for manslaughter. According to Jones's self-published autobiography (which is probably as much of a fable as any memoir by Jack Kerouac or Ernest Hemingway), he began his street career at fifteen as an arsonist and contract killer. ("I could easily kill somebody and not lose a second of sleep," he wrote. "That's when you know you a real O.G.") With its near-parody of ghetto argot and its author's determination to present a gangsta image, the book would be risible if it weren't about shooting people and employing children to sell drugs.

True to his crew's name, Jones was a pioneer in the use of child labor, since juveniles could not be prosecuted in adult courts. In the Jeffries Projects, Detroit's tallest, grimmest slum, the cops were pulling $2,000 rolls out of sixth graders' pockets. Selling packets stamped with the brand names Dyno, Murder One, CBS, and Check Mate (like many ex-cons, Jones had become a chess buff in prison), YBI was running up $400,000 a week in sales. The police estimated 5 percent of Detroit was hooked on heroin, and YBI was satisfying 90 percent of the demand.

"It was just like any other business, such as Ford or General Motors,"

Jones wrote. "I had an assembly line, I was rollin' so strong at that particular time that I had three hookup crews that worked an eight hour shift and hooked up dope twenty-four hours a day."

Jones bought a Corvette every week, until he owned enough to organize a Vette parade to Cedar Point, an amusement park in Ohio. He bought a DeLorean, but like most DeLoreans, it shorted out on the highway, so he traded it in for another Corvette. After four years as the CEO of a heroin ring, Jones estimated he had saved $5 million. He was the Henry Ford II, the Berry Gordy Jr., and the Lee Iacocca of the heroin trade.

YBI first came to the attention of Carl Taylor outside a Gap Band concert at Joe Louis Arena, the city's hockey rink/music hall. Taylor, a former Michigan State University football player, had a Ph.D. in sociology but was enough of a tough guy to run a security company with a contract to keep peace at big shows. When he saw a fleet of limousines pull up, he thought the band had arrived. Then five young men in matching red sweatsuits and white sneakers stepped out. Taylor thought the boys might be a track team, until he noticed the gold cables around their necks. From the police, Taylor learned they were heroin dealers, operating in his old neighborhood. Taylor had seen plenty of drug dealers, but none with so much money—at the concession stand, they paid from many-leaved discs of cash—or so much cool. Seeing a way to combine his doctorate and his street knowledge, Taylor spent most of the 1980s interviewing Detroit gangbangers, during the years when crack replaced heroin as the drug Nancy Reagan told America to turn down.

(When Butch Jones was arrested in 1982, he blamed the First Lady's visit to Detroit for bringing heat on him: "She'd gotten information that we were sellin' drugs to children, which was a lie, but that's all she needed to hear. After she got back to Washington, in no time at all, a task force was sent back to Detroit to hunt us down and break up Young Boys Incorporated." Jones was sentenced to twelve years in federal prison, which he thought was unjust, since he'd only committed state crimes. As he wrote, "either we have laws or we don't." After Jones was released, the feds pinned sixty-eight murders on him and he took another thirty-year sentence to avoid becoming the first Michigander in a hundred and fifty years to receive the death penalty.)

Detroit's heroin trade even had its own novelist. Donald Goines got hooked on heroin while serving a stint in the army, in the early 1950s. When he came home to Detroit, he was a full-blown junkie, pimping, dealing drugs, bootlegging liquor, and breaking into houses to get money for a fix. This landed him in the state penitentiary at Jackson, where he began writing blaxploitation novels inspired by his idol, ghetto author Iceberg Slim.

Dopefiend, Goines's first published book, is the story of Porky, an obese, misanthropic pusher who relishes the power drugs give him over his customers. When a pregnant woman visits his house, desperate for a score, Porky orders her to have sex with a dog. Humiliated, she hangs herself. Porky also delights in hooking an innocent department store clerk on heroin. Fired for stealing a dress to support her habit, she ends up selling her car, then herself.

In the three years after *Dopefiend*'s publication, Goines wrote like a teletype machine, cranking out another fifteen novels. His career was brief. In 1974, Goines and his wife were murdered in their Highland Park apartment, victims of the same street violence the author had chronicled. Since his death, Goines's books have sold over five million copies. His novel *Never Die Alone* was made into a movie starring DMX, and he has won a place as a godfather of rap, inspiring lyrics by Nas, Tupac Shakur, Grand Puba, and Ludacris.

Crack was Detroit's second-generation drug. Heroin created the gang culture that sold the new drug, and the underclass of fiends who consumed it. Crack was made for the eighties—it was a bigger rush than heroin, and it was smoked, rather than injected, sparing the user the risk of AIDS. Crack was much more popular, and much more profitable, than heroin. As a result, the competition to sell it was even more violent.

John Givans, who'd been a young man living near Chene Street during the Detroit riot, joined the army in 1984. After three years in Germany, he mustered out to look after his declining grandfather. As a welcome home, Givans's best friend invited him to share a bag of weed and a pint of Hennessey, just like they'd done before he went into the service. But this time, Givans's best friend had something new to smoke. He called it a rock. Everyone up and down Chene was smoking it now. It made the women even skinnier than junkies.

"I saw girls that I went to school with that looked like they were seventy, eighty years old," Givans remembered. "No teeth. They looked like Jewish POWs from the Holocaust."

A mile east of Chene, at 1350 East Grand Boulevard, was a four-story vintage apartment building known in its respectable days as the Broadmoor. The Broadmoor would become the most renowned dope house in the history of crack. The Chambers Brothers, a family of poor blacks from the Arkansas Delta, had migrated to Detroit looking for factory work. They discovered they could make a lot more money dealing drugs. The brothers got their start selling nickel bags and pills from a party store owned by a family friend on Chalmers Street. (The friend had opened the store after receiving a $20,000 severance check from Ford.) When crack hit the Midwest, in the mid-1980s, the brothers were well capitalized enough to expand their line.

"I saved some money," Billy Joe Chambers explained to a radio interviewer decades later, after he'd done a twenty-piece in federal prison. "When the heavy stuff came, which was cocaine, I had the money to jump. It exploded into one of the world's largest epidemics, not just in Detroit. This was something flagrant in every state and city. It was pretty much like running a business. You've got to keep cars on the road. You've got to keep houses supplied. Money piles up every day. You've got girls everywhere. You've got people trying to get on the payroll. You're buying whatever you want, you're eating whatever you want, you're going wherever you want. And all the time, you've got the police gunning for you."

The Chambers Brothers sold drugs from dozens of bungalows on the East Side, but they made the Broadmoor their flagship location, just as the Hudson's in downtown Detroit had been the flagship of the department store chain, until it closed in 1983. People would no longer come into the city to buy clothes, but they would come in to buy crack. Slinging rock was the most profitable trade the East Side had to offer. In their best year, the Chambers brothers grossed $55 million, more money than any legitimate merchant in Detroit.

The Broadmoor was nearly vacant when the Chambers Brothers took over. They offered the manager $1,000 a week to ignore the crack dealing in his building. That was a lot more than the $250 a month the landlord paid him, so he took it. The house, which became known to local crackheads as the Boulevard, was organized like a department store: $3 rocks on the first floor, $5 rocks on the second floor, $10 rocks on the third floor, $25 "boulders" on the fourth. There was a barter room where tapped-out baseheads could exchange guns and TV sets for rocks, and a "pussy room" where young women could trade their irreducible product.

Crack was in every family on Chene Street. Givans's uncle sold crack for the Chambers Brothers, then did time in a federal prison because he wouldn't roll over on his bosses. One of Givans's young neighbors, Lester Guyton, didn't have enough to eat because his mama was spending her bakery paycheck on crack. Lester and his brothers and sisters subsisted on sugar sandwiches, mayonnaise sandwiches, or food pantry cheese because their mother smoked up the grocery money. When she smoked up the rent money too, they were sent to live with aunts and uncles. The drug followed them to their relatives' houses, where crack-heads would pry off loose bricks to sell for a dime. When Guyton was thirteen, he began selling crack himself.

"I went from crack to selling cocaine," he said one day on Chene Street. "Right here in this neighborhood. I said, 'I'm going to be legit with mine.' I worked at McDonald's. It ups your clientele. I used to sell weed at McDonald's. You have a regular job, it covers you. Drugs tore this neighborhood up. I did it. I used to sell drugs to my girlfriend's mama. You had people who knew each other their whole lives, killing each other because one guy was making more than the other guy."

Crack even made Detroit the birthplace of carjacking, a term coined by the *Detroit News* in 1991 after a twenty-two-year-old drugstore clerk was killed for her Suzuki Sidekick. That was the year the city's murder rate hit its all-time high of sixty per one hundred thousand (and also the year the population dropped below one million for the first time since 1920). The crackheads had stolen everything that didn't move, and now they were stealing anything that did.

The Chambers Brothers were in and out of business in three years, busted by the FBI. After the police confiscated a home video of the brothers flashing thousands of dollars in cash and passed it on to a TV news reporter, they became the face of crack in Detroit. Not even Al Capone could have withstood that much heat. But during their domination of the drug trade, a Harlem journalist named Barry Michael Cooper visited Detroit to write an article about the city twenty years after the riots. Cooper dubbed the young dealers "new jacks," and he called his story, which appeared on the front page of the *Village Voice*, "Kids Killing Kids: New Jack City Eats Its Young."

"Detroit's violence knows no boundaries," Cooper wrote. "It's among the high-rise office buildings downtown, the upper-middle class homes and condos on the West Side, the poverty-worn projects on the East Side. Detroit is like that nightmare where your legs become paralyzed when the monsters are chasing you; you can't escape."

Cooper adapted his article into the screenplay for *New Jack City*, the *Public Enemy* of the crack era. The scene was shifted to Cooper's native New York, but Nino Brown was based on Larry and B. J. Chambers, and "the Carter"—the apartment complex Nino converts into a crack tower—was obviously Gotham's version of the Broadmoor.

Carl Taylor was a source for Cooper's *Village Voice* story and consulted on *New Jack City* until walking off in a fit of local pride when he found out the movie would take place in New York. ("Detroit's not even on the radar," he complained. "It either happens in Los Angeles or New York; New York is the shit.") Taylor was six foot four, wore horn-rimmed glasses and suits, and looked like either Sonny Liston gone to seed or Biggie Smalls after a fitness regimen. He was a professor at Michigan State University, but when journalists called, he'd growl and say, "This better be important or I'm goin' back to my old business: breakin' bones."

Taylor could talk like a blaxploitation hero because he was an academic star: his book, *Dangerous Society*, had been excerpted in *Harper's* magazine. It was timely. The Crack Wars were at their crescendo. New York was experiencing its worst violence since the Civil War Draft Riots. Los Angeles conceived gangsta rap, the *Iliad* of the war between the Bloods and the Crips. But even in 1990, its *annus mortis* of 2,605 murders, New York was only half as bloody per capita as Detroit. While never surpassing the 1974 record of 714, Detroit had the nation's highest murder rate for most of the eighties and nineties, and was never challenged among cities of a million or more people. (Detroit fell out of that league not so much because the population was being killed off, but because no one who could afford otherwise wanted to live among such violence. Only a building-by-building canvass, organized by city hall, located a million people for the 1990 census.) The entire country was in an economic slump in the early nineties, which contributed to the crime wave. But Detroit had been in an economic slump for a quarter century. As Coleman Young, then in his fifth, final, and most cantankerous term as mayor, liked to say, "Detroit could be your town next." Now that everyone else's town was Detroit, thanks also to a decade of Republican neglect for urban America, the rest of the country was more fascinated with Motown than at any time since the Supremes broke up. After Ze'ev Chafets published *Devil's Night and Other True Tales of Detroit*, ABC News came to heap pity on America's basket case. Young insisted Detroit was as safe as most cities, then kicked the reporter out of his office for preparing a "hatchet job." It was great TV.

As Taylor wrote in *Dangerous Society*, "the new underclass has been growing since the 1960s. The 1970s and 1980s in Detroit have been years of economic depression. Teen unemployment has been record-setting. Most agree that what delinquent ghetto youth desire has been beyond their means."

It's an obvious observation that the drug trade replaced the auto industry as Detroit's number one employer of high school dropouts. But the factories helped create that class of dropouts. Henry Ford, who once said, "I hire an autoworker from the neck down," dispatched his recruitment agents to the South to hire unlettered men who'd be so grateful for work they wouldn't cause labor trouble. Education was never important to blue-collar Detroiters, because the shop was always hiring, and it paid better than teaching. By the mid-1980s, the graduation rate in the Detroit public schools was 25 percent. The auto industry also created a market for heroin and crack. Drugs were available in all the shops. Some of the guys on the line wanted a narcotic heavier than Crown Royal to take their heads out of their monotonous jobs, and they had the money to pay for it. Teenagers who might have hired in at Ford's a generation earlier didn't feel like they'd missed a thing.

"Fuck that factory rap," a fifteen-year-old told Taylor. "We going to sell some dope and get paid. Then we'll go into the studio and make our rap record and be *stars*. All I want to do is get paid and show all them suckers at school that school ain't shit. Me and the boys getting paid and we ain't wasting our time doing no lame-ass factory gig."

Crack didn't come to my hometown until the end of the 1980s. Lansing was always a few years behind the big city. Unlike Flint, which was only fifty miles from Detroit and shared an identical industrial culture, Lansing was too far away, too white-collar, and too well policed for the gangs to bother with.

Paradoxically, crack's arrival in Lansing was the consequence of an antidrug campaign. The Tri-County Metro Narcotics Squad, the local narcs, went on a marijuana offensive so successful it dried up the weed supply in town. People still wanted to get high, though, so they started smoking crack. And once you start smoking crack, it's hard to stop.

Crack came to my home in Lansing. It came right into my bedroom. The winter I graduated from Michigan State University, I rented a room from an old school friend, a girl I'd known since I was six years old. Andrea's father owned a house on the Grand River, where she lived downstairs and I lived up. In grade school, Andrea had been the girl whose penmanship the teacher expected us to imitate. In junior high, she dyed a purple stripe in her buzz-cut hair, wore a dog collar for her school picture, began listening to the Psychedelic Furs, acquired a boyfriend who looked like a young Johnny Wadd, and sold me my first joints. By the time we were twenty-two, she was tending bar in a tavern next door to a biker club which had a sign warning visitors "IF YOU DON'T KNOW IF YOU'RE WELCOME—YOU'RE NOT." One afternoon, I was sitting at my desk, reading a book, when I heard Andrea creak up the stairs.

"Close your eyes and put out your hand," she commanded.

I obeyed, and felt a silty object drop into my palm. Opening my eyes, I beheld a bag of cocaine the size of a garlic bulb.

"I'm holding on to it for a friend of mine," Andrea explained.

I reacted the way any young writer would have.

"Can you introduce me to this guy?" I asked.

She did, and "Jimmy Oliver," the *nom de drogue* I assigned him, became the subject of my first magazine story. It appeared in *Z* and was then excerpted in *Utne Reader*.

When Jimmy Oliver walked down South Washington Avenue in Lansing—past the biker bar, the old train depot, the grassy field where Diamond Reo had stood until it burned down in 1975—the skinny girls chanted, "Hey, Heavy D, what you got for me today? Got some heavy boulders? Shake 'em and they sound like dice?"

Jimmy was nicknamed Heavy D. Like the rapper, he was so fat he filled an easy chair from arm to arm. He strolled around in washed-out black jeans, flannel shirts, sneakers with dirty creases, and who-cares-about-fashion black plastic glasses. His only concession to the B-boy look was a wispy gold chain around his neck.

"I give less than a shit about style," Jimmy told me the first time we met, in the living room of my house. Jimmy sat on the couch, completely wired, and talked for three hours into a tape recorder I'd balanced on the arm. "I've made the money to buy wardrobes that could damn near match Michael Jackson's. I don't spend a lot of money on clothes, I wear clothes that cover my ass. If people don't like the way I look"—*smack!* He slapped his knuckles against his palm. "That's too damn bad."

A few years before, when crack was still a novelty, Jimmy had been a rich young drug dealer who could afford to blow $12,000 over a weekend, party with prostitutes, and pick up the dinner check for a dozen of the fake friends his drug money attracted. Now he was just broke. He'd started smoking his own product, which was the fastest way to lose money in the drug business.

"I don't do it as a habit," he said, even though he was doing it three times a week. "But lately, it's becoming more and more frequent and I'm trying to stop that because for the longest time, I could walk around and hold an ounce worth in my pocket and never touch it. Then I said, 'What the hell, I've done so good for so long. Let me just take a little bit here and there.' That little treat turned into a little problem."

Jimmy lived with his mother in a ranch house on the south side of town, a neighborhood whose quarter-century-old houses, built for

Oldsmobile's final hiring boom, were already decaying, the consequence of their bum-rush workmanship. Rust wept against the grain of aluminum siding. Snow whisked through gaps between garage doors and driveways. Crackheads from a nearby housing project were making raids on the party stores, and people had been robbed for drugs in their homes. To get to his drug deals, which netted him $300 to $400 a week, Jimmy drove his mother's car. She worked days, as a clerk. Jimmy worked nights. Not many months before, he'd been arrested for possession of marijuana. The cops found two joints during a traffic stop near Detroit. He was sentenced to nine months' probation, which involved going to a drug class and lying to the counselor that he'd only smoked four joints in his life.

Ever since he was eight years old and saw people selling pot on TV, Jimmy had wanted to be a drug dealer. Thinking it might be a good way to supplement his allowance, he went to a field near his house, plucked a leaf of what he thought was marijuana, "cured" it, and rolled it in strips of the giant paper inside Cheech and Chong's *Big Bambu* album. The kids at elementary school loved it, even though they were buying ragweed.

"They said they got high," Jimmy recalled. "They would have smoked oregano and said they got high."

As a sophomore in high school, Jimmy and a friend were recruited by a dealer who needed franchisees among the student body. The reward was one joint for every five sold. It didn't take long for Jimmy and his partner to figure out that was a rip-off and buy their own bag of weed. They sold three ounces a day—a quarter-pound on football Fridays. It was very, very seldom that he wasn't high the entire school day.

Jimmy claimed to have a high school diploma. His friends weren't so sure. There's no doubt he learned a trade, though. After leaving school, he graduated to selling thirty or forty pounds a week, earning $200 to $300 a pound. Business was so good, he even put his father to work after the old man was fired from the Buick-Oldsmobile-Cadillac plant. The arrangement didn't last long. Jimmy ended up firing his father for the same drunkenness and fuck-uppery that had ended his career in the auto industry. The old man bought so much gin and gave away so many joints they had to stop doing business. Jimmy loved his father, but the old man had been in prison for his son's birth and was just the kind of loser Jimmy saw himself turning into in ten years, if he didn't get himself straight.

To make his income look legitimate, Jimmy worked as a janitor in a nursing home and, for a time, operated a band saw in a steel mill. Work plus dealing didn't leave much time for sleep, so he sometimes ate acid for two weeks at a time to stay awake. At the nursing home, he came in stoned, worked two or three hours, then crawled into a broom closet to sleep away the rest of his shift. When the boss told Jimmy, "You don't give a shit about this job," Jimmy pulled a roll of cash out of his pocket and peeled away singles, fives and twenties until he revealed its rich core of hundred-dollar bills.

"Man," he told his boss. "Man, don't start pressing me about this job again, 'cause I don't need that petty little paycheck you give me. That paycheck you give me, I'll piss on that."

Once Lansing discovered crack, it turned out to be such a ride to Valhalla that nobody wanted to smoke a joint that only took you as high as the clouds. Like a good businessman, Jimmy started selling the new drug. The trick to making money on crack was to bait the customer with a potent rock, then cut the strength as the night wore on. His rocks usually sold for $20 apiece. The first would contain $25 to $50 worth of cocaine. The potency would drop as the crackhead began to "fiend"— hunger for more rock. As a nineteen-year-old, he thought crack could do for Jimmy Oliver what bootleg whiskey did for Joseph P. Kennedy— make him a millionaire with a mansion, an army of bodyguards, enough money to feed the hungry, house the homeless. He connected with a Mexican dude named Johnny who dealt cocaine by the pound, stored fifty-pound bales of marijuana in warehouses, and turned deals that netted him $30,000. Johnny was Jimmy's main supplier, and Jimmy was Johnny's loyal lieutenant—until Johnny OD'd on a coke binge and drowned in a motel tub where a friend tried to revive him with an ice bath. When Johnny was buried, all Jimmy got were his scales and his gun. They were small compensation for losing his shot at becoming a badass.

THE JANUARY NIGHT Jimmy invited me out on a drug deal was so cold it hurt to sit on a vinyl car seat. So cold the streetlamps glittered through the thick darkness. Police cars steamed outside Quality Dairy convenience stores while the cops went inside for coffee. Snowmobiles shaved double incisions into the frozen Grand River. If you inhaled the sharp air too vigorously, your nostrils flapped shut. That cold.

"This is going to be my last deal for a while," Jimmy said as we stood in his mother's kitchen, the kitchen of a woman too tired to clean and too poor to hire someone to do it for her. This was no crack house—Jimmy's *Silver Surfer* comic book lay among stacks of papers on the dining table. On the wall, under a window, his mother had posted her "Rules for All-Night TV Watching and Game Playing." They included washing the dishes.

Jimmy's mother, a heavy woman with a pancake complexion, knew her son smoked crack but tolerated it because Jimmy brought money into the house. After all, her boyfriend smoked it, too. When she began to suspect Jimmy was fiending, she glared at him and said, "You'd better leave it alone." To protect his mother, Jimmy kept big deals away from the house. Because he had someone to pay the rent, he wasn't a lifer in the Life.

"I can leave drugs alone, I don't have to make my living off it," he said. "They're already on welfare, or they've burned up all their chances of getting on welfare. They can't get a job because it's been so long since they've had one, or they've got no marketable skills. The only thing they've got left is drugs or stealing."

We were waiting on a customer named Joey, who showed up around nine o'clock, after Jimmy finished fixing bagels and sandwiches for himself and me. Joey was a skeevy, skinny twenty-year-old with greasy broom-corn hair, dressed in an imitation-satin Detroit Tigers jacket and jeans washed out to the color of an August sky. He'd brought his "beams," a pharmacist's scale wrapped in plastic. Joey handed the scale to Jimmy and began rapping a telegraph skein of mumbles and obscenities.

"This's gonna be fuckin' good stuff, right?" he asked. "It's gonna be the right weight?"

"Uh-huh," Jimmy said flatly. "You got the money?"

Spelunking in his pockets, Joey found $200, handed it to Jimmy.

"All right," Jimmy said. "I'm gonna make the buy. You guys meet me in the parking lot of Joe's Diner in a half an hour and I'll have the bag for you."

A few minutes later, Jimmy and I were on our way downtown in his mother's car. He dropped me off at a Quality Dairy a few blocks from his connection's house, explaining, "The guy I buy from doesn't like new people around."

The Quality Dairy was in the middle of Lansing's central drug business district. Less than two weeks before, a Latino man had been shot to death at the car wash across the street as he tried to drive away from what was probably a drug deal gone sideways. If you idled your car on one of the side streets, someone would run over, tap on the window, and ask, "What you need?"

Jimmy was gone about ten minutes. At the dealer's house, he'd bought seven grams for $150, which meant he'd clear $50. Jimmy bought a box of baking soda at Quality Dairy. As we drove away, he pulled a tiny plastic bag from his coat pocket and dropped it in my hand.

"This is it," he said. There was a lot of power in that little pouch. Cocaine inspired armed robberies, prostitution, murders, and just plain desperation. A guy had once offered to sign a $600 car over to Jimmy to pay for less powder than this.

"I know men that have sold their bodies for rock," he said. "That's *thoroughly* pitiful."

On the way to the drop, Jimmy stopped at my house, set up the beams on the kitchen table, and cleaved off three-quarters of a gram, replacing it with baking soda. That was his finder's fee, but Joey wasn't supposed to know.

Joe's Diner was on West Saginaw Street. Lansing's broadest thoroughfare, it passed another GM plant that has since been demolished. Back then, the factory lamps were the only constellation visible from the diner parking lot. On the way, a police car appeared in our rearview mirror. I spent more time watching the rectangle that showed us where we'd been than the one showing us where we were going. Nothing in life would have terrified me more than seeing the rack atop that cruiser suddenly turn red, white, and blue.

The restaurant was closed. Joey and his friend were waiting in their car. Jimmy parked alongside and Joey climbed into his backseat, where he received the scales and the bag. This place was too public to weigh the coke, but he did open the bag to smell it. Satisfied, he stashed it in his pocket.

When you write about factories closing, you can't just write about the forty-year-old guys who lost their jobs; you also have to write about the twenty-year-olds who never got jobs. Honest work, or even honesty, may have been too much to expect from Jimmy or Joey. They traveled lower paths than most, but they came from familiar Lansing stock: guys who graduated from getting high and fucking up in high school drafting class to getting high and fucking up as a janitor or a lawn-care worker. Guys who lived with their divorced moms and disappeared into the dark every evening when a friend's used Impala pulled up in front of the house, who rode off somewhere to get drunk on Mickey's or Boone's

Farm, or high on pot and crack, then reappeared at two in the morning and slept 'til ten. They floated at the edge of maturity's whirlpool, waiting to be sucked in by a pregnant girlfriend, a fed-up mom, or just the realization that it might be cool to have a job and money and a house. A generation earlier, GM would have taken them in. The General had taken in Jimmy's ex-con pops. But in 1990, they were slinging drugs to supplement their $4.75-an-hour jobs.

Back at Jimmy's house, we headed down to the basement, which had once been Jimmy's bedroom. Now it was his smoking den, its furnishings and accessories illustrating the threadbare disorder of a crackhead's life. Blankets, clothes, couch cushions, and wooden pallets were jumbled on the concrete floor. Jimmy unzipped a leather case and pulled out a truncated rifle.

"This is my sawed-off twenty-two," he said. "I've rode with this across my lap many a night; it made me feel a lot better."

On the way home, Jimmy had picked up a box of Chore Boy scouring pads and a bottle of rubbing alcohol, two items necessary for cooking and smoking cocaine. The rest of the equipment—an old T-shirt, a glass pipe, a glass El Producto Queen cigar tube, a square of silk, a hemostat—was as essential to the basement as pots and ladles to the kitchen.

Jimmy rocked up his three-quarters of a gram and prepared to smoke. The pipe was a glass tube, wide open at both ends. It belonged to Jimmy's mother's boyfriend. The Chore Boy pads were a filter to prevent him from sucking in the melting rock. He burned off the brass so he wouldn't inhale "a poison hit."

Jimmy lit the wick, lifted the tube to his lips, held the fire under the glass. When the flame hit the pipe, the chip crackled, and Jimmy sucked hard, pulling cocaine smoke into his lungs. Like a pot smoker, he pursed his lips to hold in the cloud until he could hold it no longer and exhaled a colorless puff. Suddenly, Jimmy looked as free and relieved as a diver who has just broken the surface and is breathing sweet air. He hit pipe after pipe—over a dozen draws. He called it "Chasin' Jason," smoking until he found that orgasmic hit that melted him into the chair.

"Chasin' Jason's simple," he'd explained to me once. "It's catchin' him that's a bitch. A couple of times I've caught him, had him stuff a mudhole in my ass and take off again."

As he chased Jason—lighting, inhaling, holding in the smoke—an inner storm generated raindrops of sweat on his forehead and temples. Leaning into the pipe, he looked intense, determined, even businesslike, as he pursued that big rush. Finally, on about the tenth hit—*bam!*

"That's the one everybody wants," Jimmy said. "They call 'em ringers, 'cause it makes your ears ring."

After Jimmy inhaled the last big blast of the night, he still had a good-sized chunk of crack left over. It was two in the morning. The day's work was done. The night's rewards rattled in Jimmy's head. Everything was tied to the rock.

"I've got this in my pocket, " he said. "I can do one of three things with it: I can smoke it up and it'll be gone in ten minutes, I can go get sex with it, or I can sell it."

Jimmy was already high, and he'd copped fifty bucks on the deal. That left the middle option.

"I know hundreds of girls who will trade some draws for this stuff," he said. "Good, bad, and indifferent."

Before he sold to Joey, Jimmy had sworn he'd made his last deal, at least until he got off probation for that marijuana bust. It's rarely that easy to leave the game though. In the months after, he was still setting up acquaintances with small amounts of cocaine. He was still on the pipe, too. In fact, he'd smoked up coke he was holding for dealers and was waiting for the income tax return from his janitor job so he could pay them back.

Unemployed, in debt, and living with his mom, Jimmy was a long way from the days when he'd rolled with Johnny and the Mexicans and sampled every hooker who came through Lansing—over two hundred in all, he said. But of the million dollars that had passed through his pocket, he didn't think he'd wasted a cent.

"For as much money as I've made and spent and burned, I'll have a lot to show for it," he told me that night in my kitchen. "I've got memories, good times, parties that seemed like they'd never end. I haven't got shit now; I ain't even got a car. I'll probably be like the rest of the leftover hippies. Sittin' around, gettin' high, thinking about all the things I could have done with my life, and remembering all the things I did."

IN 1990, Michigan elected a Republican governor. In his first budget, John Engler cut heating assistance, medical care, aid to families with dependent children, day care, and aid to senior citizens. He eliminated General Assistance, a welfare program that supported 83,000 childless men and women. The cuts took effect on October 1, 1991, just as autumn began to turn crisp. In 1991, the entire nation was in a recession. Michigan was always hit hard by economic downturns. This one was no exception.

"There are jobs out there," the governor told our four hundred thousand unemployed. At the same time he claimed work was available, Engler eliminated Job Start, a training program for ten thousand youths who would otherwise have been on welfare. His director of social services called the cuts "a really interesting social experiment."

In Detroit, the newly homeless crowded into abandoned buildings, occupied a vacant housing project, and built a tent city, which they called "Englerville," in a public park. The Detroit police tore Englerville down twice before it was reconstructed outside a Methodist church. In Copemish, a village in northern Michigan, a woman died of an aneurysm after cutting her dosage of high blood pressure medicine in half, trying to stretch her supply after the state stopped paying. Two Detroit men tried to heat an abandoned building with a barbecue grill. They asphyxiated in their sleep. And in Pontiac, a family dried its clothes on the space heater they plugged in after their gas was cut off. The clothes caught fire. A two-year-old, a four-year-old, and a six-year-old burned to death.

The state capitol—a soft-boiled egg wearing a Prussian helmet, surrounded by Civil War statuary and northern catalpas—rose to its ovoid pinnacle above a green common in the center of Lansing. But of course, it belonged to everyone in Michigan, from Monroe in the Lower Peninsula to Ironwood in the Upper. In early December, during a whirling snowstorm, a group of homeless men from Detroit pitched a tent on the capitol lawn. A large sky-colored tent, the sort raised by a one-night-stand circus, it was equipped with cots, food tables, a TV, a radio, and, for warmth, old-fashioned propane heaters made of tin. They called themselves Michigan Up and Out of Poverty.

"Englerville USA" looked like the camp of an army that had buried its dead after a battle. It was nicknamed Operation Michigan Storm, after the previous winter's invasion of Iraq. The men who lived in the tent wore camouflage combat fatigues and carried walkie-talkies, looking like a troupe of cold-weather Schwarzkopfs.

"We wear these uniforms, one, to be visible, and two, because it's war on the poor," said the group's minister of information, James Ford. Ford had been a $3,000-a-month cologne salesman at Hudson's, until he'd quit to take a job as a regional representative for Aramis, a career decision that would land him on the streets. Aramis laid him off before he had worked long enough to qualify for unemployment. By August, he was evicted from his high-rise apartment. For months before discovering Michigan Up and Out of Poverty, Ford slept in cars, abandoned buildings, and shelters. Homelessness had not fully abraded his sales-man's polish, so he was appointed spokesman.

When a delegation from Tent City tried to visit Engler's office, its members went in uniform. The camouflaged emissaries were met by members of Engler's staff, who asked the group to write a letter request-ing a meeting, and, oh, to leave their address.

"They had the audacity to ask us for our written address," an incredu-lous Tent Citizen named Kenneth Shaw said later. "We're right across the street. Englerville, USA."

That winter, I was unemployed myself. In the two years since I'd graduated from college, I hadn't been able to find a full-time job. So I'd pieced it together. I wrote newspaper articles for $25 a byline. I chopped weeds in a parking lot, rented movies in a video store, delivered maga-zines and telephone books door-to-door, and chauffeured a shady "trader" who had lost his driver's license for speeding. I wasn't afraid of work, but money, it seemed, was afraid of me. Tent City was the most exciting thing to come to Lansing since a women's bowling tournament three years earlier, so I hung around, taking notes that I hoped to turn into another magazine article. (Like my article about Jimmy Oliver, it would appear in Z, under the department heading "The Streets.") I was stand-ing outside the tent, a week or so before Christmas, when Engler walked past with a posse of aides.

"Mr. Ford says 'Merry Christmas,'" Kenneth Shaw called out.

"Merry Christmas," the governor replied.

"When are you going to come out to the tent city?"

Engler walked on, probably weary of browbeating. Earlier that day, twenty-five nuns had serenaded him with songs of faith and protest, in-cluding "Kumbaya."

Tent City had a five-hour permit, but once it went up, its leaders vowed to keep it up until Engler restored money for health care, job training, and education and instituted a "Helpfare" program to en-courage people on the dole to work. Engler's spokesman (one of my high school classmates) called Ford and his lieutenants "professional activists."

"They're not really homeless," he said. "If they are truly homeless, then they could be in a shelter."

This enraged Ford. After only a few months on the street, he looked healthy and smooth featured but whenever someone questioned his poverty, anger bled through his fraying salesman's manner.

"There's only one man in here who's not homeless," Ford shouted when I quoted the governor's spokesman to him. He hit me with a Chuck D stare. "If this tent was knocked down, I'd have a long walk back to a city I'm familiar with. If you don't think there's homeless, talk to this guy over here."

Ford motioned to a thin black man with whittled cheeks and crooked, gapped teeth. The man, dressed for winter in Velcro sneakers, green polyester trousers, and a thin black jacket, walked over with a rickety gait.

"Talk to this reporter, man," Ford said.

"Naaaaw, I can't do that," he groaned.

"Yeah, you can. You got as much right to talk as I do."

So the man sat down on one of the wooden folding chairs that ringed the propane heater and told me his story. His name was LeVerne Boone. He had fought in Vietnam, then worked on the assembly line at a Ford plant in Mount Clemens. Debilitated by physical and psychic combat wounds, he collapsed on the line in 1978. Unable to continue working in the shop, he found a job at Burger King but was eventually fired.

"I've been homeless ever since '89," he said in a quiet voice. "I had all my stuff set out on the street two times last year, two times the year before that."

Boone pulled a letter from a stack of worn papers he carried in his waist-length winter jacket. (The fabric was too thin, he said, but he used "psychology" to will himself warm.) It was from the Michigan Department of Social Services. Dated September 22, 1991, the letter informed him that his welfare benefits had been cut from $173 a month to $51 a month.

"I never did see that fifty-one dollars," he said. Until the cuts came, he had been living with a girlfriend, but then she kicked him out.

"I guess she wanted someone else," he said, shrugging.

Boone slept in parks and under bridges, or stayed up all night in a hospital waiting room. When the tent city rose on the capitol lawn, he was one of the first Lansing homeless to take shelter there.

"It gave me a lot of positive ideas about myself," he said. "Gave me hope. It opened the door where I met some very important people from the House [of Representatives], and they listen to me, and know what's going on with the brothers and sisters. Any time you get somebody with political office to stand up with you, that means a lot. That's the greatest feeling in the world."

Since the Detroiters had their own tent city, at the Methodist church

back in their hometown, they hoped Lansing's homeless would eventually take over the capitol tent. Ten days after the raising, the locals had
begun to take on some responsibility. LeVerne Boone especially experienced a revival. He had become a spokesman for the protesters and
pointed proudly to a newspaper article in which he'd been quoted. When
the Detroit chapter of the Revolutionary Communist Youth Brigade
asked to march outside the tent, Boone told them no.

"We don't need that kind of trouble here," he lectured a young man.
"We got homeless people in here and if you young people want to be
with our coalition, you got to follow our agenda. You're just gonna be
be-boppin' around here in your leather jackets."

To a man slumped in a chair, Boone said, "You can't let them tell
you you're nobody . . . a man who has a wife and four kids. Come on,
man, hold your head up! You got nothing to be ashamed of 'cause
you're homeless."

This was on a Saturday afternoon. The tent was thronged with newspaper reporters, Young Communists in berets and Yasser Arafat scarves,
homeless men in military uniforms, middle-class fellow travelers who
worked as legislative aides and social workers in the surrounding state
office buildings. A folksinger led a chorus of "Amazing Grace" (Lansing
was said to have the second-most-vigorous folk music scene in the nation, after Cambridge, Massachusetts, probably because it has a similar
concentration of academics, earnest liberal Protestants, and lesbians).
Local sympathizers donated food, which the homeless wrapped in foil
and cooked on the lids of the propane heaters.

By night, though, the tent was nearly empty. Most of the Detroiters
had slipped away to motel rooms rented by the American Red Cross. A
small group sat around a heater, watching TV, while others stretched out
on cots. The wind outside was stinging. Gusts shook the canvas and blew
through the tent's seams. Everyone's breath was frosty and everyone's
toes were numb, even men who could afford boots.

At eleven thirty P.M., the tent flap opened and Lauro Valles entered,
leading a shivering giant who had been sleeping without coat or gloves
in a parking ramp. The man looked as though he'd been rescued from a
snowbank. His face and hands were blush red and he held his arms stiff,
as though he were in chains. He was laid on a cot. Several men piled blankets on him, then began massaging his limbs. A fellow homeless man
took down the giant's story: He was from Battle Creek and had acciden-
tally boarded a bus to Lansing, forty-five miles away. Lacking the fare to
return home, he had spent the last three days on the street. (Later, a

woman would recognize the drifter as a Vietnam veteran who had been in and out of mental hospitals since the late 1960s.)

"Do you need anything?" he was asked.

"Coffee and a cigarette," he said weakly, clutching himself and shivering.

"All the shelters were closed," one of the Detroiters said. "They close at six. If this man didn't come into Tent City, he'd have froze to death. Because Tent City is open twenty-four hours to people in need."

Valles, the man's rescuer, was a Latino wearing a tall Bolivian hat. The others called him "Chief," because of his deadpan face. Between nine o'clock and one in the morning, he took four people off the frigid streets.

Less than a week after that cold night, Tent City was dismantled by the state of Michigan. As had happened to them many times before, the homeless were evicted by a landlord. Their tent's owner refused to accept another week's rent, which was being paid by the campaign fund of a Democratic legislator. The capitol's groundskeeper also said the propane heaters, along with 230 bales of hay stacked outside the canvas walls for insulation, were the makings of "a barbecue situation."

Tent City didn't last long, but its appearance on the capitol lawn proved Coleman Young's prophecy. Tent City was the Occupy movement, an entire generation before it arrived on Wall Street. Its instigators were lower-class, uneducated, black, and Michiganders—four categories of people who felt the consequences of postindustrial America's economic inequality years before they filtered up to middle-class, college-educated white New Yorkers.

After the circus of the unemployed left town, Lansing's homeless returned to their usual hideouts: the City Rescue Mission beneath the neon cross, where a hot meal cost only a sermon about sin. If they had a few dollars, they slept at Jan's Rooms, the flophouse next door. If they were thirsty, they drank next to the fish ladder on the Grand River. There, they could hide in the bushes along the bank if the cops came by, or ogle the dancers from the strip club at the end of the park, who came outside for a smoke break on a summer evening shift. Michigan's homeless had one advantage over the homeless everywhere else in America: the ten-cent bottle deposit meant a dozen empties could be transformed into a full can of Colt 45 malt liquor. To accomplish this dregs-into-beer miracle, men would stir garbage bins, listening for the hollow clank of aluminum. They toted the empties in trash bags, bending beneath the load. The best thing was, they could redeem their discoveries at the party store, for credit. It was a one-stop job, cans for beer, with no cash involved in the transaction.

I turned twenty-five in the winter of 1992, and it seemed the members of my postautomotive generation couldn't buy or beg their way into a decent job. The nation was in its first Bush recession (that was George I, the lean patrician with the plate-glass spectacles whose administration also brought us the Gulf War, gangsta rap, the Seattle Sound, and the Los Angeles riots). General Motors was exactly halfway between one of its decennial hiring binges, when it replaced a worn-out crew of gray-haired Bob Seger look-alikes with a fresh group of dark-haired Bob Seger look-alikes. (Seger, in his middle age, put on weight, cut his hair, and began wearing wire-framed glasses, which made him look *exactly* like a UAW retiree. This allowed him to perform "Makin' Thunderbirds" with a straight face, even though he was from Ann Arbor—the least-blue-collar city in Michigan—and had never operated a machine more complicated than a microphone.) By 1992, the average autoworker was forty-six years old, which meant an approximate hire date of 1966. When GM began hiring again, it allowed every worker to recommend one applicant. This meant, of course, that the $20+/hour shop jobs became the inheritance of a working-class aristocracy.

At roughly the same age Don Cooper had built his house on three acres, I was earning $4.25 an hour at Video to Go.

A year before, the video store manager would have looked at my résumé (B.A. English, Michigan State University) and asked, "Why would someone like you want a job like this?" But this was the fall of 1991, and it was understood that these were desperate times. And desperate men were desperate to shelve copies of *City Slickers*.

I quit the video store after the manager accused me of treating the job as a joke. After that, I stood beside a conveyor belt, separating trash at a recycling plant; canvassed for the city directory; hoisted cinder blocks at a cement factory; and delivered windshields. At least I could tell my parents and friends, "There are no jobs out there," and receive a sympathetic reply. If I had tried that dodge in 1966, I would have heard "[Fill in any business in the Yellow Pages] is hiring. Go down there and help build the Great Society." In the sixties, there was so much work that the hippies had to construct an alternate system of morality to justify their indolence. "I'm not going to work to support a system that's carrying on an immoral war in Vietnam and pigs blah Mao blah." Back in the hippie days, being too lazy to get a job was intellectually rigorous. (This was the difference between a Generation X-er in San Francisco and a

Generation X-er in Michigan. They felt they'd been born too late for the Sexual Revolution. We felt we'd been born too late for the Industrial Revolution.)

In spite of the auto industry's decline, young people could still find assembly-line work in Michigan. It had nothing to do with cars, though. During my summer as a minimum-wage jerk-of-all-trades, I answered a newspaper ad for "assemblers" and ended up putting together Easter fruit baskets for Meijer, the supermarket chain. Some of my co-workers had serious experience working on the line. My supervisor had been laid off from a factory. He was building baskets because "it beats watching soap operas." The guy who wrapped the baskets in cellophane was an ex–Oldsmobile shop rat who had lost his job when he refused a transfer to GM's Saturn plant in Tennessee.

"In Lansing, they give you just enough to get by," complained a friend of mine who drove a forklift. "Enough to live on, but not enough to save and move on to something better."

That summer, I finally came to the conclusion that eventually strikes every son of a dying town: life is elsewhere.

Before I left, General Motors gave me another reason to go. In 1991, the company lost $4.5 billion, the reddest year for any corporation in American history. As a result, GM would have to close eleven more plants. The biggest would be in either Arlington, Texas, or Willow Run, Michigan. The Willow Run plant had been constructed during World War II by Henry Ford, to build B-24 Liberator bombers. More than any other industrial facility, Willow Run had contributed to Michigan's title as the Arsenal of Democracy. GM bought the plant, and now four thousand workers built Buicks, Chevrolets, and Oldsmobiles there.

GM closed Willow Run. The workers in Texas were willing to accept ten-hour shifts, which meant lower overtime costs. It was rumored that President Bush had lobbied GM's chairman, promising to push for the North American Free Trade Agreement if his home state's plant stayed open. Every plant GM closed was in the Rust Belt. Moraine, Ohio, lost an engine plant to Mexico. Danville, Illinois, lost a foundry; Tarrytown, New York, lost 3,456 jobs building Chevy Luminas, Pontiac Trans Sports, and Oldsmobile Silhouettes; Flint lost a V-8 engine plant that employed 4,000 workers.

When the workers at Willow Run heard the announcement from a GM executive, they threw coffee cups at the stage and cursed out the messenger in the suit and tie.

"There was no way I could work," said a thirty-four-year-old auto-worker who'd gotten his job in 1977, the last of the salad years. "It was just like somebody just ripped my heart out. Maybe I should go work for the Japanese. They're the ones with the smart management."

But the quote I never forgot was an epitaph written by a columnist for the *Detroit Free Press*. The Michigan Way of Life—boats! Cottages! Waterbeds! Motorcycles! Painted vans! Florida vacations! Deer hunting trips! Durable marriages!—had been based on the fact that a young man could get a job in an auto plant and keep that job for thirty years or until his body gave out, whichever came first. After Willow Run, a newspaperman dismissed that dream with three words:

"It is over."

9.

The Smell of Money

Decatur, Illinois, sweetens the world. If, in the past thirty-five years, you've drunk a 7UP, a Dr Pepper, a grape Nehi, a Squirt, a Pepsi, or an Orange Crush, you know the cloying taste of the high-fructose corn syrup produced by the A. E. Staley Manufacturing Company, which is to Decatur what Ford is to Detroit, what Harley-Davidson is to Milwaukee, what John Deere is to Moline. The city and the company are inseparable. When, in 1920, Decatur fielded a franchise in the new National Football League (an outfit founded in the broken-nose towns of the industrial Midwest), it was nicknamed the Staleys and coached by a Staley employee, George Halas. The Staleys won their first game, 20–0, over the Moline Tractors, won that fall's professional football championship, then moved upstate to Chicago, where they were renamed the Bears. Drive into Decatur on one of the four-lane prairie highways that approach the city from every cardinal and ordinal direction, making it the focus of a cats' cradle of asphalt, and you'll pass signs that proclaim, "Pride of the Prairie" and "Original Home of the Chicago Bears." A sugar substitute and a football team are Decatur's contributions to American culture.

The process that produces such sweetness, however, also generates a starchy aroma that is the chief olfactory sensation on the east side of Decatur, where the Staley factory, a smoky puzzle of pipes and chimneys, unfurls its banners of steam. The odor is as inescapable as the weather, and as various. On fair days, it smells like a toasting corn flake; on foul, like a lump of falafel burning in the oven. You can leave Decatur, but the smell goes with you, clinging to the cilia of your nostrils. When visitors or newcomers mention the stench to a native, they receive a defensive response—"That smells like money to some people," or "I just say it's someone's bread and butter and let it go at that." The words are spoken in tones that make the outsider understand that mentioning the smell is as uncalled for as asking about the heritage of a teenage daughter's baby, or about a son's unexpected return from basic training. Some things should be discussed only by family. Academic studies have found that Decatur's children suffer high rates of asthma, but those studies do not appear in the local newspaper, the *Herald & Review*.

Decatur's other pungent industrial concern is the Archer Daniels Midland Company. ADM was for decades dominated by Dwayne Andreas, a tiny millionaire who moved his company from Minneapolis to Decatur because in addition to its corn, it is also the Soybean Capital of the World. (The radio station is named WSOY, the Soy Capital Bank is the town's lending leader, and on Eldorado Street, pronounced *El-duh-RAY-do* by settlers who had only read about the Mexican War in a newspaper, is the Soy City Motel.) Were there knighthoods in America, Andreas would have been dubbed Sir Dwayne. One of America's most effulgent political donors, he has vacationed in Florida with Thomas Dewey, Hubert Humphrey, Bob Dole, and Tip O'Neill. At his mansion on a bluff above Lake Decatur (actually a dammed-up bend of the Sangamon River), he entertained even more powerful company: Mikhail Gorbachev. Near the end of his Soviet leadership, when the USSR had become everything George Orwell predicted in *Animal Farm*, the world's leading Communist slept under the same roof as Decatur's leading capitalist.

Lairds such as Andreas can only exist atop peasant societies. Decatur is a city without a middle class. When I moved to Decatur in the early 1990s, to take a job as a newspaper reporter, there was Sir Dwayne, a crust of white-collar lieutenants who lived in Frank Lloyd Wright Prairie houses and belonged to the Decatur Country Club, and below them, a vast proletariat. In the neighborhood between the corn and soy processing plants were square bungalows, jacketed against the elements in aluminum siding. Rottweilers and dirty-maned chows patrolled behind cyclone fences, barking hammering alarms whenever a rare pedestrian passed along the dirt shoulder of the street. The chain-link fences enclosing the yards were hung with sullenly humorous signs: "THIS PROPERTY GUARDED BY WORLD'S MEANEST ATTACK DOG," or for those allergic to pets: "PROPERTY INSURED BY SMITH & WESSON." In the driveways were plastic tricycles, tyke-sized BMX bikes lying on their sides, pickup trucks carrying smoke-windowed caps on their backs, Camaros and Firebirds from model years past.

Decatur is either the southernmost Northern city in America or the northernmost Southern city. As an industrial town, connected economically to Chicago and its soybean-trading pits, Decatur is part of the Rust Belt. But most of its industrial workers have roots in Southern Illinois (the whites) or Brownsville, Tennessee, (the blacks), which makes it part of the Bible Belt. Wednesdays were church nights. A "cookie patrol" picketed downtown's only adult bookstore, handing out wholesome baked goods to horny men. According to the "Letters" page of the *Herald & Review*, Scripture both prohibited interracial marriage and required gun ownership. Although Abraham Lincoln's first Illinois cabin was just outside Decatur, the city's racial structure had been imported from the South as well. Few whites were outspokenly racist, but racial epithets had not disappeared from conversation. More common were expressions such as those of an old police sergeant who lamented, "They just have a different culture, that's all." Closely linked to their roots, Decatur's blacks never developed a professional elite, unlike Chicago's. Barbecue wagons sold ribs and chicken on street corners every summer. Old men fished in gravel pits, sitting on overturned buckets. A twenty-one-year-old woman without a baby was an old maid.

Decatur was the most urban farm town or the most rural metropolis. The countryside didn't serve the city, the city served the countryside, converting its crop to corn syrup, table syrup, cornstarch, animal feed, ethanol, and soybean oil. In the summers, Decatur teenagers "walked beans," pulling weeds from between the rows of soybean plants that look like overgrown clover, fluttering in the unbroken prairie wind. (Central Illinois is so flat and so farmed-over that the landscape is a map of itself. You find your way to the next village by driving toward the grain elevators shining above the dirt horizon.)

In 1902, a Baltimore starch manufacturer named Augustus Eugene Staley was induced to buy a factory in Central Illinois with the promise that "all the corn you'll ever need is within seventy-five miles of Decatur." Staley handed the business—and the brick mansion he'd built in the middle of Decatur—to his son A. E. Jr. The paternalistic heir believed that one of his company's raisons d'être was providing jobs for Decaturites, even during hard times. Once, the story goes, Gus Jr. saw a tramp walking past the factory. Grabbing a broom, he hurried outside and hired the man to sweep floors.

"I knew A. E. Staley Jr. personally," said Mike Griffin, who worked twenty-eight years in the Staley plant. "He was a decent person. Mr. Staley regarded it as his responsibility to keep Decatur employed."

A.E. Jr. gave Griffin a job. Griffin was a coal miner's son from Kincaid, Illinois. His grandfather had been involved in the Mine Wars of the 1920s, when striking miners killed 19 strikebreakers in Herrin, 150 miles south of Decatur, in the region of the state known as Little Egypt. The perpetrators of the Herrin Massacre were acquitted by sympathetic local juries—how else was a family man supposed to treat a scab who had taken his job? Griffin's brother worked in the mines, but Mike didn't want to go down there himself. A man lost his identity in that hole. In a family portrait of four generations of Griffins, standing outside the opening of the Pawnee Mine in Kincaid, the faces were so black it was impossible to tell great-grandfather from grandfather from father from son. After dropping out of high school, Griffin joined the marine corps, which sent him to Vietnam in 1965. Returning stateside a year later, Griffin got engaged to a woman he'd met at Camp Lejeune, so he needed a job. His stepmother's brother-in-law knew someone at Staley, "and they hired [him], partially because [he] was a veteran."

Since Staley believed in doing its own maintenance, rather than jobbing out to a nonunion company, Griffin apprenticed as a millwright, getting the education he had not been provided in a mining town or the marine corps. He learned mathematics, blueprint reading, and drafting at Richland Community College, a campus surrounded by a soybean field and within Staley's radius of olfactory influence, at least when the wind was blowing north.

Four years after Griffin joined Staley, his union, Allied Industrial Workers Local 837, walked out for eighty-two days when Staley demanded it give up the right to strike over grievances and instead submit to binding arbitration. The union surrendered, and seven workers were fired for sabotaging company property along the picket line, but most of the survivors didn't take the defeat personally.

"They were tough," Griffin said, "but you could work things out."

To Griffin, the relationship between the A. E. Staley Manufacturing Co. and its hometown began to lose its sentimental feeling when A. E. Jr.'s health failed and none of his sons would take over the family business. Instead, the heir was a company attorney who merged Staley with Continental Foods, moved the headquarters to a suburb of Chicago, and outsourced packaging of consumer products. Instead of leaving Decatur in bottles and table jugs, Staley syrup left in fifty-five-gallon drums and tank cars for Chicago, where the company could hire low-wage immigrants to bottle it.

In 1988, Staley was purchased by the British sugar conglomerate Tate

& Lyle, which had built a fortune on Caribbean cane plantations. While the company's business interests had matured since then—by the time it took over Staley, Tate & Lyle was the world's largest sugar manufacturer, with interests in shipbuilding, finance, insurance, and rum—its attitude toward labor had not.

Staley's workers began to sour on Tate & Lyle after the death of a maintenance engineer named Jim Beals, who suffocated when propylene oxide filled a cornstarch processing tank he was repairing. The fatal gas leaked into the tank from a reactor that was supposed to have been shut down during maintenance. There were two reactors in the starch building. The old rule had been that whenever one was under repair, both had to be idled to prevent an exchange of chemicals. When Beals and his co-workers pointed out the safety regulation, the supervisor told them, "We don't need to shut that down. Those reactors are separate. We can isolate this one from the other one and do the work."

At the time, the president of Local 837 was Dave Watts, a carpenter who was as broad, gruff, and industrious as a *Lord of the Rings* dwarf. Watts's mustache, its black and white whiskers an illustration of middle age's tensions, traced a tight frown on his square, rubicund face. Like Griffin, Watts was a Vietnam veteran who had been hired right out of service. He'd been elected president because the union's contract was expiring in 1992 and the members thought he was just the hard-ass to stand up to their new British overlords.

"Let's get one thing straight," the bargaining committee was told at the first meeting of its first contract negotiations with Tate & Lyle, "we're not running a welfare operation here."

Computerization had made many union jobs obsolete. Tate & Lyle didn't need 750 people to read gauges and twist valves and, unlike the Staleys, wasn't motivated to pay them for the good of Decatur. During the negotiations, Tate & Lyle insisted the union give up its eight-hour day and instead work twelve-hour rotating shifts: three days on, three days off, switching from days to nights after a month, then back to days the following month. To Watts, that was a nonnegotiable demand. The eight-hour workday was the founding principle of the labor movement. Giving it up would cost his members thousands of dollars a year in salary and disrupt their family lives by forcing them onto a schedule eccentric from the nine-to-five, Monday-through-Friday world.

Watts believed Tate & Lyle was trying to provoke a strike. Unlike an auto parts plant, or a paper cup factory, Staley couldn't get rid of its union by moving to Alabama or Mexico. Staley processed corn and soybeans, and Decatur was the capital city of a fecund prairie. Staley couldn't take the corn to the Third World. Watts didn't want to strike, because a strike would allow Tate & Lyle to hire scabs. In late 1992, after the union voted to reject Tate & Lyle's offer, the company simply imposed a contract that required all plant employees to work rotating shifts. After consulting with labor experts, Watts devised a strategy to force negotiations by slowing down production. The scheme was called "working to rule," and it took advantage of the new managers' unfamiliarity with the Staley plant by stipulating that workers would only perform tasks directly ordered by a supervisor. Since the union was working without a contract, it was up to the frontline bosses to define the workers' duties.

"If I was running the air compressors, if I saw the air pressure start to drop in the plant, do we need another air compressor on?" explained Art Dhermy, who worked in the co-generation plant, which provided power for the entire factory. "I'd wait for management to notice and order me to turn one on. What we were trying to do with the work-to-rule was to show them, without us, product doesn't get out."

The co-generation plant had been working rotating shifts for four years, so Dhermy knew what his union brothers and sisters were in for. The hardest part was doing "the turn" from day to night or night to day. It was like recovering from jet lag once a month. If Dhermy was going from days to nights, he would stay up a little later every evening, to adjust to the six P.M.–six A.M. schedule. Going from nights to days was more difficult. The first morning off, he'd set his alarm for three hours' sleep, then spend his first day off "like a zombie," so exhausted he had to go to sleep early. With their new three-day weeks and three-day weekends, workers were forced to stop coaching Little League and drop out of bowling leagues. They could no longer attend church every Sunday or watch their children's basketball games. They were also working 120 hours more each year, while earning $8,000 less. In a *Herald & Review* article on rotating shifts, Mike Griffin complained that the hours were "ruining [his] sex life."

The new schedule and the new salary made the workforce cranky. Passive resistance gave way to militancy. On lunch breaks, workers marched through the plant singing "Solidarity Forever." Company-issued walkie-talkies became an in-plant radio network of union news and inspirational oratory, with workers reciting passages from Martin Luther King's "I Have a Dream" speech. The *Midnight Express*, a newsletter exposing safety violations and incompetent managers, was secretly passed around the plant. Whenever a union member was reprimanded, a fellow worker blew a whistle and the entire department followed him into the boss's office. Tate & Lyle tried to improve morale with birthday cakes. On Mike Griffin's birthday, he told his department, "I better not see one of youse eatin' this friggin' cake. You know what they're doing. If you want to be a whore, go get a street corner, but don't do it here." Then he threw his cake in the trash.

Profane and unreconstructed, a unionist born into a legacy of labor violence and blooded in Vietnam, Griffin transferred his enmity toward coal-mining scabs and the Vietcong to Staley management and the American professional class in general. To the union, he transferred the loyalty he had learned in the marine corps: never abandon a comrade. As a shop steward, he sent grievances directly to the chief executive officer, Larry Pillard, and organized two-hour grievance hearings involving the entire night maintenance crew. Griffin was fired in the spring, accused of allowing a co-worker to fall into a hole by not covering it properly. The real reason, he said: "I was a pain in their ass." The next day, he began picketing the plant, hoisting signs that read "I'M A VICTIM OF CORPORATE GREED" and "I'M A VICTIM OF LARRY PIL-LARD AND HIS LIMEY BOOTLICKERS."

Dan Lane, another Vietnam veteran turned union militant, was fired for taking a supervisor's order too literally: directed to remove all union signs from the plant, he sawed the Allied Industrial Workers logo off a plywood placard displaying Staley's partners.

The work-to-rule campaign was effective in slowing down production—the Staley plant was processing 80,000 to 90,000 bushels of corn a day, compared to its usual 140,000—but Tate & Lyle still refused to negotiate. In late spring, the entire workforce walked off the job for 32 hours over a burned-out lightbulb.

A few weeks earlier, chlorine bleach had spilled inside the plant. The workers decided to respond to the next health-threatening incident with a "safety stand-down"—a plant-wide walkout to the union hall, where they would hold a meeting to discuss the problem. The burned-out bulb was it. The incident began when a production worker was ordered to change the bulb. Following the work-to-rule principle, he refused, pointing out that company policy required an electrician to do the job. Instructed to write a work order for an electrician, the worker refused. According to the company safety manual, only management could write a safety work order. The standoff lasted several hours. Finally, the worker was told, "You're going home."

A signal went out over the in-plant radio: "Code Bronco P-3"—a fellow worker was about to be fired. The man who broadcast that message was fired, for "improper use of company property."

The day shift abandoned the plant. Instead of reporting to work, the night shift reported to the union hall.

The next morning at six A.M., the workers were back at the plant gates—but they didn't go inside. Instead they held a rally—unionists and their families, a thousand strong, wearing red shirts, the livid color of labor rebellion, going all the way back to the Paris Commune—marching in circles, chanting, "Union!" and "Solidarity!" At seven A.M., the start time *before* Tate & Lyle imposed their b.s. contract, the day-shift workers tried to reenter the plant. They were told to go home, because they'd reported to work an hour late. Management tried to force every worker to sign the rejected contract before returning to the plant. The workers refused, pointing out that the National Labor Relations Act prohibits employers from bypassing the union by bargaining directly with employees. At six P.M., the night shift was allowed back into the plant. But the truce lasted only eight days.

It has been said (by Jean-Paul Sartre, although it seems strange to quote a French existentialist philosopher in a story about labor strife on the Illinois prairie) that three o'clock is both too late and too early to do anything interesting. At three in the morning, on Sunday, June 27, 1993, the quietest of the week's 168 hours in a churchgoing city, a mechanic was summoned to Staley's dry starch department for what his supervisor promised would be a "real quick" five-minute job. When the mechanic arrived, he was told, "You are going to be locked out. I will escort you to your locker. You will get your personal belongings, but you will not shower or change your clothes. I will escort you to the gate or a holding area."

Watts was awoken by a knock on the door from the shift's shop steward.

"What do we do?" the man asked.

"Get everybody to the union hall," Watts ordered.

At dawn, Watts climbed atop a van, lifted a bullhorn to his mouth, and addressed an outdoor rally. The picketing began that morning, outside the Staley headquarters, a ten-story ziggurat that was the lone vertical monument on Eldorado Street, a.k.a. the Levee, the main drag of Decatur's blue-collar east side, notable also for the Soy City Motel, Mister Donut, and several taverns.

That summer, the picket line became another Eldorado Street land-mark. On Lockout Day, a yellow line was drawn across the gate to es-tablish the new boundary between A. E. Staley and the Allied Industrial Workers. It codified in paint the union's exile. On the narrow curb be-tween the line and the Levee, picketers set up an American flag and this handwritten sign: "AIW 837 LOCKED OUT." The settlement grew to include a wooden shelter, with the placard "GOD SAVE THE QUEEN FROM HER GREEDY RUTHLESS BUSINESSMAN" bolted to an outer wall. The shelter was mounted on wheels and shifted back and forth six inches each hour, to comply with a local ordinance banning permanent structures from the public right-of-way. Every evening, the Solidarity Car, a junky sedan spray-painted with labor slogans, cruised up and down Eldorado, honking its single emboldening note over and over again.

Picket headquarters was across the street and behind a dirt parking lot in a brick garage labeled "War Room." On a company calendar that marked the days of the lockout, "A. E. Staley Mfg. Company" had been scribbled out with a pencil. Written underneath, in thick red marker, was "TAKE & LIE," the postlockout variation of Tate & Lyle. Nobody referred to the company as Staley anymore. Staley had died with A.E. Jr. Tate & Lyle was a cruel and brutal stepfather who'd moved into the house and demanded to be called "Dad."

I first visited the picket line after the Fourth of July. It was high sum-mer. The prairie sky—a blue hemisphere in that flat, treeless country— was the backdrop for a few transparent clouds that looked like chalk marks from beaten erasers. The lockout still felt like a vacation. Larry Pearse, a skinny, mustached man in a baseball cap and a polo shirt, was on the three P.M.–to–seven P.M. shift with picket partner Buzz Glasco. Three hours to go, according to Pearse's digital watch.

"You can always tell the day Buzz walks picket," he said, nodding at a constellation of sunflower seeds on the asphalt.

Glasco raked his thick fingers through a family-sized bag of seeds, picked out the meat with his teeth, and spit out the shells—always to-ward the road. To spit toward the plant, regardless of his sentiment to-ward Tate & Lyle, would have projected a strand of his union-affiliated DNA across the yellow line, which would have constituted trespassing. The law regarding private property was subordinate to the First Amend-ment, however. Whenever a heavyset female guard marched military-style along the line, picketers called out, "Miss America!" and tried to bait her with a Twinkie hooked to fishing pole.

"We spend so much time out here in the sun, we're thinking of holding a tanning contest," said Glasco, inspecting arms the color of roasted chicken. "I'll tell you what: this is the best tan I've had in twenty years. May not win, but it's the best."

A pickup truck with a Clinton/Gore sticker rolled past. Pearse and Glasco lifted their hands in unison, as though they were marionettes on the strings of the same puppeteer. A middle-aged man on a bicycle pantomimed honking as he pedaled past.

The picketers had been pelted with cigarette butts. They had been sworn at and flipped the bird. A kid in a pickup truck screamed, "I'm going to get your job!" On the other hand, the afternoon shifts from Hardee's and Kentucky Fried Chicken had delivered leftovers. Strangers offered hot coffee and soft drinks. On a rainy afternoon, a man pulled up to the curb and asked, "Do you guys need umbrellas?"

At five o'clock, a group of union boilermakers returned from a day of work repairing the co-generation plant. As their cars crossed the Yellow Line onto Eldorado, a few waved sheepishly, but most averted their eyes. Crossing the picket line was a trial for members of other unions. In the first days of the lockout, a trucker showed up at the War Room in a quandary.

"I'm a union truck driver, I can't cross," he said to the picketers. "What do I do?"

A call to his office resulted in an ultimatum: cross the line or clean out your locker. The trucker went to lunch to think it over. An hour later, he regretfully drove through the gates. The picketers understood. The man had a contract, a job to do, probably a house, a wife, a son, a daughter.

Picket duty was four hours a week; picket pay was $60. After the lockout, Tate & Lyle refunded the workers' final health insurance premiums. The same coverage the company had provided for $25 now cost $325. Tate & Lyle was also fighting the workers' unemployment claims. Already, the suddenly unemployed were canceling their cable and newspaper subscriptions, cutting off their phones, cutting each others' hair or letting it grow long, now that they didn't have to go to work. For $15, you could buy $50 worth of groceries from Catholic Charities: fresh meat, vegetables, and fruit. If you were already poorer than proud, Second Harvest gave away canned goods, and trucks arrived at the AIW hall with donations from unions all over the Midwest. Everyone stopped drinking Pepsi, not because it was expensive but because it was sweetened with Staley corn syrup. The fact that store brands or Kool-Aid were cheaper was simply a pecuniary benefit of a principled boycott.

Pearse, who was forty-seven, had spent more than half his life at Staley. He had been planning to retire when he was fifty-five, to become a rare-coin dealer. The lockout had not only given him the time to pursue the new business, it had made that pursuit a financial imperative: the following week, he would be taking his collection to the American Numismatic Association convention in Baltimore. There, he would attempt to sell coins he had once considered precious but whose economic value was now more consequential than their sentimental value. The coins were nothing but money now.

"I've had things that I've put back for a number of years that I'm wiping the cobwebs off of," he said. "They're not as important as they were a year ago."

"I'm probably a little more prepared for this than the rest of 'em," Glasco said. "If it goes on past November, yeah, I'd probably have to tighten my belt a little bit."

If it went on past November, the pickets would go on, too.

"If we left things," said Pearse, "that would be like a soldier leaving the Tomb of the Unknown Soldier. It'd be an abomination."

DAVE WATTS KNEW his little union local in Decatur, Illinois, had little chance of defeating a multinational sugar corporation with headquarters in London. Watts had only eight hundred members, diminished from twelve hundred when he had been elected to the presidency, due to retirements and outsourcing of maintenance jobs. Watts had less money in his strike fund than Tate & Lyle's chairman, Sir Neil Shaw, earned in a month. Had Watts been thinking purely as a negotiator, he might simply have tried to negotiate the best possible exit package for his workers. That was the only area where Tate & Lyle was willing to compromise. But some union—even if it was an undermanned union in an unknown factory town—had to take a stand for labor. What was happening to Watts's workers was only a local iteration of what had been happening to workers all over America since President Reagan had fired the air traffic controllers. In just those dozen years, union membership had declined from twenty million to sixteen million. When Watts had hired in at Staley, 30 percent of American workers had belonged to a union. Now it was 15 percent. The Staley workers had lost wages, health benefits, safety regulations, even the eight-hour day, the labor movement's natal cause. Now the AIW had to let other unions know that they were next.

Mike Griffin had been married for twenty-seven years. Until the lockout, the only nights he and his wife had spent apart were the nights she spent in the hospital giving birth to their three children. After the lockout, Griffin became a Road Warrior, traveling by van to union halls and campuses, telling Decatur's story and screening *Deadly Corn*, a thirty-minute video about the health hazards of rotating shifts and industrial chemicals. The Road Warriors raised $3.5 million for the lockout fund. Griffin could afford to vent his grievances against Tate & Lyle full-time because his children were grown and he had paid off his house, in anticipation of this labor trouble.

A few weeks after the lockout began, Staley began advertising for replacement workers in the *Herald & Review* and a dozen other Midwestern newspapers. To protect the scabs from unionists, the company rented motel rooms and catered meals in the plant. There was, however, no way to get in and out of the plant without passing a picket line. Union members wrote down license plate numbers. At first, they tried shaming the scabs, listing their names on placards, beneath the rubric "SCABS OF THE WEEK."

When shame didn't work, the union tried personal pressure. Decatur is small enough that everyone knew a locked-out worker *and* a scab. Griffin found out that the son of a parishioner at his Baptist church was scabbing. He called the father on the phone.

"My son needs a job," the man protested.

"That's a fine Christian attitude," Griffin retorted.

"This ain't about Christianity. I support my son."

"Well, Darrell," Griffin said, "you and I are no longer friends. If you see me somewhere, don't speak to me."

Most of the locked-out workers were in their forties and fifties—too young to retire, but too old to begin new careers. Hired in the 1960s and '70s, they'd formed a baby-boom blockade against Generation X-ers who were sick of working at Mister Donut and eager to move across Eldorado Street into the plant that offered the best blue-collar wages in Central Illinois. I hung out with an alternative rock band whose bass player and guitarist were both working at Staley.

"Fuck the unions in this town," the bass player said.

So when shame and personal pressure didn't work, the union escalated to intimidation, vandalism, and strong-arming. Compared to the massacres, assassinations, and shoot-outs of late-nineteenth- and early-twentieth-century labor disputes, the Staley lockout was a fistfight. But for cultural, geographic, militaristic, and generational reasons, it was more destructive than most modern-day strikes. Because Staley had hired so many workers between 1965 and 1975, the union was full of Vietnam veterans, who had just reached the age when they were taking over the leadership. Dave Watts was forty-five years old when the lockout started. Their military service made them militant, but the nature of their war added an extra layer of class resentment onto the usual labor-management enmity. They'd fought for their country. Their college-educated antagonists in the Staley corporate offices had been exempted from the draft.

And so trucks drove slowly down country roads past the homes of rural scabs. Bullets were fired through windows. Tires were slashed. Headlights were shattered by cables strung across driveways. Scabs were beaten up. The union's religious allies, especially a friendly Catholic priest, insisted on a policy of nonviolence. Publicly and officially, Watts adhered to that. But to his more belligerent members, he said, "Do what you gotta do; I don't want to know. There are a lot of ugly but necessary things that have to be done, but I don't want to know about them."

The first time I saw a nail jack was at the police station. Due to my low seniority, I was the newspaper's Saturday-night cop reporter. My job was to spend an hour bullshitting with the desk sergeant and maybe get him to read me the crime reports. On one of those evenings, an officer walked into the sergeant's room carrying a paper tray filled with barbed metal objects that looked like tiny steers' horns, joined with a dab of solder. They'd been found in the driveway of a Staley replacement worker.

"What are those?" I asked Sergeant Coventry, who was a year from retirement and could afford to be friendly with a newspaperman.

"Nail jacks," he said. They were designed to penetrate a tire tread. Then he began laughing. "You smell a story, don't you?"

Of course I did. Sergeant Davis, who was built like a Soviet weightlifter and whose nickname was "the Gruffest Man in the World," made it clear he did not want me to write one.

"You're just going to teach people how to make these things," he grumbled. "I don't want that happening in my hometown."

As long as the members of the Allied Industrial Workers had been employed at Staley, the police had considered them upright Americans and even gave them the respect of one blue-collar worker to another. (As much as cops respect anyone who's not a cop.) Now that the millwrights and corn processors were unemployed street protesters, the cops lumped them into the same troublemaking scum as ghetto blacks and chickenshit antiwar marchers. A police officer's job is to preserve order. Naturally, they dislike anyone who makes that difficult. But the cops also resented the AIW because they couldn't form a union themselves and agitate for higher wages or more officers. The cops had a "Policeman's Benevolent" to care for the wives and children of sick and wounded officers.

"If I weren't a police officer, I'd start an antiunion movement in this town," Sergeant Davis said. "They've been using children in their demonstrations. That's putting little kids in danger."

"People said the same thing about Martin Luther King," I said.

"Sheeee-it," Sergeant Davis swore. "Martin Luther King had more class than all the unions in this town put together."

Another sergeant opined on the work ethic of Decatur unionists.

"I know people who used to work in that plant. They'd come in and go to sleep under a box. They'd work two or three hours and then they'd just bag out. I think they're getting everything they deserve there."

On the first anniversary of the lockout, the bad blood between the cops and the union finally turned violent. The labor dispute had dragged on for eighteen months, going back to the work-to-rule campaign. The union needed a dramatic event to persuade its members that the struggle was worth another year of unemployment. Decatur was showing signs of economic distress: two new pawnshops were collecting hunting rifles, necklaces, guitars, bows, wristwatches, and other blue-collar toys. Locked-out workers were openly blackballed in help-wanted ads at employment centers. Companies specified, "Will not consider applicants involved in labor disputes." Dave Watts's wife worked as a nurse at both Decatur hospitals to support the household. Mike Griffin's took a job as a waitress. Art Dhermy's wife owned a cake shop, but it didn't earn enough to make ends meet, so she got a full-time job selling baking equipment while Art baked and frosted the cakes. Still, the Dhermys had to refinance their house, lowering their monthly nut but extending a mortgage they'd been only three years from paying off.

"There was lots of people that lost their homes, lots of divorce, lots of bad medical situations, because the first thing Tate & Lyle done was cancel everybody's health care," Watts said. "If you had a toothache, if you had a health crisis, you were shit out of luck."

For the anniversary demonstration, the union decided to march down Eldorado Street and stage a sit-in at the main gate, blocking trucks and scabs from entering the plant. They would use the tactics of Martin

Luther King and Mohandas Gandhi to temporarily stop corn processing in Central Illinois.

The night before the march, Dan Lane's brother called to tell him he'd heard the union was "going to be taught a lesson." As he dressed in his red solidarity T-shirt on the morning of June 27, Lane expected to get beaten up. By then, he looked like a radical. Since his firing at Staley, Lane had grown a beard—beards were prohibited by Tate & Lyle, and uncomfortable in the humid plant—and wore a bandanna around his lengthening hair. He was beginning to think like a radical, too. Not only had Lane been reading about the civil rights movement, he'd been hearing about it firsthand from black union brothers. They'd never been friends inside the plant, where workers separated into ethnic cliques, but now that they were sharing Road Warrior rides to distant union halls, Lane heard stories of parents denied the right to vote, of uncles and cousins lynched. Having gone straight from high school to Vietnam, where he served from 1965 to 1969, Lane had missed his generation's protest movement. Now, twenty-five years after his peers had chanted antiwar slogans, he had a cause to which he could apply that movement's lessons.

It was hot that day. Ninety degrees. The asphalt was soft and the heavy air stank with the malty odor of roasting corn. Not much shade in the sparsely arbored prairie city, so the day felt like the inside of a glass terrarium. Labor's red line numbered two thousand demonstrators wearing cardboard signs with contradictory rhetoric: "ILLINOIS IS A WAR ZONE" covered one man's chest. But another insisted, "THIS IS NON-VIOLENT CIVIL RESISTANCE." The vanguard banner read "STOP A.E. STALEY COMMUNITY BASHING," but hundreds of union sympathizers had traveled from as far as New York, and all carried signs with their own alphabetical affiliations: URW, USWA, UAW. (Flint's Local 529 was there to share in the militancy. So were UAW workers from Caterpillar, whose Decatur and Peoria plants had walked out as part of a nationwide strike earlier that week.) When the marchers reached the main gate, they were confronted with the yellow line—and beyond it, another line of Decatur police officers, blocking the factory entrance. As the crowd chanted, "Cross that line! Cross that line!" locked-out workers began, one by one, to trespass on their old workplace. Lane was one of the first across. Halting three feet from the police, he turned around and shouted, "Solidarity!" to the crowd, which responded in kind. At one point, Lane was jostled forward and felt a nightstick against his shoulder blade. He sat on the pavement, back still turned to the officers. Moments later, the police unholstered pepper-gas canisters and aimed a stinging aerosol fog at the seated unionists. Lane ducked his head and turned away from the caustic cloud, only to be sprayed from the other side. One officer grabbed a demonstrator, turned him on his back, and sprayed him in the face as though applying Raid to a giant, helpless beetle.

Lane, who had been hoping the police would *join* their march, felt suddenly alienated from the law, from his old employer, from his hometown. "What the hell is going on?" he thought as his face and eyes burned. Around him, demonstrators were pouring cold water onto pepper spray victims, who included a TV reporter and several children. Lane had worked at Staley for twenty years, spent twenty years contributing to the company's profit margin by following orders, trying to be creative, offering suggestions, and now he was sitting outside on the hot asphalt, choking on gas.

"Why are they doing this to me?" he thought. "I've got a family they don't give a crap about. They don't give a crap about me. How can this be happening? Why would you treat somebody like this?"

The union filmed the demonstration and used the footage as propaganda. It was the climactic scene of *Struggle in the Heartland*, a thirty-minute video the Road Warriors began showing at union halls. The union even procured a letter from a Massachusetts police department, accusing the Decatur police of overreacting.

Less than a month after the Eldorado Street march, the workers at Decatur's Bridgestone/Firestone plant went on strike. The company's new Japanese owners—eager to rid themselves of the union they'd been stuck with when they bought the tire company—had demanded rotating shifts, lower wages for new workers, less vacation time, and worker contributions to the health plan. Thus, in the summer of 1994, one out of every fourteen workers in Decatur was involved in a labor dispute. Staley was locked out. Caterpillar was on strike. Firestone was on strike. At Macon County Board meetings, the Democrat who delivered the invocation now included a prayer "for those who are striking and locked out." At Decatur city council meetings, the reminder was more direct: unionists in red T-shirts filled the gallery every week, demanding the city tolerate their pickets.

For Mayor Erik Brechnitz, a conservative stockbroker, the leadership of Strike City, USA, was an ibuprofen headache. His own son was a replacement worker at Staley. When the union discovered this, it began referring to the mayor as "Brezhnev." At the Decatur Celebration, a summer carnival of carousels, elephant cars, and musicians who had retired to Midwestern midways (Tiny Tim; the Mamas and the Papas, with only one original Papa), someone dumped beer on the mayor's white hair. The mayor's Jaguar shattered a headlamp when it ran into a chain stretched across his driveway. The unions bought billboards on all the main roads with the legend "You Are Now Entering A War Zone" bracketed by vines of barbed wire. When distinguished visitors flew into Decatur, city officials plotted roundabout routes from the airport, so their guests wouldn't see the embarrassing messages.

Brechnitz, though, was less contemptuous of the union than most of Decatur's elite (Dwayne Andreas jocularly suggested that the AIW fire its leadership). The labor disputes were bad for his city's image—even the *Wall Street Journal* was writing about the union's Adopt-a-Family program—so Brechnitz secretly tried to negotiate a settlement. His partner was Decatur's congressman, Glenn Poshard. Poshard looked like the Wizard of Oz, down to his fine white mustache, and was either the northernmost Southern Democrat in Congress or the southernmost Northern Democrat. Hailing from the same Bible Belt coal-mining country as many of the Staley workers or their fathers, Poshard had grown up among people who decorated their parlors with three portraits: Jesus Christ, Franklin D. Roosevelt, and John L. Lewis, the one-time Southern Illinois resident who was president of the United Mine Workers of America for forty-one years. In matters of personal morality, he was antiabortion and antihomosexuality. In matters of economic morality, he believed there were few higher acts of patriotism than buying an American product built by a unionized worker. Brechnitz talked to Staley, Poshard talked to the union, and they got together to discuss where each side would give.

Poshard had resisted his own party's campaign to pass the North American Free Trade Agreement; he saw Decatur's labor troubles as the "flashpoint" for a new economic globalism that discarded family and community values in the name of profit. Poshard had also become something of an Anglophobe after dealing with Tate & Lyle and Balfour Beatty, a British firm building a dam on the Ohio River with nonunion labor. Those companies, he believed, were devoted to the financial Darwinism of former prime minister Margaret Thatcher, who had broken the coal-mining unions in England and Wales.

"To me, Decatur was a microcosm of what was sweeping the entire world, with the multinational corporations," he would say much later. "The bottom line was profit, a lot of it was greed, but the sense of community that the old American corporations had developed with the Staleys and so on, it just tore apart, and these guys were struggling not just to keep their jobs but they were struggling to get that sense of community back, to have a company or a corporation that loved and understood and saw it as a complete family. When Tate & Lyle came in there, all of that sense of community, they didn't even want it. I read extensively about the new corporate culture that was coming into the country as a result of the multinationals. Decatur was probably the most prolific example of how that clashed with the America that used to be."

The America that used to be. Decaturites were traditional people. One of their first questions to newcomers was, "Do you have a church home?" The most beloved restaurant in town was a diner that served thirty-six varieties of pie. The most popular nightspot was a club that played 1950s rock and roll. Its parking lot was crowded with hot rods, its dance floor with fifty-year-olds who had outgrown their leather jackets and poodle skirts but wore them anyway. "It's nostalgia for Decatur's heyday," a friend theorized. Indeed, downtown stores sold T-shirts with the label "I remember . . ." beneath photos of vanished Decatur landmarks, such as the Transfer House, where the streetcars changed tracks, or Fans Field, home of the minor-league Decatur Commodores until the city fathers declared it unsafe to host a rock concert, thus giving the San Francisco Giants an excuse to move the team. Conservatives are often accused of a futile nostalgia for the social order of the 1950s, but at least in Decatur, there was also an attempt to maintain the economic order that made such a world possible. Mothers could stay home with the children because their husbands could support a family on union wages. If a girl got in trouble, the boy who'd caused it could hire in at the factory and earn more money than she could collect on welfare.

Decatur was not a progressive city—culturally, it was twenty years behind the rest of America—and there were local leaders who saw the unions' intransigence as a refusal to embrace the modern, global economy.

"They just won't adjust for the new way of doing things," the city manager—a bureaucrat appointed to run Decatur's day-to-day business—told me one night. (Soon after, he fled Decatur to manage a suburb of Detroit.)

The question of who was more progressive, the companies or the unions, depends on your historic framework. If resistance to the new world order had grown out of a desire to avoid returning to the penury of their grandfathers, their great-grandfathers, and the ancestors who had sneaked off the manor in Sussex in the middle of the night to jump ship for America, then the union's conservatism was simply a desire to prevent the return of a more genuine conservatism, in which the many toiled to provide pleasures for the few. Or, as the wife of one locked-out worker put it, "Some people aren't getting what they need so other people can have what they want."

Poshard and Brechnitz made no progress in resolving the lockout. In Poshard's opinion, Tate & Lyle had no interest in negotiating. The company had so much money it could afford to wait until the last worker pawned the last spoon in his kitchen drawer, then crawled across the yellow line, begging to have soup poured into his mouth. Brechnitz thought the company and the union were so far apart they could never settle on a contract.

Poshard expected such disdain from British industrialists. He was more frustrated by the indifference from politicians in his own Democratic Party. When President Bill Clinton gave a speech at Knox College in Galesburg, Illinois, Poshard brought a group of Decatur union leaders to meet with Secretary of Labor Robert Reich. To a room full of workers in danger of losing their jobs and their homes, the Harvard economist gave a nebulous philosophical speech about the relationship between labor and business. Reich never gave a direct answer to any of the workers' questions, nor did he give any indication that the Labor Department would intervene in Decatur's labor disputes. The workers left feeling deflated; Poshard left feeling the meeting had been useless.

"Clinton's got plenty of time for gays in the military, but he doesn't have any time for us," I once heard a worker grumble.

(He was getting at an important historical question. For the past twenty-five years, American politics had been dominated by issues such as busing, affirmative action, women's rights, guns, abortion, prayer in school, and gay rights. The Democratic Party, which since FDR had been the champion of the working stiff, was now dominated by overeducated liberals—like the Clintons—more concerned with protecting the interests of blacks, homosexuals, career women, and pregnant teenagers than the interests of labor. It's the reason the white working class defected to the Republican Party—if the Democrats weren't going to stand up for their right to have a job, at least the Republicans would stand up for their right to carry a gun. But this period during which we stopped talking about economic issues and started talking about social issues is coterminous with America's Great Divergence in financial equality. The Republicans encouraged it, and the Democrats did nothing in response but shift their donor base from unions to socially liberal Wall Street bankers.)

Poshard got another reminder of his rank in the new world order when he and forty anti-NAFTA congressmen tried to meet with Mexico's chief negotiator on the treaty. The man wouldn't see them, but when Poshard attended a meeting at ADM headquarters, he found the Mexican negotiator sitting in Dwayne Andreas's executive suite.

"I just thought at the time, 'What kind of commentary is this on American life?'" Poshard would say. "Forty congressmen who have honest questions about this contract with Mexico can't get an answer even in our nation's capital, but I can go to ADM in Decatur, and the guy's there at their request. It shows you how much power the corporation had at the time. Multinational corporations, they're not loyal to any country. They're loyal to the profit margin that they make, and being an American corporation, or being a British corporation, the loyalty is not even to the community; it's multinational, and they will go wherever they can make the most money, and I don't think that's a complete picture of what a corporation, especially an American corporation, should be."

In the new world order, patriotism was a quaint value, to which only the backward held steadfast.

The governor of Illinois campaigned for reelection in Decatur and told the workers he couldn't help them, either. The governor was a man whose hair could have withstood a Category 3 hurricane, a man who ironed creases in his blue jeans. A shaggy delegation of big-bellied workers ambushed him outside the Macon County Republican headquarters. The governor stood in the eye of the crowd, with his fingers forming a cowcatcher, and repeated the same five words, over and over again: "This is a federal matter. This is a federal matter."

The only politicians who offered any help were the congressman and the mayor. And they couldn't help at all. This was no surprise to Sergeant Davis. In his own night-shift-desk-sergeant argot, he demonstrated that he understood globalization as well as anyone in Congress.

"Shoot," he said. "Do you think the chairman of a company in London cares what the mayor of a podunk town like this has to say? I don't think so."

Editorially, the *Herald & Review* was not sympathetic to the unionists. Our editor wrote opinion pieces lecturing the workers that their "struggle is over" and suggesting that "competitiveness" required them to accept twelve-hour shifts and unlimited subcontracting. Shortly after the lockout began, our publisher refused to run a full-page ad purchased by the Allied Industrial Workers, on the grounds that it libeled Staley. (The newspaper did run a Staley ad, rebutting the union's rhetoric.)

Since the establishment newspaper was hostile, the union began publishing its own strike journal, the *Decatur Free Press*. The *Free Press* was agitprop, on rag newsprint, but it had a sense of humor, born of aggrievement. When Dwayne Andreas won the Horatio Alger Award, given annually to self-made men by the Horatio Alger Association of Distinguished Americans, the *Free Press* invented a series of corollary prizes for its enemies in Staley management: the Horatio Auger Award, for screwing workers; the Horatio Flogger Award, for whipping employees; the Horatio Algae Award, for behaving like pond scum.

The *Free Press* was written and laid out by Mike Griffin and Dan Lane in the same one-room office that housed the Road Warriors' headquarters. It was a clubhouse for the most militant workers, with plank bookshelves supporting heavy volumes of Martin Luther King's speeches and Mohandas Gandhi's writings. I went there to write a story about the *Free Press* (published over the objections of my editor, who said, "We've heard enough from these guys") and then began stopping in regularly, mainly to hear Griffin riff on the Decatur establishment, America's economic system, and working-class pride.

"That publisher of yours, he looks like a giant *pe*-nis," he growled. Central Illinois is Upper Kentucky, so Griffin sounded like a redneck insult comic as he mocked the fact that at the pinnacle of our publisher's six feet four inches was a bald scalp as pink as a thumb. The president of Staley deserved to be "buried with his ass sticking out of the ground so wild dogs can hump him for all eternity." Griffin was mean-spirited, but only toward people with a lot more money and power, so his commentaries were crude satire. His philosophy of class relations, however, was right out of *The Communist Manifesto*.

"The laboring classes and the ownership classes have *nothing* in common," he said. Then, lest I conclude he was a Marxist, he added, "I believe in capitalism, but I believe in *controlled* capitalism."

It was an important distinction in that place and time. As a result of the labor trouble, there were a lot of people in Decatur who *didn't* believe in capitalism. Decatur is an obscure city, even for Central Illinois. Springfield is Lincoln's hometown, Champaign has a Big Ten university, Peoria is the emblem of Middle American squareness. Decatur is unknown outside its own state, which is why Tate & Lyle could bust a union there without drawing the attention of NBC, CBS, ABC, *Time* magazine, the *New York Times*, or the *Guardian*. The "Decatur" dateline was, however, appearing in *People's Weekly World*, *In These Times*, *Labor Times*, and other Old Left publications carrying the torch of the 1890s, 1930s, and 1960s. From Buffalo to Chicago, from Brooklyn to Detroit, word went out on the radical grapevine that Decatur was to the 1990s what Haymarket Square, Homestead, and Flint had been to decades past. Decatur was soon visited by a plague of socialists, who preached revolution to the working classes.

Dave Watts welcomed his new left-wing allies. In their political zeal, they did the grunt work of a union campaign: raising money, making phone calls, licking envelopes, stapling picket signs. There was tension, though, between the factory workers and the middle-class revolutionaries. Even college-educated radicals who took jobs at the Chicago steel mills in the 1970s were derided as "colonizers" by their white, ethnic, working-class linemates. In Decatur, the cultural gap was even wider. The socialists were postmodern urbanites dropped into a rural, traditional community. They were every bit as internationalist and post-Christian as the Thatcherite executives at Tate & Lyle, but they'd chosen the other side in the debate over economic globalization.

"They're not patriotic," one union member observed. "They're not God-fearing."

The first colorful conflict between the socialists and the working stiffs took place when members of the National Women's Rights Organizing Coalition showed up at the UAW hall to lecture striking Caterpillar workers on labor militancy. The young hipsters from Michigan and New York wore oversized flannel shirts (this was the autumn of 1994), safety pins in their noses, and hair dyed in hues that look natural only on lizards or tropical birds. The travelers handed out fliers encouraging workers to take over their unions and practice "mass militant picketing." Seeing this as an incitement to violence, the unionists tried to guide the radicals off the grounds, but the kids refused to leave.

"Go ahead," one shouted. "Let your union bureaucrats sell out, and you follow. Let the union bureaucrats lead you to your death."

Then UAW members threatened to call the cops.

"The same police that gassed you this summer," a radical spat back.

They were finally allowed to stay, with the understanding they could hand their literature only to workers who expressed an interest in reading it.

Then there was the evening a Cuban woman spoke at the AIW hall. While a socialist translated, she described how her country had suffered from the American embargo. The speech was intended as a lesson in worldwide class solidarity. Before it began, a thin, pretty, long-haired socialist sat down beside me and asked how much I knew about the embargo. She was trying to educate me, I suppose. Me and everyone else in Decatur. The guest speaker did not go over well with one of union wives, who thought it was Communist indoctrination. Like all the baby boomers in the room, she'd grown up with the Cold War, which had ended just five years earlier.

"I still remember the Cuban Missile Crisis," the union wife said sharply. "We all thought we were going to get blown up. I'm not ready to forgive Fidel Castro for that."

Almost every day, Watts had to tell one of his members, look, forget about the fact that these people dress like folksingers or refuse to eat meat or won't say the Pledge of Allegiance. They're getting our message out across the country. Stay focused on that.

"A lot of that radical stuff turned me off, because that's not the kind of guy I was brought up and raised to be," Watts said. "Some people, that's their mentality, but it wasn't mine. Even worse, though, was the everyday plant worker that wasn't strong union, that just worked every day, raised in the Midwest, and would go to church, all of that stuff really turned them off, made 'em afraid, and took them out of the fight, rather than drew them in. It wasn't their kind of people. 'That's not what I want to be, that's not the way I want to act, that's not how I want to look.' Most union organizations, whenever there's an outsider, they shun them away. We opened the floodgates. That was my motto, my goal, and my desire. We need the resources, we need the people, and we need to know something. And I didn't care if you were walking in the door a socialist, or walking in the door a Communist. If you had experience, come on in."

Decatur didn't exactly meet the socialists' cultural needs, either. The only bookstore was a Waldenbooks at a shopping mall. You had to drive forty miles to Champaign to see a movie that didn't star Tom Hanks, Julia Roberts, or Clint Eastwood. The socialists didn't go to church, didn't hunt, didn't fish, and didn't attend classic-car rallies.

"It's not a college town, so it's rather dull," a socialist told me when I tried to interview him for the newspaper. Then he added, "Can you not quote me? We don't want people to know we're here."

Despite their aversion to Decatur, one of the socialists ran for mayor. Although she didn't meet the residency requirement, having lived in Decatur for less than a year, she received four write-in votes nonetheless.

In that same election, Watts ran for Decatur city council. One of his TV ads referred to a magazine article that had named Decatur one of the four worst cities for young people. I cannot remember the name of the magazine, but I remember exactly what it said about Decatur: "Classic Rust Belter three and a half hours from the nearest happening city." (That same month, another magazine came out with the ten worst jobs for young people. Newspaper reporter led the list, illustrated by *Seinfeld*'s Michael Richards hunched over a typewriter. As a twenty-eight-year-old newspaper reporter in Decatur, I began questioning my life's course.) Watts made the runoff but finished fifth among six candidates in the general election. His campaign to bring labor militancy to city hall was popular only in the factory-rat precincts of the smoky, industrial east side. Even the Democratic politicians shunned him as a one-issue candidate. "They'd say, 'You're doing the right thing, I'm proud of you, but I can't support you.'" Mayor Brechnitz quit as a result of the labor strife and was replaced by a union-backed candidate. As a souvenir of his public life, Brechnitz framed a photo of himself with his back turned toward a group of red-shirted union gauleiters. His arms were folded, his mouth pulled down at each corner. It illustrated Decatur's class estrangement.

The Miller Brewing Co. stopped buying high-fructose corn syrup from Staley when its three-year contract expired at the beginning of 1995. Factory work inspires a lot of drinking, and enough union halls unscrewed their High Life taps to convince Miller that its beer was making Milwaukee infamous in the labor movement. Even though Miller accounted for 11 percent of Staley's sales, losing that contract did not convince the bosses to negotiate. So the union went after Staley's biggest customer, Pepsi. At Chicago's most visited tourist attraction, Navy Pier, the union's local supporters climbed up on the roof and unfurled a banner over the entrance, while wearing T-shirts that read "Pepsi Destroys Decatur Families."

Dan Lane had been radicalized by the tear-gassing outside Staley's main gate. The pepper spray had permanently burned away a patch of skin on his face; he could feel it sting when he stood in the sun or when he exercised. Lane was growing his hair and wearing a bandanna, just like the hippies he'd been so shocked to see when he came home from 'Nam. Pepsi, Lane realized, might determine the winner of Decatur's labor dispute. Convincing Coke and Pepsi to replace sugar with corn syrup had made Staley worth buying in the first place. If Staley held on to Pepsi, it would have fuck-you money until the great-grandchildren of the locked-out workers were old enough to walk a picket line. If Staley lost Pepsi, it would turn into a money-leeching lamprey on the corporate body of Tate & Lyle. To draw attention to the boycott and to inspire his union brothers to endure a third year without work, Lane decided to fast. As Gandhi had fasted in India. As Bobby Sands had fasted in Ireland. Before he stopped eating, Lane wrote a letter to Wayne Calloway, CEO of PepsiCo:

> Dear Mr. Calloway,
>
> There is no doubt in my mind that if PepsiCo would withdraw its business, Staley would come to realize the serious consequences of terrorizing our community. It is my family's and my hope that you, sir, will sever all ties with A.E. Staley. Until that time, I will fast . . . The lives of 750 families, including my own, are in your hands.

"During the war, I risked my life when my country called upon me," Lane told his wife and children. "Now I have to risk my life for my union and for the labor movement."

Taking a room at the rectory of St. James Catholic, which was pastored by a priest allied with the locked-out workers, he reduced his diet to juice and broth. Too weak to continue delivering the paper route that provided his only income, Lane lay in bed praying and reading the Bible, John Locke, Ralph Waldo Emerson, and Henry David Thoreau. Even as his strength diminished, he traveled to the AFL-CIO convention in New York, where he made a speech asking all of labor to boycott Pepsi.

"By God," he shouted with as much strength as his drained body could muster, "if I can do without food for sixty days, then you can do without Pepsi! If I can do without food for sixty days, you can do without Frito snacks! If I can do without food for sixty days, you can do without Taco Bell, Pizza Hut, and Kentucky Fried Chicken!"

In response, three thousand unionists chanted, "Boycott! Boycott! Boycott!"

Lane's fast lasted sixty-five days. He ended it only after a personal phone call from AFL-CIO president John Sweeney, who promised the national organization would use all its power to help the Staley workers win a fair contract.

The union's greatest public demonstration was another march down Eldorado Street, on the second anniversary of the lockout. Jesse Jackson finally came down from Chicago, answering years of pleading. The teachers joined that march. The nurses, the ironworkers. The autoworkers. The rubber workers. The Progressive Labor Party. In red T-shirts, white polo shirts, blue denim, each of the five thousand marchers was a stitch in a living banner that carried itself over the viaduct that vaults traffic over the Staley rail yards. At the pinnacle of the arch, a worker stopped to peer through the chain-link fence, down at the tracks stitched into the bald earth.

"Look out here," he said. "You used to be able to see all kinds of people working here. Now it's just a ghost factory. The softball diamond is gone. I lost my pride in working at Staley after the last contract expired. When I hired in, we had two thousand at the union. If we ever go back, it's only going to be three hundred fifty. If they ask me to come back and load corn syrup into tank cars, I don't think I'll do it for long. I can't take those twelve-hour shifts for long."

As they turned the corner onto the Levee, the marchers were a host, blurred by distance, by the heat reflected from the asphalt. The audible vanguard was a blurry beat from a sound truck, resonating off the street at its top register. A gospel diva belted out union hymns with the passion of a singer on strike from the church choir: "Hear that union train a-comin' / We'll be comin' by the thousands / We'll be marching through Decatur."

The chants were unamplified, so it was blocks later before they reached the distant ear.

"We are!" a man shouted, and everyone in the circle of his voice shouted back, "Union!"

Jesse Jackson was in the front rank—where else would Jesse Jackson be?—chanting his assonant rhymes.

"We'll march until victory is won. Say, 'I want to work. I need to work. I need to get paid for the work that I do.' We're marching not for welfare but for fair share."

The march paused for a moment of silence at the main gate, through which the night shift had been led out two years before, where workers had been tear-gassed a year before, then continued to the Civic Center, where Jackson's speech was broadcast to the lawn on loudspeakers.

"The race doesn't go to the swiftest," he said. "It goes to 'hold on.' This struggle is worth our lives. We can hold on just a little while longer."

They could hold on a little while longer, but they couldn't hold on longer than Tate & Lyle. In July, three weeks after Jackson urged forbearance, the union voted down a contract offer that required twelve-hour rotating shifts and did not offer amnesty to workers fired during the work-to-rule campaign, including Lane and Griffin.

"Our members have demonstrated that they are committed to this fight and that we will not allow Staley to starve us into submission," Watts told the press. "We will step up the pressure on Staley by reaching out to our supporters nationwide to continue the efforts against Pepsi."

Nothing, not even a demonstration outside PepsiCo headquarters in Purchase, New York, could break the soft drink company's contract with Staley. That December, though, Watts's four-year term as local president expired, and he was defeated for reelection by a rival who promised to "end this within a week of taking office." It ended even sooner than that. A week and a half after voting out Watts, the workers voted to accept a contract with rotating shifts and only 350 union jobs—fewer than half the workers who'd been marched out of the plant three and a half years before. Everyone else got a severance check—up to $30,000 for thirty years.

On Main Street, a union household's yard had displayed a wooden sign that kept score of the lockout's length with numbered boards, hung from pegs. The tally ended at 908 days. Just as Watts had feared, the union lost.

"The last six months, there was a lot of dissenting going on in the membership," Watts said. "It was because they're tired, they're broke, their cars are gone, some of 'em lost their house, some divorced. Everybody's not seeing an end to this thing. I was committed to go on as long as it took, but we didn't have the deep pockets of these corporations, the support of the city council and all of the organizations that are antilabor. The chance of little old Decatur coming out on top of this thing, it was the David-and-Goliath situation."

Of the four Staley workers I knew best and about whom I have written in this chapter, only Art Dhermy went back to work at Staley. When Dhermy returned to work, in February 1996, he went through a three-day orientation, during which he was told he would be fired if he ever used the word "scab" in the plant. Of those 350 union jobs, only 147 were filled by veterans of the lockout. The rest went to workers who had replaced them during the labor dispute.

"Those things will not be tolerated," a manager warned Dhermy, even though Dhermy had been careful not to cross that linguistic line.

"What won't be tolerated?" Dhermy asked. If they were threatening to take his job, he wanted the reason spelled out.

"You can't call 'em by that name."

"What name's that?"

The manager refused to say it.

The replacement workers tried to bait Dhermy by addressing each other as "scab," then asking him, "Isn't that what you called us?" He never uttered the "s" word, but he did spit leaf tobacco juice on the boots of those who fit the description.

Even when they finally started showing up at union meetings, Dhermy referred to them as "half brothers" and "half sisters" and joined votes to defeat their motions. (It wasn't "scab" and it wasn't on Staley property, so he was Okay.) Despite getting his job back, Dhermy spent the next decade and a half recovering financially from the lockout. He had spent $8,000 in savings, sold stock he'd been hoarding for retirement, and refinanced his house at a higher rate.

"I'd been planning to retire when I was sixty-one, but I couldn't," he said. "I pretty well got everything paid off that I was in the hole, but the thing is, by getting that paid off, I haven't been able to put anything aside for retirement."

Through the millwrights' union, Mike Griffin found work at factories around the Midwest, including the Caterpillar plant in Peoria and a nuclear power plant in Nebraska. Some of the jobs kept him away from his wife for six weeks at a time. ("I couldn't have stood going back to Staley. I would have choked the piss out of a scab the first day.") Griffin's brother-in-law, a millwright at Firestone, had crossed the picket line during his union's strike. Only death reconciled them. Griffin went to the funeral, out of respect for his sister. During the lockout, he left the Baptist church he had attended for twenty-seven years. Some of the parishioners were executives at Caterpillar and Staley, and as a result, the congregation would not take sides in the lockout. Griffin has not belonged to a church since. A union does the Lord's work.

"I still believe in God," he said. "I still believe in my fellow man. I still believe in the union. I'm union through and through. I'm talking about standing up for my fellow workers and standing up against the boss when he puts you in harm's way, and standing up for the poor."

Needless to say, Griffin hopes that the union president who succeeded Dave Watts is buried with his ass sticking out of the ground, so the wild dogs can hump him for eternity.

Dan Lane divorced his wife, moved to suburban Detroit, and remarried.

When the lockout ended, Dave Watts was forty-eight years old and a grandfather—too old, too much the family man to leave Decatur. Although still officially local president when the contract was approved, he refused to validate it with his signature. An official from the international had to sign. Watts resigned from the company and the union and went to work as a home remodeler. He had to work for himself, because nobody would hire the working-class militant who'd led the Staley lockout. Watts was so bitter about the news coverage of the lockout that he stopped listening to WSOY, canceled his subscription to the *Herald & Review*, and even quit attending church because the newspaper's labor reporter served as a lector. Watts was poorer. He'd lost friends. He couldn't find another job. He was taunted on the street. And he'd lost a contract dispute that, he believed, so intimidated the labor movement that Caterpillar and Firestone wouldn't vote to strike even if their wages were cut in half. As part of the campaign to destroy unions, his career and his reputation had been destroyed, as though by a remote missile, to increase the profits of a company six thousand miles away. After the lockout ended, the only part of Dave Watts's life that was better was the most important part.

"It almost cost me my marriage," he said. "She, like all the rest of them, she could see all the pain we were going through trying to fight a losing battle, the loss, the monetary and hope and all those things that were being flushed down the toilet. She said, 'It's time to move on,' long before it was over."

10.

"We're All Going to End Up in Chicago"

W hat did Chicago do right?" a woman from Cleveland once asked me.

In the 1990s, Chicago was the only Midwestern industrial city to gain population—and not just for that decade, but for *any* decade since the middle of the twentieth century. In 1950, Chicago was the second-largest city in the United States, while Cleveland was sixth. By 2010, Chicago was third, but Cleveland was forty-fifth. A young man who arrived in Chicago in the mid-1980s to work as a community organizer among laid-off steelworkers left in 2008 as president-elect of the United States and the representative of a new type of global citizen. Barack Obama, son of a Kenyan father and an American mother, had lived in Honolulu, Jakarta, Los Angeles, and New York, but rose to world power in Chicago. Three years later, Oprah Winfrey, one of the richest, most famous women on the planet, filmed her last talk show at the United Center, a sports arena built for the crowds who wanted to watch Michael Jordan, the most world-renowned athlete since Muhammad Ali, play basketball. In its search for America's best pizza, *GQ* magazine named a storefront pizzeria in Chicago. Chicago's Steppenwolf theater, founded in a church basement by actor Gary Sinise, premiered the play *August: Osage County*, which went on to Broadway and a Pulitzer Prize for its author, Tracy Letts.

Donald Trump built a tower surmounted by a $9 million penthouse in the Loop. Two decades before, the Loop had been a bustling business district by day, but its after-five attractions consisted of block after sketchy block of Italian beef stands, adult bookstores, and dank taverns. The surrounding area is now the fastest-growing neighborhood in Chicago, and two-thirds of its residents have college degrees.

Why, then, did Chicago not fulfill the obituary written for it in 1980? Why did it become an Alpha World City, in the same league as Paris, Mumbai, Shanghai, Frankfurt, and Sydney, while Cleveland became the Mistake on the Lake, and Detroit became *the* destination for European art photographers documenting urban decay?

The woman's real question was, "How can Cleveland imitate Chicago's success?" I had hoped to provide an answer in this chapter, but the answer is "Cleveland can't." Neither can Detroit or Milwaukee or Buffalo or Indianapolis. There can be only one Midwestern metropolis. Chicago's success is not only inimitable, it comes at the expense of every other city in the region.

The North Side of Chicago is such a refuge for young economic migrants from my home state that its nickname is "Michago." At a now-defunct bar called the Gin Mill, a green neon sign flashed "WELCOME TO EAST LANSING" at twenty-two-year-olds who'd used up four years of eligibility in their frat houses but wanted to keep partying. In 2000, a quarter of Michigan State graduates left the state. By 2010, half were leaving, and the city with the most recent graduates was not East Lansing or Detroit but Chicago. Michigan's universities once educated auto executives, engineers, and governors. Now their main purpose is giving Michigan's brightest young people the credential they need to get the hell out of the state. In the 2000s, Michigan dropped from thirtieth to thirty-fifth in percentage of college graduates. Chicago is the drain into which the brains of the Middle West disappear. Moving there is not even an aspiration for ambitious Michiganders. It's the accepted endpoint of one's educational progression: grade school, middle school, high school, college, Chicago, with perhaps a gap year of low-wage slacking between the last two stations. Once, in a Lansing bookstore, I heard a clerk say with a sigh, "We're all going to end up in Chicago." An Iowa governor traveled to Chicago just to beg his state's young people to come home.

Every University of Michigan B.S. who moves to Chicago is one less engineer for Detroit. It's another consequence of globalization, the same force destroying the middle class in Decatur: just as money and education have become concentrated among fewer people, they've become concentrated among fewer cities, too. Chicago is one of the winners.

I met Joe Lambert at a fund-raiser for Young Chicago Lakefront, the youth auxiliary of the 44th Ward Democratic machine. I'd discovered the group during the 2004 presidential campaign, when they'd gathered in a bar to heckle Vice President Cheney's speech. Everyone wore a shining button-down Oxford, everyone gripped a beer bottle as though it were the handle that would keep them from tumbling out the door. They had political jobs, but they were *West Wing* types, all angling to be the next George Stephanopoulos, or the next Rahm Emanuel, who was at that time a congressman, representing Lake View.

A long arm waved from the bar. I remembered Justin. He was a young man from a conservative Dutch Reformed community in Iowa who'd moved to Chicago, announced he was gay, and broken his family's heart by becoming a Democrat.

Justin handed me a business card. He was a spokesman for Governor Rod Blagojevich. In Lake View, coming out was good for your political career. It was the city's gay neighborhood. Halsted Street, the main strip of the Boys' Town district, threw a Pride Parade every summer. The mayor had marched in it. The mayor loved gays. Gays kept up their houses and never moved to the suburbs "for the schools." Even the alderman was gay, appointed for that very quality.

A young aide to the state senator waved a sheaf of tickets.

"The senator is in Springfield next Tuesday, so he's donated his Cubs tickets." The whole bar was paying attention now. In Lake View, a Cubs game is a social coup akin to the opera in Gilded Age New York. "I've got four tickets for anyone who can tell me what the Twenty-Fourth Amendment says."

"Poll tax!" I stabbed.

That was it. The aide came down from the bar and handed me the tickets. I passed my spares to the people standing closest.

"See you next Tuesday," I told them. "Meet me at the Harry Caray statue."

ONLY LAMBERT SHOWED UP. He had taken the afternoon off from a consulting company that installed sales tax software for businesses. He walked off the L, shouldering the same backpack he'd worn as a Michigan State accounting major less than a year before.

A spring cloudburst chased us into the stadium. By the time it cleared, the groundskeepers were dragging their huge plastic handkerchief across the sodden infield.

Since there wasn't going to be a ball game, Joe and I walked down Clark Street to a University of Iowa bar. All the Big Ten rivalries have contracted into these few blocks of Chicago. We ordered pints of microbrew and Lambert told me about his hometown, Houghton Lake, Michigan, a blue-collar resort for autoworkers who want to spend a weekend up north but can't afford a Lake Michigan cottage.

"There's a lot of people around here who are small-town Iowa and Michigan and Indiana," he said. "This is their big break."

Joe had tried to stay in Michigan, he'd tried. He thought Lansing would be a good place to start his career, but the only job he could find was at Enterprise Rent-a-Car. So he expanded his search, to Seattle, San Francisco, Boston, D.C. . . . and Chicago. A faculty adviser told him about an opening at the consulting firm. He rode Amtrak's Blue Water line to Chicago for the job interview and got a phone call the next day.

"I think I took my final on a Wednesday, and I moved to Chicago on a Monday," he said.

Joe shared a $2,300 apartment with a project manager for a credit card company and a woman who'd just finished graduate work at Harvard. Both were twenty-seven, nearing the end of the Lake View lifespan. The living room's centerpiece was a long white couch, positioned for the best view of the forty-seven-inch high-definition television. Empty Netflix sleeves flopped over the TV's top. An Xbox was umbilically linked to the control panel. The shelves behind were crammed with DVDs, as glossily colored as the spines of anime books.

The books were in the bedroom. He'd been reading *America (The Book)*, Bill Clinton's *My Life*, *Che Guevara Reader*, *Animal Farm*, and a few novels by Chuck Palahniuk. Dangling from a nail next to the bookcase was a VIP pass to a John Kerry rally.

In Lake View, it is possible to live on a block more homogenous than you'd find in any small town. Not only is it segregated by race—almost everyone is white—it's segregated by age, too. Rarely do you see anyone younger than twenty-two or older than thirty-five.

"Honestly, there are not many families here," Joe said. "I've only got a couple friends who live in buildings with families. Most of the people in my building are young single people like me. Some as old as twenty-seven. I know one guy who moved to Denver, he was twenty-six, twenty-seven, he was starting to think about the next phase of his life. This area, it's intensely individualistic, and everyone's moving on to the next thing."

That was in 2005. When I saw Joe again, five years later, he was twenty-eight and had moved on from Lake View to Wicker Park, a Brooklyn-like neighborhood of rock and roll nightclubs, martini bars, and denim boutiques. (When MTV filmed a *Real World* season in

Chicago, it rented the kids a building in Wicker Park.) We ate at Big Star, a taco joint modeled on Austin, Texas, which is more familiar to most Wicker Park residents than the Chicago neighborhood of Austin, only a few miles west on Division Street. Lambert had a new job, with an accounting firm, and was engaged to a woman from Boston. In the Rust Belt states, there's a rule of thumb that once kids are gone for five years, they're gone forever. After twenty-seven or so, they start breeding, building nests.

"Do you think you'll ever move back to Michigan?" I asked Joe.

"Honestly, I love the city," he said. "There's nowhere else I'd rather live. It's one of those things that the more time I spend here, the more I love about it. I travel a lot for work, and I've been to all the other cities, and it's one of only two metropolises in America. For everything that Michigan has going for it, they've squandered a lot of their resources. When the auto industry moved out, they had nothing to fall back on. Chicago is in a prime position to take advantage of that, because it's centrally located, in the middle of all the Big Ten schools, it's got white-collar jobs. I get calls from alumni saying, 'I'm thinking about moving to Chicago.' I say, 'By all means, come here. It's been great to me.'"

Chicago had also been great to Ryan Wiltshire, a twenty-six-year-old aerospace engineer who grew up in Northwest Detroit, a lower-middle-class neighborhood at 8 Mile and Telegraph. In Chicago, he was selling transmission distribution products for General Electric and living in a brownstone two-flat in Lincoln Park. His apartment was across the street from an outdoor café, where we went for coffee. We'd been introduced by the president of the University of Michigan Alumni Club's Chicago chapter. When I asked Wiltshire whether he'd have an easier time finding a U of M classmate in Chicago or Detroit, he seemed startled by my obtuseness.

"I think I'd have a much easier time *here*," he said. "I can think of a handful, on one, maybe two hands, that stayed. And they wanted to stay. If I got the opportunity, I'd love to stay in Michigan. I looked for a job there, but there's only one or two very small companies that hire aerospace engineers. There's actually a big U of M scene here. There's three or four bars that people go to on football Saturday."

Twenty-six-year-olds like walking from their apartments to the historic nightclub where the Smashing Pumpkins played their first record-release party, passing a dozen taverns along the way. Twenty-six-year-olds—even twenty-six-year-olds from Detroit—like public transportation, because a) cars are expensive and generate greenhouse gases that contribute to global warming, and b) you can't read the *New York Times* on an iPhone while you're driving.

"I like the density and just the kind of things that culminated here," Wiltshire said. "Michigan is a commuter state. There aren't activities for someone my age. In Detroit, any time I want to see someone, I have to jump in the car."

Ryan was nostalgic for Detroit, but he was not optimistic about living there again.

"All I hear about Detroit from its glory days is from my parents and grandparents," he said. "My great-grandfather moved up from South Texas to work at Ford for five dollars a day. We still own a house in Detroit but there's not much there for me. The neighborhood has changed. It's not the kind of place I want to live. A lot of people have lost their jobs, lost their houses. Still, most people want to move back and try to rebuild the Detroit that was there. Maybe not today, maybe not tomorrow. But someday."

IN THE SUMMER of 1995, I had taken the advice of that forgotten magazine and left Decatur for the nearest happening city, three and a half hours away.

Young Michiganders are tugged at by two cities: Detroit and Chicago. As a boy, I wanted to live in Detroit. As a young man, I ended up in Chicago. How that happened explains a lot about the fortunes of the Midwest's metropolises in the 1970s, '80s and '90s.

Michigan is a peninsula (two, in fact). The root of that word is *"insula"*—Latin for "island," and a good description of the inhabitants. Michiganders vacation up north, driving deeper into the rustic dead end that separates the state from the rest of America. When I was growing up, Lake Huron was my Atlantic Ocean, Lake Michigan was my Pacific Ocean, and Detroit was my New York City. The *Detroit Free Press* was the biggest newspaper delivered in Lansing (I delivered it in the sixth grade), so I thought working there would be the pinnacle of journalistic achievement.

Detroit was, after all, one of America's top ten cities. It not only had a franchise in every major sport, it had *pre-expansion* franchises. WJR ("From the golden tower of the Fisher Building . . . the great voice of the Great Lakes") broadcast its signal as far as the East Coast. Hudson's department store was the first place I remember riding an elevator, a lift with a caged door. I heard Rush, Asia, the Band, Bob Dylan, and Neil Young in Detroit's sports arenas and concert halls.

Chicago was only 225 miles to my southwest, but since it lay on the opposite shore of Lake Michigan, it may as well have been New Zealand. I first visited in March of 1988, during spring break from my senior year at Michigan State. The season was neither winter nor spring. It was too cold to be chilly and too warm to be cold. The days were too bright to be nights but too cloudy to look like anything but dusk. My friend Jim and I saw a Nelson Algren exhibit at the public library, but when we looked for the apartment where Algren had romanced Simone de Beauvoir, we discovered it had been demolished to provide airspace for a freeway. Chicago had destroyed its past, and in its present—at least in that postsnowfall, prebloom week—it seemed as gray, as inorganic, as a set from *The Third Man* or David Lynch's bleak *Eraserhead*. Except for a change of trains in Union Station, I did not return for four years. One night, on a lark, Jim and I drove around Lake Michigan. As we rounded the bottom, we stopped in Chicago to see a high school friend who worked in a music store downtown. Jon Mark was our pioneer, the immigrant who moves to the big city and tells everyone back home the streets are . . . paved. In the early 1990s, most of my hometown friends began quitting their low-wage gigs at the restaurant or the book warehouse and moving to Chicago, in search of better-paying work. By the time I followed them, I had a friend who helped me find me an apartment (a $325 studio, the same rent I'd paid for a two-bedroom house in Decatur), a friend who helped me carry a couch up three flights of stairs during a heat wave (the heat wave of 1995, when more than five hundred elderly Chicagoans suffocated in their uncooled apartments), and a friend who got me a job (as a stringer for the *Chicago Tribune*).

THE CHICAGO to which I moved in 1995 was not the Chicago of 1980, the year Wisconsin Steel closed and the *Chicago Tribune* announced that the city was "being eaten away by economic forces as powerful as those that thrust it out of the marshes a century ago." It was not even the Chicago I'd visited in 1988, a few months after the death of Mayor Harold Washington. That Chicago still hadn't gotten over Council Wars—years of conflict between Washington and white aldermen, which reminded everyone that Chicago was the most segregated city in America, as impossible to govern as Yugoslavia.

Most Chicagoans lived on streets that were no more diverse than Ireland or Nigeria, but they at least lived in the same city. Unlike Detroit, white flight never transformed Chicago into a black metropolis. There were several reasons for this. Chicago is a Roman Catholic city with strong parish allegiances. Its parochial schools prepared the children for the University of Notre Dame as well as any suburban academy. Mayor Richard J. Daley enforced the law requiring police, firefighters, teachers, garbage collectors, and anyone else who drew a city paycheck to live within the city limits. It was essential to his political survival because those jobs had been granted in exchange for allegiance to the Democratic Machine. Unlike Michigan governor George Romney, who marched with King and championed open-housing laws, Daley was not a liberal on race. When King marched through an all-white neighborhood in Chicago, he was hit in the head with a rock. The neighborhood stayed all white. A pillar of Daley's master plan for Chicago was to "reduce future losses of white families." As long as those white families paid taxes and voted the Democratic ticket, Daley would try to keep the blacks out of their neighborhoods. When two black students tried to rent an apartment on Daley's own block, he did nothing to stop the mob that protested their arrival. Instead, he arranged for the students' lease to be canceled. Rather than allow pupils at overcrowded black schools to attend nearby white schools, he had them taught in trailers. Although the South and West Sides were "gone," in the words of dispossessed whites, Daley's policy of containment maintained ethnic enclaves on the city's fringes. Racial redlining wasn't an option for Detroit mayor Jerome Cavanagh. Unlike Daley, Cavanagh was ambitious for higher office and needed to maintain a progressive image. Cavanagh also didn't control a political machine that could buy black votes with housing project apartments, post office jobs, and Election Day turkeys. He had to give his blacks police captains and fair-housing ordinances.

"What prevented Chicago from going the way of Cleveland and Buffalo?" wrote Adam Cohen and Elizabeth Taylor in *American Pharaoh*, their biography of Daley. "Much of the credit lies with Daley's aggressive program for downtown redevelopment."

Old Man Daley combined the tribal suspicions of an Irish tavern keeper with the municipal ambition of a Roman consul. Inheriting a downtown in which no skyscrapers had been built since the beginning of the Depression, he left it with the Sears Tower and the John Hancock Center.

Jane Byrne, who was elected mayor two-and-a-half years after Daley's death, invited the movies back to Chicago. (Feeling burned by *Medium Cool*, a documentary-style film about the 1968 Democratic National Convention, Daley had mostly kept Hollywood out, because screenwriters were no better than the journalists at making Chicago look bad. Also, the blue language and nudity of 1970s cinema offended his Roman Catholic prudishness.) In the 1980s, *The Blues Brothers*, *Risky Business*, and *Ferris Bueller's Day Off* made Chicago look like a place where a kid from the suburbs could have a good time and colorized the city's image, which had been stuck on Al Capone and the riots at the 1968 Democratic National Convention. Another event that set up Chicago's rebirth was the AIDS crisis. In the early 1980s, every young gay man wanted to move to New York or San Francisco. Then AIDS struck the saltwater coasts. A young South Sider named Tom Tunney decided he would be safer in Chicago and took a job in a hotel in Lake View, which was then a crummy neighborhood surrounding Wrigley Field. The 1980s were a low point for urban America, so gays were welcomed to the inner city. As one demographer after another has pointed out, gays attract creative types to a city by sending the message that it's a tolerant place, open to new ideas and lifestyles. When straight Joe Lambert graduated from Michigan State, he headed directly to Lake View, where he joined thousands of other newly graduated Web developers, graphic designers, publicists, and personal banking representatives. By then, Tunney was Lake View's alderman.

However, it was under Daley's son, Richard M., that Chicago became a global city. During Old Man Daley's reign in the 1950s, '60s, and '70s, he never thought about Chicago's relationship to the rest of the world. He didn't have to. In those years, when America still made everything it needed, this country was Rome and imperial Britain rolled into one.

"There was no globalization at that time," said Gery Chico, a Mexican-American lawyer who grew up near the Union Stock Yards and became Richard M. Daley's chief of staff. (The stockyards, setting of Upton Sinclair's *The Jungle*, closed in 1971, an early blow to blue-collar Chicago.) "Economies were largely siloed. There wasn't the interconnectedness of trading, with its currencies, commodities, risk devices, you name it. That's only really come about through means of technology, so when the technology revolution reached maturity in the eighties and nineties, that's what drove globalization. The fastest-moving force on the face of the planet is global business."

Chicago was well prepared for the day when trading something became more profitable than making something. To begin with, Chicago always had a more diversified economy than its Midwestern rivals. Besides forging steel and slaughtering cattle, Chicago published books, wrote insurance, traded grain futures, and issued bank loans. As the headquarters of the Mercantile Exchange and the Board of Trade, it was the Midwest's financial hub. Because of the University of Chicago, it was home to more Nobel laureates than any city in the world. And because of Chicago's geographic position as the Roundhouse of America, O'Hare was the world's busiest airport. That made it a convenient location for consulting businesses that flew employees all over the country. (The term "yuppie" was popularized by *Chicago Tribune* columnist Bob Greene, who titled an article on Chicago Seven defendant Jerry Rubin "From Yippie to Yuppie." In the 1990s, Chicago's yuppie consultants invented the linguistic device of mixing the present and future tense in the same sentence. "I'm in Phoenix all next week," they'd say.)

Professional services were Chicago's new "product." In 1986, the city's ad agencies, investment banks, law firms, benefits consultants, accountants, and management consultants employed seventeen thousand people; a dozen years later, they employed sixty thousand. Boeing announced it was moving its corporate headquarters to the Loop in the same month that Brach's closed its West Side candy factory, an emblematic moment in Chicago's transformation from a city that made things to a city that thought about things.

As the mayor's chief of staff, Chico visited Chicago's sister cities around the world and welcomed their delegations to Chicago. Young Daley cared more than his father about the city's image to outsiders. His patronage workers scrubbed graffiti off walls, tore down thousands of empty buildings, and towed abandoned cars. He planted pots of flowers on sidewalks and pedestrian overpasses, and surrounded parks with black wrought-iron fences. Nelson Algren would not have recognized the city he compared to a woman with a broken nose, nor would Carl Sandburg have seen a stormy, husky, brawling City of Big Shoulders, but Chicago had to stop looking like an industrial city before it could become an international city.

Chico, who became wealthy as a lobbyist after leaving city hall, moved into a million-dollar condo in the Metropolitan Tower, which had once housed the offices of Encyclopaedia Britannica. As a lawyer, he helped convert the Illinois Bell building to condominiums.

"When I was a kid working here in the late seventies, this town closed up at five," he said. "I mean, there was nothing down here. Maybe a few movie theaters. But the streets were cleared and the place was empty. Today, I live downtown. Along with fifty-six thousand other people and a lot of executives who find it very convenient to be in the central area."

Richard C. Longworth, the *Tribune* reporter who in 1980 had written, "There is no reason to think [Chicago] will ever turn around," now began noticing changes in his downtown apartment building. When he'd moved in, only adults lived there. Then families began arriving. By the late 1990s, "you'd go to parties and hear anecdotal stories about this great school."

But as Chicago transformed itself from a city of factories to a global financial nexus, its class structure was transformed in exactly the way globalization's enemies in Decatur predicted.

"Many Chicagoans live better than ever," Longworth wrote in *Caught in the Middle: America's Heartland in the Age of Globalism*, his book on the modern Midwest,

> . . . in safe housing in vibrant neighborhoods, surrounded by art and restaurants, with good public transport whisking them to exciting jobs in a dazzling city center that teems with visitors and workers from around the world. These are the global citizens, hardworking, well-educated, well-paid, well-traveled. And many Chicagoans live worse than ever in the old ghettos, or worse, are being shoved by gentrification out of the ghettos into destitute inner-ring suburbs. The old housing projects lying in the path of the Loop's expansion are knocked down and their inhabitants scattered to the civic winds. These are the global have-nots, separated by class and education as much as by race from any of the benefits of a global economy. In the middle are the global servants, immigrants, mostly Mexican, who perform the services—valet parking, gardening, dishwashing, dog-walking, bussing in bistros, low-level construction—that the global citizens need.
>
> All this, the rich and the poor, is on display in Chicago. Once a broadly middle-class city, where factory workers owned their homes and shared in the dream, Chicago today is a class-ridden place, with lots of people at the top and lots of people at the bottom and not that much in between.

In the late 1990s, Chicago had more murders than any American city, even more than New York or Los Angeles, whose Crack Wars had ended earlier in the decade. One of the old housing projects of which Longworth wrote was Cabrini-Green, the setting for the 1970s sitcom *Good Times*. As Cabrini-Green was dismantled to make way for the outriders of the bourgeois white invasion, an old black man made an astute observation on how his new neighbors' pursuit of professional achievement had isolated them personally. "I've never seen so many dogs," he said. (Common, the South Side hip-hop artist, had the same thing in mind when he rapped, "White folks focus on dogs and yoga.") The Pacific Garden Mission left the Loop after the winos were driven out. Tunney, the gay alderman who had helped gentrify the neighborhood near Wrigley Field, predicted, "In twenty-five years, the entire city is going to look like this. It's going to be Manhattanized. There's nothing anybody can do about it. There's too much demand for land in the city."

The classic ladder of urban renewal goes like this: artists looking for cheap digs colonize a neighborhood on the edge of the ghetto/barrio/abandoned industrial park. They are followed by homosexuals, who, because they cannot generate children, don't mind the bad neighborhood schools and have enough disposable income to paint their houses. After the homosexuals come the twenty-four-year-old personal banking assistants, market research associates, and senior policy analysts. (You'll know they've arrived when the courtyard apartment buildings are surrounded by black iron fences with security buzzers.) In the final phase, young marrieds decide not to raise their children in the same suburbs where they were raised. The young marrieds do mind the bad neighborhood schools, so they prepare the kids to test into an elite high school, which will lead to an elite college, which will lead to a job as a senior policy analyst and an apartment in a courtyard building with a black iron fence, thus shortening the next generation of gentrification by two steps.

I had mixed feelings about gentrification. On the one hand, I had grown up in Lansing in the 1970s and '80s. In those decades, it seemed no one wanted to live in a city. All my parents' friends moved to the suburbs, for bigger houses or whiter schools, and we never saw them again. Having been raised on the dichotomy that everything poor, dark, and dirty belonged in a city, while everything wealthy, white, and clean belonged in a suburb, I was glad to see rich people buying a stake in urban life. On the other hand, my second Chicago apartment was in a neighborhood in transition from Gentrification Phase 1 to Gentrification Phase 2. I paid $430 a month for a one-bedroom apartment with a steam heater that couldn't warm a dinner roll, an oven that couldn't warm anything, and a pet rat I discovered when it raced across the kitchen floor like the chuck wagon in the dog food commercial. A few blocks to my west was a neighborhood called Andersonville. Andersonville was a gay enclave, but its businesses were holdovers from the gay community's underground era: a bathhouse, a leather emporium, a twink bar, a troll bar, an X-rated video store, a lesbian bookshop. Nonetheless, it is a real estate truism that homosexuals raise property values, no matter how much they're into leather. A few blocks to my east was Argyle Street, a block of Vietnamese restaurants, run by immigrants. Andersonville won. My landlord sold to a development company that kicked out all the tenants on a month's notice and transformed the building into luxury apartments. One of my neighbors was a retired elevator inspector who had lived in his apartment for thirty-five years— since John F. Kennedy was president. When we were dispossessed, in October, the new owners shut down the boiler, forcing old Mr. Weinmann to heat the apartment with an open stove. It took him months to find a new home for himself, his wife, his daughter-in-law, and his two grandchildren. When I returned a year later, to see the display unit, *The Best of Blondie* was in the top rack of the CD holder. And if you visit Andersonville today, you'll find a gym, custom furniture stores, fashion boutiques, a running-shoe store, and *GQ*'s best pizzeria. It's at III, going on IV. Living near Andersonville made me economically homophobic. I have nothing against gays getting married, but I don't want them driving up my rent.

EVEN SOUTH CHICAGO, neighborhood of abandoned steel mills, sees its future in attracting the professional class.

U.S. Steel South Works was finished in 1992, when the structural mill and the last electrical furnaces shut down. South Works had been built in 1880, on 73 acres of lakefront property. Gradually, the mill expanded atop its own excretions, piling slag into the shallows of Lake Michigan, until, like Holland reclaiming the sea, it had created a 573-acre peninsula of limestone dolomite and phosphorous. Once U.S. Steel departed, this promontory of slag became the largest undeveloped plot of lakefront property in Chicago. Unlike other Great Lakes industrial cities, Chicago had preserved its shoreline: A city mandate written in 1836 establishing Grant Park declared the lakefront should be "forever free and clear." But the parks, marinas, and bathing beaches had ended at the gates of U.S. Steel, ten miles south of the Loop. Dismantling South Works meant Chicago could extend its greenbelt to the Calumet River. It also meant South Chicago had a chance to revive itself with the element that provided its original prosperity: water. In the late nineteenth century, water had been essential for floating in iron ore and floating out finished steel. By the late twentieth century, as Burnham had foreseen, water had become a lifestyle amenity. Those downtown Chicago condos came with lake views—something Buffalo, Cleveland, Toledo, or Gary could not provide.

However, no one wants to live on slag, no matter how close to the water. Children can't play on slag. Grass won't grow in slag. To cover the dead Plutonian surface, the city floated in 168 barges full of muck from the bottom of Peoria Lake, a wide spot in the Illinois River, 150 miles southwest of Chicago. Arriving in Lake Michigan via a network of tributaries, locks, and canals, the barges docked in South Works's old North Slip, the nautical chute that once received the thousand-foot-long *Erwin H. Gott*, the *Queen Mary* of the U.S. Steel Great Lakes Fleet. Dump trucks spread topsoil over several acres north and south of the slip— enough to build a park, but not enough to cover the entire site.

In 2009, developer Daniel McCaffery received approval from city hall to build apartments and a shopping center atop South Works's slag. McCaffery had donated a lot of money to Mayor Daley. A decade earlier, the Hispanic Democratic Organization had broken every other law in the Illinois electoral code to elect Daley's man to the city council, because the mayor wanted to decide what would replace the mill and who would build it. The Daley family's campaign to bring South Chicago under its political control had resulted in a lucrative concession for a well-connected Irish builder. Even in global Chicago, that's how things work.

When built out over thirty years, Chicago Lakeside will be the site of 13,576 homes and 17.5 million square feet of stores and offices. The North Slip will become a sailboat marina. The rocky verge of the peninsula, a bathing beach. I visited the marketing center in the old company credit union, the only one of South Works's 160 buildings that hadn't been rubbled. In the middle of the showroom floor, surrounded by Plexiglas panels, was a diorama of a quayside urban village. Model-railroad trees, in rows laid out by a Platonic arborist, followed the curve of a lengthened Lake Shore Drive. Two-inch-tall towers faced the water. I watched a four-minute promotional video narrated by TV newsman Bill Kurtis, who also narrated the movie *Anchorman*. The only greenery was indoors. Outdoors, South Works was the most khaki landscape east of the hundredth meridian. Since U.S. Steel had let nature take its course on this unnatural peninsula, a few trees had risen out of the topsoil, but they were skinny, shapeless teenagers. Mostly, the brown dust grew brittle, coppery weeds that bent stiffly in the unbroken lake winds. Far off, a coal-burning plant on the Illinois-Indiana line, a soon-to-be demolished remnant of smoggy industry, cast a locomotive cloud into the wind. Beyond, the blue silhouettes of the Indiana steel mills were piled atop the horizon-shaped curve of Lake Michigan.

Nasutsa Mabwa, the project development manager, took me for a ride around the site, her black SUV rumbling over roadbeds laid out in expectation of asphalt. Her mission, she said, was to restore the middle class to South Chicago, by persuading people who could afford to live anywhere to move down to this poor, forgotten South Side neighborhood. It was only a twenty-minute drive from downtown.

"It's going to uplift the entire South Side of Chicago," Mabwa predicted. "No one else has the access to the water. There's no land like this left. We're kind of reinventing an image that has been tarnished, and you have the media fixated on shootings and crimes. There's shootings all over Chicago. Of course we're in it because it's an opportunity for revenue. We're not going to do it for free, but after you do all of your economics, you realize that, 'Wow, this is kind of a social transformation project. This is socioeconomic change.' And then you begin to think, 'This is something that really matters. It was good, solid middle-class families, and now it's just in big disrepair.'"

A daughter of Kenyan immigrants, Mabwa had even bigger plans for Lakeside than her bosses: she wanted to bring the Obama Presidential Library there. The University of Chicago, where Obama taught law, is only three miles away. It has an academic claim, but Lakeside has a historic claim, since Obama came to Chicago to work in neighborhoods impoverished by the steel mill closings. If the mills hadn't failed, Obama would not have become president.

We drove past a desert-colored wall that paralleled the North Slip. The ore wall, where taconite and limestone were piled to await the furnaces, was, like the Great Pyramid, an artifact that had outlived its makers. Like the smokestacks at Homestead's Waterfront Mall, the ore wall would be preserved as an industrial memento. It was also too big to tear down. There would be another reminder that Lakeside sat on the bones of a steel mill: no basements. They can't be dug in slag.

No one has moved into Lakeside yet, but in the summer of '11, a bicycle club began building a velodrome, and the Dave Matthews Band held a three-day jam festival atop the slag, drawing the biggest crowd to South Works since twenty thousand worked there during World War II.

NEIL BOSANKO, the steelworker's son who ran for alderman, had spent all his six decades in South Chicago, a lifespan evenly divided between years when Prometheus was the neighborhood's patron god, and years when it was Chaos. As president of the neighborhood chamber of commerce, Bosanko had seen Commercial Avenue's department stores replaced with taquerias, fruiterias, and Nigerian groceries. Only immigrants would move to South Chicago. They had no choice but to live in places Americans had polluted and discarded. Bosanko, a Jew, had grown up among his fellow ethnics but was now one only of a few hundred remaining whites. He had raised eight foster sons and kept them all away from the gangs, except one boy who was doing time for murder. He'd run a chili parlor, because chili was fast, greasy food people could afford in South Chicago. Bosanko had visited Chicago Lakeside's marketing center and hoped to spend the final third of his life in a neighborhood ruled by Plutus, the god of prosperity. The Rust Belt era had never really ended in South Chicago. The outside world hadn't seen this neighborhood since the Bluesmobile jumped the 95th Street bridge in *The Blues Brothers*. Finally, it was about to become part of global Chicago.

"I really think that the city is treating us with respect," he said. "You will have mixed income. People are pretty free to talk about gentrification, but I want to see police here. I want to see three-hundred-thousand-dollar people moving in here again."

Bosanko envisioned a streetcar running down Commercial Avenue, just like the streetcar that carried workers to South Works. Except this one would bring urban adventurers to his neighborhood for pozole and tofu. That would be South Chicago's niche in the global city: providing an international culinary experience to young professionals.

Would South Chicago be as prosperous in Bosanko's old age as in his youth? Were those three middle-age decades an indigent aberration in the lifespan of a great neighborhood, like a spell of unemployment? Bosanko never lived to find out. Before the first brick was laid at Lakeside, he died of cancer.

11.

"Nature Always Bats Last"

The summer of 1901 was muggy, sweaty, sticky. In Brooklyn, the tenement dwellers slept on fire escapes, the slum kids freed rainbows of spray from hydrants, and the Sackett-Wilhelms Lithographing and Publishing Company, which printed the popular humor magazine *Judge*, found the humidity affected the quality of its product. Paper expanded. Colors bled together. The printer's deadlines meant it could not afford to slow the presses or reprint heat-spoiled runs.

Sackett-Wilhelms took its problem to the Buffalo Forge Company, a manufacturer of blowers and heaters, where it was assigned to Willis H. Carrier, an engineer just out of Cornell University.

Carrier's solution was to circulate cold water through heating coils. From Weather Bureau tables, he selected the dew-point temperature at which air has the right amount of moisture for the printing process. He then balanced the temperature of the coil surface and the rate of air flow to pull the air temperature down to the selected dew-point temperature. Carrier called his invention the Buffalo Air Washer and Humidifier, but we know it as air-conditioning.

Before air-conditioning, the northeastern quadrant of the United States was the most climatically desirable corner of the country. Yale geographer Ellsworth Huntington determined that the weather in the mid-Atlantic and the lower Great Lakes was most conducive to hard work and good health. "We are frequently told that the Riviera or Southern California has an ideal climate," Huntington wrote in his 1915 book *Civilization and Climate*. But then he noted, "for most people, the really essential thing to life is the ordinary work of every day . . . Hence [the cold-weather cities] are the ones which people will eventually choose in the largest numbers."

In Huntington's day, the region we now call the Rust Belt controlled the nation's industry, its finances, and its politics. Between the Civil War and World War II, almost every president came from somewhere between Chicago and Boston. But the air conditioner made it possible to export the invigorating Northern climate, without the dreary clouds and the snow. The race to the Sun Belt was on. In 1966, Texas became the first state in which half the homes were air-conditioned. As Carrier's own official biography put it, "a place like Houston could only be tolerable with air-conditioning." Before air-conditioning, Florida was the least populous Southern state, a marginally habitable peninsula of humid swamps, hard-packed beaches, alligators, rum smugglers, and Seminoles. In his essay "The End of the Long Hot Summer: The Air Conditioner and Southern Culture," historian Raymond Arsenault wrote that air-conditioning made factory work tolerable in the South, reduced infant mortality, eliminated malaria, and allowed developers to build skyscrapers and apartment blocks. By urbanizing and industrializing Dixie, air-conditioning lifted the Old Confederacy out of its century-long post–Civil War funk. By the time this book is published, Florida will be the third-most-populous state, having surpassed New York, birthplace of air-conditioning.

When Carrier started his namesake company, he located the headquarters and the factory in Syracuse. From 1960 to the turn of the century, the proportion of American homes with air-conditioning increased from one-eighth to five-sixths. That's luxury to necessity in two generations. You'd think this would have made Syracuse a wealthy city. In fact, it had the opposite effect. At its peak, Carrier employed eight thousand workers there. But in 1999, the company closed its centrifugal chiller factory—and moved the jobs to North Carolina. Four years later, it shut down the container refrigeration plant and the compressor plant—and moved the jobs to Georgia. You can hardly blame Carrier. The company was only following the market it had created. Southerners buy more air conditioners, so shipping costs are lower. Labor costs are lower, as well. Air-conditioning has not changed the South's ancestral conservatism. In the B.C. of A/C, when a Northern city was the only practical location for a factory, companies were forced to make deals with stubborn union bosses, who had the support of liberal Northern congressmen. But their population of such politicians has been much reduced as a result of air-conditioning. (New York has lost seventeen congressmen since the window unit became available, while Florida has gained twenty-three).

This is the irony of Syracuse: it popularized the product that caused its own demise, and contributed to the demise of the entire Northeastern United States. A century after Willis Carrier's brainstorm, the city that once called itself the Air-Conditioning Capital of the World had a new distinction: it was losing young people at a faster rate than any get-out-of-Dodge hometown in the United States. (Besides the factory closings, it doesn't help that Syracuse, which collects flakes from the Great Lakes and the Atlantic Ocean, is the snowiest American city outside the Upper Peninsula of Michigan. It regularly beats out Buffalo and Rochester for the "Golden Snowball," awarded each year to Western New York's snowiest city.) The defections were so serious that the loyal twentysomethings were trying to lure their classmates home with a repatriation program called "Come Home to Syracuse." That was the reason I first visited Syracuse, in the summer of 2005.

HAMELIN AFTER THE PIED PIPER'S CONCERT. Boston during Spring Break. Destin, Florida. These are cities abandoned to the elderly. Syracuse did not appear to be such a sexless, colorless, noiseless place. Its Federal Plaza was crowded with what must have been every remaining resident of childbearing age. A giant banner sagged between concrete pillars: "UPDOWNTOWNERS PARTY IN THE PLAZA." The Updowntowners, downtown Syracuse boosters, were throwing a tremendous blowout. Twenty- and thirtysomethings were so coveted they were encouraged to drink in public on a Wednesday night. I bypassed the portable bar (Coors $4) and bought a plastic cup of wine.

At thirty-eight, I was at the senior end of the bell curve, but my clothes matched. Like everyone else's, they were from Old Navy. The party uniform was a postcollegiate, premarital get-up of shorts and flip-flops for the men, frilly tank tops for the women. On the steps of the Federal Building, Shelley and the Barndogs played an FM radio revue: "Back in the USSR" (sixties), "I'm Your Captain" (seventies), "Steve McQueen" (two thousands). I looked around for someone who could tell me what it was really like to be a young person in Syracuse, because I knew I'd been penciled in for a PR whitewash the next morning, when I was scheduled to meet the board of Come Home to Syracuse on the nineteenth floor of the city's tallest building. I ruled out women. There was more flirting going on here than at a Jane Austen ball. My notebook would look like a pickup prop. After the band stopped playing and the partiers scattered, I met Chris and Jimbo. Both were twenty-seven. Both had come home to Syracuse after flailing in bigger cities.

"This is a good town if you're a cop, a teacher, a doctor, or a lawyer," Jimbo said, counting the options on his fingers. Since leaving the navy, he'd been working as a custodian while studying education, hoping to break into one of the big-four local professions.

Chris had worked as a sous chef in Atlanta but came back to Syracuse "to pay some bills, and because I couldn't stand the fucking rednecks down there. I think the Confederate Flag should be illegal. They tried to overthrow the government. People would give me a hard time when they heard my accent. I almost got in so many fights. I was talking to a guy in a bar, and he rolled up his sleeve to show me a tattoo that said 'Fuck the North.' This is a guy I might have been *friends* with."

In Atlanta, Chris had earned $16 an hour. In Syracuse, he drove a produce truck for $11.75. The work was seasonal, so he needed to find a winter job.

"This town is like a magnet," he spat. "It keeps drawing you back."

I thought about the REM song "Rockville." ("Don't go back to Rockville / And waste another year.") I'd thought about that song a lot when I was twenty-five years old in Lansing, too.

"It's a college town," Jimbo concluded. "They really fly the orange here." He was referring to Syracuse University's team colors. "It used to be a blue-collar town, but none of those jobs pay now. There's nothing for you here unless you're in college or you're married. I know a few people who moved here."

"People who went to college don't come back." Chris said. "They stay the place they went to, or they go somewhere else. Upstate New York is a dying area. I want to move to Colorado."

THE NEXT MORNING, before my appointment, I went for a walk along Salina Street, in downtown Syracuse. Redbrick towers shaded the chilly sidewalk. Syracuse's architecture is as Roman as its name: austere, classical, imposing, built to impress, not welcome. The Weighlock Building, marooned on a city street after the Erie Canal was filled in, could have been an Upper Fifth Avenue mansion. Half the storefronts on Salina were empty, unpainted for years. The other half were occupied by discount stores: CVS, Rainbow, Athlete's Foot, Oriental Mart Salon. Young men lingered on the sidewalk. A tramp with a dingy beard approached. "Where's the shelter at?" he asked me.

A few men in suits strolled briskly through this lower-class galleria, like smart yachts trying to catch a wind that would hurry them through polluted waters. I drifted down to the Landmark Theatre, the inevitable empty movie house. A marble-and-wood ticket booth was curtained with burgundy velvet. At my feet was the Syracuse Walk of Fame. I recognized many of the names beneath the tarnished brass stars—L. Frank Baum, Rod Serling, Grace Jones, Bob Costas, Dick Clark—but Peanuts Hucko must have been obscure even to locals. (He was a big-band clarinetist.) The message stamped in the sidewalk: Syracuse was a place to be from. In a few minutes, I would learn why anyone would want to stay.

"OUR MOST DUBIOUS DISTINCTION is that the Syracuse MSA has lost more of this age bracket than any other community in the country," the woman with the plaited brown hair was saying.

"It's perceived lack of opportunities," said the husky one with the wedding band. "Because of the relative size of the geographic region, someone who's from Syracuse may not know about job opportunities in Oswego."

"There are great opportunities for a young person our age who wants to be actively involved in the community," the blond prince asserted. "It's a perfect laboratory for a Northeastern city that's gone through its rough times and is poised to redevelop."

Emma, Michael, and Ben were all twenty-six years old, but they already dressed and talked like the civic elders they would one day become. We were in a nineteenth-story conference room, antiseptically chilled by Carrier. Through a dusty window, I could see the green platter of the Onondaga Valley—a bed of trees garnished with brick cupolas and glowing glass towers.

Their pitch went on for an hour. Then Michael looked at Ben: "Should we give him the tour?"

"Let's give him the tour."

"We'll give you the tour. Then we'll take you to Dinosaur Bar-B-Que. It's the best barbecue you'll ever have."

Michael and Ben led me across Salina Street, to the spot where the Erie Canal once ran through Syracuse. In commemoration, a city block had been filled in with water, as though the hydrants had burst. Children waded calf-deep, like brown cranes. The water bleakly reflected a statue of Christopher Columbus, hero to the local Italians.

("You'd be hard-pressed to find another city where the body of water it was built around is gone," Ben would tell me later. "It was filled in 1920, because the canal was not looked at as a viable means of trade. If they had been thinking ahead eighty years, they might have thought of the benefits of having a waterway running through the middle of town as a quality-of-life amenity.")

We got into Michael's SUV and drove past the ochre brick Hotel Syracuse—"our grandest and oldest hotel," Ben said sardonically, nodding at a broken glass door behind a sawhorse. The War Memorial arena looked like an amusement park designed by Nikita Khrushchev, but it was *the* symbol of Syracuse's zenith. Inside, the Syracuse Nationals, led by Dolph Schayes, the greatest Jewish basketballer, won the 1955 NBA title.

The Nats moved to Philadelphia in 1962 and changed their name to the 76ers. Big-time sports never returned to Syracuse. The War Memorial was home to professional wrestling and minor-league hockey. Now the Syracuse Orange were the focus of local pride. Outside Las Vegas and Miami Beach, Syracuse is the only city where an orange blazer is considered tasteful.

"We also won the NCAA football title in 1959," Michael said.

"In '60," Ben said, correcting him.

"The '59 team, they won the 1960 Cotton Bowl. I have a room devoted to Syracuse sports in my home."

"He's actually an unofficial mascot," Ben said.

"I'm the voodoo doctor. I put on an orange top hat and face paint and put a hex on the other team."

"It's too bad," Ben said, "that we don't have time to show you the traffic light on Tipp Hill."

"What's so special about a traffic light?" I asked.

"It's upside down. The green light is on top. Tipp Hill is an Irish neighborhood. It was named after county Tipperary, because of the rolling hills. The people didn't like the British red on top of the Irish green, so the kids threw stones at it until the city reversed it."

At the corner of Tompkins and Milton Streets was a bronze statue of a man in a floppy workingman's cap telling Irish tales to a boy with a sagging slingshot.

"My great-uncle was a stone thrower," Ben said. "Fifty years later, they were grand marshals of the St. Patrick's Day Parade."

Then Ben made a confession: his grandfather, a Tipp Hill Irishman named William Francis "Billy" Walsh, was a former mayor of Syracuse who had also represented Central New York in Congress. His father,

James Walsh, now held the same congressional seat. This was essential information for understanding Ben Walsh, but he rarely had to tell anyone. Everyone in Syracuse knew that was why he rode an elevator to the nineteenth floor every day, rather than driving a produce truck, like Chris. He was an Onondaga Valley aristocrat. What young person with a lineage like that would leave Syracuse?

(Most people who come home to Syracuse do so for family reasons. Even the boosters concede you trade career for lifestyle. But there are financial enticements. In 2010, according to the National Association of Home Builders, it was the nation's most affordable housing market, with 97.2 percent of homes sold affordable for a family earning the city's median income. After Nate Desimone and his wife had a daughter, he submitted his résumé to the Come Home to Syracuse website, found a job as an executive recruiter, and bought a four-bedroom house for two and a quarter. Then there was Kathy Chappini, who came home to Syracuse from Maine—and got a $5,000 grant to open a candy store.)

Dinosaur Bar-B-Que was not the best barbecue I've ever eaten. (I live in Chicago, you know.) The highlight was actually the men's room, where the patrons were encouraged to cover the walls with what an academic once called "latrinalia" but we would call "dirty writing" or graffiti. I left Syracuse having seen an alligator in a fedora, carrying a harmonica labeled "Hohner Big-Ass Blues."

WHEN I SAW Ben Walsh again, five years later, he was working inside Syracuse's city hall, a Romanesque Revival building of pebbled buff stone, with a turret and a tower wearing peaked red caps. It was an architectural brother of the Gilded Age's Protestant temples. Ben was executive director of the Syracuse Industrial Development Agency, the body in charge of finding new life for the shells of the city's abandoned factories. Not only had Carrier left, so had Allied Chemical, Chrysler, General Electric, and Fisher Body.

The Air-Conditioning Capital of the World may have lost its title to the Confederates and the Chinese, but it was still home to skilled tradesmen and engineers who had refused to uproot themselves from Central New York. Where else did it snow enough for cross-country skiing?

"You can lament the fact that these industries are gone, but that's not to say their legacies are negative," Ben said. "A lot of things they brought to our community define us today."

To see how high technology has replaced mass production in Syracuse, I visited Bitzer Scroll, which occupies a good-sized corner of the old Fisher Body plant. By promising to fill it with high-tech business, the city had persuaded General Motors not to tear the plant down.

A German-owned company, Bitzer Scroll manufactures compressors for chillers and commercial air conditioners. Heavy-duty jobs. The most important component is the scroll—a cylinder with a whorl-shaped groove cut into one end. Driven by a crankshaft, the scroll compresses refrigerant from a liquid-vapor mix to a pure vapor. Since the correct depth of the groove is measured in microns, it must be designed and produced by engineers and skilled tradesmen. The assembly line, in a building whose address was still 1 General Motors Drive, was in a room where UAW workers once put together dashboards and interior moldings. Girders holding up the distant, Sistine ceiling were the only reminder that this had once been an auto plant.

Richard Kobor, the facility's president, was a former Carrier engineer who had spent seven years working for Bitzer in Germany. His bosses tried to open a compressor plant in their native country but couldn't assemble an engineering team. Germans are wonderful engineers, but their mathematical qualities do make them rigid.

"You can't get people to change from a company across the street from your company, and it's impossible to get someone to move from Munich to Stuttgart," said Kobor, a loud, blunt executive whose Corvette Z06 occupied a prime space in the parking lot. "This wouldn't be here if this could be done in Germany. Syracuse is where the engineers were that had the experience in the product."

Kobor got $1.4 million in incentive money from the state and hired several engineers away from Carrier, including his plant manager, Michael McKee. McKee had managed Carrier's Syracuse chiller plant, until it moved to Charlotte in 1998. As a salaried employee, McKee was offered a transfer down south. The hourly employees were left behind, replaced with local, nonunion labor. Unimpressed with the educational system in North Carolina—many of his workers had rudimentary reading and math skills—McKee was glad to return to Central New York, whose scholastic heritage goes back to the religious revivals of the mid-nineteenth century. (Syracuse University, Colgate University, Cazenovia College, Hobart and William Smith Colleges, Hamilton College, Utica College, Elmira College, and Alfred University are all liberal arts colleges with roots in the Second Great Awakening, the evangelical movement that was so powerful in Central New York that the region became known as "the Burned-Over District," because there was no one left to convert.) The Syracuse workforce is 20 percent more educated than the national average, according to the Metropolitan Development Authority.

McKee took me on a tour of his plant, working backward through the process, from a craftsman polishing a scroll to the upright stainless steel cabinet where the scrolls were inscribed in cast iron, a process that took an hour. This quiet, clean, high-tech manufacturing was Syracuse's work now.

"Syracuse has always had a heavy industrial base," McKee said. "Certainly in the last ten years, the area's taken a hit with the large companies. There are small companies that have grown and continue to do well, but certainly, when you look at, starting back in the early nineties, General Motors pulling out of here, Carrier in the late nineties closing the large chiller plant . . . Crouse-Hinds is now a division of Cooper. They still do electrical boxes, but they're a fraction of what they once were."

Among its sixty production workers, Bitzer Scroll employed a handful of Carrier refugees, including a machinist. Unlike Carrier, which had been organized by the Sheet Metal Workers International Association, Bitzer Scroll was an open shop. Kobor had some strong opinions on unions and made sure I heard them before I left. He'd just been to Flint, to look at an auto plant scheduled for demolition.

"The UAW sure had a lot to do with it," Kobor said. He had a voice so loud it created its own echo. In his office, trying to convince a visitor of the folly of collective bargaining, it sounded especially hard and argumentative. "Is everybody around here who's dying union? *Yes*. Are there companies in the area growing? *Yes*. Are they union? *No*. That's a big deal. Until unions unionize China or Mexico, it's very difficult to have a surviving business here that's a union business. We don't have the flexibility. But you know, most of it's management. Management caused the unions by treating people so badly. Are you going to write about unions in your book?"

I promised Kobor I'd get both sides of that story. And the next day, I did.

GARY GALIPEAU DROVE into the Denny's parking lot in a black Ford F-150 with the Empire State plate "NAZGUL." If J. R. R. Tolkein's Black Riders had driven pickup trucks instead of galloping around Middle Earth on dark-haired workhorses, this was *exactly* the color, make, and model they would have ordered from the showroom.

"I've had this plate on four trucks," Gary said. "Always a black four-by-four. I was a fan long before the movies."

In his early sixties, Gary was stocky and bald, but he was bald in the authoritative way John Glenn, or his on screen alter ego, Ed Harris, is bald. His head made hair look like an affectation unworthy of a mature man. With him was his wife, Barbara. Gary and Barbara had met while working at Carrier. They'd been recommended to me by the business manager of Sheet Metal Workers Local 58, because no couple in Syracuse had a more distressing story about what happens when a corporation divorces you in middle age. Perhaps no one in the Rust Belt did.

Gary had grown up on the west end of Syracuse. When he'd hired in at Carrier, at age nineteen, the sign on the plant still read "AIR CONDITIONING CAPITAL OF THE WORLD." Barbara was from Downstate—Long Island—and sounded it. She'd moved to Syracuse to attend the university, dropped out, and got laid off from an industrial laundry.

In 1978, when Barbara was laid off from the laundry, it was still possible to jump from factory to factory. Barbara didn't know anything about Carrier. She and a friend were simply driving around Syracuse, looking for work, when they spotted the big factory on Thompson Road.

"Must be jobs in there," Barbara said.

They walked up to the security office and announced, "We want to fill out an application."

"Listen, honey," the guard said, "we're taking applications at one o'clock."

So Barbara and friend went to lunch and returned in the afternoon to fill out applications with hundreds of other job seekers. Three days later, she was offered a job on the window unit assembly line, spraying glue on the fiberglass insulation for four hundred air conditioners a day.

"After five years, you'll be golden," Barbara was told. "You'll have a job for life."

The year after Barbara was hired, Carrier was bought, in a hostile takeover, by United Technologies. After promising to keep the headquarters in Syracuse, UTC moved it to Hartford in 1986.

"That was the downfall," Barbara said. "Then we lost one part of the business after another, to either down south or Tennessee."

In 2004, Gary and Barbara lost their jobs when Carrier moved the last of its Syracuse manufacturing jobs to Singapore. There, even the most skilled workers were paid only half the $27 an hour Gary had earned as a metalworker. The couple were lucky their jobs had gone to Asia rather than Georgia. That that made them eligible for Trade Adjustment Assistance—extended unemployment benefits from the federal government. A clause in the union's collective bargaining agreement required Carrier to reimburse its discarded workers for four years of tuition and books, if they completed their courses with a C average. Congressman Walsh and Senator Hillary Clinton worked out a voucher program, so the local public colleges waived their fees until Carrier paid in full. Barbara went to Onondaga Community College for a two-year degree in health information technology, "which is a fancy way of saying medical records."

Even with the degree, Barbara couldn't find work in the health care field, so she took a job at Goulds Pumps, a sump pump manufacturer. It paid $12.47 an hour, a substantial drop from her job in production controls at Carrier, but decent money by the standards of Central New York in the A.D. of A/C.

At this point in the story, Gary stood up and excused himself from our breakfast table. He hadn't finished his French toast. The coffee wasn't making him antsy. He knew what Barbara was about to tell me, and, as the man who loved her, he didn't want to relive it.

On Barbara's ninth day at Goulds Pumps, a loose thread on her glove wrapped itself around a drill press, taking Barbara's hand with it. Her index finger was torn off at the first knuckle. The nailless digit was a stub of glossy flesh. The amputation kept Barbara out of work for eight weeks. When Barbara returned to work, she found the factory so distressing that she soon took a medical records job in a hospital, paying $2.50 an hour less.

After earning a degree in human resources management, Gary found that fifty-eight was too old to start a new career and that he lacked the salesmanship for insurance. Fortunate enough to draw a full pension from Carrier, he was able to take a part-time job behind the meat counter at Wegman's, a supermarket. It filled the health-insurance gap between the end of Carrier and the beginning of Medicare. Syracuse's preeminent vocations are now education and medicine—the training of the young and the preservation of the old. Where nothing is left for the middle-aged or the middle class, it is difficult to be both. (The largest individual employer in the area is the Oneida Nation's casino, which hired 150 former Carrier workers as bartenders and janitors.)

"I like to tell people we can't base an economy selling hamburgers and insurance policies to each other," Gary said. "There's a certain satisfaction within producing something tangible, something you can hold in your hand and say, 'I made this.' In fact, to my way of thinking, there's a gratification there you can't achieve any place else. At a time, I was regarded as a craftsman in metal. A lot of my learning for that particular field was passed down. Tribal learning from those who went before me. I would love to pass down what I have learned. I'm sixty-two years old, and I'm probably the youngest of the metal fabricators who knows how to make a Pittsburgh Lock Seam using brake valves. That's an example of tribal learning that when I die will be gone."

Having met in the factory, Gary and Barbara are a couple who can complete each other's philosophies of labor. Barbara did, at 10:50 in the morning, in a Denny's overlooking exit 35 of the New York State Thruway.

". . . And I think when he's talking about manufacturing, that sense of satisfaction that at the end of the day"—she meant this literally, not figuratively—"you can look at what you did. You can measure it. You know you did something. I work in an office now. We deal with medical records. I really can't look at a body of my work and say, 'This is what I did today.' I never have that same sense of satisfaction."

THE CARRIER PLANT was just across a traffic circle from my motel, the Red Roof Inn Syracuse, so I jogged over there in the evening. The banner still boasted "WORLD'S LARGEST AIR CONDITIONING COMPANY," but the white panels of its outer walls were already yellowing, like the pages of an unread book. An American flag, tattered at its tassled fringe, hung over the entrance. I ran through an open gate. There was no security guard to stop me. In a far corner of the parking lot, cattails grew from a dank slough. The weeds reminded me of a saying I had heard from Gary. "There are unbreakable rules when it comes to man's interactions with the planet: Number one, gravity always wins. Number two, nature always bats last."

12.

Lackawanna Blues

Before I visited the ruins of Bethlehem Steel's Lackawanna Works, on the shore of Lake Erie, I purchased a pocket guide to wildflowers. I wanted to test Gary Galipeau's maxim that nature always bats last, by finding out which plants it sends to the plate first. As I had discovered at the old Fisher Body site in Lansing, there are gardens that thrive on neglect.

In the thirty years since its day-after-Christmas death sentence, Lackawanna Steel had been untouched by wrecking crews or landscapers. It was an open-air terrarium for the study of how quickly our discarded places become feral. I can't say "return to nature," because the land had lost its virginity over a century ago. Only the hardiest posthuman weeds can thrive in asphalt, slag, and dirt poisoned by sulfur. Lackawanna is an American Macchu Picchu or Angkor Wat, except the verdure is inclining up its slopes in full view of history, recorded by ruin pornographers, such as myself, with digital cameras. Atop the neoclassical administration building, with all its gables, periscope windows, and half-shell cornices, the bronze roof had oxidized to an aquatic green. The grid of windows in the storehouse, where the mill's supplies and materials were received, was broken out in a crossword puzzle pattern. Between the frontage road and the chain-link fence, peppergrass burst from the ditches. I drove my Ford Focus across the railroad tracks, ignoring this warning: "NO TRESPASSING: PRIVATE PROPERTY. VIOLATERS WILL BE PROSECUTED. OWNER: TECUMSEH REDEVELOPMENT, INC." By now, I was familiar enough with empty factories to know the sign could be disregarded without legal consequences, or even an uncomfortable encounter with a security guard.

That was how little anyone cared about this land, which could no longer grow anything edible, produce anything salable, or support a home that was livable. Another sign, six words beneath an arrow, directed me to "IRON CITY PUBLIC SCALER SLAG PRODUCTS." Ignoring that as well, I parked the car and climbed out with my camera, my notebook, and my *Peterson First Guide to Wildflowers of Northeastern and North-central North America*. These are my field notes:

- Spotted knapweed: furzy lavender flowers, pinecone-shaped buds (Peterson: "this one lines our roadsides and field edges in many places from June to August.")
- Goldenrod: pillar of blade-thin leaves, supporting a head of pin-sized yellowish buds. (Peterson: "It blooms from July to September along roadsides, in fields and in clearings.")
- Chicory: purplish crown. (Peterson: "This alien that grows as commonly in the sterile ground along our road shoulders is much too pretty to be dismissed as a weed.")
- Yarrow: crown of tiny, fire-stemmed daisies. (Peterson: "Yarrow is another of the many dozen plants that now grace the roadsides and field edges throughout much of eastern and central North America.")
- Flattened can of Genesee Cream Ale, its logo bleached to near-illegibility.
- Tim Hortons coffee cup.
- Tangled gray cable, embedded in dirt like a root.
- Mayweed: tiny daisy heads on barbed stems. (Peterson: "From Europe and [has] found our roadsides congenial.")
- Toadflax: called "butter-and-eggs" because of the yolk at the center of its yellow petals.
- Steel rail.
- Crickets in my right ear, traffic in my left ear.
- A dolly, once painted green, with horn-shaped handles.

(Because of these unsupervised weeds, Buffalo has the highest pollen count in the nation, yet another side effect of deindustrialization.)

An arboreal generation must be synchronous with a human generation, because the trees had grown to adulthood. They were tall enough to screen my view of the mill, making it an interleaving of sooty bricks and greenery, but they were not as tall as the chimneys and peaked towers. To reach the largest tree, I walked over a sewer drain and across an asphalt platform—the employee parking lot, I guessed. My shoes crushed chunks and crumbs of red brick, pebbles of asphalt and slag. A whitetail deer bounded through the goldenrod, toward the shelter of a long, low building.

The tallest structures on the site—the tallest in Lackawanna, and taller than all but the most aspiring in Buffalo's Art Deco downtown— were the eight white windmills of Steel Winds, a wind farm on the grounds of Lackawanna Steel. On this hot afternoon, when the lake was as smooth as a wading pool, their white blades were still, like the wings of gulls poised in flight. When the propellers turned, they looked like the arms of yoga students, performing endless side bends. Steel Winds has become a symbol of Buffalo, shown during national broadcasts of Bills games. (The Bills games in Buffalo, that is. The Bills play twice a year in Toronto, leading to local suspicions that the team is planning to sneak out of the country. In the 1960s, Buffalo was the fun city of the Golden Horseshoe, as the western bell-end of Lake Ontario is known. Toronto? A fussy-lipped outpost of Presbyterianism. Now Toronto, with its Caribana Parade and its Chinatown, is the fun city, while Buffalo turns a shade grayer each year. Buffalo's bookstores sell copies of *Eye*, Toronto's entertainment weekly.)

The blades collected Bethlehem Steel's only remaining resource: the wind off Lake Erie. The ground was too polluted to build on. The beach looked gray. It was a terminal shore—at the end of America, and the end of its life. Where the cliff face had been cut away, the strata were shot through with sparkling threads of metal. In the ore slip, tires and timbers washed against the stamped metal wall. The littoral slope, seeded with grass so it wouldn't fall into the lake, was scattered with slag pots, a residue of steelmaking that looked like enormous metal tarts and leached arsenic into the soil. An accidental sculpture garden, the slag pots were monuments to steelmaking. Hundreds of feet overhead, pinwheeling blades squeaked on their axles. Each windmill generates 2.5 kilowatts a day—enough to power one thousand houses in Lackawanna, Buffalo, and Hamburg. One of the largest urban wind farms in the world, Steel Winds pays the city of Lackawanna $20,000 per turbine, per year. They can't replace the mill, which funded 75 percent of the municipal budget, but they're more lucrative than a 1,600-acre brownfield. It's been so successful that the project's owner, First Wind of Massachusetts, has since installed six more turbines. Steel Winds can now illuminate, toast bread, grind coffee beans, charge cell phones, operate computers, and transmit

The Big Bang Theory to 14,000 homes—more than remain in Lackawanna. At the rate Steel Winds is expanding and Buffalo is contracting, it will power the entire city by 2030.

After a car maker or a steel mill wears out a factory, extracts all the tax breaks a treasury will bear, and accumulates more obligations to its workers than the stockholders will bear, it flees town like a deadbeat husband, leaving a worn-out, exploited patch of land no one else will touch. An industrial city follows the same life cycle as a prizefighter or a prostitute. Its native beauty, the freshness of its earth and water, the youth and strength of its people, are used up and discarded. Then it's on to the next town.

Since Bethlehem Steel left, Lackawanna's number one claim to fame is the Lackawanna Six, a cell of young Yemeni-Americans who trained with al-Qaeda in Afghanistan. Their recruiter, Kamel Derwish, was born in Buffalo but spent much of his childhood in Yemen. Derwish returned to New York in 2000, shortly after the bombing of the USS *Cole*, in Aden harbor. The attack was celebrated by Lackawanna Muslims as righteous revenge on an American warship violating Arab waters.

Lackawanna had one of the first Muslim settlements in America. The first Yemenis arrived in 1912, although the colony didn't take root until the 1950s, when Eastern European steelworkers felt American enough to insist that someone darker clean the vats and stoke the furnaces. Drive around Lackawanna today and you'll see the Yemenite Benevolent Association, the Lackawanna Halal Market, and the Lackawanna Islamic Center, a mosque inside an old Ukrainian Catholic church.

Derwish came home to a Lackawanna less prosperous and more dilapidated than the steel village of his earliest years. The young men of the First Ward, Lackawanna's Arab quarter, were the sons of steelworkers and autoworkers but had slid down the employment ladder into jobs as telemarketers, social workers, car salesmen, and cheese factory employees. Born in the United States, they were worried not about assimilating, as their fathers had been, but about losing their Muslim identities. A harmless teenage gang called the Arabian Knights turned into the cell that gathered in Derwish's apartment to eat pizza and discuss how the Koran should dictate their personal behavior, as well as their views on world events.

Derwish "spoke with purpose," wrote Dina Temple-Raston in *The Jihad Next Door: The Lackawanna Six and Rough Justice in the Age of Terror*, "and in a town where aimlessness was the norm, that in itself made him unusual."

In the spring of 2001, Derwish persuaded six young men to follow him to an al-Qaeda training camp in Afghanistan. There, they were personally greeted by Osama bin Laden and taught to fire Kalashnikov rifles, so they could fight for the Taliban. Their adventure in jihad lasted two months. Arrested a year and two days after the planes crashed into the World Trade Center, the Lackawanna Six were the first native-born terrorist cell prosecuted during the Global War on Terror. Sentenced to between six and ten years in prison, their case brought suspicion on Muslims in the United States in general and Western New York in particular. Yet, years after they traveled to the Middle East, you can still see girls in black hijabs studying at the Lackawanna Public Library. Steel was not the most durable product of the mill by the lake. More durable are the tribes who gathered here to forge it.

IN THE EARLY 1950s, New York Governor Thomas M. Dewey decided to build a cross-state superhighway, roughly following the course of the Hudson River and the Erie Canal, the aquatic turnpike made obsolete by the railroad and the automobile. To oversee the New York State Thruway Authority, Dewey named urban planner/neighborhood wrecker Robert Moses, who would have built a highway over Eleanor Roosevelt's tomb if the first lady had lain beneath the quickest route from Lower Manhattan to Albany. In Buffalo, Moses ran his highways right along the water. Interstate 190 is a cliff's edge above the Niagara River. The Buffalo Skyway is a highway on stilts, a concrete roller coaster climbing and dipping through the air over Lake Erie. At the time, Buffalonians didn't mind. Their waterfront was a slum of dilapidated wooden shanties, saloons, and brothels for beached sailors. The lake and the river were alimentary canals for the steel mills and tanneries. Who wanted to live alongside such moral and chemical pestilence?

Bonnie Eschborn was a little girl growing up in the Riverside neighborhood when Moses drew his highway on a map of Buffalo. Riverside Park was the last urban space designed by the renowned landscape architect Frederick Law Olmsted. Olmsted built a white-block casino and a classical bathhouse for the swimming pool. Stone steps terraced the grassy slope declining to the waterfront.

The highway interposed six lanes of asphalt between Olmsted's work and its namesake feature. It also provided a quick route out of town for workers at the Chevy engine plant in Tonawanda, just across the city limit from Riverside. Autoworkers had been Riverside's burghers, but with an interstate running past their plant, they could now live in the South Towns, the new suburbs down the lakeshore from Buffalo.

Eschborn was the founder of Rediscover Riverside, a group devoted to reuniting the neighborhood with the river. Among her ideas was re-routing Interstate 190 inland, along an unused rail corridor. Eschborn met me in Riverside Park, beneath a miniature stone lighthouse.

"Before the highway, everybody used the park, everybody," she said as we embarked on a walk around Riverside. "Now we're totally discon-nected from it. After the highway came through, I don't remember even doing anything on the riverfront. The waterfront was always the focus of where jobs can be. My mother said when they were building the thruway and knocking down the shanties, people were thrilled. Back then, there was no emphasis on being close to the water. I think people were happier that they could go places fast."

Before the highway, Riverside was populated by blue-collar Poles and Italians, "who competed to grow the lushest garden on the block. There were bars on every corner doing home-cooked meals and a lot of busi-nesses here, a lot. Not too many people who work at the plant live here anymore. Now what we have is the newer, younger, undesirable drug addicts. People come out at two in the morning, screaming. If I walk in my neighborhood, I'll get attacked by pit bulls."

Riverside's remaining businesses are a tattoo parlor, a liquor store, and a deli (the Western New York term for a minimart) trading in fleece baby blankets, oversized T-shirts, submarine sandwiches, and chicken fingers. (The Red Bird Variety Store—"Novelties, Gifts, Seasonal"—was gated over, a five-buck store that couldn't make it in a dollar-store neighborhood.)

"This we don't like," Eschborn commented, "delis owned by Arabs. Not that we have anything against Arabs, but they bring in crime and drugs. We want to push that back where it came from: East Side of Buffalo."

The only remnant of the old neighborhood is Tony's Barber Shop. A union placard and an American flag hang by the chair where Tony cuts hair with scissors and a straight razor for ten bucks. Old men page through the *Buffalo News* and complain that the president is planning to spend $5 million to build the Muslims "a musk, or a mosque, whatever they call those frickin' things."

Buffalo had tried to drive out the lowlifes by building a highway along the waterfront, but now lowlifes were the only people willing to live in an inner-city neighborhood cut off from the water.

We got into Eschborn's sedan and drove toward the falls, stopping at a park in Tonawanda, where the highway swerved east of the Niagara, leaving a pod-shaped salient of riverfront. A bicyclist pedaled a macadam path. A yoga flyer was stapled to a kiosk. Cicadas reached the peak of their bell-curve buzz, uninterrupted by traffic.

"This is what we had," Eschborn lamented. "We can turn part of the thruway into this. These houses are one hundred thirty thousand dollars. I'd be lucky to get sixty for mine. Riverside is a lost community. It's fifty-four streets nobody knows about. Nobody cares about it."

After Eschborn dropped me back in Riverside Park, I walked down to the Niagara. I was followed by a woman in an Adidas T-shirt, green plaid pajama bottoms, and dirty sneakers, her breath sweet with bourbon. Becky had been sitting on a bench until she saw me wandering through the park. We crossed a skyway. The heat of auto exhaust radiated through the concrete.

"I don't like the thruway," Becky said. "I never did since I was a kid. My mother hated the sound of the thruway. She hated the noise."

We descended a ramp to a twenty-foot stripe of greenish-yellow grass between the thruway and the river. Overhead, above a concrete wall, cars strafed past like low-flying turboprops. Down below was a tiny lighthouse—a lamp propped on a pole painted with graffiti as high as the taggers could reach. Around its base, empty bottles and chunks of timber were encased in surface scum. In modern Buffalo, *this* was a riverfront park.

"It's peaceful down here, ain't it?" Becky said. "We come down here a lot to relax. Some people get mad and yell at our music, though."

It's been said that Robert Moses's "dead gray hands are still strangling the city of Buffalo." If so, this is where he dumped the body.

DOWNTOWN BUFFALO also wants its waterfront back, but like Riverside, it doesn't have much space to work with. The docks and granaries crowd the water's edge, leaving behind flaking brick towers overspanned by the Buffalo Skyway. The skyway separates the water from the HSBC Arena, where the Sabres play hockey, and Niagara Square, site of Buffalo's twenty-something-story city hall, an Empire State Building of municipal governance.

Buffalo is trying to rebuild its "inner harbor," the mouth of the Buffalo River. This was the birthplace of Buffalo, the nautical intersection where the Erie Canal ended its 363-mile run from the Hudson River to the Great Lakes. Once that ditch was dug, Buffalo was transformed, in 25 years, from Niagara frontier village to the largest inland port in the nation. Eventually, it became the transfer point for more western migrants than Ellis Island.

I've got a mule, her name is Sal.
Fifteen miles on the Erie Canal
She's a good old worker and a good old pal
Fifteen miles on the Erie Canal
We've hauled some barges in our day
Filled with lumber, coal and hay
And we know every inch of the way
From Albany to Buffalo
                              —THOMAS S. ALLEN,
          "LOW BRIDGE, EVERYBODY DOWN"

That same artificial estuary could also be the site of Buffalo's rebirth, figured Erich Weyant of the Erie Canal Harbor Development Corporation. After the corporation was founded in 2005, U.S. representative Brian Higgins obtained $350 million to rebuild the inner harbor from the New York Power Authority, which had, fittingly, once been chaired by Robert Moses. The NYPA had made millions from power generated by Niagara Falls, so Higgins negotiated a relicensing agreement that returned the money to his hometown.

"Buffalo's been disconnected from its waterfront for fifty years or more by public improvement projects, infrastructure, thruways," Weyant told me on an afternoon walk along the river mouth. "In the past twenty or thirty years, people have wanted to return to the waterfront. We've got a mix of low- and moderate-income housing down here. People are now thinking of water as recreational rather than industrial."

We walked through the dank shadow of the skyway, which cut a strip of sunshine out of a summer afternoon. Once we stepped back into the light, Weyant led me to a stunted boat slip with limestone walls. This was the original terminus of the Erie Canal. During Buffalo's sudden urbanization, the canal was rerouted to Tonawanda, but this remnant, buried and forgotten in the 1920s, was rediscovered during waterfront excavation. The land was peeled back 320 feet—intended to be 1/5,280th the length of the original canal, but a bit short. One hundred and eighty-five years after it had been the focus of downtown Buffalo, it was the focus of Canalside, a tourist trap invented to reunite Buffalonians with the city's reason for existence. We passed onto Central Wharf, a wooden boardwalk where seagulls dove for French fries from an outdoor restaurant. It had an unpopulated Coney Island–in-September feel. Most of the attractions were still aquatic—a naval museum with three retired World War II vessels, a kayak livery, sailing classes—but Weyant envisioned a freshwater replica of Baltimore's Inner Harbor.

"We want to build a faux canal system, to give people an idea of what it was like to have water downtown," he said. "We want to have a Buffalo maritime museum, so people can visit historic boats. We want a cobblestone-street district, and we're hoping to put in a retail/restaurant mix. We're also working with cultural groups to tell the story of Buffalo. We could have an exhibit on the Underground Railroad."

I asked Weyant what he thought of Bonnie Eschborn's dream of diverting the highway from Riverside.

"It's been discussed for years," he said. "But that's a huge—our project is three hundred fifty million dollars. I can't even imagine what that would cost."

"If they built it today, though, do you think they'd put it where it is now?"

"Back then, the waterfront was an area of murder and bloodshed and human trafficking and prostitution," he said. "But look at what Boston did with the Big Dig—it's all submerged. With people looking at the water as something to use, it would have been placed differently."

On a boat trip up the Buffalo River, I saw what the Saint Lawrence Seaway had left behind. It was a gray summer morning, but a cloudy day in Buffalo is a dozen shades of gray. Lake Erie had boiled up a piebald quilt of lint, static, bruise, gruel, and black powder smoke. Despite missing the exit three times on my attempt to descend from the skyway to the waterfront, I was early and waited fifteen minutes before a boat sidled up to the jetty. Dipping a toe onto the idling vessel, I jumped aboard. The boat gouged a frothing J on the river and roared upstream, ahead of a ginger-ale wake. A kettle-corn odor settled in my nose.

"What's that?" I asked the pilot. His name was Mark. He wore a University of Buffalo cap and his beard was transparent white.

"That's the Cheerios," Mark said.

The General Mills plant fills millions of boxes a year, but it's the last living link to Buffalo's title as America's Granary. As the river uncoiled, we passed another grain elevator, as tall as a housing project. Its concrete walls had flaked away, exposing a network of steel bones.

Every bend of the Buffalo River revealed another empty elevator, each bearing the faded logo of a brewery run dry: Schmitt's, Cook's, Carling, Fred Kuck Malting. The gray cylinders were tombstones for Buffalo beers.

"Don't they look like castles?" Mark marveled. "They just go on as far as the eye can see. Down in Youngstown, Ohio, they took a grain elevator and made a shopping mall out of it. I keep threatening to paint them white and start a drive-in movie theater."

The sky was packed with fleece. On the bank, four men emerged from a door at the bottom of a tower. Farther on, boys dipped lines into the water, angling for fish too toxic to eat. A heron swept the surface on dragonfly wings. The trip felt tranquil and eerie at the same time, as though *The Wizard of Oz* had been remade as a dystopian science fiction movie and we were floating through the monochromatic ruins of the Emerald City.

"Why doesn't anybody use them anymore?" I asked Mark.

"They haven't been used for decades," he said. "Nineteen-twenties-ish. The whole industry, because of trains, became obsolete."

"So why aren't they torn down?"

"The cost of tearing them down would be frightening."

And nobody wanted the land. Other cities were building condos and shopping malls on the water. Buffalo still thought of its river as a damp industrial access road.

"There's very few things that Buffalo has done perfectly," Mark said. "They have perfectly separated the citizens from the waterfront. Buffalo is the last city of its size I've seen to regentrify. They keep moving farther and farther out."

EVERY GREAT LAKES CITY hopes that all the college students, all the factories, all the congressional seats that have disappeared to the Sun Belt, will someday come home—for the water. Not to sail on, not to look at out the window of a condominium—but to drink.

For the last half century, the Great Lakes states have been on the losing end of a migration that would have baffled our nomadic ancestors. Ignoring thousands of years of prophetic wisdom, going all the way back to Moses and Aaron, Americans have been moving away from fresh water and into the desert. In the most recent census, the two fastest-growing states—Nevada and Arizona—were two of the driest. Michigan, the state with the most drinking water, actually lost people. Some of those migrants were looking for work, following factory jobs down south. Others just couldn't stand another gloomy Northern winter. Those cold-weather refugees have been learning that the climate so well suited to year-round golf is not as well suited to providing millions of people with life's most essential element: H. Two. Oh.

In the late 2000s, Atlanta endured its worst drought in a century, inspiring Georgia governor Sonny Perdue to pray for rain. Lake Lanier, the reservoir that waters the endlessly growing colossus of metro Atlanta, shriveled to a shiny puddle. Georgia restricted car washing and lawn watering and shut off outdoor fountains.

At the same time, San Diego experienced its driest summer in recorded history. The hills were charred from autumn wildfires. California was so tapped out that the state tightened pumps carrying water from the Sacramento River to San Diego, and water authorities urged San Diegans to tear up their grass, replacing it with cacti and succulents.

These developments were viewed with some satisfaction by Northerners.

"They can have all the water they want," said Hugh McDiarmid Jr. of the Michigan Environmental Council, pointing out that the Great Lakes contain six quadrillion gallons of surface freshwater, or 20 percent of the world's supply. "All they have to do is move here."

There's plenty of cheap land. In Buffalo, I met a young Harvard Law graduate who had bought a house for $5,000, paying his mortgage and taxes by renting out the upper floor. Living for free allowed him to use his expensive degree at an immigrant aid society. Buffalonians have been waiting decades for this crisis.

"When the 'bomb' goes off—in 1990, 2010, or whenever—it could lead to the biggest rush since Sutter's Mill," Paul Jays of the *Buffalo Courier-Express* wrote in 1981. "But the 'gold' will be fresh water and cities like Buffalo—in what might be called the Water Belt—will be sitting right on the Mother Lode."

The South's water shortage was also regarded with some alarm, because every once in a while, someone looks at a map, draws an imaginary line from Chicago to Albuquerque, and thinks, "Wait a minute! If we can pipe oil across Alaska, we can pipe water from Lake Michigan." Bill Richardson, the former governor of arid New Mexico, had his region's plight in mind when he told the *Las Vegas Sun* that Northern states need to stop hogging all the water.

"I want a national water policy," Richardson said. "We need a dialogue between states to deal with issues like water conservation, water reuse technology, water delivery, and water production. States like Wisconsin are awash in water."

With that envious remark, Richardson tapped into the greatest fear of every Great Lakes politician: that all those folks who fled to the Sun Belt would try to take the water with them. Richardson was not the first desert chieftain to look covetously at the lakes. In 2001, President George W. Bush tried to talk to Canadian prime minister Jean Chrétien about piping water to Texas. Chrétien wouldn't discuss it. Three years later, trying to win Michigan, Bush declared, "We're never going to allow the diversion of Great Lakes water."

Water is an even more emotional issue in Michigan than in New York. In New York, the Great Lakes are an upstate concern, peripheral to New York City residents; in Michigan, they define the state, geographically, culturally, and historically. Michiganders see themselves as guardians of the lakes and have raised holy hell about issues as minor as exporting bottled water from local springs. When a Georgia congressman introduced a bill to study the nation's water use, two colleagues from Michigan condemned it as the blueprint of a Sun Belt plot to steal the Great Lakes, thus draining Michigan of its last remaining economic resource.

"My constituents are not going to support diverting Great Lakes water, particularly to areas of the United States that have lured jobs and people from Michigan," snarled Representative Candice Miller, R–Lake Huron.

In other words: You wanted to go live in that sand box. Don't come crying back to us when you can't find anything to drink.

Taking water from the Great Lakes is not the same as taking coal from West Virginia or oil from Alaska. The Great Lakes are not giant reservoirs to draw on whenever the nation needs a drink. They're an ecosystem. It has been said that exporting water from the lakes would be like exporting sunshine from Arizona. Draining the lakes would destroy fish spawning grounds and steal water from farmers. Thanks partly to the same climate change that's had the South thirsting, the lakes are as shallow as they've ever been, which would require dredging harbors. They haven't frozen over in recent winters, and no ice means more evaporation.

"Water diversion is the third rail of Great Lakes politics," says Peter Annin, author of *The Great Lakes Water Wars*. "It's the one issue that unites Democrats and Republicans. Bill Richardson's 2008 presidential candidacy ended because of his comments. You throw Ohio, Illinois, Michigan, Pennsylvania, New York out of the mix, it's really hard to win an election."

To seal off their water from the rest of the nation, those states, along with Minnesota, Indiana, and Wisconsin, negotiated the Great Lakes–St. Lawrence River Basin Water Resources Compact, which bans large-scale transfers of water outside the region. After ratification by all eight governors, it passed Congress and was signed by President Bush on December 8, 2008. The compact's framers pushed for approval before 2012, when the Southwestern states would, as happens every ten years, gain more congressmen at the Midwest's expense. (New York and Ohio lost two seats apiece, while Michigan, Pennsylvania, and Illinois each lost one; Texas gained four; Florida, two; Georgia, South Carolina, Utah, Arizona, and Nevada one. The Water Rush is at least another census away.)

The South needs water. The Midwest needs people. Maybe it's time the two regions worked something out. Think of how much less energy we'd expend moving the people to the water, instead of moving the water to the people. Beckoning the Sun Belters home is not an idle appeal. The Great Lakes basin is home to thirty-three million people. But its water can support millions more. William Frey, a demographer who has studied the Sun Belt migration for the Brookings Institution, thinks the South's water shortages may "spur a U-turn" in that decades-long pattern. Moribund Upstate New York may finally have a chance to recover all those kids who buggered off to California with their SUNY master's degrees.

ON THE EVENING I left Buffalo, I returned to Riverside Park, for a sunset ceremony. A dozen people stood in the grass, where the land begins to subside toward the river. All held percussion instruments, or at least solid objects that could be clicked together rhythmically. One woman held a wooden spoon and salad tongs. Another held a pair of sticks shed by one of Riverside Park's tenured elms, which are so thickly and exhaustively branched that the loss of a few twigs won't alter their network of veins cast in wood.

"This is the only place on the eastern coast where you can see the sunset over a body of fresh water," Bonnie said. Then she thanked me for bringing my notebook. "We can only get the media to come out when we have a murder."

The Niagara River flows north from Lake Erie to Lake Ontario, and Buffalo is on the east bank. (This also places it east of Canada, a geographic quirk not quite as remarkable as Detroit's location north of Windsor, Ontario.) We looked over Strawberry Island, hollowed to a cay by the mining of sand and gravel for the concrete that built Buffalo. Beyond was Grand Island, the last barrier between New York and Ontario.

It wasn't a beautiful Great Lakes evening, not one of those Lake Michigan sunsets that are ephemeral strata of salmon and smoke. The sun's withdrawal was more felt than seen. The light mellowed from noon white to eight o'clock orange. The air cooled, until the entire park felt like shade.

Drumming away the light was the idea of Mercy Delacruz, who had seen a similar ceremony on Venice Beach, when she'd lived in Southern California. Mercy played an African djembe, a profound counterpoint to a snare drum and a tambourine.

In Los Angeles, drumming had been "more of a meditative thing," Mercy said. In Buffalo, it was a shamanistic exercise to drive away demons—the drunks and muggers who haunted Riverside Park. In its own way, it, too, was a communion with the water, a plaint for a reunion.

13.

The Second Great Recession

Ted Michols watched Slavic Village fall apart. A retired trade magazine editor, a bachelor, a man who likes to sit on his porch and watch Classen Avenue passersby he's known fifty years, Michols has lived his entire life in a little square house his grandfather bought in 1923. It's the kind of house that used to be good enough for everyone in Cleveland: eight hundred square feet of domesticity in the middle of a pond of grass where a Virgin Mary is flanked by floral suns of marigolds and an American flag. He shared it with his brother, another bachelor who died in 2005. Now he's alone. His old school friends want to know why he never followed them to the suburbs. To them, Slavic Village is the Old Neighborhood, but no longer the neighborhood they grew up in. "It's changed," they say delicately. That's Cleveland code for "the element moved in," which in turn is code for "black."

Michols stayed because Slavic Village is Polish—unlike many urban neighborhoods, where integration is the period between the arrival of the first black and the departure of the last white, Slavic Village only changed halfway. At Seven Roses, the cabbage-and-pierogi buffet on Fleet Avenue, the newspapers and lunchtime gossip are about doings in Kraków and Warszawa. And staying in Slavic Village meant staying in the parish of Immaculate Heart of Mary, where he had been baptized.

"The one good thing about living here is you have a lot of friends," Michols said. "We were working on the sidewalk, about ten people stopped and talked. You don't get that in the suburbs. People don't talk."

But he had fewer friends than before the housing crisis. The house next door disappeared first. The couple who lived there had paid $17,500 for it, in 1977. At that price, they should have been sheltered for life, but

230

"they liked to buy stuff," Michols observed, so they borrowed and borrowed against their equity until, in 2004, they lost it to the bank. A fireman picked it up for $25,000. Like a slumlord, he painted it and rented to a woman on Section 8, who was so clueless about housekeeping that Michols had to mow her lawn. From owner to low-income renter, the house was moving down in the world. Eventually, a corner of the foundation collapsed, causing the floor to sink four inches. The tenant moved out, and the house was demolished, leaving in the grass only the outline of its basement. The same thing happened across the street, where an absentee landlord bought out an owner and rented to tenants who sold drugs. After they set the house on fire, Michols went to court to have the place demolished.

Frugality was easy for Michols. Having inherited his house, he'd never made a mortgage payment. Having no children to educate, he never thought of borrowing. So he was astonished by the appliance repairman who divorced his wife and abandoned his house, owing $83,000. And by the speculators who were paying double what the old-line neighbors knew the properties were worth.

"Sometimes, we'd look at some of those homes and we said, 'This is going for eighty-six thousand dollars? What is going on?' The bank wasn't looking at applications."

As the loans went bad and the houses emptied, the scrappers arrived, tearing out furnaces, aluminum siding, and water pipes right in broad daylight. To discourage scavengers, signs reading "THIS HOUSE DOES NOT HAVE COPPER PLUMBING" were posted in windows. But Classen Avenue became such a magnet for thieves they even broke into occupied houses. A kid from down the street tried to burgle Michols, but Michols chased him off. Only a neighbor who mowed the vacant lots prevented Classen Avenue from reverting to presettlement prairie.

Clevelanders have a saying: "Cleveland's pain, the nation's gain." It means "A lot of shitty stuff happens here, but we hope the rest of America can learn from our misfortune and avoid the same crap." The foreclosure crisis that would drag the American economy into its deepest slough since the Great Depression arrived first in Cleveland, and nowhere was it more severe than Slavic Village. The 44105 zip code, which covers southeast Cleveland, was the scene of more housing speculation than any place in the country. Unfortunately, the rest of America wasn't paying attention.

Slavic Village was settled in the late nineteenth century by Poles,

Czechs, and Bohemians who'd been imported to break a strike by native-born workers at the Cleveland Rolling Mill. They worked ten hours a day, six days a week, for wages that kept them just a bit more comfortable than barnyard animals, and built $400 cottages with even smaller mother-in-law cabins out back. Slavic Village was sooty, it was overcrowded, but it was also one of those self-contained ethnic ghettos that perpetuated Old World languages and customs for decades after *babcia* and *dziadek* arrived on the ship from Danzig. The church where you were baptized, the department store where you bought your communion dress, the high school where you finished your education, the factory where you spent your working life, the tavern where you spent your after-work life, the house where you raised your family, the hospital where you died, and the graveyard where you were buried were all within a few miles of each other. Unto the third generation, children grew up speaking Slavic languages at home, hearing them during Mass at St. Stanislaus (Polish) or St. John Nepomucene (Czech), and arguing in them at the Alliance of Poles, the Czech Sokol Center, or the Bohemian National Hall. The storefronts on Fleet Avenue and Broadway were labeled with poorly envoweled names: Stepke's Hot Shop, Glinka's Tavern, Divorky Hardware. Nobody minded a small house, because the tavern, the church, and the social hall were extensions of the living room.

That all changed after World War II, of course. Slavic Village's children moved to inner-ring suburbs such as Garfield Heights and Parma. (Parma is Cleveland's Cleveland, the butt of local jokes about pink flamingos and bathtub Madonnas. *The Drew Carey Show*'s original theme was "Moon over Parma" and in 2010, a radio host spoofed Jay-Z's "Empire State of Mind" with "Parma State of Mind.") The suburbanites returned for polka bands and pierogi-eating contests at Slavic Village Fest, but when their parents died, the middle-aged offspring had no interest in their childhood homes. They sold out to absentee landlords, who rented to Section 8 tenants. By the 1990s, Slavic Village, which had never actually been a village, was no longer entirely Slavic either. It was more than 50 percent African-American. After the slumlords came the speculators, the house flippers. Ohio had some of the weakest lending laws in the nation. Slavic Village, a neighborhood full of unwanted dwellings, was ground zero for exploitation. Between 2000 and 2010, Slavic Village's population dropped 27 percent, on its way down from its all-time high of seventy thousand to twenty thousand. During a time when banks were willing to write mortgages to *anyone*, for any amount of money, there was cash to be squeezed out of empty houses.

Here's how one scam worked, according to Tony Zajac, an aide to Slavic Village's city councilman Anthony Brancatelli. When Zajac's aunt was eighty-nine, her son moved her into a nursing home. He put a "PRIVATE SALE" sign on her ten-room house, offering it for $40,000. The buyer took out a $90,000 mortgage, stating on the purchase agreement that she intended to use the balance for rehab. Instead, she split the money with the mortgage broker and the appraiser who had conspired to falsify the home's value.

"They took the fifty thousand dollars and split it to line their pockets with gold," Zajac said. "Three years ago, Aunt Mary and her son were sued by the lender, Deutsche Bank. They falsify the income of the purchaser and they fly. They leave the house once they got the money."

Then there were flippers. They paid old women $40,000 for their houses, then turned around and sold them for $60,000 to suckers whose greed was inflamed by "Get Rich Quick in Real Estate!" infomercials, and by the inflated real estate market of the late 1990s, when properties were doubling and tripling in value. Hapless bargain hunters purchased houses on the Internet, only to find them boarded up and stripped of every metal fixture. A California artist looking for a cheap home/studio bought a Slavic Village house that turned out to be condemned. (After many trips to housing court, he brought it back up to code.)

The lenders were so aggressive they went door-to-door on the East Side of Cleveland, pointing out loose shingles, collapsing chimneys, or sagging porches. Money from a second mortgage could repair any of those defects, the door-to-door brokers told the homeowners. They never mentioned the adjustable rate.

Anita Gardner's sons fell for that scam. Gardner, who worked thirty-one years as a heavy-duty machinist and welder at TRW Automotive, bought a two-story house on the East Side for $21,000 back in the early 1970s. It was almost paid off when she was diagnosed with Chiari malformation, a brain disorder that left her too ill to work or even walk up the stairs to her bedroom. So she bought a one-story home, a converted liquor store, and signed the old house—"My Buckingham Palace, a place where I could cover the walls with my paintings and close off the world"—over to her two thirtysomething sons. When Gardner had moved in, every house was owned by an autoworker or a steelworker with a wife, four or five children, and a new car. Then J & L Steel, the neighborhood's largest employer, closed in 1999. The blue-collar workers moved out, and the mortgage brokers began moving in, attracted by the remaining residents' financial desperation. Having lost their paychecks, these dispossessed factory rats were told they still had a source of income, in the houses they'd bought cheap and paid off with union wages and frugality.

"This couldn't have happened if people had good jobs," Gardner said. "Or why would they change their mortgage? They were desperate for money. It was targeted. It was definitely targeted. Mortgage agents were going door-to-door, calling on the phone. It was in the air: 'You don't have to have credit. You can have nice things.'"

Gardner's sons fell for the pitch. Neither had ever been able to afford nice things. The elder brother had served eleven years on a drug charge. When he got out of prison, the only job he could find was delivering furniture for Sears. The younger brother worked as a restaurant supply salesman. When an agent from Countrywide Financial offered them a $70,000 mortgage on their mom's almost-paid-off house, they signed. Gardner suspects the agent falsely inflated the home's value in order to write a bigger mortgage. Agents received bigger commissions for adjustable-rate mortgages. The boys used the second mortgage for a shopping spree. A black Hyundai Tiburon sports car. A new couch. A big-screen TV. A refrigerator in the garage, full of beer.

The monthly payments began at $436 a month, but as the boys missed payments, it more than doubled to $950, far more than they could pay on their small-time jobs. When the past-due amount reached $4,000, Gardner's sons appealed to Mom for a bailout.

Gardner paid the arrears, plus an $800 transaction fee, plus a series of six $1,000 "good-faith payments" to return the note to its original payment plan. A Realtor friend negotiated with Countrywide to buy the house back for $25,000—which Gardner raised by borrowing on her new house. The mortgage lending crisis ate up her life savings.

"I'm out of money," she said. "This is all my retirement money. I have enough to live on, but all the money I had stuffed under the mattress, it's gone. Meanwhile, my mortgage on the new house jumps from six hundred dollars to nine hundred dollars."

Gardner evicted her sons—"they don't deserve this, they don't understand what the palace is"—but two months after buying back her house from Countrywide, she was informed that the employee with whom she'd negotiated had no authority to cut a deal.

"Why should we take twenty-five thousand dollars when we can get seventy thousand dollars?" a Countrywide agent told Gardner. "We will get the money from your son. We will prosecute him."

Countrywide sued Gardner's sons and began foreclosure proceedings on the house. Desperate, she appealed to an organization called ESOP—Empowering and Strengthening Ohio's People. As a social service agency in the nation's foreclosure capital, ESOP was devoting a large part of its resources to mortgage counseling. Having lived a middle-class life, Gardner was a little put off by ESOP's office. A room in the back of a church, with two or three people working on mismatched furniture, it reminded her of a sweatshop or a numbers runner's den. But Gardner joined ESOP's campaign against Countrywide, which had been writing shady mortgages all over northeastern Ohio. Wearing a shark's head, Gardner joined a picket of Countrywide's headquarters, where ESOP members passed out the personal cell phone number of CEO Angelo Mozilo. Busloads of protesters picketed Mozilo's country club. (They were followed, needless to say, by vanloads of TV cameras.) ESOP blew up the company's fax machine with photographs of foreclosed homes. Finally, Countrywide settled with Gardner for another $6,000. Buckingham Palace was hers again, but the rest of her street was a cemetery.

"There was seventy-six houses on the street, and now only eleven are occupied," she said.

This raises a question. Which is the greater social ill: allowing people who can no longer afford their mortgages to stay in their houses, thus undermining the credit system by letting people skip out on their payments, or evicting people from houses for which there is no buyer, thus undermining the property itself and the surrounding neighborhood? Ted Michols and Anita Gardner would say let the poor folks stay and look after their houses. Vacant houses attract criminals. Michols called the cops on a stripper trying to tear the aluminum drainpipe off a house at eleven o'clock in the morning. In a 150-foot radius around a vacant house, property values go down at least $7,000. A vacant house reduces its *own* value even more, since it's usually denuded of plumbing fixtures, boilers, carpeting, sinks, toilets, heating pipes, and any architectural sconces that can be peddled in a secondhand shop. Yellow foreclosure stickers and plywood windows are not warnings, they're invitations. After homeowners exhaust the equity, inner-city scavengers salvage the last pennies of value out of a house, until the mortgage lender ends up paying the city for demolition.

Jim Rokakis, who had been a twenty-two-year-old city councilman when Dennis Kucinich was mayor, was elected Cuyahoga County treasurer in 1996. Holding that job, at that time, made him the first politician in America to see the foreclosure crisis coming. Normally, 2 to 3 percent of the county's homes were in foreclosure. But by the end of

Rokakis's first term, that proportion had doubled. Cuyahoga County had the highest foreclosure rate in the nation.

As a freshman treasurer, Rokakis was ignorant of the mortgage industry's scams. But once he learned that fly-by-night brokers were writing inflated mortgages to buyers with no income, he convened a conference, "Predatory Lending in Ohio," at the Cleveland branch of the Federal Reserve. Rokakis hoped that Federal Reserve Board chairman Alan Greenspan might crack down on sleazy lenders like Countrywide. Greenspan did nothing, not even after receiving a warning letter from a Federal Reserve governor who attended the conference. So Rokakis persuaded three Ohio cities—Cleveland, Dayton, and Toledo—to adopt anti-predatory-lending ordinances. The ordinances were quickly invalidated by the state legislature in Columbus, which passed a law specifying that only the state could regulate banking. This, of course, lured even more lenders to Cleveland. In 2004, Ameriquest Mortgage Company, the nation's largest subprime lender, established an office of its Argent Mortgage subsidiary in Cleveland. Ameriquest had invented the "stated income loan": if a customer told Ameriquest he earned one hundred grand a year, Ameriquest would take his word for it. Why let the facts mess up a bad loan?

"The amazing statistic about Argent is their first year of operation, '04, they led Cuyahoga County in two categories—loans issued and foreclosures," Rokakis said. "So the day they opened up, they were in trouble. They were making these wild loans and they were making loans that could not be repaid."

By the time the crisis peaked, in 2006, Cuyahoga County had thirteen thousand foreclosure filings—four times its pre-2000 level. Unable to get the attention of Greenspan or Ohio governor Bob Taft, Rokakis wrote an op-ed for the *Washington Post*. By then, it was too late for the nation to gain from Cleveland's pain. From its cradle in Slavic Village, the subprime lending industry had spread throughout the entire nation and was a year away from capsizing the entire American economy. Wrote Rokakis:

> Let me tell you about a place called Slavic Village and the death of a girl called Cookie Thomas. You've never heard this story before— talk of housing markets and hedge funds, interest rates and the Federal Reserve has drowned it out.
>
> Twenty years ago, the Slavic Village neighborhood of Cleveland was a tightly knit community of first- and second-generation Pol-

ish and Czech immigrants. Today, it's in danger of becoming a ghost town, largely because a swarm of speculators, real estate agents, mortgage brokers and lenders saw an opportunity to make a buck there.

You could say it was because of them that 12-year-old Asteve "Cookie" Thomas lost her life on Sept. 1, shot in Slavic Village when she stumbled into the crossfire of suspected drug dealers. The neighborhood wasn't always a haven for criminals—not until hundreds of foreclosures destabilized the community. Houses (800 at last count) and then entire streets were abandoned. Crime increased as vacant properties offered shelter for people who had a reason to hide.

Cookie Thomas . . . haunt[s] me because [she] didn't have to die. In a sense, [her death] was foreshadowed in the late 1990s, when the dark side of the real estate industry—the predatory lenders—came to Ohio, including Cleveland's Cuyahoga County, where I serve as treasurer. They knew that the state's lax regulatory structure would give them virtually free rein. This is when we first heard terms such as "securitization," "mortgage-backed securities," "3-28s," and "risk modeling." These are code words for Wall Street strategies that made the cycle of no-money-down, no-questions-asked lending possible—the strategies that have sucked the life out of my city.

By 2006, the year the crisis peaked in Cleveland, 903 of Slavic Village's 2,944 properties were in foreclosure. Rokakis did secure passage of a county ordinance that sped up foreclosure of vacant, tax-delinquent properties. The empty houses went into the city's land bank, which often sold them to next-door neighbors, so they could expand their yards. ("If the vacant lot is next to you and you can beautify it by putting grass and cutting it and keep it nice, it adds to your property value," Rokakis said.) Others went to community development organizations. On a street as gapped and rotten as an old tramp's mouth, a group called Slavic Village Development built vinyl-sided ranch houses to replace the worn-out workingman's cottages.

Slavic Village offers an opportunity for an entrepreneurial developer. Broadway, the neighborhood's high street, is served by five-and-ten-dollar businesses: Walgreens, Wendy's, soft ice cream stands, and grimy diners serving city chicken. (The Cleveland dish of city chicken is actually cubed pork on a skewer. It was invented as a poultry substitute by

Slavic housewives too poor to afford actual chicken and is still served as a white ethnic comfort food.) What Slavic Village needs is a strip mall gathering every ghetto business under a single roof. It would include a cell phone store, a discount dollar store, a rent-to-own center, a Laundromat, a liquor store specializing in White Owl cigars and Night Train wine, a Chinese takeout with three wobbly tables and a hand-lettered "NO MSG" sign in the window, a chicken-and-fish grill where the food is served on a rotisserie that rotates through a bulletproof window, an instant-tax-refund center where a man dressed as the Statue of Liberty hands out flyers every winter, and a currency exchange charging a 3 percent fee to cash checks for people trying to avoid having their bank accounts garnished for child support and/or back taxes and/or legal fees. The mall could also support a sneaker boutique selling counterfeit Nikes (look for the backward swoosh) and three-for-five packages of cotton socks, as well as a day labor center that takes a 33 percent fee out of your wages but doesn't ask, "Have you ever been convicted of a felony?" on the application. A pawnshop is also a possibility, although pawnbrokers have been thriving since the recession began, so they might be able to afford their own building.

The wonderful thing about this mall is that it could be prefabricated and franchised out to every inner-city neighborhood and small town in the United States. Just as toothpaste and soap manufacturers are trying to profit from the economic stratification of America by developing discount products for the formerly middle class, a single poverty-pimpin' conglomerate—we'll call it PoorMart—could develop thousands of these little malls, from Bridgeport, Connecticut, to Phenix City, Alabama, to Stockton, California. After buying the properties in foreclosure sales, PoorMart would hire nonunion contractors to build the stores and recruit low-wage employees from Pakistan, India, Nigeria, and Iraq, arranging for work visas which would be voided at the first sign of insubordination. PoorMart would fill a niche too small and specialized for Walmart to occupy. As the Walton family earns billions of dollars by selling shoddy goods to people who lack the money or the transportation options to shop in department stores, PoorMart's owners would earn billions off people too poor to shop at Walmart. They'd make billions more in interest and convenience fees from people too broke to save up for a living room set or wait six weeks for their tax refunds. With its combination of retail stores and financial services, PoorMart would transmute the masses' poverty into investors' wealth.

As the birthplace of the new underclass, Slavic Village is the perfect test market for PoorMart. Unlike most urban neighborhoods—even most neighborhoods in Cleveland, where the Cuyahoga River separates East Side blacks and West Side whites—Slavic Village is racially mixed. A cross was burned when blacks began to infiltrate in the 1990s, but Catholic parishes—like Ted Michols's Immaculate Heart of Mary—and Polish immigrants prevented unanimous white flight. Slavic Village's demographics have settled at 55 percent African-American and 41 percent Caucasian. The white population has actually been growing, due to young urban pioneers seeking cheap housing and "authentic urban experiences" (e.g., Polish bakeries) they can't find in the suburbs. When Slavic Village Development built middle-income houses and town houses on the site of a closed-down state mental institution, it managed to attract black and white buyers in equal numbers, by marketing to both races. Councilman Brancatelli marketed his Fourth of July fireworks show the same way: he hires a country singer and a funk band, thus drawing a salt-and-pepper crowd of blacks, elderly Poles, and tattooed white families. While waiting in line for free ice cream and hot dogs before the fireworks, I met a man who identified himself as "Bohemian, Hungarian, Polish, Czech, and Slovenian," which used to pass for diversity in Slavic Village. He believed his neighborhood's worst years were over, now that the city was demolishing the legacies of the foreclosures.

"It's cleaned up a lot of property," he said. "There's a lot of vacant land. The crime went up, because there was drug dealers in all the houses, but they've been torn down. It's turning the corner. Plus, once you're a drug dealer, you have to have money to buy drugs. All the scrap is gone. The drug dealers are moving out to the suburbs."

THE HOUSING CRISIS that began in Slavic Village eventually bankrupted several Wall Street houses that had overinvested in subprime-mortgage-backed securities. What was bad for Wall Street was even worse for Detroit. The American automakers were already struggling in 2008. Their solvency depended on SUV sales. Only big vehicles could generate the profits necessary to pay health care premiums and pensions for millions of retirees. But once gasoline prices crested at $4 a gallon that May, even Americans stopped buying SUVs. In the spring quarter of 2008, General Motors lost $15.5 billion. GM cut off medical benefits to retired salesmen, engineers, and executives, but it couldn't cut off UAW members, whose contracts guaranteed health care for life.

Then, in September, Lehman Brothers filed for bankruptcy. The stock market lost 30 percent of its value. Automobile sales dropped by the same amount, to their lowest levels since the Iranian crisis of the late 1970s. GM stock crashed to $3.36 a share—less than a third of its value just three months before, and its most meager price since 1946. Drivers weren't buying cars. Bankers weren't making loans. The auto companies had only one place to turn for money: the federal government.

In Pinckney, Michigan, an automotive engineer named Tom Lavey watched the entire congressional auto bailout hearings on CNN. Lavey had plenty of time to sit in front of his television, because he'd just been laid off for the second time that year. During the spring, he'd ended a contract job with International Automotive Components, designing carpets for Ford cars. In the fall, Lavey caught on as a contractor with Ford, where he had worked early in his career. It paid a third less than he'd been making at IAC, but in 2008, the Big Three weren't handing out engineering jobs the way they had been when Lavey graduated from Eastern Michigan University in the 1980s.

There's a legend that when a boy is born in southeastern Michigan, his parents declare, "What a cute baby. He'll make a great addition to the auto industry." Lavey decided that himself. From the time he was seven years old, he wanted to make cars. His path was confirmed in college, where he saw a flyer listing the salaries of various careers. "Manufacturing and Auto Industry: $30,000 a year" it read. That was good money. It was security, too. How could manufacturing ever go away? People would always need stuff. The auto industry had supported his grandfather, who'd spent his entire career at Ford, and it would support him, too. Right out of college, Lavey got a contract job at Ford and saved enough money for a three-month trip to Europe.

"From 1989 to 2008, it was fat in this town," he said. "You'd get a contract, have two parts to work on."

Throughout the 2000s, though, Lavey saw signs that his dream career was not as secure as he'd imagined. There were fewer designers on each job, which meant the surviving engineers often had to stay in the office until eight or nine o'clock. And the auto companies were outsourcing computer-assisted drafting to India and the Philippines. The draftsmen were cheaper but a pain to work with. You couldn't talk to them face-to-face. Because they were on the opposite side of the world, bad designs took an entire day to fix.

Still, Lavey wasn't prepared for the brevity of his last assignment for

Ford. The job lasted exactly a month before it was eliminated during the financial crisis.

"Don't worry," Lavey's supervisor told him. "This is a budget thing. We'll have you back in January."

Two weeks later, the boss called back, with more bad news.

"Guess what?" he told Lavey. "They got me, too."

When the chairmen of General Motors and Chrysler traveled to Washington to beg for a loan (first by corporate jet, then by caravan, after congressmen criticized the mendicant auto executives for flying when it would have been cheaper to drive), the strongest opposition came from Southerners who saw burying Detroit as an opportunity to bury the United Auto Workers and the entire union movement. Senator Richard Shelby of Alabama called the American auto industry a "dinosaur" and suggested government aid would only delay its well-deserved demise.

"Companies fail every day and others take their place," Shelby said. "I think this is a road we should not go down."

The companies that would have taken GM's place—Mercedes-Benz, Hyundai, and Honda—all have plants in Alabama, where they benefit from Southern hostility to organized labor. None of Alabama's plants are unionized—perhaps one reason the state ranks forty-sixth in household income.

Senator Bob Corker of Tennessee, who represented a Volkswagen and a Nissan plant (as well as GM's unionized Saturn facility in Spring Hill), tried to force the UAW to agree to "wage parity" with the Japanese auto plants as a condition of the bailout. His attempt to cut union wages to nonunion levels was mooted when President George W. Bush decided that, like the banks, the auto companies were too big to fail and sent them $17.4 billion of the $700 billion Wall Street bailout money, enough to keep them afloat for three months.

Bush was one of Detroit's few friends in Washington during that difficult autumn. Even as two of the Big Three wheedled with the Senate Banking Committee, the House Energy and Commerce Committee unhorsed Representative John Dingell of Michigan as its chairman, replacing him with Henry Waxman of California. It was a clash between liberalism's most powerful wings—coastal progressives and Rust Belt union brothers—and it was unfortunate, because between them, the two have a solution for saving the auto industry.

If one congressman had foreseen that universal health care could be a boon to American manufacturing, it was Dingell. Rooted in the

New Deal and the industrial heartland, Dingell embodied the auto industry's traditions. Stocky, block-headed, with safety-glass eyewear, he looked like he should have been inspecting the paint job on a Buick. Every year since beginning his record-setting service in Congress, in 1955, Dingell had introduced a bill for a single-payer national health insurance system—the same bill his father began promoting in 1933.

By 2008, though, the political tide had turned against the old Detroit champion. Dingell's defense of the auto industry made him a stalwart opponent of any regulations that might discourage GM from building ginormous SUVs. He had tried to prevent California from adopting its own auto emissions standards, arguing for a nationwide plan. Waxman, a resident of Beverly Hills, was more concerned with air quality in his overpopulated state than with the plight of Midwestern factory workers. The eighty-two-year-old Dingell left the meeting at which he lost his chairmanship on crutches, demonstrating the infirmity of both his state and the industry he has defended so vigorously.

Waxman and Dingell both needed to realize that health care, environmentalism, and the labor movement are inseparable elements of saving the auto industry. Unfortunately, the Affordable Care Act that Waxman would help pass did not relieve the burden of health care costs on automakers. GM had already tried to do that on its own. During a two-day strike in 2007, the company negotiated an agreement to transfer retiree health care to an independent trust fund maintained by the UAW. GM contributed $36 billion to the fund—70 percent of its liability to retirees. It was expected to save the company $2.5 billion a year.

THE $17 BILLION BAILOUT did not provide a new job for Tom Lavey. Americans still weren't buying cars. They had no equity left in their houses, and since new housing starts had crashed from two million a year to five hundred thousand, hordes of construction workers were without jobs. Out of work for the first time in his adult life, Lavey joined the "99ers"—the hard-luck Americans eligible for ninety-nine weeks of unemployment. As a bachelor, he had no family to support, but he was nonetheless grateful when his landlord cut the rent in half. He could have paid the full freight with his unemployment check, but that would have meant eating a lot of meals at his mother's house. Lavey kept busy in his machine shop, where he made screws, nuts, and binocular housings, selling them to a science supply company for just enough money to cover his cell phone bill and fill his gas tank.

"Working in a shop, I got laid off for a week at a time," Lavey said. "But this was the first time I was told, 'Get out and don't come back.'"

He wouldn't be invited back in for almost two years.

WHEN NICK WAUN CAME home to Michigan after a tour of duty in Iraq, he intended to finish his economics degree at the University of Michigan–Flint. But first, he needed a job to pay for school. Waun was a fourth-generation factory brat—his great-grandfather had been a Sit-Down Striker, and growing up, he'd listened to his father and grandfather talk shop. In 2007, it wasn't easy to get a job in an auto plant, but Waun was a veteran. More importantly, he was a legacy. He had an in.

"Hey," his aunt asked. "You want to go work for General Motors?"

(A family recommendation is pretty much the only way to get a job in an auto plant nowadays. The United Auto Workers may as well be a hereditary guild.)

Waun was hired to work on the line at the Lake Orion assembly plant, at $28 an hour, an astonishingly high wage for a twenty-five-year old. He bought a house in Lapeer, a village in Michigan's Thumb, a protuberance east of Flint whose anatomical nickname is derived from its resemblance to the loose digit on the mitten-shaped Lower Peninsula. At night, Waun built Pontiac G6s and Chevy Malibus. During the day, he went to school in Flint.

Waun belonged to the final class of middle-income autoworkers. If he'd hired in even a few months later, he would have been offered half the money he was earning, and fewer benefits. In 2007, as part of the same national agreement in which the UAW took on retirees' health care costs, the union also agreed that nonassembly workers could be paid $14 an hour. This arrangement became known as the tiered wage system. The veteran autoworkers were called Tier Ones, while the ill-paid new hires were Tier Twos. The UAW hoped Tier Twos would become Tier Ones as soon as the companies' fortunes improved. The next year, of course, GM and Chrysler went bankrupt. As part of its prebankruptcy concessions, the union agreed to freeze Tier Two wages until 2015. During the bankruptcy restructuring, GM was forced to eliminate the Pontiac nameplate. (With Oldsmobile already dead, GM's brand ladder had been reduced to three rungs: Chevrolet, Buick, and Cadillac. Buick survived because it had become to Chinese party officials and software tycoons what the Mercedes-Benz is to Hollywood producers and Brooklyn rap stars: the car that says, "I've made it," or however they say "I've made it" in Mandarin.) With Pontiac in the brand graveyard, Waun was laid off for a year while the Lake Orion plant was retooled to build Chevy Aveos. When he was called back, GM gave him a choice: he could stay in Lake Orion as a Tier Two, or he could continue earning $28 an hour at the plant in Lordstown, Ohio, 220 miles around the bend of Lake Erie. The reason: Lake Orion would be building the Aveo and the Chevy Cruze, compact cars that sold for less than $20,000. GM could only make a profit if 40 percent of the workers assembling those cars earned $14 an hour. Because of Waun's low seniority, he would have to take a pay cut.

Waun took the transfer, which came with a $30,000 bonus. He dropped out of college eighteen credits short of a degree and rented a $450-a-month trailer in a mobile home court across the turnpike from the plant. Lordstown was home to a lot of GM gypsies who'd been forced out of their home factories.

Even before he was jerked around by General Motors, Waun had been a rabble-rouser. During his freshman year in college, he was a campus radical who thought a student should sit on the University of Michigan's board of regents. Neither the Democrats nor the Republicans would nominate him, so he ran on the Reform Party ticket. At eighteen, Waun was the youngest candidate ever to appear on a statewide ballot in Michigan—one-upping fellow Flintoid Michael Moore, who had only run for local office. As an autoworker, Waun labored in GM's two most militant cities: Flint and Lordstown. The Lordstown plant had opened in 1966 and was immediately staffed with Vietnam veterans, who were, as we saw in Decatur, Illinois, the most uncompromising labor activists of the late twentieth century. Lordstown built the Vega, Chevy's crappy attempt to crash the small-car market. The car was scheduled to debut in 1970, but that fall's UAW strike delayed its introduction. The little Vega was supposed to be America's greatest weapon against Japan since Fat Man. To rush the heavily advertised car to dealers, GM *doubled* the speed of Lordstown's assembly line. A "speed-up" had caused the Sit-Down Strike. Lordstown's workers responded by slashing upholstery, keying up paint jobs, denting quarter panels, and even breaking off keys in locks. Finally, they went on strike. The estrangement of these young, multiracial workers became known as the "blue-collar blues"; their rebellion was a "Worker's Woodstock," drawing comparisons to the antiwar marches at nearby Kent State University.

As a scion of both these Up the Company traditions, Waun began a campaign against the tiered-wage system. It wasn't just about economic fairness, although that was certainly part of it. Tiered wages were accomplishing what those Southern senators had tried to write into the auto bailout plan. Nonunion, foreign-owned plants were now setting the pay scale for American autoworkers. Not only did Tier Twos earn half as much, they had lesser benefits, bigger copays for health care, and a 401(k) contribution, instead of a pension. If GM could threaten to cut Waun's pay in half, whose livelihood was safe? There was also a quality issue. After a year at Lake Orion, Waun was named a team leader—just as the plant brought in a second shift, composed partly of Tier Twos. Tier Twos were not supposed to assemble cars. According to the agreement, that status was reserved for "non-core" jobs, away from the line. But GM was putting them on the line, and, unsurprisingly to Waun, they wouldn't—or couldn't—work as hard as Tier Ones. Some were juggling two jobs to pay their rent and came to the plant exhausted. Others decided that $14 an hour was not enough money for the hectic pace of auto work. They walked out of the plant, declaring, "I'm going back to Home Depot." If a bolt wasn't torqued right, they'd let it go down the line, rather than making the effort to tighten it. Such lax attitudes created tension with the Tier Ones. Waun saw a resentful Tier One punch his Tier Two team leader. When the Michiganders arrived at Lordstown, the lower-paid Ohioans refused to speak to them, then taunted them by wearing T-shirts popular on football Saturdays in Columbus: "Ann Arbor Is a Whore," "M Go Blow."

"They've already had problems with the Cruze, with steering wheels coming off," Waun said. "There's been a couple recalls. I've heard it brought up at the union, that it was sabotage by disgruntled Tier Two workers."

Waun filed a complaint against the Lake Orion agreement, on the grounds that it had been approved without a vote of the local membership. If his brothers and sisters had known about the Tier One/Tier Two clause, he was sure they would have turned it down.

"The membership had no previous knowledge that a 50% pay cut was under consideration until the announcement on October 3," Waun wrote in his complaint. "For the previous 12 months, charging member Nick Waun had perused every local newsletter, attended every local meeting, and frequently reviewed the local website. Though negotiations with GM were reported on, there had been no indication that significant pay cuts might be an issue at the table."

In a letter addressed to "Brother Waun," UAW president Bob King replied that not only had the international executive board rejected

Waun's complaint, but he had no standing to make a complaint, because he had transferred his local membership from Lake Orion's 5960 to Lordstown's 1112. Waun then appealed to the National Labor Relations Board, which declined to intervene in "an internal Union matter."

So Waun continued his campaign on the Internet. He became a regular poster on factoryrat.com and autoworkercaravan.com, two shoprat message boards. During a visit to Michigan, Waun participated in a demonstration against the two-tier system that was attended by one of the last surviving Sit-Downers. Bob King labeled him "the number one troublemaker in the UAW."

As I found out when I visited his trailer in Lordstown, Waun had nothing better to do. Big and soft, with a shaved head and oblong, half-framed spectacles, Waun lived in conditions that identified him as a) the tidiest bachelor this side of a wedding, b) a mustered-out soldier who still abided by barrack-room standards of neatness, or c) a man who spends most of his nights in a place he refuses to call home. Probably all three. The *only* furniture in his living room was a folding card table, on which rested his computer and a copy of *Overhaul*, auto czar Steven Rattner's self-congratulatory memoir of how he saved Detroit, despite spending only one day there and knowing far more about credit default swaps than internal combustion.

"I look at it like camping," Waun said of his austere life. "I look at it like when I was in the army. A lot of times we'd sleep in tents. A lot of times we'd sleep in trailers."

Waun couldn't travel because he'd burned all his time off visiting his aged parents in Michigan. Since his brother lives in Seattle, Waun is the closest, so he used up a month and a half of sick leave caring for his diabetic father. When his mother's heater broke down, Waun took vacation time to fix it. He couldn't sell his house, either, because it's worth less than he paid for it. Nor could he finish his degree: the school where he earned 90 percent of his credits is in Michigan. Waun didn't live where he worked. Nor did he work where he lived. It was a familiar situation for a soldier, and it was becoming familiar for autoworkers too.

"We've had guys who've had nervous breakdowns," he said. "They're facing divorce. We've had three suicides. They just couldn't face moving down here. A number of guys got into drugs. Now they're in rehab."

Waun took the transfer because had he stayed in Lake Orion, he would never again have earned $28 an hour. GM has promised to promote Tier Twos to Tier Ones, but given the economic structure of the auto industry—in which companies must pay grand retiree benefits while trying to make a profit on fuel-efficient cars—and the prevailing wages at nonunion competitors, Waun believes the company is using the system to permanently reduce its labor costs.

"We're trying to prevent it from becoming the future," Waun said. "The Tier Two was sold to the membership in 2007 as a temporary fix to their problems. Now that they're out of bankruptcy, the dog is dead, but the tail is still wagging."

The tiered wage system was not just bad for the Tier Twos, he believed. It was bad for the UAW. The union is trying to organize Southern plants, but who needs a union that can't get you any more money than you're earning now? It was bad for all American workers, because the UAW "set a standard for wages in the industrial world, and industrial America. At $28.12 an hour, people can feed a family and buy a used car, buy a decent house, and maintain a certain standard of living." It was bad for GM, because the auto plants would only attract less skilled, less committed workers. And it was bad for the auto industry, because those workers would build cars as shoddy as any Vega that came out of Lordstown in the early seventies. "People aren't going to have a vested interest in the automobile. You're going to end up with cars like my Aveo out there. After fifty thousand miles, the rear axle came off and the odometer broke."

I visited Waun late in the evening. It was his early morning, since he worked third shift, midnight to eight, at the building across the highway that was his only reason for leaving the trailer. Our interview ended as his clock-in time approached. Before I left, he gave me the phone number of a co-worker named Nadine, who had suffered even more from the tiered wage system: she'd been forced to take a 40 percent pay cut.

Nadine was a plaintiff in *Dragomier et al v. UAW*, a lawsuit filed by a group of Lordstown autoworkers who had been busted down from Tier One to Tier Two. Nadine hired in at Lordstown in 2002. After over a dozen years of working for banks and law firms, she changed the color of her collar because she was tired of sitting in front of a computer for fifteen hours a day. Building cars was an eight-hour job she could forget about when she went home. Hired as a temporary employee at 70 percent of the full-time rate, by 2008 she was earning $24.40 an hour. That June, a union representative called in thirty-five temporary employees, one at a time, and gave them all the same speech: "The company is finally going to make you permanent. The only thing is, you're going to have to take a temporary pay cut. If you don't, you'll be out of the plant by September."

When Nadine appealed to an official in the company's labor management department, the official told her, "Take it or leave it. You do this or
you'll be out of a job."

Had Nadine turned down the offer, she would have been ineligible
for unemployment. So she signed. Right away, her life went to hell, inside and outside the plant. As a single woman, Nadine had no one at
home to share expenses. She canceled her cable and her Internet. That
left her with just enough money to pay the mortgage.

"I am living like I'm on unemployment or welfare," Nadine said
bitterly. "I'm struggling to make my mortgage payments, to live. I'm
losing five hundred to seven hundred dollars a week. I can't afford to do
anything. At work, it's 'Oh, what are you doing on shutdown? I'm going to Florida.' 'Oh great, I'm trying not to lose my house.' I have nothing in common with people I work with. After I put gas in my car, pay
late bills and late fees, I have twenty dollars left to eat for a week and a
half. I still owe money on a foot surgery from over two years ago. It's
devastated my life. I've lost friends over it. I've lost family over it. I can't
socialize."

GM promised to raise Nadine's pay when it added a third shift but
ended up filling those jobs with workers from Delphi Automotive, a
parts supplier that had sold some of its operations to the company.
Workers with *less* seniority were earning more money than Nadine, which
"really raised my rage." To add insult to poverty, Nadine was still working
on the main assembly line instead of the easier, nonassembly work supposed to be assigned to Tier Twos. Whenever she got off the turnpike at
Lordstown, her dread of the upcoming shift generated "a horrible feeling in the pit of [her] stomach." All night, as she installed brake boosters, Nadine reminded herself that her situation was not the car's fault or
the customer's fault. It was the only way to prevent her acid anger toward GM and the UAW from eroding her work ethic. Really, the only
thing that kept her coming to the plant every day was the lawsuit against
what she knew was an illegal contract. If she quit, she would lose her
standing as an advocate for all the Tier Twos at all the GM plants.

"The only reason I'm still there," she said, "is that I know it's easier to
fight this battle from the inside."

TOM LAVEY FINALLY WENT BACK to work in the spring of 2010, designing floor mats for Ford. He was a contractor, meaning his company

badge was piped with a green stripe, rather than the blue stripe that identified full-time employees.

"I'm making more money than I did before the layoff, but it's not secure," he said. "Even if they give you a blue stripe, it's not secure. A lot of people don't trust the car industry anymore. A lot of engineers left to go to Indiana to work at Navistar. I've got a five-year-old car, and I'm going to drive it into the ground. I'm check to check. That's the way everybody feels deep down."

IN MICHIGAN, the 2000s are known as "the Lost Decade." The Rust Belt was the site of the nation's first Great Recession, in the early 1980s. The first was deeper than the second—in 1982, Michigan's unemployment rate was 14.3 percent, a figure not even 2009 could touch—but it was briefer, and it did not result in a permanent diminution of Michiganders' standard of living. Michigan was the only state to lose population in the 2000s. In 2000, Michigan's per capita income was eighteenth among states. By 2009, it was thirty-seventh. The poverty rate, once fifth lowest, was 14.4 percent—in the top twenty. Even the obesity rate ballooned to 31.5 percent, putting Michigan among the five fattest states, in the same league of avoirdupois as Alabama and West Virginia. In college degrees, Michigan fell from thirtieth to thirty-fifth as half the graduates left the state in search of work, like Okies with BAs and BSs, reversing the migration from the South that had built it into a megastate of the mid-twentieth century. (By the early twenty-first, Michigan would be surpassed by Georgia and North Carolina.) "There's nothing for them here," explained a retired Oldsmobile engineer whose children had dispersed to Colorado and California. The unemployment, the low education rate, and the fissured, potholed roads inspired Michiganders to nickname their state "Michissippi." It may be even more backward, as racial resentments dating back to the 1960s prevent black Detroit and its white-flight suburbs from acknowledging Michigan can no longer afford so many municipalities. That's one reason Michigan's cities are more decrepit and more destitute than any other state's. Benton Harbor, Pontiac, and Flint are so broke their operations have been taken over by emergency financial managers, appointed by the governor. Detroit is to urban blight what Paris is to romance. In Lansing, the shopping center where my family once shopped for groceries, graduation clothes, haircuts, birthday cakes, and garden tools is now anchored by a Laundromat, a Food for Less, a dollar store, and a plasma center—our very own PoorMart, where a few faded Oldsmobiles and pickup trucks with "$500/ OBO" signs float on a lake of asphalt.

The last three chapters of this book will tell the stories of three Michigan cities—Detroit, Flint, and Lansing—at the end of the Lost Decade.

14.

The Corner of Palmer and Jesus Saves

Perrien Park, on the East Side of Detroit, is a city block of unmown grass. Its rising green tide laps the legs of a jungle gym and a swing set, concealing the deck of a squeaky merry-go-round. "Keep Off the Grass" signs are unnecessary, because the grass grows waist high, almost as tall as on the prairie. Walking through the park, the only pedestrian on the concrete path that cuts a neat bend sinister through the disorderly vegetation, I spotted a house with this sign on its fence: "PUPPIES FOR SALE." Not looking for a dog, just looking to talk to a stranger in a strange city, I crossed the street. In a penned-in dirt yard, a pit bull bitch nursed her eight-week-old litter. On the verge of weaning, the mother growled whenever a puppy nipped her teats.

"You want one?" asked their owner, a bleary, redheaded man.

"I live in Chicago," I said. "I couldn't get it home."

"I go to Chicago all the time. You know Fox Lake?" he asked, naming a resort village near Wisconsin. "I know a woman there. What are you doing in this neighborhood?"

Not an unexpected inquiry. The East Side is the most depopulated quarter of the most depopulated city in the United States. Judging from Perrien Park, even Detroit city hall has forgotten it's there. Across from Joe's house was a six-unit brick apartment building, vintage pre-Depression, with six units to let.

"I'm writing a book," I said. I hesitated before making that confession, but Joe didn't seem like the type of Detroiter who would scold me for voyeurism. He encouraged voyeurism.

"Do you have a camera?" he asked.

"Just the one on my cell phone. I left my big camera at the motel."

"You've got to see the Packard plant. You can get some great pictures. My buddy owns the six-plex, the Quonset hut."

"All right," I said. "Get in the car."

If you're watching a black-and-white movie starring William Powell, Monty Woolley, or Adolphe Menjou, and a touring sedan pulls up in front of a country manor, there's a good chance that sedan is a Packard, one of the "three Ps" of American luxury cars, along with Pierce-Arrow and Peerless. In the chambers of the Packard plant, designed by renowned industrial architect Albert Kahn and constructed on thirty-seven acres of an old cattle pasture in the heart of Detroit, cars were not assembled, they were crafted. Woodworkers machined and varnished frames and trim. Coachwork was built by hand in the body shop; the chassis and undercarriage were painted with detailed brushstrokes.

During World War II, Packard, like all American auto companies, shifted to defense work, building engines for aircraft and naval vessels. Unlike Ford, Chrysler, and GM, which grew to Big Threeness after the war by selling millions of cars to a nation with blue balls for American iron, Packard never recovered from the interruption. Military work damaged its tooling, and even before Pearl Harbor, it had outsourced body building to the Briggs Body Company. When Briggs sold out to Chrysler in 1953, Packard abandoned its antiquated multistory factory and set up an assembly line in the vacant Briggs building.

The new plant was so ill suited to mass production that cars came off the line with loose wires, doors that didn't shut, radios that wouldn't play music, clocks that couldn't keep time. Packard lost $30 million that year. Five years later, it was out of business.

Detroit has been called a calamity in slow motion. What war and natural disaster wreaked on Berlin and New Orleans, fifty years of neglect has wreaked on Detroit. But Detroit has been emptied out by two social forces that, in America, are more powerful than bombs or hurricanes: racial conflict and the free market.

On the way to the plant, Joe insisted we stop at a party store.

"A guy who owes me money is there," he said.

Once Joe had his money, he directed me down East Palmer Street. We passed a brick viaduct lettered like an unfinished crossword: "MO OR CITY IN U TR L PARK." At a telephone pole with a crosswise board painted "JESUS SAVES," I turned right, down an alley whose east side was defined by a three-story factory. A Quonset-hut skyline defined its west. An ochre pit bull walked a butterfly path between them.

"That's my dog Bruno," Joe said.

Nearly sixty years after the last Packard left, the building still contained enough steel, timber, and rope to provide income for a tribe of scrappers who worked and lived there. Joe pushed aside a chain-link gate barring a Quonset hut's bay door. An RV loomed in the doorway. In the darkness, in the depths, was a vintage Cadillac.

"They do a lot of body work here," Joe explained.

The chief body man was sitting in a lawn chair with a bottle of Wild Irish Rose between his feet. His name was Al, and he lived in an apartment somewhere in this garage, with his roommate, Greg, a black ex-junkie.

"Are you going to heaven?" Al shouted rheumily at me.

"I don't know," I said. "Only God knows."

"Do you believe Jesus Christ is the son of God and your personal savior?" Al demanded.

"Yes," I said.

"Then you're going to heaven!" he shouted. "You should know that!"

Al unscrewed the bottlecap to pour another inch of bellicosity into himself. Following his bibulous example, Greg pulled a half pint of vodka out of his shorts, leaning on a cane for balance as he lifted the bottle.

"So when are you going to show me around this place?" I asked Joe.

"You haven't quite met my terms," he said.

"I'll buy you a beer *after* we go," I promised.

We set off down the alley, toward the berm of rubble blocking its far end.

"In here," Joe directed, guiding me through a doorless doorway into a room I can only describe as a gallery of destruction. The floor was covered in soaked and yellowed papers, timbers broken raggedly in half, bricks pried from walls, garbage bags, cinder blocks, plastic water bottles. (Beer and pop bottles would have been collected and redeemed for their deposits, in the spirit of stripping the plant down to its last dime of salvageable material.) The graffiti was as intricate as Islamic design or the most heavily decorated New York subway car of 1977. "DECAY," read one message. (The British graffiti artist Banksy had visited Packard, either to validate it as one of the world's great spray-can art collections, or to validate himself by working among urban blight impossible to find in Europe, where socialistic governments don't allow cities to fall apart. Banksy painted a boy holding a bucket of paint, next to the words "I remember when this was all trees." Suddenly valuable, the wall was cut away and peddled to an art gallery. The producers of the third *Transformers* movie filmed several crash/explosion scenes at the plant.)

We inched up a ramp, Joe stopping every few feet to aspirate a high-G whistle that reverberated in the empty room. Was he communicating with a confederate, hidden behind one of the pillars that formed a grove of concrete trunks? Following a stranger through an abandoned building—especially a dipsomaniac, pit-bull-breeding stranger—only a fool wouldn't be wary of a mugging. Detroit is both the friendliest and deadliest big city in America, for the same reason: it's poor. If poor people have anything to share—beer, tobacco, food—they'll share it with you. If they don't, they'll knock you over the head and make you share what you have. If I talked to a stranger about his dog in Bloomfield Hills, suburban hometown of Mitt Romney, he wouldn't invite me to the country club. But I wouldn't have to worry about getting jumped, either. I had to hope Joe was showing me Detroit's generous side.

In the next room, we encountered a bearded young man burdened by a college student's backpack. He was staring at a clipboard.

"This is kind of like real-life Dungeons and Dragons," I said.

Now that our expedition had a third member, Joe played it like a trucker who's just picked up a spare hitchhiker.

"Do you guys want to go up on the roof?" he asked me and the bearded kid, a broad-faced Pole from Hamtramck named Bartosz. "If you do, we're going to have to negotiate a fee. I don't do this for free. I know this place like the back of my hand."

Joe flashed his florid knuckles.

"How long is the tour?" Bartosz asked.

"About half an hour."

"How about five dollars?"

Joe hedged.

"I'll buy you some beer," I offered again.

"I'll buy you some beer too," Bartosz said.

"Okay," Joe said. "That sounds good."

Joe whistled as he entered each cavern, mumbling, "The boys might be here." Finally, we arrived in a roofless arena known as "the Boathouse," a dumping ground for speedboats and fishing boats whose owners who couldn't make the payments and wanted to report a theft. Michigan has more licensed watercraft than any state, so why wouldn't some of them end their voyages three miles from the river? Discarded itself, the plant collects discards—commercial, animal, and human. A brand-new pickup truck had been driven into an empty elevator shaft. Its hood was tilted into darkness, but its tailpipe angled toward the sky. The sun set its glossy golden paint aglow.

"This thing has current tags," I said, whipping out my cell phone to photograph the license plate.

"Don't take a picture of that," Joe said, warning me. "It's probably an insurance job. It won't be discovered for three or four months. By then, they've got the money."

We climbed a stairwell of which nothing remained but chipped concrete stairs. On the roof, cottonwood trees grew from puddles in the asphalt. I looked over a ledge at an elementary school whose last pupils had left high school by now. Over another ledge was the only business in sight, the Packard Motel, a $50-a-night hostelry.

"What brought you to this place?" Bartosz asked me.

"I told Joe I was writing a book, and he told me I had to see this place."

"Oh, you're writing a book," he said. "I thought you were just some asshole from Chicago."

"You can do one and be the other," I said. "What are *you* doing here?"

"I've heard about this place ever since my family moved here from Poland, but this is the first time I've ever been here."

There's a term for what Bartosz and I were doing in the Packard plant: urban exploration, the pastime of breaking into abandoned buildings for voyeuristic purposes. Urbex—its shorthand name—was popularized and promoted in the zine *Infiltration*, published by a Canadian trespasser who called himself Ninjalicious. *Infiltration* offered tips on scaling barbed wire fences, crawling through windows, disabling alarms, and evading security guards. Ninjalicious eventually compiled the handbook *Access All Areas*, as essential an urbex accessory as a flashlight or a digital camera.

The Rust Belt, of course, is the heartland of urban exploration. Besides Detroit, the other golden cities are Chicago, Cleveland, Buffalo, and Gary—all places where manufacturing wealth paid for Gothic masterpieces which were left to rot when manufacturing disappeared. Buffalo's grain elevators, for example, are too expensive to maintain and too expensive to tear down—a perfect situation for urban explorers. Gary's City Methodist Church looks as though it was shaken by an earthquake—rubble covers the floors, and the brick walls have split open, offering arbored vistas. City Methodist is so popular with photographers that Gary is considering preserving it as a "ruin garden." Gary Screw and Bolt, where trees grow through fissures in the concrete and ten-foot-high drifts of old work uniforms molder on the shop floor, is such a trip into the Ozymandian future that it was featured on the History Channel's

Life After People. Packard is not even Detroit's number one urbex destination: that would be the Michigan Central train station. The station is more convenient to the hostel, and its dome-ceilinged Great Hall is a work of architectural beauty whose disintegration is more poignant than that of a functional automobile plant. (Actor Michael Cera sneaked in while filming *Youth in Revolt* in Detroit, telling late-night talk show host Jimmy Fallon he heard "terrifying" gunshots.) Urbex tourism is a conundrum for Detroit. The city can't promote these attractions, for reasons of public safety and public image, so it discourages the tourists. "No Trespassing" signs are one method. Shame is another. Detroiters call photographs of their city's collapse "ruin porn." Ruin porn was actually pioneered by Detroiter Lowell Boileau on his website The Fabulous Ruins of Detroit, which compares Detroit to Zimbabwe, Ephesus, El Tajin, Athens, and Rome. However, it was most successfully exploited for commercial and artistic purposes by photographer Andrew Moore, who spent three months among the ruins to produce *Detroit Disassembled*, a $50 coffee table book and a traveling exhibit that I happened to see at the Akron Art Museum. Its most arresting images were a Dali-inspired photograph of a melting clock, found in an old school, and an empty mental health ward in which someone had scrawled "God has left Detroit."

Detroit's intelligentsia took offense to Moore's exhibit. In late 2008, when the auto industry nearly went bankrupt, Detroit was lousy with American, French, and British journalists seeking signs of hope in a downtrodden city. (They all ate at least one meal at Slow's Barb-B-Q, a popular restaurant near the old Tiger Stadium with a 90 percent white clientele.) Since then, it has been an artistic law that any portrayal of Detroit by a writer or photographer from outside Detroit must be rebutted by a blogger, journalist, or academic from inside Detroit. The most well-thought-out reaction to ruin porn is the essay "Detroitism," by Wayne State University professor John Patrick Leary, in the online magazine *Guernica*. Leary identified the three types of Detroit stories: the Metonym (about the auto industry), the Detroit Lament (about "derelict buildings"), and Detroit Utopia (generally about white hipsters planting community gardens next to their $5,000 homesteads).

> Detroiters often react testily to this kind of attention (as I do), even when it is done skillfully and with good intentions, as much of it is . . . Ruin photography, in particular, has been criticized for its "pornographic" sensationalism . . . So much ruin photography

and ruin film aestheticizes poverty without inquiring of its origins, dramatizes spaces but never seeks out the people that inhabit and transform them, and romanticizes isolated acts of resistance without acknowledging the massive political and social forces aligned against the real transformation, and not just stubborn survival of the city. And to see oneself portrayed in this way, as a curiosity to be lamented or studied, is jarring for any Detroiter, who is of course also an American, with all the sense of self-confidence and native-born privilege that we're taught to associate with these United States.

Of course, using the term "ruin porn" can also be a way to evade responsibility for the city's shabbiness by scolding outsiders for noticing it—which is what Bartosz was getting at when he called me "some asshole from Chicago." After that, I told everyone I met in Detroit I was from Lansing, which at least made me a fellow Michigander.

(When I asked a Detroit journalist to review this chapter for accuracy, he corrected a few errors, then criticized me for spending all my time in a tumbledown neighborhood. "Ruin porn in text form," he wrote. "Visiting [East English Village] or Palmer Park or University District or Green Acres would have screwed up [your] whole outlook." In East English Village, a well-preserved middle-class neighborhood near the Grosse Pointe border, a sturdy, five-bedroom Tudor-style brick house sells for $89,900. So I should point out that the neighborhood surrounding the Packard plant no more represents all of Detroit than the South Bronx represents all of New York City.)

WHEN WE DESCENDED to the alley, a white van, with a lawn mower lashed to the top and the legend "Peacemakers International" on the sliding door, had arrived.

"Uh-oh," said Eric, a scrapper who had emerged from one of the buildings. "It's Pastor Steve."

"Maybe I can pretend I'm not here," Joe said.

Pastor Steve was a reformed junkie and unreformed biker who preached in a storefront church on Chene Street. He wore his gray hair thin on top, long in the back, but the mullet was more Andrew Jackson than nineties hockey player. In sunglasses and jean shorts, he looked ready to attend a picnic for retired Hells Angels. After meeting Joe through a prison ministry, while Joe was doing time for drunk driving, Pastor Steve brought him to the East Side, adding a parishioner to his flock.

"This place is the heart of hell," Pastor Steve told me when he found out I was writing a book. Pastor Steve loved publicity. He ran back to his van and fetched me a photocopy of a cover story on his church that had appeared in *Metro Times*, Detroit's alternative weekly. It labeled him "Desolation Angel." "Even the cops will tell you that. This neighborhood is Detroit in a handbasket. The people around here are involved in everything: drugs, prostitution, you name it. I started getting high in the early sixties. Then, it was marijuana, speed—beatnik stuff. The heroin started coming in in the mid-sixties. That was the bomb. That destroyed Detroit. Before that, drug dealing was just out of someone's apartment. You had to go to Black Bottom to get it."

Pastor Steve invited me to his church. That Sunday, he was visiting land he owned up north. But the Sunday after . . .

"I don't believe in denominations," he said before driving off. "I want to start a movement of all Christians in Detroit."

At the party store, I bought Greg a forty of Keystone Ice: a malt liquor bomb in the shape of an artillery shell. Bartosz bought Joe a pint of vodka. Both bottles were passed around, and once they were empty, the entire alley chipped in for pizza. Joe rode shotgun, directing me to the pizzeria, but he was so drunk he nearly dropped the pizza box in the parking lot. Back in the alley, Joe wouldn't get out of my car. For the rest of the afternoon, he sat stupefied in the passenger seat, looking like a crash-test dummy, and equally insensible. When I asked for directions back to Perrien Park, he answered in a sleepy mumble, as though not even he knew what he was trying to say.

"How am I gonna get him home?" I appealed to Eric, the scrapper.

"Just follow my truck."

In front of Joe's house, we each grabbed an arm, dragged Joe across the street—his flailing feet taking one step for every two strides we covered—and chucked him into his grassless yard. Joe stumbled past his dogs and crawled up the steps.

"I was in there once," Eric said. "You do *not* want to go in there."

"Do you live down at the plant?" I asked.

"Naw. I grew up around here, but I live in Hazel Park"—a suburb just north of 8 Mile Road. "I come down there every day, though. You can still make some money out of that place. I sold two pipes for thirty-three dollars. I need to get some money to pay a lawyer. I've got a marijuana case. Have you ever been across the Mackinac Bridge?"

The Mackinac Bridge joins Michigan's Lower and Upper Peninsulas. Since Eric mentioned it in the context of a legal hassle, I guessed he hadn't gone elk hunting in the UP. In that most isolated salient of the Midwest, entire counties subsist on guarding prisoners from Detroit. Michigan's drug sentences are some of the harshest in the nation, and the maximum penalty for murder is life without parole, so Detroit contributes permanent residents to Marquette, Newberry, and Munising.

"Crossing the Mackinac Bridge is no fun when you do it in belly chains," Eric said.

I HAD DISCOVERED CHENE STREET, and from there Perrien Park, and from there the Packard plant, through Gary Wozniak, an entrepreneur attempting to transform the East Side into an agricultural homestead. I had discovered Gary through one of my old high school classmates, who was doing his PR. That's networking, Detroit style. It's a city of 713,000, but the professional class of architects, city planners, journalists, publicists, and urban agriculture advocates is small enough to fit into an auditorium, which it often does, at symposia titled "Detroit by Design" and "Powering Up the Local Food System." At one such function, Wozniak ran into Mayor Dave Bing, the former Pistons basketball star who had been elected to succeed ex-mayor Kwame Kilpatrick, thrown out of office for carnal, fiscal, and criminal offenses that violated too many provisions of the Ten Commandments and the Michigan Compiled Laws to enumerate here. Within two weeks, Gary had a meeting in Bing's office. Forty-five minutes after that, he had the mayor's support for a network of garden plots and tilapia farms in the vacant lots and vacant buildings of the East Side. He planned to call it Recovery-Park.

Gary was the chief development officer of SHAR—Self Help Addiction Rehabilitation—which had started as a halfway house for drug addicts. A recovering addict himself—from a little bit of everything: crack, heroin, alcohol—he planned to employ ex-junkies and ex-cons at his farms, because nobody needs an education to pick tomatoes. The grandparents of today's East Siders could have told them that. They'd moved north to escape from sharecropping, and now their descendants were about to end up right back in the dirt.

Gary was already operating a pierogi bakery based on a Polish grandmother's recipes, in the kitchen of an old elementary school. His two employees, both addicts with criminal records and mouths as gapped as any East Side street, earned $8 an hour plus benefits to turn out 150 dozen pierogis a week, in such all-American flavors as jalapeño and strawberry cream cheese. They were sold at the People's Pierogi Collective in Eastern Market, Detroit's weekend farm-to-table emporium.

"Our biggest challenge with our client base is jobs," Gary explained. "Seventy percent of our clients can't read or write on an eighth-grade level. Seventy percent are felons. The official unemployment rate in Detroit is thirty percent. The unofficial rate is fifty-five percent. It's more challenging here than in other cities. Farming is something that is teachable. You don't have to read and write. It doesn't matter if you have a record."

We drove around the East Side in Gary's truck. Past entire blocks that were rectangles of grass. Past an empty elementary school on which a world-renowned Detroit street artist had painted square faces that looked like African masks. Past the site of Northeastern High School. It was as eradicated as thoroughly as Carthage, but unlike Carthage, the land beneath was still fertile. Gary planned to grow lettuce in hoop houses there. We drove past a public school for pregnant girls, where a chestnut horse galloped around a paddock. Then to the Chene-Ferry Market. A farmer's market closed twenty years, it is near collapse because scrappers have cut away so many supporting pillars. On the other side of Ferry Street, men sat in lawn chairs outside a party store, beneath a mural of the Scooby-Doo gang in the Mystery Machine. They drank from paper bags and talked. It seemed that these refugees from Alabama and Tennessee had, over time, transformed the neighborhood into a replica of their native villages. The only difference between the East Side and the rural South was reliable cell phone service. The twentieth century had simply been an urban interlude here.

"The neighborhood that we're in was one of the most densely populated in the city," Gary said. "At the height of its residency in the 1950s, it had eighty-nine thousand people. It now has four thousand." (I did a little research of my own on that. In 1980, the census tract that includes the Chene-Ferry Market contained 2,571 residents, of whom 58 percent were white. By 2009, it contained 623 residents, of whom 90 percent were black. The ratio of occupied to vacant homes went from 9–1 to 2–1 and the average property was worth $11,200, half its 2000 value.)

At the end of the 2000s, Detroit supported nearly 250 community gardens, producing 330,000 pounds of food. It is the world's leading agricultural city, and not just because it has so much empty land per person. The flat, humid farmlands of southeastern Michigan are capable of growing over two hundred fruits and vegetables—the usual apples, tomatoes, peppers, lettuce, carrots, and beets, as well as such exotica as bok choy, curly kale, collard greens, and mizuna.

Farming is also the solution to a social problem. Detroit, in commercial if not horticultural terms, is a food desert. It's hard to buy a cantaloupe after dark. In all of Detroit's 140 square miles, there's not a single chain supermarket. No Kroger. No Meijer. No Farmer Jack's. One night, I got out of a meeting at nine P.M. and wanted to buy oranges and bananas for the next morning's breakfast. I had to drive all the way past 8 Mile Road, passing several fruit markets just closing their doors. The trip took me five miles out of my way. Detroit has 1.5 square feet of grocery space per person—half the industry standard. As a result of paying markups in convenience stores (following the principle that everything should be more expensive for the poor), Detroiters spend 13 percent of their income on food. The average American spends 9.4 percent. (Although 30 percent of Detroiters subsist on the Supplemental Nutrition Assistance Plan, what used to be known as food stamps.) Also, Detroiters get crap for their money. In most corner stores, the only vegetables are potato chips, the only fruit is a Little Debbie banana flip, and the only meat is beef jerky. That's why Americans in the top 20 percent income bracket eat seven times as many fruits and vegetables as those in the bottom 20 percent. A program called Detroit Fresh is attempting to bring the orchard to the inner city by placing fruit baskets in gas stations and party stores.

Detroit also has a tradition of growing food to get through hard times. During the Panic of 1893, Mayor Hazen Pingree encouraged his constituents to plant gardens, which became known as Pingree's Potato Patches.

Detroit's largest and most successful urban garden is D-Town Farm, a seven-acre plot in Rouge Park, on the city's far west side. It's run by the Detroit Black Community Food Security Network, a neo-Africanist movement that sees agriculture as a form of independence for Detroiters. (In Detroit, every issue, *especially* issues as elemental as where you live and what you eat, has a racial angle.) On one of my few trips away from the East Side, I spent a morning raking soil and planting collard greens at the farm. The compost bins were painted red, green, and yellow, the colors of the Ethiopian flag. A tire tread decorated with Egyptian hieroglyphics was marked "Quad 3." A sign by the gate said simply "KAZI," the Ashe-Yoruba word meaning "life force." A tiny plot grew medicinal herbs: burdock, red raspberry leaf. The city donated the land.

Michigan State University donated the deer-and-rabbit fence that kept out the pests who'd nibbled away most of the first season's crop. From the United States Department of Agriculture came four hoop houses, inexpensive greenhouses covered in milky plastic sheeting, which added a month to the growing season for the farm's specialty crops: bok choy, mizuna, and lettuce whose earthy flavor is startling to anyone who has only eaten chilled leaves from the grocery.

The Detroit Black Community Food Security Network's director was Malik Yakini, a dreadlocked schoolteacher who began every work session with a spiritual circle.

On the Saturday I farmed, a group of students from Puerto Rico and Argentina also showed up.

"We should be glad for our international visitors," Malik said as birdsong chipped at the morning. "Some of us don't realize the magnitude of what we're doing. In two or three years, we'll be saying, 'I was with D-Town Farm.'"

Malik ended with the invocation "*Imara*," a Swahili word meaning "strong." After three hours of hoeing and planting, he told me more about the farm's mission.

"The fact that Detroit has so much vacant land and the dire economic condition caused people to look at gardening as a way to feed themselves," he said. "Detroit has the potential of growing a much greater proportion of its own food. What a lot of us talk about is trying to reach the 10 percent benchmark. Part of what urban agriculture has to prove is it can be an economic growth industry, not just that it's cute."

The network sold its crops at farmer's markets that called in neighborhoods where it was otherwise impossible to buy fresh food. But D-Town Farm could not sell its produce as cheaply as the grocery store chains. Its $1 pound of greens cost 30 cents at Kroger. Urban agriculture's only competitive advantage is that Kroger refuses to do business in Detroit.

"We've done a pretty good job of learning how to grow crops," Malik said. "Now the business end has to be viable. Our penetration is very small. This battle to provide greater access, to get people to utilize the consciousness they have, it's a tough struggle."

MALIK YAKINI HAD BEEN ABLE to talk the Detroit city council into giving him seven acres of a remote park. Gary Wozniak was having a tougher time convincing East Siders that their neighborhood ought to be plowed and cultivated for the first time since the French *habitants* abandoned their riverfront strip farms in the eighteenth century. Every month, SHAR held a meeting in the basement of a Catholic church. Along the walls, Gary set up aerial photographs of the neighborhood, outlining exactly where he planned to plant his crops. Dozens of black folks filled the folding chairs, including the state senator Coleman Young II, bastard son of the bachelor mayor.

Gary gave a speech about a Community Benefits Agreement that would guarantee East Siders got jobs on his farm. The audience regarded Gary skeptically. He could not have looked whiter. He was Polish. His white flesh covered a three-hundred-pound body and glowed on the crown of his shaved head. He lived in Utica, a 94 percent white suburb in 93 percent white Macomb County, far beyond 8 Mile Road. Despite his good intentions, Gary represented one of black Detroit's deepest fears: that one day, the white man would return and repossess the city the blacks had struggled to keep going for forty years. Some statistics: Detroit's population loss since the early 1950s would constitute the tenth-largest city in the United States; its *white* population loss would form the sixth-largest city.

"We have endured," one woman declared, rising to make a tribal claim for her neighborhood. "We've been here through fires, robberies, dilapidated houses. We've been here and we're going to stay. If you're coming into our community, you need to get with us."

Gary protested that he'd been holding community meetings for over a year and had conducted a door-to-door survey of two thousand residents. In Detroit, though, it was hard to determine who represented the community.

"We've been here all our lives and we don't have block clubs," proclaimed a heavy man in blue jeans and a work shirt. "I got the only house on my block, so I *am* the block club."

The residents' chief complaint, besides the fact that a suburbanite was making decisions about their neighborhood, was that they didn't want to live next to a farm. Farms meant manure and pesticides. Farms belonged in the country. Accepting one would mean giving up their notion of themselves as city dwellers and of Detroit as a city.

Janice Harvey, a lifelong East Sider, tried to defend the project to her neighbors.

"There is a question, do you want to live near a farm, in a farm?" Janice asked the audience.

"No," they chorused. "No! No!"

"And if not, what do you want to live near, besides housing, because everybody wants to live near housing."

An old woman stood up.

"All of a sudden, everybody want to put farms in here," she complained. "What about housing? We're an industrial city. We want houses!"

Janice did not explain that housing was not a profitable use of land on the East Side. In 2011, nobody was building houses *anywhere*. Property values were wallowing all over the country. Nowhere were they wallowing deeper than inner-city Detroit, where houses were selling for less than $20,000. What builder could turn a profit in that market? To sell a house in Detroit, you had to find someone who wanted to live in Detroit, and over the last decade, people had been leaving for heaven, the suburbs, or Alabama at the rate of fifty-five a day. The demographers predicted Detroit would bottom out at half a million, one-quarter its peak population. Janice didn't say any of that. She said: "One of the reasons we have so little as we have is we are not together."

THE NEXT AFTERNOON, Janice met me at a Coney Island diner on the corner of Mack and Mount Elliot Avenues. The Coney Island—a wiener with both tails overlapping the bun, smothered in loose chili and mustard—is a delicacy invented in Detroit and as central to its culinary identity as crab cakes are to Baltimore. A Coney dog, a basket of French fries, and a can of Vernor's constitutes a complete Detroit dinner.

I arrived at the diner early, allowing me to witness a confrontation between the Asian owner and a customer who insisted he was entitled to a can of pop with his order.

"The sign outside said you get a pop with your meal," the customer argued.

"Only from eleven to two," the owner pointed out.

"Well, it didn't say that."

After much aggrieved shouting, the man got his pop. But even as he drank it, another argument was taking place at the counter of a takeout joint or a party store somewhere else in the city. The owners were always Asian or Arab. The customers were always black. Only one thing would have shocked me more than seeing an African-American standing next to a cash register of a liquor store: seeing an Arab buy a can of beer there. Detroit's politics are based on the postcolonial relationship between the black city and the white suburbs. In his last election before going to jail, Kwame Kilpatrick had won a come-from-behind victory by campaigning on the slogan "Our Mayor" (not *Theirs*) and spreading the word on the street that his mulatto opponent was the son of an Austrian war bride. For the electoral whipping he received, the hapless opponent might as well have been all white. At the retail level of racial resentment, though, most of the animosity is directed toward foreigners. Outside a Chinese restaurant, I heard a man complain, "The Asians lost the war, now they're trying to win the economic war, by ripping off black people and white people." Chaldeans, the Iraqi Christians who own most of the liquor stores, are referred to as "motherfucking Caledonians." The Arabs return the suspicion by doing business behind bulletproof glass that, were it ice, would be thick enough to drive a four-by-four across.

As a fellow American and English speaker, I rarely received dirty looks on the East Side. There was the guy in the park at the corner of Chene and Ferry who suspected I was a cop because "it's not normal to see a white person sitting out here," but that had more to do with the *kind* of white person I am—clean-cut, bespectacled. Plenty of poor white folks showed up at Pastor Steve's church for free clothes, but no one suspected *them* of being undercover.

LIKE HER NEIGHBORS, Janice Harvey wanted housing, too. So many houses had disappeared from the East Side during her seven decades, and with them all the other appurtenances of urban life. First went the white people, most of them Italian. Then after the "rebellion" of 1967, the bakeries, the movie theaters, the bowling alleys, the schools, and the supermarkets closed. Finally, the next-door neighbor moved out. Then the man on the corner. A film of the neighborhood's history would run forward for 266 years from the arrival of French explorer Antoine de la Mothe Cadillac to the riot, then backward at triple speed. Janice's block consisted of three houses, followed by three vacant lots. Dot, dot, dot. Dash, dash, dash. The missing houses had been abandoned, lost for back taxes and bulldozed, or burned down by absentee owners.

(After 1967, Janice also started seeing the bulletproof glass and behind it, the Levantine faces, "'cause black folks weren't about to take that chance.")

Living in the Motor City without a car, Janice bought her office supplies, computer supplies, and cleaning supplies online, bought her food at the markets that marked up prices as the fruit spoiled. Once a month, she took a bus to a suburban mall. ("They got everything out in the suburbs," she marveled. "You go down those Mile Roads, and they got all kinds of devices.")

"We're well suited for housing," Janice said of her neighborhood. "GM people need houses, all the sports arenas. We're right here in the midst of everything. There's no reason we can't bring back the fabric of the neighborhood. There are folks who had to leave because the houses fell down around them. They would come back to be near family. They can't afford a hundred-and-fifty-thousand-dollar house."

Until the housing market recovered, though Janice didn't mind living near a farm.

"I could see it as a temporary Band-Aid for vacant land to be cared for, and when the dollars are there again, we can build," she said. "People are concerned about odors and rodents, but it makes a monkey out of doing nothing. It's stimulating some conversation on what else can we do?"

AT THE CORNER of Palmer and Jesus Saves, Eric the scrapper was cutting apart an elevator frame with a propane blowtorch. Inside the shaft was one of Packard's spookiest vistas. Bricks knocked out of the wall had left a hole with digital outlines. Staring back through that glassless window was a graffito face, its mouth puckered in surprise. From the right distance and the right angle, the outline of the face and the edges of the hole aligned perfectly, as though a man were trapped back there. Adding to the image of confinement, the elevator cage had collapsed over the opening, once Eric cut away its supporting struts.

To protect his eyes, Eric wore a pair of metal sunglasses. Work gloves covered less than half his bare forearms. Eric's jeans were heavy with dirt and sweat. With his stringy hair, ropy frame, and gaunt forty-five-year-old face, he looked like a junkyard Iggy Pop. As his focused blue flame burned through the steel, a fountain of miniature fireworks sparkled on the metal.

Eric tossed a cut away beam onto a clanking pile. The cage door sagged, until it dangled from a chain beyond the blowtorch's reach.

"There's probably three, four hundred dollars here," he said. "This is going to be melted down and turned into a car, turned into a toaster, whatever. This is the hardest work I've ever done, and I've worked seven days a week. I can only do this for two or three more weeks and then I have to figure something else to do."

That sounds like a lot of work for $400, but it was the only work that suited Eric: he was a felon, he didn't like "dealing with a boss," and he'd dropped out of school at fourteen to learn how to wield a blowtorch in his father's auto body shop.

"There's scrap yards all over town. It's metal. Doesn't matter how dirty or rusty it is, they'll take it."

As Eric carried the propane torch and tank back to his truck, a goth scrapper with a silver nose ring and gray face tattoos ran out of a building across the alley. In one hand, he carried a circular saw. In the other, a coiled rope.

"Look at this!" he shouted. "I'll bet this hasn't been seen by human eyes in eighty years. This is good quality hemp. You could probably smoke it."

It seems astonishing that, after five decades of scavenging, there is *anything* of value left in the Packard plant. But the freelance dismantling of Packard is a microcosm of the scrapping of an entire neighborhood. There are no longer enough jobs to support the citizenry, so the citizenry is consuming every last bit of leftover wealth it can find. It's a given that any abandoned house will be stripped of its copper pipes and its boiler. The crews don't always wait until a house is abandoned. Crackheads pry bricks off houses, sell them for a dime apiece. East Siders have returned from two-week vacations to find their homes looted.

"Once somebody knows you're not living in a house, they will take *everything*," a former neighborhood resident told me. "The windows, the plumbing. My mother moved to the West Side because they were shooting every day, shooting the windows. She said she'd rather move to a safe neighborhood than stay where she's been the last twenty-five years. She was thinking of renting the house or giving it to the church. Once someone knew we weren't living there, they stole the stove. They stole my six-thousand-dollar gym, and then they burned the house up."

Eric threw the propane tank into the bed of his truck.

"You know," he told me, "when you started coming around here, I thought you were a cop, 'cause you were asking so many questions."

"I'm not a cop," I said. "I'm an author. I showed you that book I wrote, *Young Mr. Obama*, with my picture on the cover."

"Yeah, but they coulda had that printed up," he said. "That's the kind of thing they do to make you undercover."

WEDNESDAY AFTERNOON, Chene Street. Chene Street, in high summer, is a timeless place. Nobody moves fast, because nobody has any place to go. On Chene Street, there is no place to go. The only businesses: a liquor store, run by Yemenis, selling cans of beer and bottles of sweet wine that slow the street people even more; a deli and a gas station that stay open only because they're close to the General Motors plant across the highway.

The plant is officially known as Detroit/Hamtramck Assembly, but everyone calls it Poletown, after the ethnic ghetto that was torn down to make room for it in 1981. When GM chose Detroit as the site of its first new auto plant in Michigan since the 1950s, Mayor Coleman Young was so eager to accommodate the company that he rammed a "quick take" eminent domain law through the state legislature, then used it to condemn fourteen hundred houses and sixteen churches. Poletown, Young said, was marked for demolition because it surrounded the recently closed Dodge Main plant, the only suitable site for an auto factory. Young's critics accused him of serving up Poletown because it accomplished two political ends: portraying himself as the mayor who was reindustrializing Detroit, and ridding the city of thousands of white voters whose political philosophy went no farther than the third letter of the alphabet: Anybody But Coleman. The news media loved the conflict, because it gave them an opportunity to portray urban working-class ethnics as victims, not racists. Poletown flipped the embattled-white-neighborhood narrative on its head. These hardworking Catholics were defending their parishes not from infiltration by poor blacks, but from destruction by a powerful black mayor. This time, the *blacks* were the racists, not the whites. Ralph Nader, who had made his name by taking on GM, returned to Detroit for another round, organizing the Poletown Support Team to help residents fight eviction. The left-wing *Village Voice* ran a cover story condemning Detroit for giving tax abatements to GM. William Safire, the *New York Times*'s house conservative, praised the Poletowners for defending their property rights. The story reached a picturesque crescendo when a SWAT team evicted bitter-end parishioners from the basement of Immaculate Conception Church. A *Detroit Free Press* photographer snapped a picture of a seventy-year-old woman in crepe-soled shoes shouting from the back of a paddy wagon. That fall, Young was reelected to a third term, by his biggest margin ever.

Detroit/Hamtramck Assembly eventually employed six thousand autoworkers, but it was another disaster for the East Side. Chene Street had once run straight through to Hamtramck. Now it dead-ended into an auto plant, cutting off the neighborhood from the Midwestern Warszawa to the north.

"When they put that in, it completely sealed off Chene Street from Hamtramck," said Marian Krzykowski, the Chene Street historian. "It was a nail in the coffin. It was devastating. It was a working-class, diverse, viable area. There were a lot of businesses. It was alive. Once that plant came in, that was the end. For the next twenty years, they just went down, down."

None of those six thousand autoworkers moved into the neighborhood; anyone earning UAW wages could afford a house in the suburbs. (Managers in Detroit auto plants observe a "thirty-mile rule" when determining a safe distance to raise their families from Detroit.) Chene Street is now bleak enough to have provided the view out the window during Eminem's bus ride in *8 Mile*.

I bought a Daily 3 lottery ticket and a scratch-off at the deli. (The lottery terminal was perfectly located in the intertidal zone between the auto plant and the ghetto.) Then I walked south on Chene. The Eastown Bar's roof tiles had burned away, exposing blackened joists that a strong wind could have crumbled to ash. Carved below the flat roofline of another building: "W SMUCZYNSKI." A windowless storefront church whose only sunlight struggled through bulletproof glass blocks. The Black Bottom Social Club, booming dance music. On the walls of an empty hip-hop clothing store (Rocawear, Sean John, Phat Farm) an artistic war was taking place. Guerilla art from a local commune competed with gang graffiti. It was the Yes Farm's faceless red yogi, emanating rising-sun stripes, versus the tags of the Scorpios, 4 Life, East Side BG, and Black Gangstas. (What had happened to the cleverly named Chene Gang?)

In Chene-Ferry Park, I sat down next to a man drinking a can of Milwaukee's Best Ice and scratched the gray latex off my lottery ticket with a quarter. Then I gave the quarter to the beer drinker.

"If you win the lottery, come back with a drink," he requested. "You drink?"

I do, but not in the way he meant it, not as a pastime.

On the way back up the street, I paused in front of a bakery so freshly arsoned it smelled like cinders, and exhaled cool air. The Yes Farm had struck here, too, replacing the pastries with concrete layer cakes, painted pink and turquoise: Miami Beach colors for black-and-white Chene Street. Oscar Watkins, a fifty-year-old man wearing all his worldly possessions, stopped there, too. For two bucks—the price of checkbook journalism on Chene—he narrated the street's commercial history.

"This was Max's Furniture Store, before it was converted into a bakery," he said of the building in front of us. "That was Kowalski Sausage, then it turned into a T-shirt shop. Over there was a bank. Then it was a Coney Island. Then it went out of business."

Oscar himself had been a fixture on the street since 1984, shortly after the GM plant opened. He'd intended to get into the auto industry himself, but after he could no longer afford tuition at a technical school, and his mother died, he "got weak, started selling crack and heroin." He said, "I know the Chambers Brothers. I was my best fuckin' customer. Before I knew it, I had a motherfuckin' jones." Unable to find a job because of a retail fraud conviction, he'd turned in bricks, aluminum, and pallets at the Chene-Ferry Market, when it was a recycling center.

"Now I just do the hustle," he said. "One of my son's friends is moving out and he's paid up until the third of next month, so I can stay at his place. Rest of the time, I stay at vacant houses here and there."

On my way back up the street, a man ran out of Peacemakers International—Pastor Steve's church—calling after me, "You got a cell phone? There's some guy laying in the grass."

On our way to investigate, we passed the Milwaukee's Best Ice drinker, walking in the opposite direction.

"Hey," he asked me. "Can you give me a ride home?"

"I gotta deal with this," I said, to put him off.

We searched the lot but didn't find anyone lying drunk among the weeds.

"You know, I think that guy who walked past us was him," the man said. "I remember when he still had his mind."

The last thing I did before leaving Chene-Ferry Park was buy a camera for three dollars. I didn't need a camera, especially not a point-and-shoot film camera, but I wanted to talk to the gaunt man who was trying to sell it, and I thought three dollars would be an icebreaker. Here at the very bottom of the economy, even human interaction has a financial component, especially when someone like this author, who looks like he has disposable income—or at least loose change—appears on the scene. Because at the corner of Chene and Ferry, everyone needs money, all the time. Let the investment counselors at T. Rowe Price talk about thirty-year bond yields and long-term financial planning. The guys who hang out at Chene and Ferry measure their financial goals in minutes and hours. Habitually destitute, they are looking for just enough to pay for the next $5 rock of crack, the next $1.99 can of beer, the next 99 cent bag of potato chips. Besides a camera, I got this story for my three dollars:

"Do you mind if I drink? I keep it in the bag. I'm solo. I just come out here and sit under the tree. My name is J. C. Hood, all good in the neighborhood. I've been over here since '07. My people have a house over here they let me stay in. I'm upstairs and my uncle downstairs. It's an old house, almost on its last legs. No utilities, no heat, no water, no lights. No phone. I got a propane heater and a bed. I eat out and I bathe out, at the Capuchin Soup Kitchen at Mount Elliot and St. Paul. I get my clothes from Crossroads and Capuchin. I earn about five thousand dollars a year, hustling. I collect cans at Tigers games. Any kind of major event, I'm gonna try to catch it. I ride my bike, man, for hours, looking for stuff. I found a pair of boots. I can get five dollars. Houses, doors be open. You go in there, you can find a lot of stuff. Foreclosures, people just leave their stuff there. I've found TVs, stereos. I eat and take a bath and try to hustle, get money for cigarettes or something, and then my day is over.

"I went to high school in Alabama. I moved up to Detroit when I was twenty-two, to stay with my father. I went to prison for petty armed robbery. I used a knife. I got eighty-one dollars. When I ran around the corner, I thought I'd got away but my man was on me. When the police drew down on me, I thought, 'Man, I should have kept running.'

"I got five to fifteen years. I did all of it. I've been to every joint in Michigan. I learned a cooking trade, but the people in the restaurants, they be afraid to hire me. I worked in a 3M welding plant, but they fired me for poor work performance. I was having incidents with the other guys. On the job, people will try to get you fired. I'm unemployed. I collect food stamps. I'm trying to see what my disability's going to be. The correction officers bent my hands back when I was locked up. I also suffer from depression. I've had a rough life. I've turned my life over to the Lord, and I think I'm over that drug thing.

"People get kilt down here. Not recently. It is mellow, but if you carrying the wrong kind of attitude, you gonna have problems.

"I love Detroit. I wish I could be beneficial to the city and state but I really haven't figured it out."

DETROIT/HAMTRAMCK ASSEMBLY brought blight to Chene Street. Of all GM's plants, though, it's the best hope of reversing the blight the auto industry's failure has visited on the entire state of Michigan. Sacrificing a neighborhood to save a city, or a state, is the sort of tough executive decision that separates visionary mayors from panderers to the sensibilities of liberal do-gooders. At the end of burned-out Chene Street, GM is building the Chevy Volt, its hybrid electric car, the car designed to a) end America's dependence on foreign oil, and b) make General Motors look as environmentally and technologically progressive as the Europeans or the Japanese.

The first time I saw the Volt, it was only a battery. This was in November 2008, the same month that GM CEO Rick Wagoner went to Washington, D.C., to beg Congress for a bailout. I was in a sterile testing room at the GM Tech Center in the Detroit suburb of Warren. Andrew Farah, the Volt's chief engineer, handed me a lithium-ion power pack in a plastic sleeve. Farah had big hopes for that flat, rectangular fuel cell. Hopes that it was, at last, the innovation that would reverse General Motors' decades-long degeneration from 50 percent of the U.S. market to landlord of the largest vacant lots in Flint, Saginaw, and Lansing.

Before the Volt, GM had not thought up an original idea since it put a V-8 engine in the Oldsmobile. This was GM vice chairman Robert Lutz's reaction to the Toyota Prius: "Hybrids are an interesting curiosity and we will do some, but do they make sense at $1.50 a gallon? No, they do not."

Hybrids do make sense at $4 a gallon, but of course, Toyota had cornered that market. Now, for once, stodgy old Papa Jimmy was going to be first at something. As Toyota was the hybrid company, Chevy would be the electric company. As Prius was a metonym for a hybrid, the Volt would become *the* electric car.

"I want that brand right on my forehead," Farah said, pointing at the space above his safety glasses.

Farah worked on GM's first failed attempt at a battery-powered automobile: the EV1, subject of the documentary *Who Killed the Electric Car?* The EV1's problem: the battery weighed 1,200 pounds. To wring 40 miles out of a single charge, the car was a two-seater, with no trunk.

"You had to build the car around the battery," he said.

The lithium-ion battery weighed a third of that. The Volt would be an "extended-range" vehicle. Once the charge ran down, a gasoline engine would take over. But it wouldn't power a drive train, as on a traditional vehicle. It would power the electrical system running the car.

Because an electrical system is 50 percent more efficient than a drive train, the energy required to drive 40 miles on battery power is less than a gallon of gasoline. Fueling the Volt costs 2 cents a mile. At $4 a gallon, a gasoline-powered car costs 13 cents a mile.

One of my old high school classmates was so eager to buy an electric car that he flew to New York (like so many other newfangled ideas, the Volt was first marketed in the coastal states before working its way inland to the cautious heartland), bought a car, and drove it back to Michigan. As Matt Stehouwer reported on his blog, voltfansite.com, in his first three weeks of driving to work, he covered 627 miles on 4.2 gallons of gas. The only problem? Matt, a technology manager at Michigan State University, was told to stop "stealing electricity" by charging his Volt on campus. So he charged the Volt at home, at night. The local utility gave him a 25 percent discount on electricity drawn between eleven P.M. and six A.M. *and* a $7,500 rebate to match the $7,500 tax credit he received from the federal government. As a result, his monthly lease payment was $250, the electricity was $25, the gas $20. When Matt had leased a Chevy Malibu, he'd spent $200 a month on gas, so he figured his net cost for owning a Volt was fifty bucks a month.

Matt and his Volt met me in the parking lot of a Sears on the East Side of Lansing. The car was tricked out with a "VOLT 974" license plate and a garish green hood, patterned with stylized leaves and the word "Volt," so he can proselytize to fellow tech nerds. He'd testified about the Volt before the Michigan House of Representatives and was interviewed on WJR, Detroit's fifty-thousand-watt radio station. ("I haven't seen a vehicle attract this much attention since I ran into someone on a Segway. Lot of 'em want to know how much I spend on gas a month. I tell 'em, 'I don't even *look* at gas prices.'")

Matt let me drive the car. On the highway. There is something anodyne about a Volt. It's a car for people who need to get somewhere but would to like imagine they're not getting there in a car. As satirist Neal Pollack once wrote about the Volt's nemesis, the Prius, it's "the concept of the car as energy-saving household appliance, something as utilitarian as a low-flow dishwasher." The Volt makes no noise. It emits no exhaust. A graph of its acceleration would follow a perfectly flat forty-five-degree incline, because it has no gears. There's no lag between second and third, but neither does the Volt communicate any feeling of power to its driver. The car barely offers a physical experience at all. Unlike every other vehicle in its price range, the Volt is not a luxury car or a muscle car. The cramped backseat is divided by the battery pack into two buckets. Volt buyers aren't spending forty grand on aesthetics or mechanics; they want to make a social statement. Chuck Frank, an apostate Chevy dealer from Chicago who became one of the Sierra Club's most generous donors, bought a Volt "because [he] wanted to reinforce [his] environmental credentials." Matt didn't care about the environment; he wanted to screw OPEC.

"The energy is made by Americans, the car is made by Americans, and most of the parts are made by Americans," he said. "You're going to see a lot more Volts soon. Five dollars a gallon will force people into more economical cars. I keep telling my kids that they will not drive a gas car."

GM sold only 7,671 Volts in 2011, about three-quarters of its 10,000-car goal. Sales were so bad that Detroit/Hamtramck Assembly's Volt line shut down for five weeks in the spring of 2012, so dealers could sell off some of the 150-day backlog. (During that layoff, former president George H. W. Bush bought a Volt for his son Neil, which may help overcome Tea Partyish hostility to a car that doesn't run on gasoline, qualifies for a tax credit, and was built by "Government Motors.")

In year one, the car's sales were less important than its Chevy name-plate. Even though the Volt is a tiny, expensive toy for environmental and technological fanboys—a $20,000 car for twice the money—GM made the right decision by rushing it into showrooms before the Chevy-, Honda-, and Toyota-driving masses could afford to buy one. Eventually, lithium-ion batteries will be cheaper. Eventually, apartment buildings and gas stations will install charging stations. Eventually, gas will cost $5 a gallon. When all that happens, a lot of people will buy electric cars. GM hopes that brand on its forehead is big enough to make them buy Volts.

THURSDAY EVENING, Fort Street and Jefferson Avenue. Because the Packard Inn was the East Side's only hostelry, I was staying in Cork-town, near the grassy lot representing the footprint of the old Tiger Stadium. My hotel's parking lot was surrounded by a barbed wire fence, with a gate that squeaked aside when I swiped my room key. Before sup-per, I went for a run toward Hart Plaza, the spot along the Detroit River where Cadillac, the city's founder, landed in 1701. (Detroit is the third-oldest city on the Great Lakes, after Sault Ste. Marie and Macki-nac Island. All three occupied equally strategic positions for the French fur trade: the Soo controlled canoe traffic between *lacs* Huron *et* Super-ieur, Mackinac between Huron *et* Michigan, Detroit between Huron *et* Erie.) Downtown, all the traffic lights were blank. Cars lined up ten and twenty deep at the intersections. The next day, I planned to do some historical research at the Detroit Public Library on Woodward Avenue, the city's longest, widest thoroughfare (Detroit is the best city in America for making a U-turn, because the streets are so broad and so empty). The library was closed, due to the power outage. I crossed the street to the Walter P. Reuther Library of Labor and Urban Affairs, at Wayne State University. The lights were out there, too. All Wayne State was dark.

The Detroit Public Lighting Department, the decrepit municipal utility, had shorted out under a hot-weather load. The blowout shut down most of Detroit's public institutions, including city hall and the courthouse. *That* was my WTF moment in Detroit. *That* was the moment I thought, "I'm glad my boyhood dreams of Detroit didn't come true." It wasn't the crime, or the arson, or the abandoned buildings, or the wild foxes denning among the weeds. Detroit was as incapable as Port-au-Prince or Lagos of keeping all its lights on all the time. The lighting company only collects half its bills, but even if it collected all the money, it couldn't afford the $250 million necessary to modernize the system. The customer base is shrinking, but the grid stays the same size. That's modern Detroit's malady: it is no longer a functional city. It's the lower-class district of a metropolitan area. The middle class has fled north, east, and west (and would flee south, too, if not for the international border), taking along the department stores, the supermarkets, the basketball team, the white-collar jobs, the movie theaters and concert halls, and prevented the poor from building a train to chase after them. (The suburb of Troy vetoed a terminal for a light rail line that would have followed Woodward Avenue out of Detroit, calling it a "heroin train.") There is just no way that three-quarters of a million maids, busboys, bus drivers, scrap collectors, schoolteachers, artists, home health care aides, and secretaries can generate enough tax money to maintain an infrastructure built for *two million* autoworkers, engineers, dentists, accountants, professors, and electricians. Detroit levies a 2.5 percent income tax on residents and a 1.25 percent tax on commuters. Yet I know a woman whose neighborhood hires a private plowing service in the winter, because it's the only way to guarantee snowless streets.

"I wouldn't move back to Detroit even if someone gave me a free house," I once heard from a white riverboat captain who grew up on, then escaped, the city's Southwest Side. "The garbage never gets picked up there."

The fewer services Detroit provides, the more residents it loses. The more residents it loses, the less it can afford to provide services. Highland

Park, the city-within-the-city that is Detroit distilled to a few square miles of weedy streets, recently tore out 90 percent of its streetlights, because it can no longer pay the electric bill. Meanwhile, tony Oakland County, on the other side of 8 Mile Road, has one of the highest per capita incomes in the nation. Detroit can only become a city again by following the examples of Toronto and Indianapolis and consolidating the old urban core with the suburbs. That's not likely to happen; the whites would complain about sharing tax dollars, the blacks about sharing power. (Detroiters are jealous of their control over the area's water system.) Detroit and its suburbs will continue to revolve around each other like twinned planets, one black, one white, never touching but never able to break free into broader orbits.

Janice Harvey had given me Detroit's side of the urban-suburban antagonism: "Every time they want to talk regionalism, I get an attitude," she said. "They owe Detroit an apology. They left us, they deserted us, they consumed us, and the courts said our infrastructure had to save them. They left their trash, they caused us problems, they burned their houses."

In 2012, the Detroit city council voted to accept a consent decree, which gave an unelected board oversight over Detroit's finances. It was seen as the best way to avoid a state-appointed emergency manager with dictatorial powers. Benton Harbor and Flint, two other cities with large black populations, have been run by emergency managers, who are supposed to clean up the mess left by corrupt and/or incompetent mayors— Kwame Kilpatrick was corrupt and/or incompetent (he turned down a multimillion-dollar donation for new schools because he would not have had complete control over the money), but Detroit's problems are deeper than the misrule of any hinky, kinky politician.

Detroit may be the most American city. Europeans are fascinated by Detroit because their socialistic societies would never allow a city to rot. There's no such thing as white flight in England or Germany, at least not on a metropolitan scale. And government-planned greenbelts prevent the urban sprawl that encourages escape from used-up cities. Detroit would even be impossible across the river in Canada, whose social planning does not allow cities (or individuals) to fail as they do in the United States. (In the song "American Woman," the Canadian band the Guess Who tells the title character, "I don't need your ghetto scenes.")

"It's unique," remarked an Irish tourist I met at Hostel Detroit. He was in town for Movement, the electronic music festival that attracts fans from all over the globe. "It went from being nothing to being the richest city in the world to this in a hundred years. There's no other city like it in the world."

ON FRIDAY EVENING, Mike Hartnett stood on St. Aubin Street outside a restaurant named the Polish Yacht Club, overseeing the parking of Lincoln Navigators, Chrysler Sebrings, and Cadillac Escalades that were notably well polished and undented for the East Side.

The Polish Yacht Club is always busy on Fridays, because it serves fried perch, an end-of-the-week sacrament for Roman Catholics. It was founded as a tavern in 1909, by an immigrant named Stanislaus Grendzinsk, who named it the Ivanhoe Café after its telephone exchange. (During Prohibition, Grendzinsk turned the tavern into a restaurant, serving fish because, at ten cents a pound, it was cheaper than meat.) Sometime in the pre-riot 1960s, a patron instructed the bartender to tell his wife he was "at the Polish Yacht Club." The joke caught on. The regulars printed up cards, designed a pennant, bought captain's hats and sailing jackets, and held annual elections for commodore. The winners' photos are all displayed on the back wall of the dining room. There's not a black (or, to be fair, Anglo-Saxon) face among them. The back room is the Pope's Corner, commemorating a 1970s visit by Karol Cardinal Wojtyla, Archbishop of Kraków, who had distant cousins in Hamtramck. Behind the bar, bottles were topped with Dixie cups, a rotary phone awaited a wife's summons, and a sign demanded "BE NICE OR LEAVE!" For most customers, the fish fry is a visit to the Old Neighborhood.

"I'm basically like a scarecrow," Mike explained. "When people come down here, they want their cars looked after. What they used to do, they would break the window, take everything inside, and then open the door. The alarm wouldn't go off until then. We had three cars stolen. You've got a lot of nice cars here. Cadillacs. They're not used to that in this neighborhood. They'll be waiting in the weeds."

The Polish Yacht Club is one of the last places in Detroit to absorb white ethnic saltiness. Surly humor is the default civic mood of Buffalo, Milwaukee, and Chicago, but I didn't get hit with it in Detroit until my second visit to the Yacht Club.

"You're Patti, right?" I said, reintroducing myself to the founder's great-granddaughter Patti Galen, a short, round forty-nine-year-old.

"That's still my name," she said in a po-faced monotone.

Patti, a cop's wife, had grown up in the neighborhood and lived in Detroit until 2001, when the city stopped enforcing its residency requirement. The white cops moved to the suburbs, taking their white-cop attitudes with them.

"People in this neighborhood keep telling me I look like a cop," I said to Patti.

"No," said the woman who slept with a cop. "You don't look like a cop."

A man at the bar offered the opinion that Mike's scarecrow act wasn't as necessary as it used to be, now that there were more weeds, and fewer criminals to hide in them.

"I used to drive people down here and scare the *shit* out of 'em," he boasted. "Now there's hardly anything left to be scared of."

There are white people moving into the East Side. Young urban pioneers have colonized an entire block of Farnsworth Street, in the shadow of St. Hyacinth, the neighborhood's last surviving Catholic church. It is an unusual block for this part of Detroit, because every house is occupied. The first time I walked it with Gary Wozniak, I did not encounter any white people, but I saw everywhere signs of their presence: the outer wall of a house decorated in red, blue, green, and yellow stripes; a hand-painted "SLOW CHILDREN" placard, nailed to a tree; foreign cars parked along the curb with bumper stickers for the Detroit Waldorf School and the "Kill Your TV" movement. On one corner of Farnsworth and Moran was the Yes Farm, the art collective that competed with the graffiti taggers on Chene Street. On the other corner, the Farnsworth Community Garden, where the homesteaders raised their crops. A flyer requested volunteers to build beehives.

"In the summer, it's almost like San Francisco," Gary said. "There's people on the porches drinking beer, smoking weed. It's like a hippie commune, which is cool."

The East Side is the perfect hippie environment, because it is simultaneously premodern and postmodern. You can go back to the land *and* attend all-night raves in empty factories. The $12,000 houses offer grace from mortgages and material pressures. The second time I walked the block, I met a Yes Farmer, a young man from Oakland County who worked in a print shop downtown. His background was typical of Farnsworth Street. Most white people who grew up in Detroit have either moved out or are trying to get out. Only suburbanites romanticize the city.

"They're all young, hip-hop, techno, hippie," said Patti Galen at the Polish Yacht Club. "Tattoos, piercings. They all have visions. They want to change the world. They made cement cakes and put them in the window of the bakery on Chene Street after it burned down. They were smashed up in a day. You can't change this neighborhood."

(When I attended Mass at St. Hyacinth, a parishioner asked whether I was "one of the urban farming kids." It was a sign of the archdiocese's desperation in a city where the white population has declined from 1.6 million to 75,000. The newcomers are the kind of white people who go to goth clubs on Saturday night, not Mass on Sunday morning. St. Hyacinth's congregation seemed to consist of legacy suburbanites who parked their sedans in a gated, guarded lot, huddled in the first few rows of the sanctuary, then drove back to Livonia. Weekday masses had been canceled, since the celebrant died. Only a portly midvocation priest from Poland remained. "The church may be in danger of closing if we don't get more people," the parishioner explained.)

The urban pioneers are part of a movement called "Rust Belt chic." I first heard that term in Youngstown, Ohio, from a thirty-three-year-old college graduate named John Slanina. Slanina had taken his Youngstown State degree to the Netherlands, then to Atlanta, but he'd brought it back, along with an urban aesthetic evident in his chunky glasses, goatee, and red sneakers. While working at the University of Delft, Slanina started a blog called *I Shout Youngstown!* to tell the people back home, "Hey, there are all these neat things in the Netherlands that you can emulate." Then he decided to move home and emulate them himself.

"You can get a house in a nice neighborhood for forty thousand," Slanina said of Youngstown. "And you don't need to hang around the Kiwanis Club for twenty years to have an impact on what's going on here."

(Youngstown's mayor and congressman were both in their thirties. The older generation of politicians—including imprisoned congressman James Traficant—had been discredited by their ties to the Mafia.)

In no other city has the term "Rust Belt" been so embraced—but only by those too young to have lost a job on Black Monday, the September day in 1977 when Youngstown Sheet and Tube announced it would close by the end of the week, laying off five thousand workers. The Rust Belt Theater Company produces work by Youngstown playwrights. The Rust Belt Brewing Company crafts Blast Furnace Blond Ale, and the Artists of the Rust Belt build mobiles out of steel salvaged from scrap yards.

For Slanina, Rust Belt chic is also a way of carrying on the urban, Slavic-American culture into which he was born. It's *slivovitz*, pierogis, and pepper-and-egg sandwiches. It's polka karaoke at Polish happy hour, Slovak language lessons and ice hockey in an old steel mill. It's a wedding with a kolaches, pizzelle, and baklava on the cookie table—"a fantastic example of Rust Belt chic and classic Youngstown."

If it's true that every trend skips a generation before returning to fashion, then the young people who embrace Rust Belt chic are celebrating their World War II–era grandparents' urban, blue-collar lifestyles and rejecting their baby boomer parents' flight from the cities and from their ethnic heritage. In the 1970s, polka, bowling, and Hamm's on tap at the Polish National Alliance were *not* hip: they were symbols of a reactionary culture, the white ethnic hard hat. Vilified as a blindly patriotic bigot by upper-class liberals and black militants alike, lampooned on *All in the Family*, forced to pay for the racial sins of someone else's ancestors by sacrificing his children to forced busing, his career to affirmative action, and his tax money to welfare, he retaliated by buying a ranch house in an inner-ring suburb and voting for Ronald Reagan. Slanina's grandfather was a steelworker. His parents were schoolteachers.

Plenty of Rust Belt cities are trying to repatriate the grandchildren of steelworkers, although the return to urban living is a creative-class movement, not a working-class movement. After NAFTA passed in 1993, the small textile shops on Cleveland's industrial East Side began moving to Mexico. The city noticed that artists looking for cheap studios were moving into the old brick factories. So in 2000, the city council rezoned a light industrial district for live/work spaces.

The live/work ordinance was one reason downtown Cleveland gained 1,300 residents in the 2010 census, making it the only growing neighborhood in a city that lost 83,000 people. Councilman Joe Cimperman— the loquacious politician who tried to unseat Dennis Kucinich in 2008—helped pass the ordinance. Artists' lofts don't employ as many people as factories, Cimperman says, but they're "a hell of a lot better than vacant." The artists who occupied a shut-down elementary school opened their studios once a month to give art lessons to the neighborhood kids, "kids who were doing drugs, having sex, setting cars on fire."

The live/work ordinance "was almost like a blessing by the city," Cimperman said. "The artists realized that we cherished them. That they weren't squatters. I think the fact that we finally have a policy for bringing people back to the city is kind of generational. People in my generation—you know, you don't really realize your population is declining when you are in it. But you see these buildings and you are thinking, 'If there's one artist in there, why wouldn't there be ten?'"

Detroit is experiencing the same contradictory population trends as Cleveland. While Detroit lost a quarter of its people in the 2000s, the population of under-thirty-fives with college degrees increased 59 percent. In Detroit's case, that's significant because they're the first postriot generation, who grew up without their parents' antagonism toward blacks, Detroit, and black Detroiters. They're the reason the city's white population increased in 2008 and 2009, for the first time since the early 1950s.

Sarah Szurpicki grew up in the suburbs and studied environmental science and public policy at Harvard. When she got married, Szurpicki and her husband bought a three-bedroom Mies van der Rohe condo in Detroit's Lafayette Park, for $70,000. Szurpicki is a founder of GLUE, the Great Lakes Urban Exchange, a network of twenty- and thirtysomethings in Detroit, Buffalo, Pittsburgh, Milwaukee, St. Louis, and Cleveland who trade ideas about redeveloping their Rust Belt (a term GLUE embraces) hometowns. I brunched with Sarah at the Russell Street Deli, a restaurant across the street from Eastern Market. Most of the diners appeared to be hipsters. Needless to say, so did all the waitstaff.

"The younger generation is not as racially divided," she told me as we ate omelets from the veggie side of the deli's menu. "A lot of it is pop culture. If you grew up in the eighties, *The Cosby Show* was on TV. We didn't fight those battles during and after the riot. We don't carry those scars."

After brunch, Sarah showed me her condo. It was severely square, severely glassy, and severely narrow—modern in the way that only the architects of the 1950s and the 1960s understood modernism. The back door opened onto the park. Sarah pointed across the grass at a school.

"And there's even a school right here in the neighborhood for when our kids are old enough," she said.

At the time, that elementary school was 98 percent black, and the Detroit public schools had a 25 percent graduation rate. It's one thing to attract young people looking for a hiatus from suburbia. Convincing them to raise families in the city is another. Ben Schmitt, an ex-reporter for the *Detroit Free Press*, passed the first gut check—sending his daughters to kindergarten in Detroit. But when a flagstone crashed through the front window of his house in East English Village, Schmitt short-sold his home—worth $100,000 less than he'd paid for it—and moved his family to his native Pittsburgh.

"For a while I believed in [Detroit]," Schmitt wrote in an op-ed for the *Pittsburgh Post-Gazette*, after he was safely out of Detroit and in a new career at a marketing firm. "I purchased a home in one of the city's stable neighborhoods nine years earlier because it felt real. I scoffed at other colleagues and editors who drove to work on the freeways and never spent a minute in the city they covered.

"But when I heard my daughters' screams that evening, I knew I was gone. No more compromises."

ON SATURDAY MORNING, Pastor Steve led a prayer service around a wooden cross rising from a pot of orange lilies in a landscaped lot across Chene Street from his church. His vestments consisted of a gray cutoff T-shirt, knee-length khaki cargo shorts, a turquoise belt, black socks, and black sneakers. His congregation—some black, some white, all too poor to live anywhere but the East Side—stood in a loose circle.

"God is doing something on Chene Street, and you're drawn by the precious Holy Spirit," Pastor Steve told them. "Drug addicts, prostitutes, criminals out of the system, people that are bound by alcohol and sexual practices, we thank you, Lord, for bringing them to us. Thank you, Lord, for bringing us to Chene. Thank you, Lord, for bringing us to the heart of hell."

A bearded man in a "John 3:16" T-shirt, a fringe of hair blowing over his ears. A short stout woman propped up by a cane. A black kid wearing a T-shirt depicting an old English D—the emblem of Detroit—shaped like a hand grenade. Pastor Steve called this place the heart of hell, but it may have been closer to heaven than anywhere in Michigan. To live on Chene Street was to have failed by all social, financial, and legal standards. These people would never make it out to the suburbs. Their only hope for personal advancement was to become angels in the next world. (Pastor Steve lived in the suburbs: he'd moved to Utica, the same town as Gary Wozniak, after his wife was mugged.)

Pastor Steve continued. "Probably represented here is every kind of crime you can imagine. Every background from drug dealing to homelessness, to prostitution, to people who are highly educated who think they're good old boys. Sometimes, they're the hardest to reach. When you're in this area, remember where you came from. Don't be afraid to break bread with anyone."

SATURDAY AFTERNOON, the biker apostle roared up to Chene-Ferry Park on a flatulent Harley with a glossy Jesus painted on the fuel tank.

Removing his black helmet, which proclaimed "FAITH" beneath a silver sword and shield, Pastor Steve groomed his white beard, smoothing strands that depended from his chin like a Hebrew's *payot*. Fishing-lure earrings dangled from his lobes. Silver and turquoise rings sparkled on his fingers. On the north side of the plaza, the church had painted the same sunrise emblem as the Chene-Ferry Market, but with purple rays, an orange cross, and the motto "LOVE WINS."

The occasion was the Peacemakers International Singing Contest. A guitar, bass, and drum combo—the musical accompaniment for every storefront church—was setting up on a temporary stage. I recognized several people I'd met on the street. Joe was walking one of his unsold pit bull puppies. Oscar Watkins sat on a bench, preparing to sing "Amazing Grace." The church handed out commodities every Tuesday—a schedule known up and down Chene Street—and its front door was always open, so anyone could page through the piles of old clothes on fold-out tables. Oscar had lived for several months at Jesus House, a home for recovering junkies run by one of Pastor Steve's white-boy sidekicks, a husky young man who'd beaten a cocaine habit with God's help.

"I gutted the basement and made it my room," Oscar said of his stay at Jesus House. "I was saving and paying my taxes and then they accused me of getting high. Fuck it, if you think I'm getting high, I might as well get high. I think there's some racism there. Some of the white guys had different privileges. Pastor Steve's a good guy and all that. He's doing good for the community, but there's more than meets the eye. They don't like me down there. They know I speak my mind. Steve keeps trying to get me to go back to Jesus House. He calls me 'deacon.' I don't see no deacon. It'd be a waste of my time, anyway. I'm fifty years old. I ain't got that much time. I'm gettin' tired of these streets, though, the heroin. Just when you do good, that's when the devil steps in. Paul said in the Bible, 'I'm the chief of sinners.' I feel like that."

Before the singing started, Pastor Steve bowed his head and raised a palm to heaven.

"Lord Jesus Christ, I believe in all my heart that you're the son of the living God, and you died for my sins. I open up my heart, Jesus, to you."

Joe answered the altar call. So did his puppy. At least, the dog was dragged up there on a leash.

When the contest began, the first performer declared that God had commanded her to sing, not in our language, but in the spirit. I wish I could transcribe the lyrics of her wordless psalmody, but it was in the tongue of angels, not humans. Oscar was next, with a penetrating rendering of "Amazing Grace." The truest artists are not those with the grandest voices, but those whose voices make the singer indistinguishable from his song. Frank Sinatra was never more convincing as a brokenhearted loser than Oscar as the wretch who narrates the hymnal's greatest hit, a hymn that makes more sense coming from the mouth of a homeless drug addict than a nylon-robed choir in a church with a $5,000 weekly collection plate. There was no collection at this service, because nobody had any money. A thirteen-year-old sang a verse of R. Kelly's "I Believe I Can Fly." In the alley behind him, a spindly, bearded man in laceless shoes, who believed no such thing, searched a garbage bin for the last salvageable discard on the block.

Finally, Joe sat up on the speaker and took the microphone.

"I'm gettin' some feedback," he mumbled. Four o'clock on Saturday afternoon was not likely a sober hour. "I've got just a few words to say."

Joe moaned the first word of a hymn—"Shiii-lohhh." The rest was as incomprehensible as the woman who'd sung in tongues.

ON SUNDAY AFTERNOON, at three o'clock, Detroit's home of the blues is a vacant lot at the corner of Frederick and St. Aubin streets. This is the site of John's Carpet House, a music festival that rises from the weeds during every fair-weather weekend. It got started in a house across the street—when there was a house across the street. John Estes, a blues musician, ran his own juke joint—just opened up his doors and let anyone come inside and sing. So many sang that John built an addition, just for the bands, insulating the walls with carpeting. Hence the nickname. Carl Carlton, who nearly won a Grammy for "She's a Bad Mama Jama," played in the Carpet House. So did some of the Motown stars who stayed in Motown after Berry Gordy took the label (and all the royalties) to Los Angeles. Martha Reeves (who became a city councilwoman after her recording career ended), the Contours, Alberta Adams, Thornetta Davis. Forty years after Motown, John's Carpet House was their only stage.

After John died, crack dealers took over his house. The neighbors firebombed it, to fumigate the drug trade, and the city bulldozed the cinders. The music moved across the street, into a vacant corner lot, but the name didn't change: the show was still called John's Carpet House, even though the house was gone. In exchange for the space, John's old friend Pete Barrow mowed the grass once a week.

An hour before showtime, Pete—a big man with a straw hat and a mustache that followed the contours of his frown—began setting up the temporary wooden stage, an old deck covered with carpet scraps. Pete swept the carpet with a push broom and uncoiled the orange cords connecting the amplifiers and the sound board. The cars—every damn one of them American—began arriving, parking on the perimeter of the field until it looked like a drive-in picnic, leaving the grass in front of the stage open as a dance floor. The mobile barbecue wagons lit their grills and the saucy smoke drifted all the way to Chene Street. Hand-lettered signs advertised "WING DINGS $3.00. HALF SLAB $9.00. WHOLE SLAB $15.00."

"Anybody who's anybody in Detroit plays here," Big Pete explained. "We try to stick strictly to blues. I don't want no mess. We had one guy tried to rap. I told him, 'Don't play none of that hip-hop shit. You stick strictly to blues.'"

As blues fans unfolded chairs beneath the canopies of wild trees, rippling motorcycle engines announced the disembarkation of Big Pete's "security force"—the Outcasts, the Detroit Gentlemen, and the Hell's Lovers. The Hell's Lovers wore their philosophy—"Ride for Peace"—on the backs of their leather jackets. The mamas' jackets advertised the pussy magnetism of motorcycles by declaring their wearers "Property of Hell's Lovers." A Detroit police car cruised up and down Frederick Street to keep the street clear of motorcycles, but its hood was etched with abrasions and its rearview mirror was cracked. The cops looked less threatening and less sexy than the bikes.

The music: Leilani, two women in matching zebra-print blouses, sang Roberta Flack's "Feel Like Makin' Love" over a karaoke track. Mr. Romance, a man wearing a bling cross and a backward baseball cap, surprised the entire meadow with a version of K'Jon's "On the Ocean" that started down around his ankles before writhing through his vocal cords. Then a Caucasian gentleman in a zoot suit bastardized Robert Johnson by singing "Come on, baby, don't you want to go? / Well I really love Chicago, but take me home to Detroit."

(This was an actual blues number, but it was clear that Big Pete's definition included rhythm and blues, this great musical city's greatest musical contribution to the world.)

Then came Harmonica Shah. Harmonica Shah was a bluesman: the harmonica belt around his waist had holsters for seven harps, one for each musical key: A B C D E F G. When he sang his cheatin'-woman ballad "I Heard You Was at the Casino," he blew his sorrow through the reeds. During "Hey, Detroit"—"Detroit ain't no hippie town / If I feel like this tomorrow, I'll be Mississippi bound"—an old man in a striped suit and two-tone shoes danced around the meadow, intensifying the music by inhaling from a joint pinned in a roach clip. After the set, I ran behind the speakers to a) buy a copy of Harmonica Shah's CD *Tell It to Your Landlord*, and b) meet Harmonica Shah.

Harmonica Shah was a Muslim in a Christian city (albeit the city where the Nation of Islam was founded) and a blues singer in a soul town. He had this in common with his fellow Southern blacks: he'd moved to Detroit to work in an auto plant. After Ford fired him for absenteeism, he picked up the harmonica while driving a taxicab.

"I got fired out of Ford's, I got serious about the harmonica, and I traveled around the world," Harmonica Shah said. "White folks just started sending me around the world. The white people kept the blues alive. Black people were ashamed of it. When they did Motown, they wanted to get away from the old wagon wheels and cotton farms, and sound modern."

Even in Detroit, though, there was always a stage for the blues: in a storefront, in a soup kitchen, in a vacant lot.

"We could take a picture and say, 'This is a blues festival in Mississippi,' and now people wouldn't know the difference," he said.

It was July, summer's lushest month. John's Carpet House was surrounded by green fields crosshatched by cracked side streets, like township sections in miniature. Across the many squared-off meadows, a food processing plant resembled a ruined castle. Standing in line for a Porta-John, I was advised I could do my business more quickly in the "slop house," a wild stand of brush growing on the grave of a bungalow.

As evening came on, the streets teemed with bikers, drinkers, and smokers, all attracted to the East Side's only free entertainment (although Big Pete passed a bucket to pay the house band). I saw Al and Greg, the Packard plant's odd couple. Greg supported his wizened legs by leaning against a lawn chair. And just when the scene could not have looked any more like Ernie Barnes's Saturday-night dance party painting "Sugar Shack," a half-dozen men on horseback rode through the crowd. They were dressed as Civil War soldiers, members of a drill team that had performed elsewhere in the city that afternoon. Big Pete tolerated plenty of wild human behavior at his weekend joint, but at that species he drew the line. He grabbed the microphone, interrupting a hot trumpet solo.

"Lookie here," he shouted. "We got five or six horses out there, bucking at people. We can't have them horses here. They could hurt somebody and then we'd be in a world of trouble. Please get them horses off the lot."

By showcasing African-American culture in a setting that was at once inner-city and pastoral, John's Carpet House is not just quintessentially Detroit, it is *uniquely* Detroit. These blues, this barbecue, the empty fields, the cars, the horses, composed a scene that could not exist anywhere else in the world. Detroit is a great place to spend a summer vacation, if you know where to find the empty spots on its map.

BY MONDAY, at noon, Anthony Hardy had set up his canopy in a weedy parking lot on Chene Street. The red hots were plumping in the hot water basin of his stainless steel food cart. I'd met Anthony the day before, selling hot dogs at John's Carpet House. Since there was no restaurant on Chene, Anthony decided to improvise his own. His only competition was the deli near the plant, but Dan and Vi's didn't sell hot dogs or Coneys, and how could you call yourself a real Detroit restaurant without serving Coneys? Also, it was owned by Italians.

"I came out here because between the freeway and Gratiot Avenue, Dan and Vi's is the only place to get something to eat," Anthony said. "The Coney Island burned down. It used to be a Comerica Bank. I'm fifty-eight going on fifty-nine years old. I'd rather sell hot dogs and sausages than dope. I don't have time to do time, so it's easier for me to sell hot dogs and sausages."

Anthony was most worried about competition from "the camel jockeys," as he called Detroit's Arab merchants. As immigrants, he believed, they were exempt from taxes for their first seven years in America. He'd also heard they demanded fellatio from female customers.

"The Chaldeans here, they have this philosophy that they can do what they want, say what they want about our women, but if you say anything about the women in their religion, they'll cut your head off."

(Chaldeans are actually Maronite Christians, but even in metro Detroit, which has enough Arabs to support an Arabic radio station, people who should know better think they're all Muslims.)

Two men wearing Wesco Oil patches on their work shirts bought two Coney dogs apiece, squirting fluorescent pools of mustard into the greasy chili. Then two men from the neighborhood sat down on coolers. Anthony's canopy was the only respectable hangout on the street. The park and the wall outside the liquor store were for unemployed drunks. When John Givans (who is quoted elsewhere in the book, talking about the riot and the crack trade) told me he had lived in the same house since 1961, I knew immediately which house he meant.

"It's that one with the cyclone fence and the peaked roof, near John's Carpet House, right?" I said. "The best-looking house in the neighborhood."

"That's it," he said. "My grandfather built it. He was the first black wrecker in Detroit. When we moved in, it was all Yugoslavian and Polish. It was us and one other black family in the neighborhood. I'm the last one left."

John had two daughters, aged seven and eleven. He wanted to move them to a farm in the country, where the schools were better. But his house wouldn't fetch enough to buy a farm, and he was suspicious that the white people were trying to clear out the East Side to provide cheap land for the condo dwellers.

"This neighborhood is like a jungle," said Lester Guyton, a young ex-marine (the judge said it was the military or jail, for selling weed) who had shown up to provide the extra mouth necessary for three-cornered bullshit. "It's like Guatemala. The property here is too rich. They're trying to get the black people that live here out of here, to make room for white people from downtown."

"My gas bill is eight hundred dollars a month in the winter," John complained. "They tell me confidentially there's no way I can burn that much gas. They're trying to drive me out."

Anthony, who had a conspiracy theory about the Arabs, joined in on the conspiracy theory about the whites.

"When they ran the I-75 freeway through Black Bottom, a lot of people screamed foul," he said. "An old white lady done tole me. I said, 'I'm gonna get me a house in Detroit.' She said, 'You can have it, because we're moving out. But we'll get it back later.' They're trying to shut the East Side down, to get everybody who's not of the Caucasian persuasion out of here."

John Givans grunted.

"The city services out here are nonexistent," he said. "It's almost like a farm now. I got rabbits, pheasants, raccoons. If I could get rid of the crime, I'd never leave."

15.

Flintstones

The 9/11 Memorial Corner occupies three of the four lots at the intersection of North and McClellan Streets, on the vanishing North End of Flint. A cross between folk art and patriotic kitsch, its backdrop is a pentaptych of the Manhattan skyline, with the Twin Towers still the tallest stalks in that architectural garden. A ceramic angel spreads her plaster wings atop the middle panel, while in the grass—more tightly barbered here than in any of the surrounding yards—a statuette of the Virgin Mary bows her head toward the ground. Written on a billboard are the names of every police officer and firefighter who died that Tuesday morning. A winding path of cinder blocks bears a hand-painted roll call of all the soldiers who never came home from Afghanistan. "OUR (heart) AND (praying hands) GO OUT TO THE WORLD. GOD BLESS 9- 11-01 AMERICA," reads the message on a concrete foundation, road-mapped with weeds. I wasn't walking long among this roster of the dead before a small, tattooed woman appeared on the porch of one of the block's three remaining houses and walked across the street.

"I just want to take some pictures of this," I explained. "I've got a camera in the trunk of my car."

"Take all the pitchers ya want," she said. "This is fer the public."

Suzie Fitch curated this site, checking the Internet for casualties every day, recording the sad news with a fine-tipped brush.

"We just lost two this weekend," she said. "We lost forty-seven in April."

"What about the soldiers in Iraq?" I asked.

"Iraq din't have nothin' to do with 9/11," Suzie said. "I can't wait until the war is over. I wish we never gone into Iraq. We should finish

Afghanistan first. We had to go there, no ifs, ands or buts. They're the ones who kilt us."

A pickup truck pulled up across the street. Suzie's husband, Moose, home from hanging drywall, walked over to join us. Moose wore a ponytail, a graying beard, and a T-shirt with the face of a similarly bearded man still at large in the Middle East. "WANTED," it read. "OSAMA BIN LADEN."

The 9/11 Memorial Corner could not exist anywhere but a city like Flint. Where else could the Fitches have acquired so much vacant land for their patriotic crèche? It is within sight of Buick City. The factory that was supposed to bring Japanese efficiency to America had been closed for a dozen years, leaving behind a neighborhood of shuttered taverns, party stores and stringy people sitting on slanted porches. A Realtor's sign was planted on the front lawn of UAW Local 599 headquarters. An auto plant that had once employed twenty-eight thousand was now attended by a few dozen demolition experts working for RACER, the land trust that took over GM's vacant properties after the bankruptcy. As the houses surrounding Buick City emptied out, the Fitches bought up vacant lots from the Genesee County Land Bank, which sold them for as little as $25 to neighbors willing to cut the grass. The couple had expanded their yard nearly to the end of the block. The only corner they didn't own was squatted on by a dead-eyed house that had become a dumping ground for old mattresses; it remained upright only because the city couldn't afford to bulldoze it. The Fitches didn't own the land across the street, but Moose mowed the lawns anyway, so drug dealers couldn't hide their stashes in the weeds. One hundred years after GM's founding, Flint was at the far end of its historic arc. The Vehicle City had been built to produce automobiles, but once the plants wore out, it was being disassembled at the same geometric rate at which it had risen. In the damp, lush climate of Lower Michigan, verdure is relentless, crawling through every sidewalk fault, packing every empty space with thick grass. Already, trees were encroaching on the yards Moose tried to keep clear—trees broad enough for drug dealers to hide themselves behind. Carl Sandburg's poem "Grass" seems appropriate for the Memorial Corner, since it's about war dead. "Two years, ten years, and passengers ask the conductor: / what place is this? / where are we now / I am the grass. / Let me work." But it also seemed appropriate for Flint itself, disappearing under vegetation.

Before the Fitches built their memorial, "the neighborhood was using that corner as a public dump site," Moose said. "We still find a lot of stuff down there. You get tired of looking at garbage because people just don't care. They don't take pride in their country that I saw as a child."

Moose and Suzie had met in Chicago, her hometown, then returned to Flint, his hometown, because he needed to be close to his children by an earlier marriage.

"When he brought me here, he's like, 'Wait 'til you see Flint,'" she said. "'It's happening. It's goin' on. It's a mini-Chicago.' And I come here and I'm like . . ."

"I was embarrassed," Moose confessed. "The whole time I was gone, it went to hell."

"We're gettin' out of here," Suzie said. Then she jumped in the air and stamped on the sidewalk. *"I am not gonna die in Flint, Michi-kin!"*

Moose had appeared in Michael Moore's anti-Iraq War film, *Fahrenheit 9/11*, after the filmmaker discovered the 9/11 Memorial Corner on a hometown visit. Unsophisticated Moose didn't know Moore from D. W. Griffith, but he'll show off his Corner to anyone, so he allowed the director to film them driving around the North End in Moose's pickup.

"They said they were taking pictures of memorials to 9/11, and the movie was going to be about honoring those folks of 9/11," Moose would say later. "He came up to my wife: 'This is the best thing we've seen in the city of Flint.'"

Once the movie came out, though, Moose felt he'd been a victim of journalistic trickery. This was Moose's quote as it appeared in *Fahrenheit 9/11*: "Look at the neighborhood I live in. Most of 'em are abandoned. That's not right. You want to talk about terrorism? Come right here. President Bush, right here. He knows about this corner."

Moose's words give the impression that he was talking about the North End, and blaming gangbangers for terrorizing the residents. In fact, Moose said, Moore combined two unrelated quotes. The second half was a response to the question, "Who do you want to visit this corner?"

As a result of his *Fahrenheit 9/11* appearance, Moose was tracked down by *another* Flint documentarian. Kevin Leffler had grown up in Moore's hometown of Davison, and even worked with Moore in the early 1970s as an operator on the Davison Hotline. But like a lot of Flintstones, Leffler thought *Roger & Me* depicted Flint as a pitiable parade of dreck, terrifying investors who might have brought in businesses to replace General Motors. So he self-produced *Shooting Michael Moore*, a combination of interviews with every Flintstone Moore had dicked over on his way to the big time and an attempt to interview Mike, employing the stalker journalism Moore introduced in *Roger & Me*.

In the film, Moose tearfully demanded to know how Moore could misrepresent his patriotic display. There was no cynicism or irony at the corner of North and McClellan, and Moose seemed hurt that a Hollywood director could introduce such notions into his carefully tended garden of Americana.

"Mr. Moore," he said, his voice welling, "how can you do this when you say you love this country and you talk for the small man? Mr. Moore, you broke our heart, just like 9/11 broke this country's heart."

Moose got emotional over two subjects—America and his wife. In his mind, Moore had violated both.

There are two high holidays at the Corner: Memorial Day and September 11. Memorial Day was coming up. If I wanted to see what the Corner meant to America, and to North Flint, I should come back then, Moose suggested.

THE BIKERS ARRIVED FIRST, a gray-haired iron cavalry called the Christian Motorcyclists Association of America. Their "Riding for the Son" vests were embroidered with Indian arrowheads—Flint's emblem— identifying them as the Flint Area Good News Riders. A biker pointed at a young woman's peace-sign tattoo.

"Do you have an Islamic boyfriend?" he asked. "That's an Islamic peace sign. A Christian cross upside down, with both arms broken. When the Jews are dead, when the Christians are dead, then the world will be encircled by Satan. They've used it since Saladin."

Moose, who was patriotic without being political and religious without being sectarian, wore a T-shirt that read, "I SUPPORT MY COUNTRY AND OUR TROOPS. PRAYER FOR THE PRISONERS AND MISSING." As the impresario of this event, he had strung fleece marine corps blankets along a wire, lit candles inside glowing cutaway milk jugs, set up a video camera on a tripod, and was now walking along the improvised plank benches and folding chairs, recruiting veterans to fold the flag. (Moose had never served in the military himself, which may be why he admired veterans so.)

"There's plenty of seats up here," he told his late arrivers. "Remember, we're all Americans, so don't be afraid."

When the audience numbered three dozen—a good crowd for an outdoor vesper, which is what the ceremony in the long late-spring Michigan evening felt like—Moose made a speech.

"Will all the veterans stand up? We're here to honor the fallen veterans, the veterans still fighting, and the families. We need to start supporting our veterans, because they give us the freedom to do this."

A rotund young pastor sanctified the Corner.

"Bless this property that has been set aside for a memorial," he said. "Bless the hands that have set every stone and raised every flag. Bless our veterans. Bless the families and those that are longing after their loved ones on a foreign shore. Bless those that have paid the ultimate sacrifice. The just died for the unjust."

The biker who'd called the peace sign a Muslim brand rose to express himself. That morning, he'd marched in a Memorial Day parade. Only one person had stood to salute the flag.

"And he was in a wheelchair!" the man bellowed. The consequence of such disrespect for the Stars and Stripes: "Sixty-one thousand Vietnam Veterans have committed suicide since the war! Twenty-one thousand are in our jails or prisons!"

Moose, who just wanted peace, seemed disconcerted by the biker's outburst, so he tried to change the mood of the gathering with a clueless-husband joke.

"Thank you," he said. "I didn't know that, but I don't know a lot of things. I'm married."

The biker cocked his arm in a sharp salute as three fellow veterans lowered and folded the flag. It was changed each Memorial Day. Flint's four seasons are hard, even on polyester. The biker handed Moose the tri-corner folded flag.

"On behalf of our government, thanks for what you've done for our veterans," the biker said.

"Thank you," Moose replied. "And welcome home, vets."

Even in late May, Michigan sunlight doesn't last forever. It mellows and dissolves. As the infiltrating darkness grayed the evening beyond the balance point between day and night, Suzie laid lilies at a wooden cutout of a soldier's silhouette, then read a poem she'd clipped from the newspaper. ("Memorial Day is a day of tears / For those who died over the years.") Finally, she led the congregation across the street to her memorial and asked everyone to recite, in unison, a name she'd painted atop a cinder block.

Most of the Good News Riders had grown up in Flint, but almost all had moved away to the old farm towns that absorbed the city's white working class—Flushing, Clio, Mount Morris. Before stomping their kick-starters, they stood around for a few minutes and talked about their hometown with a mixture of old-neighborhood nostalgia and suburban disdain.

"Highest murder rate in America," one lamented. "Fifty-nine point five per hundred thousand. The next is forty nine."

"Where do they get the money to buy drugs?" a woman asked. "Who's got money anymore?"

"They sell themselves. It'll be fifty dollars. Twenty-five for the pimp, twenty for the drug dealer, and five for them."

"This used to be one of the nice streets in town," a man said with a sigh. "When the shop was going."

THE TOPIC OF VIOLENCE in Flint is unavoidable, because Flint is the most violent city in the English-speaking world. The 2010 homicide rate quoted by that biker—59.5 per 100,000—is a figure so scandalously high that every Flintoid can cite it to the decimal. In 2010, 61 people were killed by their fellow man in Flint (or woman, in the case of an old lady who shot a teenage intruder), breaking a record set when Flint had twice as many people as it does today. The lawlessness was equal to Latin American drug capitals. To put the homicide rate in perspective, if New York City were as lethal as Flint, it would have 5,000 murders a year—twice as many as during the worst year of the Crack Wars, and over ten times as many as today. Flint has topped 24/7 Wall Street's list of the most dangerous cities over 100,000 people for several years. It won't drop off until the 2020 census, when the population will officially dip below six figures. (It was 102,434 in 2010.)

But first, it's important to write about why Flint may be the only place where the Fitches could have transformed their street corner into a veterans' memorial. Flint, which generates empty lots as multifariously as it once generated Buicks, has done more than any city to put vacant land into the hands of people who can do some good with it. It's a necessary project, because there's so much land to spare. Of 57,000 residential properties, 32 percent are unoccupied—12,000 houses, and 6,000 lots. Flint had to invent a solution for abandonment, because it was dealing with empty houses long before the foreclosure crisis struck.

In 1984, a few years after General Motors began its withdrawal, Dan Kildee was elected to the Genesee County Board of Commissioners, from a district in southwest Flint. Kildee came from a political family. His uncle, Dale, was the congressman who'd paid five dollars to sledgehammer a Toyota. A county commissioner runs for reelection every two years. In each campaign, Kildee found himself knocking on fewer doors.

"In this one section of my district, there were empty houses where I'd talked to voters two years before," he would recall. "It didn't really oc- cur to me then that this was part of some larger phenomenon, but it was just obvious to me that there was some sort of decline and abandon- ment taking place."

Elected county treasurer in 1996, Kildee quickly discovered that Flint was a major market for tax lien speculators. Lured by the "instant wealth" promises of late-night infomercials, investors—or "bottom-feeders," as Kildee came to call them—would buy liens on abandoned properties in bulk. If the owners paid, the bottom-feeders made a 15 percent return. If the owners didn't pay, the bottom feeders foreclosed. As long as the land was worth more than its delinquent taxes, the bottom-feeders could profit.

The lien was a nineteenth-century system, designed to ensure that government could get cash quickly, without waiting for tax payments. For pre-postindustrial Flint, liens were a disaster, putting houses into the possession of absentee owners who let them go to seed. Kildee's office stopped the speculation by borrowing money equal to all the delinquent taxes and paying local governments what they were owed. The county became the tax speculator *and* the landlord, renting out salvageable houses. In 1999, Kildee convinced the state legislature to change the tax law, allow- ing counties to foreclose on properties. This led to the establishment of the Genesee County Land Bank, giving the community ownership of its vacant houses and lots. The land bank has demolished 1,500 houses and sold nearly 1,000 lots to neighbors. That's how the Fitches, who are not a wealthy couple, or even a middle-class couple, acquired so much land.

Genesee County became a model for other communities that sud- denly found themselves with more land than anyone wanted. In the words of Cleveland's Jim Rokakis, "The father of the land bank move- ment in this country is Dan Kildee. But he will tell you that the Ohio land bank is the Michigan statute on steroids. They led the way and we got to tweak it."

Although the land bank has rescued individual streets from blight, it has not been able to reshape Flint by shutting down entire neighborhoods. As land bank director Douglas Weiland puts it, "We own 5,669 parcels, but we don't own an entire block." Because of the housing crisis, the county can't buy out residents, either. The average Flint home price crashed from $58,961 in 2005 to $15,372 in 2009. Paying fair market value wouldn't even provide the sellers enough money for a studio condominium. Plus, resentment still lingers from the urban renewal projects of the 1960s, when black neighborhoods were bulldozed to make way for highways.

The one section of Flint that *has* been successfully redeveloped is downtown. Saginaw Street, from the mid-1980s onward, was a midway of failure, where the plywood-to-glass ratio was at least 50-50. But prominent local investors and developers have decided to rebuild Flint from the center outward.

"Cities like Flint can't compete with the suburbs," Kildee says. "They need to offer something that is a unique urban product. If a purchaser has a choice between a suburb and a suburb in the city, typically, they're going to take the real thing. What cities should offer is something that's unique to the urban environment: a high-density, walkable neighborhood that has different types of housing that are not all McMansions built on former city neighborhoods."

Flint returned the wrought-iron Vehicle City arches to Saginaw Street, as a matter of local branding. The land bank acquired the Durant Hotel, which had closed in 1973 after a half century as the place to stay for traveling salesmen looking to do business with GM. Now, its marble-pillared lobby and checkerboard ballroom restored, the Durant is Flint's luxury loft building, with two-bedroom apartments renting for around $900 a month. Away from downtown, the land bank also rescued Fisher One, site of the Sit-Down Strike. GM wanted to tear the plant down. It's now a million-square-foot warehouse for Diplomat Specialty Pharmacy, which ships prescription drugs all over the country.

But downtown's most important development was persuading the University of Michigan to turn its Flint branch into a residential campus, rather than a glorified four-year community college. With money from the Mott Foundation—Flint's industrial legacy sugar daddy—an organization called the Uptown Reinvestment Corporation turned the Hyatt Regency into a dormitory. That was symbolic, because, like Auto-World, the Hyatt was a trashed legacy of Flint's failed campaign to reinvent itself in the early 1980s. Closed for nearly a decade, it was "dilapidated beyond belief," said an executive of the reinvestment corporation. "Broken glass, boarded-up windows, trees growing on the roof. When we walked in, you could barely move with all the rubble."

If Saginaw Street and its tributaries were all you saw of Flint, you would probably think you were on the main strip of a staid, stable city, the kind of place whose "Welcome to" sign is surrounded by Civitan and Kiwanis badges: there's a tapas restaurant, a pipe shop, a men's clothing store, a hipster T-shirt store, a Barnes & Noble in the U of M student food court, and an independent bookstore on a side street.

"The dozen or so buildings that have been redeveloped in downtown Flint really have had a transformative effect on the psyche of the community," Kildee said, explaining why Flint is an ideal place to experiment with strategies for rebuilding shrinking cities. "If you did them in Detroit, nobody would notice. We're big enough for those changes to be significant and small enough for them to be transformative."

But cross the Flint River, to the North End, and Flint is as close to anarchy as any city under the Stars and Stripes. It's a twenty-first-century Tombstone, an American Mogadishu. At the bottom of the ladder of lawlessness are the property crimes: scrappers carrying boilers down the street in broad daylight, then, once every empty house has been scavenged, stealing manhole covers off drains. Then there are the robberies. Pizzerias won't deliver in North Flint, because so many drivers have been strong-armed or held up at gunpoint. A man from New York State bought a house online, attracted by the low price and by Michigan's liberal medical marijuana law, for his multiple sclerosis. Knowing nothing about his new neighborhood, he was robbed as he moved his furniture in. Then there's the prostitution, which on some streets is so flagrant that fed-up neighbors spray-paint "NO HO ZONE" on boarded-up windows. At Dan Kildee's urging, I visited Jane Street, to see what a nearly denuded block looked like. After I drove past the dirt and rubble several times, taking pictures with my cell phone, a woman began walking toward my car, assuming I was trolling for sex. So I got out of there.

Arson is a popular form of mischief in North Flint. One morning, I read on mlive.com, Booth Newspapers' Michigan news site, that eleven houses had been torched overnight. (The *Flint Journal*, Booth's legacy paper product, is printed only four days a week.) I rushed up I-69 from Lansing to check them out before they were sealed off by fire inspectors. There was no reason for haste. To the Flint Fire Department, arson is an inexpensive form of slum clearance. The firefighters didn't attempt to put out the flames. If they had, the arsonists would have returned to finish the job, creating more alarms. They just tried to stop the fires from spreading. On Oklahoma Avenue, three houses had burned to their foundations. In the last occupied home on the block, a teenage girl was sitting on the porch.

"I got about ten minutes of sleep last night," she said. "I saw the flames about one thirty. We had to stand outside on the corner the whole time. We were there until the sun came up. My brother had to spray the house down with the garden hose until the fire department got here. It took them forever to get here. They sprayed our house down so it didn't spread. The house behind the house next door, their house melted, and they were over here yelling at us because nothing happened to our house. The house next door was really nice, but they moved out a month ago, and they already stripped the siding. We're the last one on this side of the street. My mom says we're going to move out at the end of the month. Once we're gone, they're going to strip this house and burn it down like all the others. It was three teenage boys who did this. They're the ones who've been threatening to shoot us. They came back and stood on the corner and watched."

At the top of the ladder, of course, are the shootings. Moose and Suzie called the police after their next-door neighbor—"a would-be pimp, a crackhead thief"—was shot. It took the officers fifty minutes to arrive. (I heard this exact figure from several Flint residents.) Many blamed the violence—and law enforcement's inability to control it—on the city's young mayor, Dayne Walling. In early 2010, after the police union refused to accept pay cuts, Walling laid off 57 officers—a third of the force. That fall, he laid off another 20. By the time Walling was finished cutting, Flint was protected by 124 officers, 1.2 per 1,000 residents, by far the lowest ratio in the state, and less than a third of Detroit's manpower. Murders increased from 36 to 61, making Flint the deadliest city in the country, just ahead of New Orleans, where the social order had broken down due to natural, not economic, causes. The pastor of Eliezer Church of the Apostolic Faith memorialized the dead with crosses. The names were obscured by the overgrown churchyard. ("I am the grass. Let me work.")

Convinced the police couldn't protect them, people bought guns. On a few of my visits to Flint, I hung out with a young man named Reginald Kaigler. Kaigler had graduated from UM-Flint with a criminal justice degree and spent a year as an AmeriCorps volunteer in Alaska. When he returned home, he couldn't get hired as a probation officer by the county, so he started a vlog. Kaigler filmed himself walking around town, sharing his libertarian political views on marijuana laws, immigration, subprime lending, unemployment benefits, and gun control. Like a right-wing Michael Moore, he believed that living in Flint allowed him to witness the real-life results of political ideas he deplored.

"I think Flint shows the consequences of a lot of policies that are being floated around right now," he said. "We're seeing what happens when you can't rely on credit and debt for your economy. We're seeing what happens when the credit card is maxed out. I see a lot of failed policies here, and I see a lot of people pursuing the same policies on a national level, so that's where my perspective is coming from. I feel like I can talk about a lot of things that a lot of people are considering doing."

Kaigler's YouTube channel, DEMCAD, had over 28,000 subscribers, which meant he earned enough money on advertising to pay the phone bill and the Internet bill at his mother's house. And also to buy guns. Kaigler owned a Glock 21, a Mossberg 500 pump-action 12 gauge, and a Mossberg ATR 30.06. Some of his video commentaries were filmed at shooting ranges, where he reviewed weapons by shooting up old video game consoles and computers. His test of a GP Walther 10 semi-automatic rifle was viewed by 70,000 gun fans.

As part of his journalistic mission, Kaigler catalogued all the murders in Flint, so he knew exactly who and what he needed to protect himself from.

"You're seeing a lot of personal robberies of the pizza guys," he said. "A lot of B and E, muggings. A lot of situations where there's a domestic dispute, where a guy kills his wife or daughter. In March, one lady, there were four guys broke into their house. There was another incident where a sixteen-year-old boy broke into a woman's house. She told him, 'I have a gun,' and he broke in anyway and she killed him. The police being out of it is a big part of the picture. If there's gunshots, it may take an hour. If I shoot somebody, I've got an hour to get away. Given what's going on in the city, and the fact that you can't rely on people to back you up, I feel it's more necessary to own a gun."

(While Kaigler was showing me around town, we stopped at an African-American cultural fair on the riverfront where I bought a T-shirt that read I (HEART) FLINT on the front, and, on the back, "GIN-U-WINE HOMEGROWN FLINTSTONE." "Flintstone"— popularized by Mateen Cleaves, Morris Peterson, and Charlie Bell, three Flint basketballers who played on Michigan State's 2000 NCAA Championship team—has replaced "Flintoid" as the local appellation.)

When Internet punditry didn't pay enough of the bills, Kaigler took a job as a security guard, patrolling apartment complexes. It paid $7.50 an hour if you didn't carry a gun, $9 an hour if you did. Kaigler carried a gun, but not just for the money.

"I don't go to the grocery store without my Glock Twenty-One," he commented. "I don't mow my lawn without my Glock Twenty-One, because there's been people who've been robbed while mowing their lawns."

Libertarians like Kaigler weren't the only Flintstones packing heat. I would meet a Baptist preacher who concealed a handgun under his sport coat. The *Detroit News* profiled a man who protected himself with a .22, a .44, and a quartet of pit bulls.

Mayor Walling had promised to reduce crime by 10 percent. When instead it went up 40 percent, he denied that his police cuts were the cause. "There will never be enough police to sit at every kitchen table to stop these conflicts from escalating into violence," he said.

Moose Fitch thought that was nonsense.

"They had the mayor on TV. They were asking 'im why Flint's the most violent city in America, whether it's because he cut the police. He said it's a community problem," said Moose, scoffing. After the police took two weeks to respond to his breaking-and-entering complaint, Moose gave up on calling them for anything but gunfire. "They're cuttin' cops and firemen right and left, but they ain't cuttin' their own salaries. They ain't cuttin' services to rich areas."

The pastors—including the pastor who carried a gun—were trying to do something about the murders. Flint has a high number of churches per capita: Baptist, Nazarene, Church of God in Christ, African Methodist Episcopal. The statistic is both an indication of the religiosity of people a generation or less removed from the Bible Belt, and of Flint's depopulation, since many congregations have dwindled to a few dozen parishioners, or less. The pastors lobbied the city to sponsor a chapter of CeaseFire, a violence intervention program that's been successful in Boston, Chicago, and North Carolina. Flint needed any help it could get: state troopers were patrolling the streets to make up for laid-off cops. The police department agreed to work with CeaseFire, and a former GM executive named Rick Carter set up an office in a Catholic church. That summer, CeaseFire and the police were planning to "call in" kids who'd been caught dealing drugs but hadn't committed a violent crime. The kids would be given a choice: get straight, or go to jail. If the juvenile delinquents went through a job training and a substance abuse treatment program, the county prosecutor would give them a pass.

"These are kids who are hanging out with the wrong crowd, getting involved in their own kind of activities," Carter explained. "The community is extending an olive branch. Instead of having law enforcement throw the book at you, we are going to try to work with you if you are willing to turn your situation around."

(CeaseFire called in seven j.d.s; two stuck with the program. The backsliders were remanded to the criminal justice system.)

The pastors were as close to the violence as anyone, because they had lost members of their flocks and, in one case, their families. In a conference room at the church, Carter introduced me to Reverend Ira Edwards of Damascus Holy Life Baptist Church and Reverend Jeffery Hawkins of Peace Missionary Baptist Church. Edwards had baptized a young man on Sunday, then preached his funeral a week and a half later.

"I have a great-grandmother who is taking care of her granddaughter because the mother is in prison for driving a car in a drive-by shooting," Edwards said. "Her little sister's father is on the run because he shot someone. We have one other young man, the niece of one of my members, who was being robbed and shot the guy that robbed him, but because [the victim] had an illegal pistol, the guy died and he goes to prison, too. We have one young lady who joined the church with her family after about a year of coming, and her boyfriend joined and was baptized on Sunday, at Bible study on Wednesday; he was dead on Friday because of domestic violence. She said, 'I'm not taking any more.' She killed him. I have a congregation of probably less than sixty people. If I've got that many in just my small congregation, I really feel for the others."

Hawkins's connection to the killings was even more personal: two of his sons had been shot to death in drug-related murders. In Flint, though, that didn't make him unusual, or even unlucky. Everybody knew somebody who'd been murdered. Hawkins had always preached against the street life, but after his sons died, he became a warrior against violence.

"It was one of those things where you are on a battlefield trying to fight for others and you become a victim of it yourself," he said. "It appeared that could have been one of those things that I said, 'You know, this hit home too much for me. I'm going to back off.' Well, that wasn't the case. It hit for me where I said, 'I am going to become really aggressive now to make a greater change than ever before.'"

Edwards tried to compete with the gangs by holding Friday Family Nights at his church, with Bible Bowl and Twister. He took his young parishioners bowling and invited them to fish in the stocked pond behind his house. He offered job counseling and drug counseling. But as prominent as he was in his community—a pastor is like an African-American rabbi, responsible for the temporal *and* the spiritual uplift of his people—he could not put a preacher at every kitchen table, to paraphrase the mayor. And like the mayor, he believed that was where the violence in Flint began.

"My belief primarily is the lack of concern from the parents," he said. "I made this statement Sunday in church. You know Ray Ray and Pookie don't have a job—why do you keep letting them bring these twenty-four-to-forty-two-inch flat-screen TVs in here? Why do you let them drive around with a car with four thousand dollars in tires and wheels, and don't ask where he got it from? They don't care where it's coming from, but as soon as that child gets picked up . . . I told them yesterday, if your child gets caught up in this stuff and he refuses to take the deal that's being offered, don't come and get me to come and get him when he's getting arrested, because I am not going down there."

A few days later, I attended a CeaseFire meeting in the gymnasium of one of Flint's largest Baptist churches. The purpose was to announce the "scared straight" plan to the community. The chief of police was there. Mayor Walling was there.

On my way out of the meeting, I ran into one of the pastors I met at the CeaseFire office in the parking lot. He was dressed in a Sunday preaching suit. I told him I'd just met a woman who bought a gun after her house was broken into.

"Shoot," he said, patting the breast of his coat. "I've got a concealed weapons permit."

"*You've* got a gun?"

The pastor snorted. "Not on me," he said. "But I'm not going to be a victim."

If the preachers were armed, then who in Flint *didn't* have a gun?

DAYNE WALLING WAS A RHODES SCHOLAR who had returned home to Flint at age thirty-two and been elected mayor three years later, because what else is there for a Rhodes scholar to do in Flint? Although he was pale, bulbous and graying at the temples, he still looked like a young man, in a blue suit whose sleeves overlapped his shirt cuffs.

Flint, the first American city with a black mayor, and the first to pass an open-housing ordinance by popular vote, was just as likely to elect a white mayor as a black one, and just as likely to throw him out when he couldn't reverse the murder rate or bring back the jobs General Motors had spirited away. Walling was finishing the term of Don Williamson, a car dealer who resigned rather than face a recall election when it was discovered the city had an $8.3 million deficit, not the $4 million surplus he'd claimed. Williamson would not have been the first Flint mayor kicked out because he failed to balance the budget. Woodrow Stanley— Flint's third black mayor—was recalled because of financial mismanagement: he missed federal grant deadlines and failed to cut a deficit which grew to $30 million after Buick City closed. In the previous decade, city hall had been occupied by four elected mayors, two interim mayors, and an emergency financial manager appointed by the governor to balance the city's budget. Running Flint requires the financial acumen of William Pitt the Younger, the law-and-order bullying of Benito Mussolini, the city-building vision of Romulus, the labor negotiating skills of

Franklin D. Roosevelt, and the industrial efficiency of Otto von Bismarck. Obviously, no politician has all these qualities. Any politician who had even *one* probably wouldn't settle for mayor of a bankrupt city of one hundred thousand and counting backward. Flint is ungovernable, yet Flintstones continually punish mayors who can't govern it.

(The Rust Belt is a cradle of boy politicians too callow to win in more orderly cities. In Youngstown, after Congressman James Traficant was expelled from the House and imprisoned for bribery, racketeering, and tax evasion, he was succeeded by a twenty-nine-year-old staffer, Tim Ryan. Youngstown's voters threw out Traficant's generation of mobbed-up leadership and elected a 34-year-old mayor, Jay Williams. The president of Youngstown State University's board of trustees was also in his 30s.

"There was kind of a reboot," one Youngstowner commented. "There definitely is a youth movement here."

There's a youth movement all over the Rust Belt. It's far easier for an ambitious Generation Xer or Millenial to achieve civic prominence in Flint, Youngstown, Buffalo or Pittsburgh than in New York, Chicago or Washington, D.C.)

In his campaign for a full term as Flint's mayor, Dayne Walling had six opponents. When you're in charge of the nation's murder capital, you can't expect to return to office by acclamation. The field was seated together at an NAACP mayoral forum in the spacious wedding reception hall of a North End Baptist church. The seven men were a perfect reflection of Flint's demographics, as though selected to fill a quota. Three whites, three blacks, one Korean. Furthermore, race didn't seem to be an issue. Earlier that day, I'd stopped at Mayor Walling's campaign office to pick up a stock of glossy brochures: every volunteer was black. Flint couldn't afford to vote along racial lines because it was looking for only one quality in a leader: protection from murderers, arsonists, rapists, and burglars. Tribalism was too far up the hierarchy of needs. Walling's best-funded rival, a white developer who had moved in from the suburbs to campaign for mayor, parked an old state police car in front of his campaign headquarters. Inside, I met a volunteer who'd gotten involved in politics after his brother was shot to death during a robbery. He'd bought a house in Flint—"Twenty-five thousand dollars," he said, incredulous at the figure; "it was way overpriced"—and might have run for mayor himself, if he hadn't blown so much money on real estate.

"They still haven't caught the guy who killed my brother," the man said. "There were two witnesses, and they haven't arrested anybody."

The debate began before the mayor even arrived. A black man

stormed through the aisles between folding tables, chanting, "Walling sucks! Walling sucks!" He was guided to a seat, where he was told to shut up and allow the candidates to give their own versions of why Walling sucked.

"Every municipality in the state had a chance to vote on whether they wanted their public safety cut," said a white candidate named David Davenport. "It's sad that we had to lose ninety lives because somebody decided to take away your democratic right. You say we're number one in homicides? What do you expect when you come in and lay off fifty-six officers in a city that's number three?"

Then a black candidate—Darryl Buchanan, a former city council president—picked up the attack on Walling.

"His administration allowed a serial killer to roam free for a hundred and ten days," Buchanan said. "His actions showed he didn't care about the North End."

In the spring of 2010, an Israeli Arab named Elias Abuelazam began approaching old, weak-looking black men on the streets of Flint. He asked for directions or help with his car—and then stabbed them. In Flint, murders of black men are a weekly occurrence, so Abuelazam killed five and slashed eight more before the police realized there was a pattern to his attacks. That may have been why he chose black men as his victims and Flint as his hunting ground. Had Abuelazam stabbed young white women in the Washington, D.C., suburbs—where he lived before moving to Michigan and beginning his spree—his crimes would have been profiled on *Nancy Grace* after victim number two. Because murder was so common, it was allowed to become even more common. Abuelazam, who contributed to Flint's record-breaking homicide total, was arrested while trying to board a plane to Israel and is now serving a life sentence in a Michigan prison. Before the killer was caught, Reginald Kaigler filmed a vlog post in which he declared, "I'm going to be more cautious. It sort of reminds me one of the reasons why we should be able to carry our weapons openly."

In defense of his leadership, Walling hearkened back to a humiliating episode in Flint history. In 2002, after Mayor Stanley was recalled, Flint was placed under the control of an emergency financial manager, who had the power to make spending decisions without consulting the mayor or the city council. With another Republican governor in office, there was talk a state takeover could happen again.

"You've seen what's happened to this community when the spending goes wrong and we lose control of our entire community and the democratic process," the mayor said. "That's not going to happen while I'm your mayor. We're going to reduce the deficit and we're going to have the biggest public safety force we can afford."

Just as there had been a racial subtext to the accusation that Walling allowed a serial killer to run loose because he didn't care about the (mostly black) North End, there was a racial subtext to this boast. Emergency managers had mainly been appointed to replace governments with black leaders: Pontiac, Inkster, Benton Harbor, the Detroit public schools, and Highland Park. The white governor in Lansing wouldn't do that to a white boy. Between Oxford University and Flint, Walling had worked as a grant writer in the Washington, D.C., mayor's office. Only he knew how to go outside the community for help. Just that month, he'd brought Labor Secretary Hilda Solis to Diplomat Specialty Pharmacy, the drug dispensary in the old Fisher One, where she announced the appointment of Youngstown, Ohio, mayor Jay Williams as director of the Office of Recovery for Auto Communities and Workers. (Talking about the plant where the Volt was built, Solis made a very creditable effort to pronounce Hamtramck. "Hamtrack" isn't bad for a California girl.)

"There's sixty firefighters and police officers who would not be able to come to work for our community if it weren't for my administration going to the foundations, going to the federal government for grants, and getting these investors in our community," Walling said. "The state is investing in the city of Flint right now. The Michigan State Police invested in our county jail to free up space that we haven't been able to pay for in our community. If incompetent leadership comes back in, our community's only recourse is to hope and pray that somehow that administration can win a case in front of the Supreme Court."

The people of Flint bought it: in November, Walling was returned to office with 56 percent of the vote. Less than a month later, Governor Rick Snyder appointed an emergency manager, with dictatorial powers to eliminate Flint's $7 million deficit. Flint became a ward of the state. Walling was mayor in name only, with 60 percent of his old salary and a seat on the manager's advisory council. The city council was allowed to meet once a month, to review items on the Manager's agenda.

The emergency manager law was written to rescue cities from corrupt or incompetent mayors. Walling, a cross between a Webelo and a *West Wing* policy wonk, was not corrupt. Nor was he incompetent. It would have been impossible to balance the budget of a city that's lost half its people and over 90 percent of its middle-class jobs without making it look even more like the set of *Escape from Flint*. If a city is too poor to afford democracy, it's not a city anymore.

16.

"This Is Not Your Father's Oldsmobile"

D avid Hollister had been mayor of Lansing for less than a year when General Motors's vice president for local governments walked into his office on the ninth floor of city hall. The office overlooked the Michigan state capitol, a snow-globe version of the original in Washington. Hollister had spent twenty years in that capitol, as a Democratic state legislator. State government was one leg of the stool that supported his city's economy. The second leg was Hollister's alma mater, Michigan State University. The third, and the strongest, was Oldsmobile. At one time, Oldsmobile had employed twenty-five thousand workers in Lansing, including Hollister's father, a high school dropout who had hired in as an assembler and worked his way up to tool-and-die maker. According to the WPA's *Michigan: A Guide to the Wolverine State*, Lansing's trinity of employers meant that "the political activity of a state capital, the rumbling tempo of an industrial city, and the even temper of a family community are curiously blended." In postclassical language, this had been abbreviated to "the Three C's: Capital, Campus, Cars."

Oldsmobile's identity, however, was no longer inseparable from Lansing. The Oldsmobile sign, which once glowed above the Grand River in grapefruit neon, had been taken down in 1985, when GM reorganized itself into two divisions. The guys on the line didn't work at Olds anymore, they worked at B-O-C. Officially, that stood for Buick-Oldsmobile-Cadillac. Gripers called it Big Old Cars, or the Big Operation of Corruption. To strip Oldsmobile of all independence from the parent company, the engineers and executives had been transferred from Oldsmobile's boxy administration building to GM headquarters in Detroit. But General Motors still operated three auto plants in Lansing, and it was those plants the vice president had come to talk to Hollister about.

"I've got some good news and some bad news," the executive said.

"What's the good news?" the mayor asked.

"Well," the vice president answered, "we are going to be celebrating the one hundredth anniversary of the Oldsmobile, and we are going to have a yearlong celebration, and it's going to be culminated with a week celebration here in Lansing. We are going to be launching three new cars—the Aurora, the Intrigue, and the Alero. These are centennial cars. And the good news is the Alero will be made in Lansing. It will bring work to the assembly plants."

(Oldsmobile, founded in 1897 by Lansing's Ransom Eli Olds, was, true to its name, the oldest American auto nameplate.)

"Well, this is all very good news," Hollister said. "What's the bad news?"

"The life cycle of the centennial cars is about five years, and at the end of the five-year run, we are going to close the Lansing facilities."

Hollister felt as though he'd been punched in the stomach. GM was going to throw Lansing a party and then preside over its funeral, for the same reason: it had been building cars there for nearly a century. Lansing's auto plants were obsolete. Olds Main, the plant on the river, dated back to 1901, when the state granted R. E. Olds the fifty-acre Michigan Central Fairgrounds, including the horse-racing track, on which he tested cars. The Fisher Body plant had been purchased from bankrupt Durant Motors in 1935. The painted, trimmed bodies were shipped across town to the assembly line in the Main plant, an inefficient arrangement that crowded the one-way streets of Lansing with sighing diesel trucks and cost General Motors $20 million a year.

No American auto company had built a new plant north of the Mason-Dixon line in over a dozen years, since Detroit flattened Poletown. Having used up Lansing, GM was going to move on to a Southern state with more open land and lower labor costs, leaving behind hundreds of acres of polluted real estate. Same game the company ran on Flint. Losing three auto plants wouldn't turn Lansing into a setting for *Life After People*, because it was not as dependent on building cars as Flint. But Lansing would be a poorer city, and it would no longer be a city that made things. As the twenty-first century approached, Hollister hoped to turn Lansing into an advanced manufacturing center. That would require both the brains of professors and the hands of skilled tradesmen.

There was another difference between Lansing and Flint: Lansing didn't have the history of labor trouble that had caused GM to walk away from the Vehicle City. In 1937, a month after the Flint Sit-Down Strike, workers at Reo Motors staged their own sit-down, but that strike did not leave behind the same screw-the-foreman legacy. Lansing was not a purely blue-collar town, which leavened class conflict. But Lansing's autoworkers also descended from different stock than Flint's. Flint's auto plants began booming in the 1920s, after nativist Republicans in Congress halted immigration from Europe. So the Buick was forced to recruit unlettered sharecroppers from the South. Lansing's autoworkers were more likely to be Yankees or German Catholics, two groups more devoted to hard work and education. Modern yeomen, they worked a full shift in the plant, then spent another eight hours tending their farms.

"That many entering the first auto plants in Lansing came primarily from native-born, rural backgrounds affected management and working-class culture in the early factories," wrote Lisa M. Fine in *The Story of Reo Joe*, a study that explains why Lansing's autoworkers were never attracted to radical labor movements. "The farmers' conservative and capitalistic values account for the relative tranquility of the hinterland . . . Both the prosperity on the land and the personnel from the land created the conditions for the start of the automobile industry in Lansing."

Even today, Lansing autoworkers disdain the antagonism of their Flint brethren. A tool-and-die maker who transferred from Oldsmobile to Flint is convinced GM decided to close his new plant when one of the workers mooned executives making an on-site visit.

"God bless them," said a former president of a Lansing UAW local, "but they have a legacy of being more militant. We have a legacy of getting along."

"I couldn't believe the difference that sixty-five miles made," said a cost estimator who was transferred from Olds to Buick. "Oldsmobile was always spic-and-span. When I moved to Buick, it was a pigpen. They were stepping over pallets and defective parts."

"We never had a local strike," a plant designer said. "We had one where Fisher Body shut down for an hour. Flint was always an adversarial relationship. When the Oldsmobile forge plant started making differentials, we brought in a guy from Chevrolet Flint who had experience. He didn't talk to anybody in the factory. He had no communication with the hourly guys whatsoever. He got kicked out of our factory in less than a year."

GM had a "hard" problem in Lansing—obsolete, inefficient factories—
not a "soft" problem of surly employees. Even though he'd been told his
city's abandonment was inevitable, Hollister thought he could convince
GM to rebuild in Lansing. Along with the president of the largest UAW
local, he created the Keep GM Committee, which met every Monday
morning at seven o'clock. It was Lansing's first order of business. They
visited Toledo, which had torn down several neighborhoods to prevent
GM from moving a Jeep plant to a cornfield fifty miles outside the city.
To put a body shop, a paint shop, and an assembly line under one roof,
GM needed two hundred acres, so Hollister hired an engineer to find
two hundred acres. And he used the launch of the Alero as a civic moment
to convince GM that Lansing and the Oldsmobile were inseparable.

In the mid-1990s, Oldsmobile was a car with an image problem. R. E.
Olds had sold out to General Motors in 1908, but his car was so successful it took GM nearly a hundred years to screw it up. But screw it up GM
did. During the seventies and eighties, Oldsmobile was moving over a
million units a year, making it the nation's third-most-popular brand. As
the middle car in GM's brand hierarchy, its reputation was correspond-
ingly middle-class and middle-aged. According to market research, the
average Olds driver was a sixty-two-year-old who wanted to advertise
that he'd achieved a respectable but not ostentatious standard of living.
Cutlass Supremes and 98s were seen in the parking lots of every public
golf course, Congregational church, and state-college football game,
and helped define the era's look of squared-off sedans.

GM's decision to consolidate its divisions was made by chairman
Roger Smith. Smith is just as much a villain in Lansing as he is in Flint,
but for different reasons. Oldsmobiles had always been designed in Lansing. Now they were designed by a Buick-Oldsmobile-Cadillac team
that reported to Detroit. As a result, Buicks, Oldsmobiles, and Cadillacs
became indistinguishable—a collection of shoe boxes with tires.

"That era in the eighties, when they were the slab-sided, front-wheel-
drive cars, those babies looked terrible," said Oldsmobile historian
James R. Walkinshaw, co-author of *Setting the Pace: Oldsmobile's First
Hundred Years.* (His chapter on the eighties is titled "Fall from Grace.")
"And they all looked alike. I wouldn't have bought one, personally.
That's all part of that Roger Smith thing. We lost the capability to solve
problems in-house. We couldn't get freshened body styles, so our cars
became old, stodgy."

Don Cooper, who was nearing the end of his thirty-two years with
Oldsmobile, thought the car went bad when the "Oldsmobile" sign

came down. He continued to call his workplace by its birth name, even as most of his co-workers switched to "B-O-C."

GM tried to turn Oldsmobile into an American BMW, specializing in sporty luxury cars. That was a niche nobody needed. On the sporty end, Oldsmobile lost sales to Pontiac, which was building the Fiero, the Firebird, and the Trans Am during the eighties. On the luxury end, it lost sales to the Buick Skylark, the Buick Regal, and the Buick LeSabre. By the end of the decade, the million-selling Oldsmobile was selling fewer than seven hundred thousand cars.

Oldsmobile. Even the name sounded stuffy. The marketing brains in Detroit decided the way to make Oldsmobile a youthful and exciting car was to tell people it was a youthful and exciting car. Thus, they approved one of the most memorable and least effective slogans in advertising history: "This is not your father's Oldsmobile." Produced by the Chicago ad agency Leo Burnett (let's share the blame here), the ads starred William Shatner and Ringo Starr—celebrities who, like the Oldsmobile, had last been exciting in the 1960s—getting into their real-life children's Cutlass Supremes. (Has anyone born after Babe Ruth left the Yankees ever owned a Cutlass Supreme? Seriously.)

"My father drove a starship, so it's only natural I'd drive around in something space-age," Melanie Shatner said in a 1988 ad. "My Oldsmobile Cutlass Supreme, totally redesigned for the future. It's powered by a fuel-injected V-6, monitored by an onboard computer. I guess some things are just meant for the next generation."

Ooooh, a V-6 engine. So much for the Rocket.

(*Star Trek: The Next Generation* had premiered the year before, so Oldsmobile was trying to associate itself with the reboot.)

"This is not your father's Oldsmobile" became an eighties catchphrase even more enduring than "Where's the beef?" while reminding the world that the car was driven by exactly the kind of people its name suggested. Since not even baby boomers would buy Cutlass Supremes or 88s, Oldsmobile got rid of those cars altogether, replacing them with the streamlined Alero, Aurora, and Intrigue. (Oldsmobile's general manager even suggested renaming the brand "Aurora." When that didn't fly, he just left the name off the cars.)

The Alero was the good news that GM's vice president had brought to Mayor Hollister's office. When the first Alero came off the line, to the accompaniment of a high school band blatting "God Bless America," Hollister was not only in the plant, wearing safety glasses and a hard hat, the city bought a car for the mayor and every cabinet member.

GM had not publicly announced it was leaving Lansing, but all the workers knew, since no new cars were planned after 2000. The city paid for "LANSING WORKS—KEEPING GM" billboards on I-96, the highway every GM executive drove between Detroit and Lansing.

The executive who oversaw the Alero's rollout was so impressed he tipped off Hollister that GM was looking to build a new factory "for an unknown new project."

"Given the momentum you've developed, you ought to at least aggressively go after this, and not just be satisfied with the Alero," he said.

Even the GM vice president who had brought the bad news into city hall told Hollister, "You might have a shot at this."

Hollister's engineer came up with a plan to build a new plant on the Grand River as the old plant was being demolished. GM wouldn't have to buy new land and wouldn't be responsible for cleaning up a brownfield. They took the plan to the office of Rick Wagoner, who was then vice president of North American Operations but would later become famous as the CEO who flew a private jet to D.C. to beg Congress for a bailout after the Wall Street shitstorm of 2008. Wagoner bought it. (Larry Dungey, my high school classmate who'd joined the army because he couldn't go from high school to the assembly line, telling his shoprat dad, "You can't just walk into General Motors today," now worked in that plant as a fireman. His wife worked on the line for even more money, allowing them to raise their children in a vast suburban house.) Then the mayor learned that GM was looking for 1,200 acres, to replace Fisher Body and another nearby assembly plant. Lansing didn't have 1,200 empty acres and could not have produced it by tearing down a blighted neighborhood, because Lansing didn't have as much blight to offer as Flint or Detroit. So Hollister annexed a chunk of a rural township, out where the two-lane roads form squares, a mile on each side.

While Hollister was persuading GM to stay in Lansing, he received a visit from a Leo Burnett executive who knew the community through his work on the "This is not your father's Oldsmobile" campaign. The man owned the Sultans of Springfield, a Class A Midwest League baseball team, but was looking to move it, because the capital city of Illinois wouldn't build him a stadium. Lansing built him one, on a vacant lot where the city had recently torn down its one-block-long red-light district, which consisted of an adult bookstore, a gay bar, and a used-record shop whose owner made ends meet by selling pot. (Lansing can only support so much vice.) Oldsmobile bought the naming rights to the stadium, and the owner christened his fugitive team the Lugnuts, sup-posedly in honor of the city's automaking heritage. (Most Lansingites thought the nickname was patronizing and insulting. I would have preferred the Shoprats; the mascot could have been a giant, bewhiskered rat in a baseball cap, Detroit Red Wings T-shirt, and sagging blue jeans, who disappeared after the bottom of the third, spent the middle innings in Gus's Bar, and returned before the ninth inning to punch out. The adman was no marketing doofus, though. The Lugnuts cap, featuring a smiling bolt—a bolt!—became the bestseller in minor league baseball.)

Lansing needed a new identity, because in 2000, GM announced it would cancel the Oldsmobile after four more model years. The In-trigues and Aleros—the Oldsmobiles that dared not speak their names—attracted some younger drivers, but at the expense of senior citizens who had cherished the Cutlass, which was as roomy and comfortable as a pair of Sansabelt slacks. Exercising its exceptional talent for destroying its own market share, GM had alienated Oldsmobile's most loyal cus-tomers without minting enough new drivers. By the turn of the century, Oldsmobile sold only 294,000 vehicles.

When Olds's death sentence was announced, I considered buying an Alero, just so that, for once in my life, I could floss the local whip.

"Why do you want to buy an Oldsmobile?" my brother asked. "You won't be able to get parts."

"Um, I think you've got it backward," I told him. "They're getting rid of Oldsmobile because its parts are the same as every other car's."

I could get one cheap now. The last Aleros, which came off the line in 2004, have outlived their five-year warrantees and are sliding down the ownership ladder, to pizza-delivery guys and community-college stu-dents. (The Alero does have a big fan club at the Oldsmobile reunion. The collectors skip from the 1970s to the late 1990s. The aesthetic judg-ment of time has confirmed that Roger Smith's Bravadas and Achievas were ugly as shit.)

At the beginning of his term, Hollister had thought the Oldsmobile would outlive Lansing, at least the blue-collar Lansing in which he'd grown up. Instead, blue-collar Lansing outlived the Oldsmobile. When he left office ten years later, Hollister wasn't the mayor who had lost GM. He was a mayor with two new auto plants and a baseball team.

The Delta Township plant is five miles southwest of the ruins of Fisher Body, which it replaced. The old factories were built on rivers and lakes. This one was built on a crook in Interstate 69, the highway between Port Huron and Indianapolis. It sits among a grid of blacktops that trace the outlines of surveyed sections and bear the names of centennial farming families, German and Yankee: Creyts, Davis, Royston, Dunkel. After nearly a year of badgering GM publicists, I was allowed to join the slipstream of a factory tour organized for state troopers at a nearby post. I was the only visitor not wearing a blue-and-gray uniform, and the only one carrying a pencil.

The Delta plant puts together the Chevy Traverse, the Buick Enclave, and the GMC Acadia—"crossover" vehicles, too big to be sedans, too small to be SUVs. In true GM fashion, they look almost identical: like fashionable basketball shoes, if basketball shoes were ten feet long and made of steel instead of rubber. The only distinctive feature was a rear window: trapezoidal on the Acadia, rhomboid on the Traverse and Enclave.

Like all round-the-clock factories, the plant generated its own permanent day, from a constellation of lamps hanging from a ceiling higher than a barn's. Because it has to last twenty-four hours, the light was far dimmer than the sun's, so the enormous room had a feeling of gloomy isolation. And it was quiet. The vehicles moved from station to station on skillets—wooden slabs, like sections of a parquet floor, or tiles on one of those handheld games in which you shuffle the numbers around, trying to put them all in order. When the skillet reached one end of the room, it slid sideways and changed directions, so the assembly line juked all over the building. The skillets also allowed workers to ride along with the cars until their job was finished. One woman tossed owner's manuals into glove compartments. A man in a Michigan State Spartans T-shirt (or maybe a Detroit Lions jersey—everyone was dressed in athletic memorabilia), grabbed a roof liner from a T-bar hanging over the line, swung it around, pulled it through the still-glassless front window, and bolted it in, while Tom Petty and the Heartbreakers' "Refugee" played on his work group's radio. The line moved at exactly one vehicle per minute, but the assemblers had so perfected each motion that the work seemed both tedious and leisurely, and more artisanal than industrial.

Our tour guide was himself a refugee from Fisher Body. He'd hired in when auto work was as loud, dirty, and muscular as the cars it produced.

"I go back to the Body plant," he boasted. "When we had a sunroof, the low-seniority guy used to hold the body up while the other guys bolted it in. We've made a lot of improvements in ergonomics."

The marriage area is the section of an auto plant where the body is fitted over the undercarriage, just like gluing together a plastic model of a Ford Mustang. It used to be a violent consummation, a combination of lover's leap and wrestling body slam. The body dropped from the ceiling and was sealed to its mate by big men with torque wrenches.

"They had these guys looked like bodybuilders," the guide reminisced. "When they retired, they didn't have any shoulder muscles."

In this plant, the undercarriages rode to the site of their wedding on wheeled pallets equipped with global positioning systems guiding them to their upper halves, to which they were joined with twenty-four-volt electric wrenches. That didn't even become possible until the 1990s, when the military began allowing its satellites to provide civilians with GPS. The only precomputer equipment carried over from Fisher Body was a three-wheeled bicycle with a wire basket, still the nimblest vehicle for delivering parts to the assembly line.

We approached the end of the process, the CARE line, where gray-haired workers turned the ignitions and tested the windows. (The in-plant joke was that it stood for Crippled Almost Retiree Line. "Is this a high-seniority job?" I asked the gray-hair who invited me to ride in a Traverse as he drove it over a bumpy treadmill that simulated a rocky road. "Ohhh yeah," he responded, grinning.) Our guide made a strange statement, coming from an autoworker.

"If you have to build cars," he said, "this is the way to build 'em."

If you have to build cars? Was this a more-than-thirty-and-not-even-out GM lifer who was probably driving his fourth employee-discount SUV admitting that Ralph Nader and the Critical Mass cycling movement were correct, and the automobile was nothing but an instrument of slaughter and environmental degradation, rather than the chariot of spatial freedom and economic advancement? Was our guide confessing that cars are a filthy necessity of American life? If so, in his confession was a boast: Delta Township was the only LEED Gold-certified auto plant in the world. Rainwater was stored in cisterns to flush the toilets. A quarter of the building materials were made from recycled content. The white polymer roof deflected heat, saving on air-conditioning.

On the way out, our group gathered by the vending machines in the lobby. The state police sergeant, a taut man with a fringe of crew cut around his skull, had demanded to know why I was writing in a notebook. Now he told the GM publicist, "I just want you guys to know that we're right down the road if things ever go sideways in here."

The woman, who appeared eleven months pregnant, looked startled. This was an auto plant, not a post office or a college campus.

"Well, thanks," she said. "That's good to know."

The Delta Township plant built its first car in 2006. (Grand River Assembly, which took the place of the original Olds plant in 2001, is building the Chevy Camaro and Cadillac ATS, *Esquire*'s 2012 Car of the Year. The magazine began a four-page article on the compact sedan— designed to compete with BMW, Audi, and Mercedes-Benz—by writing that it "may be the most important domestic car since the Model T.") If Delta matches the lifespan of its predecessors, it will build cars until the twenty-second century. But only two years after it opened, General Motors went bankrupt. The new mayor of Lansing, Virg Bernero, feared *he* would be stuck with the legacy as the leader who lost the auto industry. Like Hollister, his predecessor but one, Bernero was an autoworker's son. Bernero's father was an Italian immigrant fruit peddler in Pontiac, but a drunk driver ran into his truck, ruining his back, so he could no longer hoist boxes of tomatoes and peaches. He went into an auto plant, where he oiled machinery and shoveled coal into furnaces. It was less strenuous than the fruit business, and it paid well enough to support a wife and five children, and even send them to the orthodontist and the state university. Bernero knew his family had joined the middle class when they stopped paying the doctor in produce and started paying with a Blue Cross Blue Shield card.

In that ominous autumn of 2008, Southern senators were crowing over the demise of the auto industry and Mitt Romney—son of the auto company president who governed Michigan during its most prosperous decade—wrote a *New York Times* op-ed titled "Let Detroit Go Bankrupt." Bernero was frantic. He had visions of Lansing becoming a brother in misery to Flint, a diorama to scale of Detroit. As a member of the U.S. Conference of Mayors, he called the executive director in Washington, D.C.

"We need help," Bernero pleaded. "The auto industry is in a panic mode here. It's in a meltdown."

The director told Bernero the conference president, Miami's Manny Diaz, did not consider the auto industry a priority for America's mayors. Miffed, Bernero resigned and started calling the mayor of every city with an auto plant, North, South, East, or Midwest. He called Lordstown, Ohio; Shreveport, Louisiana; Arlington, Texas; Youngstown, Ohio, recruiting enough colleagues to form the Mayors Automotive

Coalition. They hired a D.C. lobbyist who helped them persuade Congress to set aside $740 million for the RACER Trust, which will clean up the properties GM left behind after its bankruptcy. (Cleaning up Fisher Body will cost $4 million to $5 million. The city would like to redevelop it into a green manufacturing zone, with high-tech businesses powered by wind turbines and solar panels.)

As founder of the Mayors Automotive Coalition, Bernero was invited on Fox News to bicker with a right-wing anchor about how much the unions should give up in the auto industry realignment. It didn't look like a fair debate: the anchor, Gregg Jarrett, was indistinguishable from a junior Republican Congressman, with a well-fed full-moon face and dark, carefully parted hair that resembled the topping on a Lego figurine. Bernero, whose kinky ethnic hair was defoliating along his browline, revealing pink scalp, wore a round Lansing pin on his broad lapel. Jarrett was even in higher resolution: he was in a New York studio, while Bernero was broadcasting on Skype from the city hall of a dwindling Rust Belt capital. But some people only need five minutes on television to become famous. Barack Obama did it at the 2004 Democratic National Convention. Susan Boyle did it on *Britian's Got Talent*. And Virg Bernero did it on Fox News, with a friend-of-the-workingman oration that anyone who has ever seen a Michael Moore movie should have expected from a mid-Michigan liberal. In abrasiveness and indignation, Bernero had the edge over his interlocutor.

"I gotta say, in all honesty, I was a little offended by your question, 'Have the unions given up enough? Has the workingman given up enough?'" Bernero began, before Jarrett had even asked him a question. "My question is, 'Has Wall Street given up enough, for the billions they have taken?' I gotta tell ya, I am sick and tired of the double standard. One standard for Washington and Wall Street, another standard for the working people in this country. It always comes down to, in order to be more competitive, we gotta take it out of the hide of the working person. Cut their pay, cut their benefits. Let me ask you, have the bonuses been cut on Wall Street?"

"General Motors has forty-seven billion dollars in future costs for UAW workers who have health care for life," Jarrett interjected at last. "They need to give up that which no other worker gets: health care for life."

Bernero entertained the interruption with grumpy impatience, then switched on again.

"If you think you're gonna make me feel guilty about the fact that I had health benefits as a kid, and I was able to have straight teeth because my dad retired from GM, and if you think my eighty-four-year-old father and other retirees like him, if you think they should feel guilty for the benefits they received, I disagree with you. General Motors and the auto companies created a great standard of living in this country. They helped create the middle class, which is now under attack, because of the outsourcing that's taken place. Since 2001, when China joined the WTO, we've lost something like two point seven million jobs to China, because of the unfair trade."

"Mr. Mayor, this is a television show, not a campaign speech," Jarrett said. "You're not the Eveready battery. We're just having a discussion here."

Bernero's tightly wound populism was such a hit that he was invited back onto Fox and CNN to debate free-market fundamentalists such as John Fund of the *Wall Street Journal*. "Is this the angriest mayor in America?" CNN *American Morning* anchor John Roberts asked before playing a Bernero clip. That became Bernero's nom de politics: America's Angriest Mayor. The following year, he won the Democratic primary for governor, with the support of the UAW, but lost by twenty points to a Republican businessman who styled himself "One Tough Nerd." Michigan had been governed by a Democrat for most of its Lost Decade, so it was a Republican's turn to preside over the state's reversion to the rural woodland it would have remained had Henry Ford not grown up in Dearborn. As I like to say, though, Michigan did not become great because of the auto industry. The auto industry became great because of a Michigander. Larry Page, who grew up in East Lansing, co-invented Google, making him as much a tycoon of the early twenty-first century as Ford was of the early twentieth. (Unfortunately, when Page opened a Google office in his home state, he put it in Ann Arbor, the state's intellectual capital and home of the University of Michigan, his alma mater.) So, when I finally got an appointment to meet my hometown's angry mayor, I pointed out that even with two new auto plants, Lansing's population of autoworkers has declined from 25,000 to 6,000—and 177 of the workers in the Delta plant were Tier Twos. Who had a plan to replace 20,000 of the best jobs in town?

"It's an evolution," Mayor Bernero said, not angry but intense, with a clipped, rapid voice, like a Midwestern minor-league hockey announcer's. "Even if the industry was here, it's more automated. We have the capability of making the same number of cars that we made with twenty-five thousand people with five thousand. So we need a bunch of

GMs. We need the green energy, we need the high tech, we need the biotech. You name it. And we've got that possibility in mid-Michigan— with Michigan State University, with some of the companies that have come out of the lab and into the community, like Niowave."

NIOWAVE OCCUPIED an inner-city elementary school that had closed for lack of students. That alone made it a quintessential Lansing business. Not even Mayor Bernero would send his children to the city's schools, which have become poorer and blacker every year since I graduated. The Harding-era craftsmanship is too good to waste, though, and Lansing is not large enough to absorb the ruins that make the more rural corners of Detroit look like the Arkansas Delta. The old schoolhouses have been occupied by yoga studios, and even an African-based academy named after Lansing's most famous escapee, Malcolm X, known in his Lansing days by his "slave name," Malcolm Little.

Niowave manufactures equipment for particle accelerators used in physics experiments, X-ray imaging devices, and missile defense systems. It's a business that requires both physics Ph.D.s, to design the machines, and skilled tradesmen, to build them. Niowave's founder, Terry Grimm, had spent fourteen years working at Michigan State University's nationally known cyclotron. But this was not a business he could have started in Cambridge, Massachusetts, despite MIT's technical expertise. Nor could he have started it in Cleveland, despite its population of laid-off machinists. He needed a major research university *and* a major industrial facility.

"There are not many places in the world that have both of those," Grimm said. "And the infrastructure. Try finding that on Long Island."

Academic colonies also lack the ethic that manual craftsmanship is a worthwhile pursuit. One of Niowave's technicians, Jeff Tarr, was a GM model maker who took an early retirement buyout when the company switched from physical prototyping to computer-assisted drafting. Niowave didn't pay as well as GM, but *nobody* paid $33 an hour anymore. When I visited Niowave, Tarr was building a vacuum plate he had designed on a computer. Niowave's products were as industrial as the Oldsmobiles he'd designed. They just weren't mass-produced. Its atom smashers were gleaming barrels with lids bolted to the top, like portholes. Its electron guns were shaped like shock absorbers. Everything was built of niobium, a metal that shields instrumentation from magnetic fields.

"What I do here is really close to what I did there," Tarr said. "It's a lot of the prototyping, a lot of the research. Being a model maker, I was always looking for the next challenge. I grew up around cars all my life. I didn't grow up around accelerators. I don't understand everything that goes in there, but I'm just happy to do my part."

THAT YEAR the Delta plant opened, and Fisher Body was torn apart in strips of rippled metal. I decided it was time to come home to Lansing. My goal in life had always been to sell so many books I could live wherever I wanted, and I'd never wanted to leave Michigan. I had moved away in 1992 because none of my jobs there paid worth a damn.

Still, I was about to turn forty, so it seemed like time to end my decade-long big-city adventure and return to a place where I could always count on Sunday dinner. And maybe, I thought, Lansing needed me more than Chicago. How could I mourn my hometown's abandonment if I refused to live there myself? I applied for a job at a small weekly newspaper. It didn't pay much, but it doesn't cost much to live in Lansing. After I was offered the position, a real estate agent showed me a sturdy two-bedroom house for $75,000.

If I had gone to work for the newspaper, I might have bought that little house. But it didn't work out that way. When I went to lunch with the publisher, to discuss the final details, I overplayed my hand.

"What about vacation?" I asked.

"Oh, we don't offer vacation the first year," he said. "It wouldn't be fair to the other staffers if I gave it to you. Maybe we can work out some long weekends."

I didn't really care what was fair to the other staffers. I cared about what was fair to me. But I'd been gone so long I didn't understand how little leverage I possessed in Michigan's job market. The day after our meeting, I e-mailed the publisher, proposing a compromise: one week's vacation the first year. Minutes later, his number appeared on my phone.

"I'm withdrawing the offer," he said curtly. "If all you're thinking about is vacation, that's no way to start a new job."

When I shut my phone, I also shut away any illusions of ever living in Lansing again. If the best my hometown could offer was a job with no paid vacation, it was no town for me anymore.

I SAT in the principal's office of Sexton High School with a copy of *Young Mr. Obama: Chicago and the Making of a Black President* resting atop my thigh. It was the book I'd written after giving up on Lansing and going back to Chicago, and it was another reason I would never move back home. But I was spending a summer in Lansing, to research this book. A week earlier, I'd met the principal at a city council meeting where the boys' basketball team was honored for winning the state championship. I knew I couldn't finish this book without visiting Sexton, and I knew I couldn't get inside the school without the principal's permission, so I offered to donate a copy of *Young Mr. Obama* to the library. The principal told me to call his office, which was probably what he told everyone he met, but now I had a ten o'clock appointment, and I was inside the principal's office for the first time in twenty-six years, since I had interviewed my own principal, as the editor of our school newspaper, the *Zodiac*.

Sexton's hallways were emptier now. No one was standing in the lobby, where Lansing's original seal—a pioneer axing a tree—was painted on the tile floor. In that quarter century, the student body had dwindled from 2,100 to 750, almost entirely because whites had withdrawn their children from the urban public schools. My school years, the 1970s and 1980s, coincided with the era when Lansing's falling white population and its rising black population were intersecting. Lansing's blacks and whites both lived prosperously, because the auto factories paid equal wages. But the blacks lived on the West Side, and we lived on the South Side.

In 1973, when a local judge ordered busing to integrate the grade schools, I was about to enter first grade. Precocious enough to read the paper, I knew buses would be coming to our neighborhood, but I didn't know what they would be carrying, until one of my friends warned me black kids would be bused to Lewton Elementary, our all-white school. At the time, the prospect of going to school with black kids was frightening. Rumors had filtered all the way down the grade ladder from Sexton that some bathrooms were controlled by blacks, others by whites, and you dared not pee in the wrong one. Militant black students had taken over the principal's office, demanding passing grades. White girls couldn't wear ponytails, because black girls carried scissors in their purses.

So my friend had a plan: every afternoon, four of us would line up outside the school and give the bus the finger. For four days straight, we acted out our not-so-massive resistance against integration. On Friday, the bus stopped. The fed-up driver stepped down. My friends fled to a nearby field. I stood in place, frozen with the fear of authority. The driver took down my name and phone number and called my mother. That afternoon, for the only time in my life, I was spanked with my pants down.

The bus was from Main Street Elementary, a West Side school near the Oldsmobile plant. (Main Street was Earvin "Magic" Johnson's alma mater. On the first page of his autobiography, he writes of growing up attending Sexton basketball games, dreaming of winning a championship for "the pride of the West Side." Starting high school in the midseventies, Magic was bused to all-white Everett, on the South Side. Thanks to busing, *they* won the state championship.) We didn't start taking classes with black kids until the third grade. Before that happened, we white kids were driven to Main Street and assigned a black "partner" for a day of total immersion with the opposite race.

That sounds as sappy as a *Davey and Goliath* episode on racial tolerance, but it worked. By the time I arrived at Sexton, the student body was 55 percent white and 40 percent black, with a few Mexicans and Vietnamese making up the balance, but there were no office takeovers, because the principal was a respected black minister, and because we'd had seven years to get used to each other, instead of being thrown together during puberty, when one's natural response to a new kid is to beat the crap out of him. There were no black bathrooms or white bathrooms. We all smoked pot in the same bathrooms. The homecoming king was a black football player, the queen a white cheerleader. We were a statewide power in basketball and golf. My classmates included Malcolm X's niece and the daughter of a Lebanese lawyer whose golf bag I'd carried at the country club. There were racial tensions, but they were over matters of culture, not turf. At a postgame dance, Bruce Springsteen's "Dancin' in the Dark" was hooted down by a crowd that wanted to hear Cameo. Dan Oberdorfer's parents would not allow him to take Janine Morris to the prom. I had to step around break-dancers to get to the library. But my only physical altercation was with a redneck who was dating my ex-girlfriend.

I knew that Sexton was unusual—that most other schools were lily-white suburban or all-black inner-city—but I didn't realize how unusual until I went to Michigan State University. Most of my college classmates had grown up in segregated metro Detroit, and the campus was constantly sparking with racial controversies: one spring, black students occupied the administration building for nine days. The young men inside that building were acting on grievances I naively thought had been settled twenty years before—we'd been through that in Lansing, but we were long past it. Since then, though, Lansing seems to have given up on interracial education. On the one hand, it opened an Afro-centric charter school named after Malcolm X. On the other, a schools-of-choice policy allows white kids to defect to the suburbs. Today,

Sexton is 66 percent white and 19 percent black. My old school is no outlier. According to the Civil Rights Project at Harvard University, public school integration peaked in 1988, three years after my graduation from Sexton, when 48 percent of black students attended integrated schools. Today, that figure is 31 percent.

I never thought of Sexton as Ghetto High. Most of us were white, after all. But the rest of greater Lansing did. "You go to Sexton?" a kid from the suburbs once said to me. "I went to a basketball game there when we played you guys. All I saw were the dark ones." In college, I tried to impress a black girl from Detroit by telling her I'd attended an inner-city high school.

"Where'd you go?" she inquired skeptically.

"Lansing Sexton."

"Can't argue with that!" she exclaimed.

Even the Detroit kids thought Sexton was a tough school. A biracial education is the only street cred I've ever had in my life. During his 2008 speech on race in Philadelphia, Barack Obama said that "segregated schools were, and are, inferior schools." I hope he meant all-white schools as well as all-black schools. And I hope he meant inferior socially as well as academically. Today, I live in a neighborhood that's one-third black, one-third white, and one-third Latino. It seems normal to me, but I'm not sure I'd be comfortable if I'd graduated from a suburban high school. *Young Mr. Obama* is a study of how Chicago's black politics elevated Obama to the Senate and the presidency. I'm not sure I would have been comfortable on the South Side if I hadn't gone to school with African-Americans. The fact that Sexton was multicultural before that term existed is a legacy of Oldsmobile, which was itself multicultural, at least at the shop-floor level. And the school itself has left a legacy of integration, among its graduates and their children. In the 2010 census, Lansing had a higher percentage of mixed-race residents with a black parent than any city in the United States. That's also what happens when you throw black kids and white kids together during puberty. My hometown fulfilled the fears of every segregationist who swore to defend Southern womanhood. It's the Miscegenation Capital of America, and proud of it.

The principal's office had two doors: one opening south, one west. The occupant, Dr. Reginald Bates, a transplant from Washington, D.C., seemed to expect trouble to come through both. My appearance in the south door was just what he'd feared.

"I have a headache," Dr. Bates grumbled as I sat down. He glared at my copy of *Young Mr. Obama*.

"You want to donate that book? I've never done this before. Let me call the librarian. Does it have any profanity in it?"

"One word."

"Let me see it."

I opened the book to a passage in which one of Obama's campaign advisers calls him "motherfucker."

"It's in the context of a journalistic quote," I explained.

While we waited for the librarian, I asked Dr. Bates how many students attended Sexton.

"Around seven hundred and fifty."

"When I was here, it was twenty-one hundred."

"I've heard that story a hundred million times. I had an alumni come in yesterday at seven o'clock, wanting to talk about the old days. That's my time to get things done. Don't come in here at seven o'clock to talk about that. Not to cut your story off."

"Closing the factory must have reduced enrollment," I ventured.

"I don't know," Dr. Bates said curtly. "That was gone before I got here. I don't have a frame of reference for that."

"Do you still have drafting or auto shop?"

"We don't have any programs for the auto industry."

What Sexton had was health care programs, such as emergency medical technician training, so its students could learn to care for their baby boom shoprat grandparents.

When the librarian arrived, I opened my book and showed her the twelve-letter word. A short, stout woman in a burnt-pumpkin skirt, she seemed more offended by the idea of rejecting a book with the word "motherfucker" than by the word "motherfucker" itself.

"Just listen to the language in the hallway," she said. "You can hear worse here every day."

That seemed to satisfy Dr. Bates.

"How's this inscription?" I asked. "'To the students of Sexton High School. Someday, one of you can be president.'"

For the first time, Dr. Bates looked at me as though I weren't there to ruin his day.

"That sounds great," he said.

IN THE HALLWAYS, the lockers were buffered with more bumps and welts than a prizefighter's face. Through the solarium windows of the lobby, I could see that the grass on the athletic fields had grown as long as Old Testament whiskers. Sexton was designed during the first year of World War II and reflected the idea, then about to give way to the atomic age, that the classical world contained the germ of all knowledge. Every few feet, I passed a wall tile, painted like a square of embellished pottery, depicting a Shakespearean character, a figure from Greek mythology, a Japanese geisha plucking a samisen. On the north wall of the school, facing the empty space where Fisher Body used to be, are grimy bas-relief sculptures of men in WPA manual poses, practicing the ten disciplines: art, chivalry, drama, education, geography, labor, law, literature, music, pioneering. For a young scholar, it was more inspiring than the functional campuses of the decades that followed, schools that looked like giant split-level houses. I was headed upstairs to the gymnasium, to meet the basketball coach. Like Dr. Bates, Carlton Valentine had grown up in Washington, D.C., but he belonged now to Lansing. Valentine had played basketball for Michigan State, in the losing years after Magic Johnson left. Not quite talented enough for the NBA, he spent five years in Sweden, then returned to Lansing, because it was his wife's hometown. As a result of a middle-aged knee injury, he walked across the gymnasium floor, six and a half feet tall, with a gangling lope, and led me into the basketball office, a room rich with the odor of old wood baking in the late-spring heat. Unlike Dr. Bates, Coach Valentine had a reference for General Motors's role in the depopulation of Sexton.

"You look across the street, the GM plant's gone," he said. "That was one of the huge reasons why Sexton was as big as it was. People worked here. They lived here. When the plant closed, they dispersed to other areas. In 2005, we had thirteen hundred kids. People transferred out of state and took their kids. The people that own the houses in this area are older now. Their kids moved to the suburbs."

Sexton won the basketball championship after it was demoted from Class A—in which it competed with schools from Detroit, Flint, Grand Rapids, and Saginaw—to Class B, in which it played hick schools, most of them all-white. Shrunken to its inner-city core, the student body had urban basketball talent with rural numbers. Three of the starters—including Valentine's son—were going on to play for Division I colleges.

Coach V and his Big Reds were heroes to the children whose families had remained in Lansing, so he was driving the players across town to teach a grade-school basketball clinic. When I was growing up, the grade school's neighborhood had been white skinned and white-collar.

Since then, it had been infiltrated by every strain of American immigration. Besides the black kids and white kids, there were Latin kids, Asian kids, and Middle Eastern kids. In my generation, race mixing had been bipolar. Now it's multipolar.

"Hold up, hold up," Coach V shouted to the children gathered around him, children whose complexions covered the spectrum from John O'Groats to the Equator. "How's everybody doing? I need eye contact. How's everybody doing?"

"Good," the children mumbled.

"That's not good enough."

"*Good!*"

Coach V shook an eight-year-old boy's hand, then gave him pointers on masculinity.

"When you shake hands, you make sure you squeeze, and you make eye contact," he instructed. "Go into it like a man."

The coach had to run off to his day job, as marketing director for an elite local gym, so I spent the rest of the hour talking to one of his players. Robert Ray Jr., whose father had been a year behind me at Sexton, was tenth or eleventh on the bench but had been profiled on the front page of the *Lansing State Journal*, because his was not a typical Ghetto High basketball player's story. With a 4.18 grade point average, Robert had won a Gates Millenium Scholarship, funded by the Microsoft founder, which provided a full ride to any accredited university in the United States. He planned to major in biochemistry at Michigan State, then become an osteopath. In twenty-five years, the school's racial composition had changed, as they would have said in Cleveland, but its image and its reputation had changed not at all. As in a white-flight neighborhood, a black population of 40 percent was far beyond the demographic tipping point that eventually results in a black population of 90 percent.

"When I started going to Sexton, they asked me, 'Have you ever seen someone get shot?'" Robert said. "We just laugh, 'cause it's nothing like that."

One of the teachers at Sexton had told me she had trouble attracting suburban kids to her regional EMT program, because of "the reputation." "Where I'm housed," she said, "it's kind of turning people off."

"Did winning the state championship do anything for the school's image?" I asked Robert.

"Not really. That kind of goes along with the picture we depict.

We're good at football, basketball, and track. They refer to us as we're good at the black sports. We're bad at tennis, golf, cross-country—the *white* sports. We're *supposed* to be good at basketball."

I drove back across town, past the high school, with the football stadium on my left, the wildflowers growing on the grave of an auto plant to my right. I crossed the railroad tracks and parked on the side street behind Gus's Bar. The burgundy Oldsmobile was on the sidewalk. I went in through the back door that led straight ahead to Gus's flophouse and turned left into the bar. It was dark at three in the afternoon—the light never changed inside Gus's any more than it changed inside an auto plant—and Gus Caliacatsos was standing behind the bar, looking like a bald Greek hobbit in his sandals. Gus knew me by now. I drank in his bar whenever I was on the West Side, and any addition to his roster of regulars was remarkable. So with my Budweiser, he also served me his personal gossip.

"I sold the bar," he said.

"You sold the bar? What are you going to do now?"

"Going back to Greece," he said. "No more this place. I've been here for fifty years. Right now, Lansing the most dumb place, because there's no jobs."

"What are they gonna call this place when you're gone? Is it still gonna be Gus's Bar?"

Gus smiled. He had one last joke for the city that had taken away his livelihood.

"His name gotta be Gus, too," he said.

ACKNOWLEDGMENTS

First of all, I want to thank my parents for sending me to J. W. Sexton High School in Lansing, Michigan. We are J. Dubbs! If they had moved to the suburbs, as so many of their friends were doing in the 1970s, I would never have had the Rust Belt cred to write this book. I also want to thank the people who guided me around the cities of industrial America but don't appear in the text. In Chicago, Rod Sellers of the Southeast Historical Museum and Bob Wisz, owner of Doreen's Pizza. In Lansing, Dave Pfaff, historian of the R. E. Olds Transportation Museum and Kathleen Lavey of the *Lansing State Journal*. In Flint, Connor Coyne, who read one of my chapters for accuracy. In Detroit, Darci McConnell, a high school classmate who introduced me to urban farmer Gary Wozniak, and Tanya Irwin, a college classmate who introduced me to the architectural marvel of the Guardian Building. In Gary, Indiana, Katherine Hodges, webmistress of the "City of Destiny" blog, who took me on a ruin tour of City Methodist Church. In Cleveland, Christine Borne Nickras, who gave me a place to stay and corrected the errors in my copy. Also, Frank Ford and Bobbi Reichtell at Neighborhood Progress and Marie Kittredge at Slavic Village Development. In Buffalo, Aaron Bartley, Mike Malyak, and Mitch Gerber. In Homestead, Daniel Steinitz of the Tin Front Café and Ron Baraff of Rivers of Steel National Heritage Area. In Syracuse, Rick Simone of Sheet Metal Workers Local 58, and Frank Caliva and Kevin Schwab of CenterState Corporation for Economic Opportunity. In Decatur, retired *Herald & Review* business writer Gary Minich, who covered the Staley lockout in the 1990s. I also want to thank David Beers and Eric Liu for first encouraging me to write about Lansing, as well as Mark Schone, Joan Walsh, and Julian Brookes for publishing my Lansing articles in Salon.

This book began as an idea by my editor at Bloomsbury Press, Pete Beatty, a fellow Rust Belt native from Ohio. It was Pete who insisted I interview Michael Stanley. I also have to thank Jasmine Neosh for typing the book, and Ike at SOS Copies and More for giving me a break on copying.

BIBLIOGRAPHY

Ackermann, Marsha A. *Cool Comfort: America's Romance with Air-Conditioning*. Washington, D.C.: Smithsonian Institution Press, 2002.

Adams, Thomas F. "UAW Incorporated: The Triumph of Capital." Diss. Michigan State University, 2010.

Adler, Dennis. *Packard*. London: Motorbooks International, 1998.

Adler, William M. *Land of Opportunity: One Family's Quest for the American Dream in the Age of Crack*. New York: The Atlantic Monthly Press, 1995.

Angle, Paul M. *Bloody Williamson: A Chapter in American Lawlessness*. New York: Alfred A. Knopf, 1952.

Arsenault, Raymond. "The End of the Long Hot Summer: The Air Conditioner and Southern Culture." *Journal of Southern History* L, no. 4 (1984).

Ashby, Steven K., and C. J. Hawking. *Staley: The Fight for a New American Labor Movement*. Urbana, IL: University of Illinois Press, 2009.

Bensman, David, and Roberta Lynch. *Rusted Dreams: Hard Times in a Steel Community*. Berkeley, CA: University of California Press, 1988.

Bluestone, Barry, and Bennett Harrison. *The Deindustrialization of America: Plant Closings, Community Abandonment and the Dismantling of Basic Industry*. New York: Basic Books, 1982.

Burns, Daniel J. *Images of America: Homestead and the Steel Valley*. Charleston, S.C.: Arcadia Publishing, 2007.

Chafets, Ze'ev. *Devil's Night and Other True Tales of Detroit*. New York: Vintage Books, 1990.

Clemens, Paul. *Made in Detroit: A South of 8-Mile Memoir*. New York: Anchor Books, 2005.

Cohen, Adam, and Elizabeth Taylor. *American Pharaoh. Mayor Richard J. Daley: His Battle for Chicago and the Nation*. Boston: Little, Brown and Company, 2000.

Collins, Michael. *The Keepers of Truth*. New York: Scribner, 2001.

Conot, Robert. *American Odyssey: A Unique History of America Told Through the Life of a Great City*. New York: William Morrow & Company, Inc. 1974.

Cormier, Frank, and William J. Eaton. *Reuther*. Englewood Cliffs, N.J.: Prentice Hall, Inc., 1970.

Cowie, Jefferson. *Stayin' Alive: The 1970s and the Last Days of the Working Class*. New York: The New Press, 2010.

Cox, Stan. *Losing Our Cool: Uncomfortable Truths About Our Air-Conditioned World (and Finding New Ways to Get Through the Summer)*. New York: The New Press, 2010.

Dandaneau, Steven P. *A Town Abandoned: Flint, Michigan, Confronts Deindustrialization*. Albany, N.Y.: State University of New York Press, 1996.

Earley, Helen Jones, and James R. Walkinshaw. *Setting the Pace: Oldsmobile's First 100 Years*. Lansing, MI: Oldsmobile Division of General Motors Corporation, 1996.

Eichenwald, Kurt. *The Informant: A True Story*. New York: Broadway Books, 2000.

Ellis, William D. *The Cuyahoga*. New York: Holt, Rinehart and Winston, 1966.

Farley, Reynolds, Sheldon Danziger, and Harry J. Holzer. *Detroit Divided*. New York: Russell Sage Foundation, 2000.

Fine, Lisa M. *The Story of Reo Joe*. Philadelphia: Temple University Press, 2004.

Fine, Sidney. *Sit-Down: The General Motors Strike of 1936–1937*. Ann Arbor, MI: University of Michigan Press, 1969.

——. *Violence in the Model City: The Cavanagh Administration, Race Relations, and the Detroit Riot of 1967*. Ann Arbor, MI: University of Michigan Press, 1989.

Forrestal, Dan J. *The Kernel & The Bean: The 75-Year History of the Staley Company*. New York: Simon and Schuster, 1982.

Franklin, Stephen. *Three Strikes: Labor's Heartland Losses and What They Mean for Working Americans*. New York: The Guilford Press, 2001.

Gallagher, John. *Reimagining Detroit: Opportunities for Redefining an American City*. Detroit: Wayne State University Press, 2010.

Goines, Donald. *Dopefiend*. Los Angeles: Holloway House, 1971.

Goldman, Mark. *City on the Edge: Buffalo, New York*. Amherst, N.Y.: Prometheus Books, 2007.

Greenberg, Stanley B. *Middle Class Dreams: The Politics and Power of the New American Majority*. New Haven, CN: Yale University Press, 1996.

Halberstam, David. *The Reckoning*. New York: William Morrow and Company, Inc., 1986.

Hamper, Ben. *Rivethead: Tales from the Assembly Line*. New York: Warner Books, 1991.

Hernandez, Treasure. *The Flint Saga*. Deer Park, N.Y.: Urban Books, LLC, 2011.

Hersey, John. *The Algiers Motel Incident*. New York: Alfred A. Knopf, 1968.

Hoerr, John. *And the Wolf Finally Came: The Decline of the American Steel Industry*. Pittsburgh: University of Pittsburgh Press, 1988.

Huntington, Ellsworth. *Civilization and Climate*. New Haven, CN: Yale University Press, 1924.

Iacocca, Lee, with William Novak. *Iacocca: An Autobiography*. New York: Bantam Books, 1984.

Ingels, Margaret. *Willis Haviland Carrier: Father of Air Conditioning*. Garden City, N.Y.: Country Life Press, 1952.

Ingrassia, Paul. *Crash Course: The American Automobile Industry's Road from Glory to Disaster*. New York: Random House, 2010.

Johnson, Elmer W. *Chicago Metropolis 2020: The Chicago Plan for the Twenty-First Century*. Chicago: The University of Chicago Press, 2001.

Jones, Butch. *Y.B.I. (Young Boys Inc.): The Autobiography of Butch Jones*. Detroit: H. Publications, 1996.

Kahn, E. J., Jr. *Supermarketer to the World: The Story of Dwayne Andreas, CEO of Archer Daniels Midland*. New York: Warner Books, 1991.

Kearns, Josie. *Life After the Line*. Detroit: Wayne State University Press, 1990.

Kestenbaum, Justin L. *Out of a Wilderness: An Illustrated History of Greater Lansing*. Woodland Hills, CA: Windsor Publications, 1981.

Klekowski, James J. *South Chicago, U.S.A.: A Photographic Essay*. Chicago: Ellis Avenue Studios, 2002.

Klinkenborg, Verlyn. *The Last Fine Time*. New York: Alfred A. Knopf, 1990.

Kornblum, William. *Blue Collar Community*. Chicago: University of Chicago Press, 1974.

Kucinich, Dennis J. *The Courage to Survive*. Beverly Hills, CA: Phoenix Books, 2007.

Langan, Michael D. *Tapped Out: A Worker's Memoir of Bethlehem Steel's Rise and Demise in Western New York*. Buffalo, N.Y.: 2010

Lewis, Michael. *The Big Short: Inside the Doomsday Machine*. New York: W. W. Norton & Co., 2010.

Linkon, Sherry Lee, and John Russo. *Steeltown U.S.A.: Work & Memory in Youngstown*. Lawrence, KS: University Press of Kansas, 2002.

Longworth, Richard C. *Caught in the Middle: America's Heartland in the Age of Globalism*. New York: Bloomsbury USA, 2008.

Madigan, Charles M., ed. *Global Chicago*. Urbana, IL: University of Illinois Press, 2004.

Meyer, Philipp. *American Rust*. New York: Spiegel & Grau, 2010.

Michigan Writers' Project. *Michigan: A Guide to the Wolverine State*. New York: Oxford University Press, 1941.

Miller, Carol Poh, and Robert A. Wheeler. *Cleveland: A Concise History, 1796–1996*. Bloomington, IN: Indiana University Press, 1997.

Mitchell, Sandy. *Images of America: Cleveland's Slavic Village*. Charleston, S.C.: Arcadia Publishing, 2009.

Moore, Michael. *Here Comes Trouble: Stories from My Life*. New York: Grand Central Publishing, 2008.

Ninjalicious. *Access All Areas: A User's Guide to the Art of Urban Exploration*. Self-published, 2005.

Pacyga, Dominic. *Chicago: A Biography*. Chicago: University of Chicago Press, 2009.

Pekar, Harvey. *American Splendor and More American Splendor: The Life and Times of Harvey Pekar*. New York: Ballantine Books, 2003.

Perlstein, Rick. *Nixonland: The Rise of a President and the Fracturing of America*. New York: Scribner, 2008.

Peterson, Roger Tory. *Peterson First Guide to Wildflowers of Northeastern and North-central North America*. New York: Houghton Mifflin, 1968.

Rattner, Steven. *Overhaul: An Insider's Account of the Obama Administration's Emergency Rescue of the Auto Industry*. New York: Houghton Mifflin Harcourt, 2010.

Rose, William Ganson. *Cleveland: The Making of a City*. Cleveland: The World Publishing Company, 1950.

Scott, William Walter III. *Hurt, Baby, Hurt*. Ann Arbor, MI: New Ghetto Press, 1970.

Sellers, Rod. *Images of America: Chicago's Southeast Side Revisited*. Charleston, S.C.: Arcadia Publishing, 2001.

Serrin, William. *Homestead: The Glory and Tragedy of an American Steel Town*. New York: Crown Publishing, 1992.

Snyder, Brad. *Beyond the Shadow of the Senators: The Untold Story of the Homestead Grays and the Integration of Baseball*. New York: McGraw-Hill, 2004.

Stakes, Damon. *Cleveland Rocks: A Bicentennial Political and Social History of Cleveland, 1796–1996*. Cleveland: York Publishing Company.

Stanley, Robert. *Once Upon a Time in South Chicago*. Self-published, 2012.

Stein, Judith. *Pivotal Decade: How the United States Traded Factories for Finance in the Seventies*. New Haven, CT: Yale University Press, 2010.

Suarez, Ray. *The Old Neighborhood: What We Lost in the Great Suburban Migration: 1966–1999*. New York: The Free Press, 1999.

Taylor, Carl S. *Dangerous Society*. East Lansing, MI: Michigan State University Press, 1989.

———. *Girls, Gangs, Women and Drugs*. East Lansing, MI: Michigan State University Press, 1993.

Temple-Raston, Dina. *The Jihad Next Door: The Lackawanna Six and Rough Justice in the Age of Terror*. New York: Public Affairs, 2007.

Tesich, Steve. *Summer Crossing*. New York: Random House, 1982.

Walley, Christine J. "Deindustrializing Chicago: A Daughter's Story." In *The Insecure American: How We Got Here and What We Should Do About It*, edited by Hugh Gusterson and Catherine Besteman. Berkeley, CA: University of California Press, 2009.

Warren, Kenneth. *Bethlehem Steel: Builder and Arsenal of America*. Pittsburgh: University of Pittsburgh Press, 2008.

Wylie, Jeanie. *Poletown: Community Betrayed*. Urbana, IL: University of Illinois Press, 1989.

Yergin, Daniel. *The Prize: The Epic Quest for Oil, Money and Power*. New York: Free Press, 1991.

Young, Coleman, and Lonnie Wheeler. *Hard Stuff: The Autobiography of Mayor Coleman Young*. New York: Viking, 1994.

Zannes, Estelle. *Checkmate in Cleveland: The Rhetoric of Confrontation During the Stokes Years*. Cleveland: The Press of Case Western Reserve University, 1972.

INDEX

ABOUT THE AUTHOR

Edward McClelland was raised in Lansing, Michigan, and lives in Chicago. His previous books include *Young Mr. Obama: Chicago and the Making of a Black President*; *The Third Coast: Sailors, Strippers, Fishermen, Folksingers, Long-Haired Ojibway Painters, and God-Save-the-Queen Monarchists of the Great Lakes*; and *Horseplayers: Life at the Track*. Since beginning his professional writing career at the Lansing Community College *Lookout*, he has written for the *Chicago Reader*, the *New York Times*, the *Washington Post*, *Slate*, *Salon*, *Playboy*, and many other publications. Find him on the web at www.edwardmcclelland.com and on Twitter at @tedmcclelland.